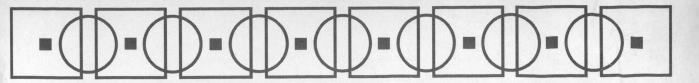

Pattern Languages of Program Design

2

Edited by

John M. Vlissides
IBM Thomas J. Watson Research

James O. Coplien
Bell Laboratories

Norman L. Kerth
Elite Systems

ADDISON-WESLEY
An imprint of Addison Wesley Longman, Inc.

Reading, Massachusetts • Harlow, England • Menlo Park, California
Berkeley, California • Don Mills, Ontario • Sydney
Bonn • Amsterdam • Tokyo • Mexico City

Cover: Photographs by Charles Mercer and Scott Mehaffey, used with the permission of the Robert Allerton Park and Conference Center, University of Illinois at Urbana-Champaign.

Frontispiece used with the permission of Bettina Steinmueller (Germany). All Rights Reserved.

The programs and applications presented in this book have been included for their instructional value. They have been tested with care, but are not guaranteed for any particular purpose. The publisher and authors do not offer any warranties or representations, nor do they accept any liabilities with respect to the programs or applications.

Acquisitions Editor: Thomas E. Stone
Associate Editor: Deborah Lafferty
Production Supervisor: Nancy H. Fenton
Cover Designer: Eileen Hoff
Production: Editorial Services of New England
Project Manager: Rojean Wagner, Editorial Services of New England
Text Designer: Ron Kosciak, Dragonfly Design
Text Figures: George Nichols
Copy Editor: Bruce Crabtree
Senior Manfacturing Manager: Roy E. Logan

Many of the designations used by manufacturers and sellers to distinguish their products are claimed as trademarks. Where those designations appear in this book, and Addison-Wesley was aware of a trademark claim, the designations have been printed in initial caps or all caps.

Access the latest information about Addison-Wesley titles from our World Wide Web page: `http://www.aw.com/cseng/`

Library of Congress Cataloging-in-Publication Data
Pattern languages of program design / edited by James O. Coplien,
  Douglas C. Schmidt.
        p.   cm.
      Includes bibliographical references and index.
      1. Computer software—Development. 2. Object-oriented
programming. I. Coplien, James O. II. Schmidt, Douglas C.
QA76.76.D47P375   1995
005. 1—dc20   95-6731
                                                                                CIP

ISBN 0-201-60734-4
ISBN 0-201-89527-7 (2, edited by John M. Vlissides, James O. Coplien, Norman L. Kerth)

2 3 4 5 6 7 8 9 10–MA–00999897

Contents

3 Special-Purpose Patterns

4 Architectural Patterns

5 Process and Organization

6 Exposition

7 Concurrent Programming/Distributed Systems

8 Reactive Systems

Introduction-1

Ralph Johnson and Ward Cunningham

PLoP was founded to create a new literature. That implies that the founders were somehow dissatisfied with the existing literature, which is true. The founders, a handful of notables in the object-oriented programming community, had come to realize that the advance of their discipline was limited by a bias in its literature. The bias, a product of the traditions of scientific publication, was to favor the new, the recent invention or discovery over the ordinary, no matter how useful. The founders' interest in the ordinary may have come from their studies of software reuse. Or it may have come from their observations that projects fail despite the latest technology for lack of ordinary solutions. What matters is that all the founders agreed to focus their attention on the dissemination of solutions. The PLoP conference is one result.

This volume is the first of a series of books dedicated to the "pattern form," our best guess at the way to share solutions. We asked authors to submit papers in the "pattern form" without actually saying what that form was. Christopher Alexander coined the term *pattern language* and explained the form well in his book *The Timeless Way of Building*. Many authors were familiar with this work, and many more were introduced to it through a series of OOPSLA workshops and Internet discussion groups. Even so, we felt authors needed considerable latitude in adapting Alexander's form to the domain of computer programs. The one thing we insisted was that each paper describe a solution, a thing that could be made to solve a problem.

You will notice as you read this volume that the authors' solutions cover an incredible range of problems. This means that you will probably not find every chapter equally interesting. We expect that as the PLoP community grows and matures that PLoP will itself splinter along traditional lines of interest. Future volumes may not demand so much versatility of their readers. For now we ask that you dig into all the chapters. Even if you do not plan to apply what you read directly, it might inspire you with new ideas of how to present patterns, and it should certainly give you a perspective on why it is so difficult to develop software.

For all this diversity in subject matter, there were some surprising agreements among PLoP authors and attendees. For one, most found that a solution, the essence of a pattern, could easily transcend the exact nature of its expression. A pattern must ultimately reside in one's own mind. So the various writing styles—from labeled sections of a standard template to running paragraphs of a more narrative style—have less to do with the success of a pattern than with some more basic elements. These include establishing a problem and its context, analyzing the forces bearing on the solution, and, most important, offering a concrete solution. Patterns that include these elements succeed.

A central feature of PLoP '94 was the writers' workshops. Instead of presenting their papers to an audience, writers listened to a small group discuss their paper and debate its strengths and weaknesses. This gave authors a chance not only to learn how they were communicating but also to discover learning alternatives to the techniques they were presenting. Writers' workshops, originated a few decades ago in the creative writing community, are an important forum where new writers learn the craft and experienced writers polish their material. We owe a great debt to Richard Gabriel for introducing us to the writers' workshop in the spring of 1994. To the best of our knowledge, this is the first time it has been used in a technical community, but it seems to work well.

So that is the vision and process that has led to this volume. We are pleased with the result and are sure you will be also. For us it is full speed ahead. Every week we see some new piece of evidence that the shift of focus that we and our authors have made will have a profound and enduring effect on the way we write programs. They will also show by example our vision of the future of software engineering.

Pattern Languages of Program Design, James O. Coplien and Douglas C. Schmidt (eds.), Copyright © 1995. Reprinted with permission Ralph Johnson and Ward Cunningham.

Introduction-2

Richard Gabriel

Repetition, Generativity, and Patterns

Repetition—a Foucault pendulum, seawaves north of Santa Cruz, the shapely, curved stride of a young woman—attracts us—a steady R&B beat, night lullabies. Repetition—rhyming poetry, pre-dawn coffee—defines our lives—suppertime, weekends, evenings out.

When we were born, the world, fresh, contained no repetitions. An infant first smiles at his mother's return not because it is her but because her presence repeats; later he smiles because the she who returns is the same she. I take my daughter to the bus stop at 8:20 AM every day, and as we stop she waits a minute then looks up the road to see the bus come over the ridgetop. She expects the bus to arrive at a particular time and feels safe and human when it does—out of sorts and stressed when it does not.

We understand all there is for us to understand through repeated parts and portions. Grammar is our regularized grunting, song is our stylized noise-making, human society is our patterned gene stuff. We live by recognizing and using recurrences, by relying on what happens over and over. Unpredictability when not sought is feared.

Recurrence works because actions, characteristics, and relations that are noticeable repeat. Every act—every thing—contains not only the noticed repeated parts but also attendant, variable portions. The recurrent parts stand out because our minds (our brains?) are constructed that way.

Repetition as mantra is how we learn: 2×8 is 16, 3×8 is 24, 4×8 is 32. When I spelled "stillness" wrong in the fifth grade, I wrote it 100 times on the board. When I play squash and mis-hit or misdirect the ball, I chant, "follow through, follow through, you idiot." A mantra of simple things. The magic of the chant—enchantment; inward song—incantation. When the rhythm of repetition begins, the body sways; when the repetition of chant continues, sometimes the chanter cannot stop. Repetition is power.

What repeats is important and reveals commonality. What isn't repeated is variable and can be highlighted or hidden. Repetition makes us feel secure and variation makes us feel free. Abstraction reveals and revels in what is common, the repetition, and what is abstract is defined by the repeated. The remainder, in science, basks behind the veil of ignorance, and the remainder, in computing, is filled in as missing. Abstraction is what we know as long as what is repeated has the magic of enchantment and song of incantation.

But, what of the mantra "follow through, follow through"? Insistence of rhythm is a mnemonic—in ancient times laws were expressed in incantatory rhythms—and remembering and teaching are what we intend by the incantation. The law of follow-through is hard to forget—it's a law, though, that makes little sense: where is its enchantment? How can advice about what to do after you hit a ball make any difference to what happens when you hit it, or before?

The advice must work—because we hear it all the time—but how can it work? Here's how: If you plan to contact the ball at a particular point, your muscles will naturally begin slowing down just before you get there—perhaps to guard against the jolt. When you try to slow down the forward motion of your arm, muscles opposed to that motion contract to counteract. Your arm, then, moves with "noise," jiggling up and down, circling around; and power moving forward drops. Amplify this by the length of the racket. Problems.

When you follow through, your arm is aiming at a point well beyond where the racket will contact the ball, so there is no deceleration. "Don't decelerate, don't decelerate, you idiot!" It might make a mantra worth repeating, but it isn't advice you can take.

This mantra generates the effect we want—just as a seed generates the flower that eventually blossoms. Just as the wind in the sand generates dune designs and sidewinding sinews and ripples of grains of sand. The power of generative activities is cousin to that of repetition. Give a person something that can be done, and it will be done. Science loves a clever explanation—the gyroscopic forces generated by the front wheel of a bicycle cause the proper lean when you turn—but the clever explanation is merely clever, and really good only for a pleasant magazine article or MIT macho talk.

Generative mantras have the psychological power of ritual coupled with the physical power of algorithm. Ritual builds on our need for repetition and predictability, ritual is the basis of superstition—if you step with your left foot at the top of the dugout, rub toward the business end of the bat with the pine rag, dig a 3-inch trench to stand in with your right toe, you will not strike out. Ritual calms—the ritual of petting a dog lowers blood pressure below resting levels, makes stutterers speak clearly.

Rituals, repetitions, recurrences: These are simply patterns, the repeated parts, the familiar signposts that tame frightening variations. You don't know what the pitcher will throw, but you know how you will prepare as you walk to the plate. Rituals, like the advice to follow through, are things people can follow.

Software—is it something we can learn to produce by scientific study? Will type systems with nice semantics make it easy to produce and maintain the 5-million-line telecom switching system? Will an additional 30 percent in performance from unboxing data in a higher-order programming language unleash productivity in the software workplace?

I don't think so. Such work will help a few dedicated researchers achieve tenure and assure a comfortable life for their long-enduring families, but you might as well tell a novice tennis player about how muscles decelerate and ask them to repeat their new stroke 20 times.

The work of the Hillside group is to remind us that people in teams and groups write software, and that in the absence of rituals and repetitions, recurrences, every step of the way for the individual is invention and creation. Software engineering is not yet engineering and won't be, cannot be, for decades if not centuries, because we cannot yet recognize the important, repeatable parts. When we do we will have patterns—recurrences, predictability.

Is it really possible we cannot yet recognize the repeatable parts? For several years I traveled to Paris every few months, and my good friend, Jérôme, would always take me to the *brasserie* where he'd order oysters. Whenever I tasted them, all I could discern was salt water, fat, and sometimes grit. Jérôme didn't skimp, and many times we had Locmariaquer oysters, but I ate the smallest polite number I could get away with.

Years later I visited Point Reyes Station in California, and my friend and I ordered oysters—Hog Island Sweetwaters. They're farmed in Tomales Bay where the river enters the bay, and they are only slightly salty. Suddenly I could taste oystertaste, sweet and lightly eccentric, muscularly hard, central. The next day—guarding against oddities—we ate oysters somewhere else, and once more I enjoyed them. The next year or so I sampled oysters whenever I could, and even when they weren't the Sweetwaters, I could taste the hint of oystertaste and could enjoy that part of it—the repeated part.

Two years ago Jérôme and I were in Portland, Oregon, and I took him to Jake's where we dined on 5 dozen oysters of many types. He smiled and ordered champagne for the two of us.

I needed to learn to recognize the repeated parts—it took years and luck. Something as basic as flavor—I had to learn to taste it. Before that, oysters tasted like poison.

Software tastes like poison. Patterns, possibly, will reveal the sweetwaters.

Patterns embody the repetitions and recurrences within software; they provide the lonely developer with rituals and familiarity, and prevent him or her from falling prey to lossage. A pattern is a simple thing to understand, the more so the more like a ritual it makes part of development. Patterns feed on repetition, provide ritual. What patterns leave out provides freedom, a point of departure for creativity.

There is no content to patterns—no one will ever produce a journal article or conference paper whose content is a pattern or pattern language—and if someone does, he's missed the point. Just as no one will ever write an acceptable biomechanics paper whose content is the advice to follow through.

If the ballplayer's ritual works it's because it relaxes him or gives him confidence. Patterns should be like these rituals—people should be able to follow them and perhaps there should rarely be reasons why or the reasons can be the topic of a real scientific paper. The content is not in the pattern—that's somewhere else; the pattern holds only the ritual part, and the pattern works by giving the developer something to do with the knowledge only that "if you do this, it will work." Such patterns are called generative patterns. Patterns work like rituals, patterns feed our need for repetition and predictability, patterns are designed for people to use in their lives—generative patterns work like magic.

Generative patterns don't require CS degrees to understand. To get their gist you don't need a mathematical background—you just do what they say and win.

How do you produce generative patterns? You don't—you find them. They are in systems written by virtuosos, they are in systems that are a dream to maintain. If a great programmer comes to you and says, "Hey, look at this code I found," that's where you'll be able to mine generative patterns. Someone invented or developed the code that contains the patterns, but that's largely irrelevant: it's that the same solution or style has been used and found habitable. We don't find a single gold atom, we find veins and nuggets—accumulation. Patterns are discovered because they are well used; they form a vein that anyone could find.

Great pattern writers are miners, they create nothing except the wonderful explanation—they are writers, they aren't scientists, or even engineers. CS departments consider them drudges, scribes, amanuenses. Pattern-writing geniuses won't get tenure anywhere, they won't advise CEOs. A pattern writer won't ride off into the sunset with the prize in his saddlebag.

When we look at Christopher Alexander's patterns, we see that almost all of them have to do with how people live in homes, towns, and cities, with other people and alone, indulging in culture or savoring spirituality. Few talk about engineering and construction. They are short on physical explanation—we don't learn why light in a room causes useful biological reactions, only that such places are alive and comfortable. Alexander draws on centuries and millennia of architecture, and he, with a group of about a dozen, spent nearly a decade finding out 253 patterns.

We hunt today alone for software patterns in 40 years of code. Have we found any patterns yet?

Anyone can write lines in verse with a rhythm and some rhyme—is it poetry? Patterns are a form—the repetition calms, the variation inspires— but are we still writing doggerel?

■ ■ ■

Kent Beck

Once there was a mountain kingdom whose economy was based on farming. Wanting to get the most out of the limited arable land, the king set up schools to teach all the inhabitants the principles of farming—photosynthesis, weather, entomology. Upon graduation, each young lad or lass was assigned a patch of land to farm and given seeds and tools. Each was allowed, even encouraged, to farm his or her own way.

The results were disaster. Understanding the principles did not keep new farmers from making terrible mistakes. Crops were planted at the wrong time, crops in adjacent fields did not work together to limit the depredations of insects, the soil was not maintained from year to year.

As the food supply shrank, the country's residents became restless. They brought their empty bellies before the king and demanded a solution. He in turn brought together his wisest advisers and gave them a choice—solve the farming problem or learn to do without their heads.

After many late-night meetings where gallons of stimulating drinks were consumed, the advisers reported to the king. "King," they said, "the education given future farmers prepares them to farm in any number of ways. Toothless old farmers know, however, that only a few farming techniques deserve consideration. While understanding the principles is important, understanding the techniques that work is equally important. Bring together your most experienced and thoughtful farmers. Have them write down what works in a book. Give this book to new farmers, that they may avoid obvious mistakes and get on with farming."

At first the book grew quickly, as new farming techniques were recognized and recorded. It looked as if the book would grow so large that no one would be able to understand it all. After a while, though, it became apparent that many techniques were duplicates of others, and that the recognition of new techniques had slowed to a trickle. The book settled down to a weighty but manageable tome.

As farmers learned to read and use the book, the kingdom's food production stabilized. Farmers could now take advantage of the wisdom of others. When they faced a situation, they weren't responsible for always inventing a unique solution; they could find a technique that solved the problem. If no technique fit exactly, they were still able to adapt techniques rather than start from scratch.

The farmers sometimes missed the crazy old days of wild invention. On the whole, though, the kingdom was satisfied. The people ate well, so they were happy. The king didn't have to listen to complaints all day, so he was happy. And the advisers had solved the problem, so they still had heads to be happy with.

The Beginning

Preface

An idea is like a seed blowing in the wind: it has little significance until it lands, takes root, and starts to grow. The idea of *patterns*, blown about the software field for two decades, has finally landed and begun to flourish. The 1994 Pattern Languages on Programming conference (PLoP '94) marked the germination of the pattern movement as the first conference dedicated to patterns in software. The following year saw publication of several pattern books, magazines rushed to print pattern articles, and patterns surfaced at mainstream software engineering and object-oriented conferences.

Then came PLoP '95, which was as different from its predecessor as a seedling differs from a young plant: it was more robust, its roots went deeper, and it was better attuned to its environment. The emphasis shifted from "What are patterns all about?" to "What makes a pattern good, and a good pattern better?" This is a profound shift, a sign of rapid maturing in people's thinking about patterns. It is a shift away from introspection toward a healthy activism. Many now appreciate that a pattern's value is in neither its discovery nor its definition but in its relevance, its quality, its impact. Patterns in software are as much about great literature as they are about technology.

Writing patterns sounds simple but isn't. The struggle is twofold: recognizing our own wisdom in recurring design problems, and communicating that wisdom effectively.

The authors of these chapters know a great deal about the struggle. It starts with reflection on the problems one has solved recurringly; then characterizing the essence of the recurring solution; and then writing the characterization down. But that's just the beginning. A pattern is invariably useless if it isn't reshaped through criticism, and that's where PLoP comes in. A paper submitted to PLoP enters a "shepherding process" where reviewers iterate with the author(s) to improve the paper. A submission may go through several iterations before it is accepted or rejected.

The struggle continues at PLoP. Papers are not *presented* there in any traditional sense. Rather, each is reviewed in a "writers' workshop," in which the author listens to readers discuss the paper. He or she is not allowed to participate in the discussion—that would contaminate the process with editorial input unavailable to other readerships. The goal of the workshop is to help the author *improve* the paper, not defend it.

The author goes home with one more chance to revise the work before submitting it for final review. Papers that clear this last hurdle are included here. Each had to survive the equivalent of thorns, storms, and locusts before blooming as a chapter in this book.

With seeds and new ideas, you never know exactly how they'll grow. Many vines have sprouted from the pattern seed, each growing independently but along one of two paths. Some grow in the path blazed by Christopher Alexander [Alexander+77, Alexander79], reflecting his seminal work on patterns of building architecture. Alexander structured his patterns hierarchically into a system he called a "pattern language." But like vines left to find their own way, these Alexandrian-style papers adapt the form to their needs: they deviate from the path when it suits them.

Other vines head in a path blazed by the "Gang of Four" (GOF), the nickname for the authors of the first book on software patterns [Gamma+95]. These pioneers discovered the value of isolated patterns that capture wisdom in object-oriented software design. Their patterns are larger, more highly structured, and much less interdependent than Alexander's. They have helped many software developers recognize and exploit the benefits of patterns, and they've inspired many more to attempt writing patterns of their own.

This book presents numerous specimens from these paths. As you study each chapter, ask yourself which path suits you best, and why. Look carefully at the style, the format, the problems posed, the forces resolved, the consequences and drawbacks of each pattern.

Then act. A vibrant pattern community requires everyone's participation. Have you found patterns that fit your work? If so, please try them out. Do you find wisdom here that's worth sharing with your colleagues? Please let them know. Can you identify wisdom you've acquired that needs documenting? Please write it down, and have others critique it. And please consider submitting it to an upcoming PLoP!

No book materializes without help from people behind the scenes, but PLoP calls for extraordinary effort. The members of the Hillside Group organized the conference. Brian Foote and his student colleagues from the University of Illinois Urbana-Champaign proved invaluable as they assembled the papers, copied and distributed them repeatedly, and helped run the event with good cheer. The shepherds lived up to their name as selfless overseers of their authoring flocks. The contributions of nonauthor PLoP participants also need acknowledgment, for PLoP is not a passive listening experience; reading multiple papers and giving careful, constructive feedback is hard work. Many thanks to you all.

As in the previous book in this series [Coplien+95], we have avoided tampering with details of form and layout in each author's work, even as we yearned for typographical coherence. So our friends at Addison-Wesley are to be doubly commended for their achievement. Deborah Lafferty guided the production effort with a gentle but firm hand; her ability to keep projects on schedule continues to amaze. Rojean Wagner and the staff at Editorial Services of New England were challenged by many an electronic format and emerged victorious. Special thanks to Tom Stone, who took a risk and gave a fledgling movement a voice.

Finally, we recognize the people most critical to this book's success, the pattern authors themselves. They have chosen to share their wisdom with the rest of us, and they sacrifice a great deal in the process. It takes courage and dedication to spend time revealing what could well be one's competitive advantage. We extend heartfelt thanks on behalf of all who will benefit from their labors.

J.M.V.

J.O.C.

N.L.K.

[Alexander+79] C. Alexander. *The Timeless Way of Building.* New York: Oxford University Press, 1979.

[Alexander+77] C. Alexander, et al. *A Pattern Language.* New York: Oxford University Press, 1977.

[Gamma+95] E. Gamma, R. Helm, R. Johnson, and J. Vlissides. *Design Patterns: Elements of Reusable Object-Oriented Software.* Reading, MA: Addison-Wesley, 1995.

[Coplien+95] J. O. Coplien and D. C. Schmidt, (Eds.) *Pattern Languages of Program Design.* Reading, MA: Addison-Wesley, 1995.

LANGUAGE-SPECIFIC PATTERNS AND IDIOMS

PART

1

Part 1 starts, so to speak, at the beginning. *Idioms* were an early precursor of patterns, often not in pattern form, but conveying key design insights for a specific language or technology. Today, idioms retain the original sense of language dependence, but they have borrowed the expository form of the pattern discipline. Many pattern taxonomies split patterns into three levels: architectural patterns (best exemplified by some of Mary Shaw's patterns in Part 4), design patterns (typified by the general-purpose patterns of Part 2), and idioms such as here in Part 1. Idioms are the day-to-day hammers and nails, bricks and mortar of the programmer. Yet programming is as much or more of a craft than design is, and idioms capture the art and engineering honed by programmers over years of experience. That we capture idioms gives dignity to programmers, too often dismissed as assembly-line workers who assemble the great works that emanate from the architecture gods. There is wonder, art, and cleverness at the implementation level, too.

Tom Cargill's patterns (Chapter 1) solve memory management problems in C++ programs. Though the patterns build on a C++ exposition, they drive at the deeper principles of lifetime and scope. Many programmers are caught up in the software traditions, like block-structured programming, that equate lifetime with scope. The lifetimes and scopes in object-oriented programs are richer than those in procedural programs: most object-oriented programs offer the class as an additional level of scoping, and many objects outlive the scope of any single member function. The object-oriented computational model pulls lifetime and scope apart. Because language subtly affects the expression of lifetime and scoping (e.g., `static` in C++), some of these issues are idiomatic and differ from language to language. Cargill focuses on the problems of balancing each instantiation with a cleanup. Note that though this is largely a memory problem, it broadens to other finalization issues as well (resetting device driver states on close, or closing out the buffers to a file when the file object goes away). The broader problem fits well within Cargill's patterns, based on C++, but it would have to be handled idiomatically in Smalltalk.

In Chapter 2, Ken Auer and Kent Beck team up to give us patterns for efficient Smalltalk programming. Many of these patterns are good tutorial expositions of time-honored optimization techniques, such as "Lazy Optimization"—from which the pattern language takes its name—and "Hot Spot" (based on "Pareto's Law"; see also Gerard Meszaros' chapter in Part 8). Yet performance tuning isn't simple; there are a few experts who seem to know how to do it right. What patterns do they know that we don't? Kent and Ken are widely acknowledged as such experts in the Smalltalk community, and they share wondrous patterns such as "Experiment" and "Object Transformation" with us. These patterns are "ah-bvious" once you read them, but they haven't yet made it into the programming mainstream. And in the spirit of the word *efficiency* in its most general sense—the most payoff with the least investment—Kent and Ken tell us when *not* to optimize, balancing forces of development cost and maintainability with performance.

Compare and contrast these patterns with Gerard Meszaros' patterns ("A Pattern Language for Improving Capacity of Reactive Systems") in Part 8.

Bobby Woolf's patterns (Chapter 3) purportedly address how to partition Smalltalk systems for source code configuration management, yet there is much more going on here than meets the eye. These patterns are as much about good architectural principles as about the development environment. The patterns even touch on organizational issues, using the architecture to facilitate independent work that minimizes coordination and communication overhead. In that sense, these patterns are reminiscent of the patterns of process and organization in the first volume of this series [Coplien+95]. Bobby's patterns weave these perspectives together seamlessly, drawing on the conventions of ENVY to express principles of structuring and relationship. This is a highly generative pattern language: not only does it solve configuration management problems, but it points the way to a sound architecture and a reasonable team organization as well.

These authors deserve a special thanks. Programming techniques don't enjoy the same kind of reverence as patterns of Architecture and Design, even though ignorance of idioms is usually more deadly than ignorance of the grand principles of architectural design. The software development community needs more patterns like these as a basis for better pedagogy in programming language education, as a shared vocabulary for day-to-day design, and as building blocks for design patterns. (Some of the patterns of Jung Kim and Kevin Benner exhibit this layering in Part 2.) Whorf advised us well when he said language shapes what we can think about: programming language-level patterns deserve a strong focus in the body of literature we are trying to build.

[Coplien+95] J. Coplien, and D. Schmidt, eds. *Pattern Languages of Program Design*. Reading, MA: Addison-Wesley, 1995.

1

Localized Ownership: Managing Dynamic Objects in C++

Tom Cargill

ABSTRACT

Localized Ownership is a pattern language that tackles the management of
dynamic-object lifetimes in C++. It forms a sequence of patterns that address
a range of design constraints. Early patterns in the sequence emphasize
simplicity and locality of the responsible code. Later patterns offer greater
flexibility, at the expense of a more complex implementation that is dis-
persed more widely.

INTRODUCTION

Problem The lifetime of a dynamic object in C++—one allocated from heap memory
(the free-store)—is managed explicitly by the program. The program must
guarantee that each dynamic object is deleted when it is no longer needed,
and certainly before it becomes garbage. (There is no garbage collection in

standard C++, and few programs can afford to produce garbage.) For each dynamic allocation, a policy that determines the object's lifetime must be found and implemented.

Each pattern in Localized Ownership addresses this single problem under various constraints.

Forces   The simplest policies for managing a dynamic object's lifetime are those that localize the work within a single component, such as a function, object, or class. A simple solution that suffices is ideal. Unfortunately, attempts to localize lifetime policies are confounded by rich object architectures that require their objects to play multiple roles in cooperation with many collaborators. What ownership policies are applicable in these more complex contexts?

TERMINOLOGY

Lifetime   The lifetime of an object in C++ is the interval of time that it exists (by occupying memory). An object is created from one of three "storage classes": automatic (local), static, and dynamic. The lifetimes of automatic and static objects are controlled *implicitly* by the program's execution. The lifetime of an automatic object ends when execution exits its block. The lifetime of a static object continues until the end of the entire program execution. The lifetime of a dynamic object continues until the program *explicitly* destroys that object, however.

Creator   A dynamic object is created by the execution of a new expression. The entity that executes the new expression is the dynamic object's *creator*. The creator may be a (member) function, an object, or a class. The creator cannot be inferred from the source code alone. In general, a new expression that creates a dynamic object is executed by a member function, that member function executes on behalf of an object, and that object is an instance of a class. Therefore, the creator of the dynamic object might be deemed to be the function, the object, or the class. In the following code the creator could be the member function f, the object executing A::f, or the class A:

```
void A::f()
{
  . . .
  new Resource
  . . .
}
```

Although the creator is determined by the intent of the programmer, the language constrains the choice. If the `new` expression is executed by a static member function, the creator is either the function or its class. (There is no object.) If the `new` expression is executed by a nonmember function, only the function may be the creator. (There is neither object nor class.)

Owner   The *owner* of a dynamic object is the function, object, or class that bears the responsibility for ending the lifetime of the dynamic object. The owner is responsible for eventually deleting the dynamic object. Upon a dynamic object's creation, its creator becomes the owner. A dynamic object may acquire an owner other than its creator, and it may have more than one owner at a time.

Ownership does not imply exclusive access to the owned dynamic object. Other parts of the program may legitimately access the dynamic object, but that access must be consistent with the owner's policy. In particular, other parts of the program must guarantee not to attempt any access after the owner has deleted the object.

OVERVIEW

Localized Ownership

The Localized Ownership pattern language contains three primary patterns, of which the first is divided into three subcases:

1. Creator as Owner
   - 1.1 Function as Owner
   - 1.2 Object as Owner
   - 1.3 Class as Owner
2. Sequence of Owners
3. Shared Ownership

The patterns are ordered by decreasing the localization of ownership responsibility: earlier patterns localize this responsibility narrowly; later patterns distribute it more widely. Localized responsibility generally simplifies design and implementation. Therefore, use the lowest-numbered pattern that suffices.

Resources Other Than Dynamic Objects

Although the Localized Ownership patterns might be used to manage other resources (such as files or database locks), they are presented here specifically in terms of dynamic objects. There are two motivating reasons for this. First, the focus on dynamic objects makes the discussion more concrete. Second, for most C++ programmers the effort expended on managing dynamic objects overshadows that devoted to other resources.

PATTERN 1: CREATOR AS SOLE OWNER

Context   The creator of a dynamic object is in a position to fully determine that object's lifetime. A narrow, specific purpose for a dynamic object suggests that its creator may be able to control its lifetime. A narrow purpose does not imply that the object is short-lived or that the creator has exclusive access to it, however.

Solution   Upon creating a dynamic object, its creator becomes its owner. That ownership responsibility is never transferred. The creator must eventually dispose of the dynamic object. If other parts of the system access the dynamic object, that access must be consistent with the owner's policy. When the identity of the dynamic object passes through an interface (typically a pointer or reference as a function parameter or return value), constraints on the object's lifetime must be part of that interface.

The three types of creators result in three specializations of this pattern.

PATTERN 1.1: FUNCTION AS SOLE OWNER

Context   An object whose access is restricted to the function that created it and to functions whose execution is nested within that function's execution is a candidate for sole ownership by that function. The lifetime of the object can be established without considering the lifetimes of any other objects.

Solution   When the sole owner of an object is a function, that function must eventually `delete` the object. The `delete` expression is coded explicitly in the function. If the dynamic object is required for only the current invocation of the function, the `delete` expression occurs before the function returns to its caller. If the dynamic object's lifetime spans many invocations, the function may retain the object from call to call, using a local static pointer, for example. Eventually the function itself executes `delete`, when the object is no longer needed.

Example   The creator function creates and deletes during a single invocation:

```
void some::SoleOwner()
{
  . . .
  Resource *res = new Resource;
  . . .
  delete res;
  . . .
}
```

Example   The following code shows a function that holds a dynamic buffer from one call to the next. On each call the function determines if the current buffer is large enough and allocates a larger one if needed:

```
void Transport::xmit(const Packet *p)
{
  static char *buffer = 0;
  static int allocated = 0;

  int sz = formattedSize(p);

  if( sz > allocated ){
    delete [] buffer;
    buffer = new char[sz];
    allocated = sz;
  }


  . . .
}
```

PATTERN 1.2: OBJECT AS SOLE OWNER

Context   The lifetime of a dynamic object cannot be tied to a single function, but it can be bounded by the lifetime of the object that created it. Creation occurs in a nonstatic member function.

Solution   If the sole owner of a dynamic object is another object, then the owner acquired it by executing one of its own member functions and must delete it before the end of its own lifetime. The last opportunity the owner object has to delete the owned object is during the execution of its own destructor. The lifetime of the dynamic object must not extend beyond this point.

Example   Stroustrup's "resource allocation is initialization" [Stroustrup91] is an example of an object as sole owner. The "Cheshire Cat" technique[1] reduces unwanted indirect header file dependencies by moving the private members of a class into an auxiliary object, to which the class delegates its operations. Typically, the auxiliary structure is dynamically allocated in the constructor and deallocated in the destructor:

```
class Server {
public:
  Server();
  ~Server();
  . . .
private:
  class Auxiliary *aux;
};

Server::Server()
{
  aux = new Auxiliary;
}

Server::~Server()
{
  delete aux;
}
```

Example   If a communications `Connection` object encounters an error, it opens a `Window` to display pertinent information. The `Connection` object lazily defers creation of the `Window` until an error occurs. If instructed to `clearErrors()`, the `Connection` disposes of the `Window`, if it has one. If the `Connection` still holds a `Window` at the end of its own lifetime, the destructor performs the delete:

```
class Connection {
public:
  Connection();
  ~Connection();
  void clearErrors();
  . . .
private:
  Window *errWin;
```

---

[1] The term was coined by John Carolan [Carolan89].

```
    void error(Text);
    . . .
};

Connection::Connection()
{
  errWin = 0;
}

Connection::~Connection()
{
  clearErrors();
}

void Connection::error(Text t)
{
  if( errWin == 0 )
    errWin = new Window;
  . . .
  errWin->write(t);
}

void Connection::clearErrors()
{
  delete errWin;   // may be null
  errWin = 0;
}
```

PATTERN 1.3: CLASS AS SOLE OWNER

Context Even though there is no single function or object to serve as owner, the ownership responsibility can be localized to a single class. The function that creates the object is either a static or nonstatic member function of the class.

Solution All parts of the class collaborate to determine the lifetime of the owned object. The implementation of the ownership responsibility is distributed across the member functions as they execute on behalf of all objects of that class. Static member functions may also participate.

Example Class `Query` illustrates Class as Sole Owner. A `Query` object provides end-user database services. `Query` objects are created and destroyed arbitrarily. All `Query` objects share a single `DataBase` server. To conserve resources, the `DataBase` object should exist only when there is at least one `Query` object. The constructor and destructor of `Query`, using static data members, implement this policy together on behalf of the class:

```
class Query {
public:
  Query();
  ~Query();
  . . .
private:
  static DataBase *db;
  static int population;
  . . .
};

DataBase *Query::db = 0;
int Query::population = 0;

Query::Query()
{
  if( population == 0 )
    db = new DataBase;
  population += 1;
}

Query::~Query()
{
  population -= 1;
  if( population == 0 ){
    delete db;
    db = 0;
  }
}
```

PATTERN 2: SEQUENCE OF OWNERS

Context   No suitable creator that can assume ongoing ownership responsibility can be found. For example, a factory creates objects on behalf of others. Once the object has been successfully created, the factory's ownership responsibility should end, but the created object's lifetime must not.

Solution   Ownership may be transferred from the creator to another owner. Ownership may then be further transferred any number of times. At each point of transfer the outgoing owner relinquishes its ownership obligation, whereupon the incoming owner assumes it. The transfer of ownership must be considered as an explicit part of the interface between the two. Although the owner may change many times, at any particular time ownership rests with only one owner.

Example The following code shows ownership transfer from a factory to a function (the transfer could as easily be to an object or class as to the incoming owner):

```
Resource *Creator::factory()
{
  Resource *res = new Resource;
  if( res->valid() )
    return res;      // transfer
  // retain
  delete res;
  return 0;
}

void Client::usesFactory()
{
  Resource *res = Creator::factory();
  if( res != 0 ){
    // transferred
    . . .
    delete res;  // eventually
  }
}
```

Example The function shown below transfers ownership to a local `auto_ptr` object. The `auto_ptr` template is part of the draft C++ standard library [ANSI95].[2] The only purpose of an `auto_ptr` object is to assume ownership of a dynamic object. The `auto_ptr` destructor deletes the object. The advantage of transferring ownership to an automatic object is that its destructor will execute under almost all control flow scenarios that leave the block.

```
void Use_auto_ptr()
{
  Resource *res = new Resource;
  auto_ptr<Resource> owner(res);
  . . .
  // use res
  . . .
} // owner deletes
```

[2] Note that `auto_ptr` is a misnomer: the object need not necessarily have automatic duration. For example, an `auto_ptr` object might be a member of a class.

PATTERN 3: SHARED OWNERSHIP

Context   When a dynamic object is shared widely by diverse components, it may be impossible to identify a single owner or even a sequence of owners for it. An object that defies simple characterization and management of its lifetime is likely to be long-lived.

Solution   Allow arbitrary owners to declare unilateral interest in a dynamic object. The lifetime of the dynamic object continues until all of the owners have relinquished their interest in it. Constraints on the owners and the owned object vary, depending on the style of implementation.

Example   A conventional reference-counted implementation of a string class [Stroustrup91, p. 248] uses shared ownership of the representation object, which in turn is sole owner of the underlying array of characters. Usually the representation class is designed to carry a reference count to support its shared ownership. That is, the implementation of the ownership intrudes into the class of the owned object. Ownership is intentionally restricted to the string objects.

Example   Reference-counting "smart pointers" [Coplien92, p. 65] also use shared ownership. As with a reference-counted string class, the mechanism usually intrudes into the owned object and limits ownership to the smart pointer objects.

Example   The following example demonstrates that intrusion on the owned object and constraints on the owners are not intrinsically part of the pattern.

Shared ownership information with respect to arbitrary objects is recorded in a global instance of class `Shared`. `Shared::adopt()` records an arbitrary owner declaring an interest in an arbitrary object. `Shared::disown()` records an owner relinquishing that interest. A `true` result from `disown()` informs the departing owner that no other owners remain and therefore the dynamic object should be deleted. Effectively, `Shared` provides reference counting that constrains neither owner nor owned object:

```
template<class R>
class Shared {
public:
    void adopt(R*);
    bool disown(R*);
```

```
private:
    map³<void*,int> owners;
};

template<class R>
void Shared<R>::adopt(R *r)
{
    if( owners.find(r) == owners.end() )
        owners[r] = 1;
    else
        owners[r] += 1;
}

template<class R>
bool Shared<R>::disown(R *r)
{
    assert( owners.find(r) != owners.end() );
    owners[r] -= 1;
    if( owners[r] > 0 )
        return false;
    owners.erase(r);
    return true;
}


Shared<Window> clerk;
```

A `Journal` object logs messages to a `Window`. The current `Window` is established in its constructor but may be changed by the `bind` member function. A `Journal` object assumes shared ownership of its `Window` by registering its ownership with `clerk` and deleting any unowned `Window`. The `Window` class does not participate in the implementation of this ownership mechanism. The other owners of `Window` may be arbitrary functions, objects, and classes; `Journal` requires only that they observe the protocol with respect to `clerk`:

```
class Journal {
public:
  void bind(Window*);
  void log(Message);
  Journal(Window*);
  ~Journal();

  . . .
```

---

³ This is the map template from the draft standard library. The class `map<K,V>` is an associative array of `V` indexed by `K`. As coded, the `<` `operator` is assumed to define a total ordering on `void*`, which is not true in general.

```
private:
  Window *current;
  . . .
};

void Journal::bind(Window *w)
{
  clerk.adopt(w);
  if( clerk.disown(current) )
    delete current;
  current = w;
}

void Journal::log(Message m)
{
  current->display(render(m));
}

Journal::Journal(Window *initial)
{
  current = initial;
  clerk.adopt(current);
}

Journal::~Journal()
{
  if( clerk.disown(current) )
    delete current;
}
```

RELATED TOPICS

Dangling Pointers

Discussion of garbage avoidance often leads to the separate but related topic of "dangling pointers." A pointer dangles when use of its value becomes invalid (at the end of the lifetime of the object it addresses). Use of a dangling pointer is undefined behavior, which often results in a program crash, or worse. A pointer that refers to a dynamic object dangles if the dynamic object is deleted (by its owner). However, dangling pointers can also arise without the use of dynamic allocation: a pointer to an automatic object dangles if the pointer outlives the object. A dangling pointer must never be dereferenced.

Reference Counting Versus Garbage Collection

Reference counting (mentioned with respect to shared ownership) is easily confused with garbage collection. The two mechanisms are not equivalent, however. There are circumstances under which reference counting reclaims memory that garbage collection misses, and vice versa. By tolerating a dangling pointer, reference counting that depends on an explicit decrement operation can recover a dynamic object that garbage collection must retain. On the other hand, a cycle of mutual references can cause reference counting to overlook a set of objects that garbage collection would reclaim.

Exception Handling

An exception handling (EH) mechanism for C++ (using termination scmantics) has been proposed in the draft standard, and implementations are becoming available. Clearly, a nonlocal goto mechanism introduces further analysis in determining that a program, including any use of dynamic memory, is coded correctly. Unfortunately, to date the C++ community has little experience with EH, and a coherent approach for the using EH in C++ has yet to emerge. It appears that object state and resource management (including dynamic memory) are the two key problems to address when using EH, and that resource management is the easier of the two.

ACKNOWLEDGMENTS

My thanks to Paul Jensen, David Leserman, Doug Schmidt, John Vlissides, and the members of my PLoP '95 workshop for their comments on drafts of this paper.

REFERENCES

[ANSI95] ANSI. *Working Paper for Draft Proposed International Standard for Information Systems—Programming Language C++*. ANSI Document X3J16/95-0091, 1995.

[Carolan89] J. Carolan. *Constructing Bullet-Proof Classes, Proceedings C++ at Work*. New York: SIGS Publications, 1989.

[Coplien92] J. Coplien. *Advanced C++ Programming Styles and Idioms.* Reading, MA: Addison-Wesley, 1992.

[Stroustrup91] B. Stroustrup. *The C++ Programming Language,* 2nd ed. Reading, MA: Addison-Wesley, 1991, p. 309.

Tom Cargill can be reached at P.O. Box 69, Louisville, CO 80027; `cargill@csn.org`.

Lazy Optimization: Patterns for Efficient Smalltalk Programming

2

Ken Auer and Kent Beck

We both preach to our clients about performance tuning and productive programming. "Make it run, make it right, make it fast," is the mantra. But as much as our clients seem to like this philosophy, in reality it makes them very nervous.

One client in particular who had received a full dose of this medicine began moving ahead nicely on a complex application that stored Smalltalk objects in a relational database. The client first got the application to work and then made sure the design for the overall framework was very elegant and flexible. Unfortunately, the system was not nearly as responsive as the user wanted. It was time to "make it fast," and time was running out.

Later, a developer pulled Kent aside and said, "You got me in trouble."

"About what?"

"You said I could tune performance after I got the design right," the developer said.

"Yes, I did," Kent replied. "What happened?"

"We spent all that time getting the design right, then the users wanted subsecond response time. The system was taking as long as fifteen seconds to respond to a query. It took me all weekend to change the design around to fix the performance problem."

"How fast is it now?" Kent asked.

"Well, now it comes back in a third of a second."

"So, what's the problem?"

"I was really nervous that I wouldn't be able to fix the performance problem."

And that's why there is a pattern called Performance Assessment. It probably won't change anything about how you program, but it will keep you from getting nervous.

Software development is like a delicate piece of chamber music. If any one instrument protrudes, the quality of the piece is ruined. You have to strike the right balance:

- You have to program like mad to get enough functionality done to make a competitive product.

- You have to thoughtfully correct hastily made design decisions to continue making progress.

- You have to make programs run fast to be competitive.

Although many performance problems stem from lack of a coherent design, many others stem from solutions that optimize readability or flexibility over resource usage. In many cases this is the right trade-off, as the costs of a system over its lifetime are dominated by how well it communicates with humans. When the program has to go fast, though, it just has to go fast.

Languages (like Smalltalk) provide power that allows us to manage complexity. They hide how much binary logic is actually being exercised behind the functionality we take for granted. This isolation from the details makes it easier to write communicative but inefficient code.

Tuning in Smalltalk is the same as in any language. You either:

- do expensive things less often or

- do less expensive things

The primary forces driving the production of efficient programs are

- Finite computers. If computers were infinitely fast and had infinite memory, we wouldn't have to worry about performance. As long as we're limited to the current 3+1 dimensions,[1] however, we will always be faced with problems

---

[1] "3+1 dimensions" refers to space (height, width, depth) and time.

that tax the available resources. Escalating expectations ensure that the strategy of waiting for the next generation of hardware to arrive is no long-term solution. A successful tuning strategy has to bow to the facts of finite resources.

- Long-term costs. Well-written, well-factored programs have the fewest defects and incur the least maintenance costs. Many performance optimizations sacrifice these long-term benefits for immediate improvements, however. A successful tuning strategy has to preserve the benefits of good programming style while still achieving acceptable performance.

- Time to market. If we had years and years to program, we might be able to produce programs that were both elegant (that is, simple to maintain) and efficient. Competitive pressures always dictate that a program be shipped before it is perfect, however. A successful performance strategy cannot take a long time to execute.

Below is a partial pattern language for creating efficient Smalltalk programs. Many of the higher-level patterns are not specific to Smalltalk at all and could in fact be applied to any language. Many of the more detailed patterns could also be applied to most languages, and most definitely to object-oriented languages. However, in the interests of brevity and narrowing our audience, we chose to illustrate the patterns by assuming that their application is to Smalltalk. Additionally, as patterns get to lower levels of detail and move into the realm of "idioms," they tend to be less applicable to a wide range of languages. The authors have a high level of confidence in the performance of these patterns when they are applied to Smalltalk. We invite experts in other programming environments to use this as a template for a similar pattern language for their own environments, and we would be surprised if they did not find their own unique, language-specific patterns (or idioms).

Figure 1 shows a graphical map of the patterns in this language. Patterns referenced but not yet published are in italics.

PERFORMANCE ASSESSMENT

Prologue   You are ready to begin developing the User Scenario in your Commitment Schedule in earnest.

Problem   **How can you begin, confident that performance won't be a problem?**

Forces   Early in program development is when you are most likely to hear the siren call of premature optimization. Once you are into the thick of development,

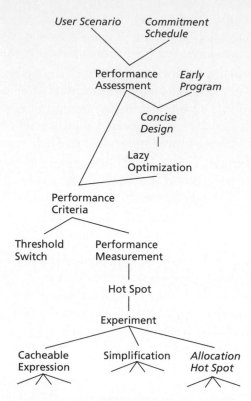

FIGURE 1 Map of patterns in the language

you will be unlikely to have the energy for thinking of anything but getting the system done and done right. Unfortunately, it is at precisely this stage when premature optimization has the opportunity to do the most damage.

Early in development is when you should listen most carefully to users' needs and take stock of your available resources. If every thought is poisoned by "Yes, but how fast will that run?" you will likely miss the chance to make large leaps in development.

At the same time, performance is a legitimate concern. If the program doesn't go fast enough, you will not get paid (or keep getting paid). You need to assure yourself and your client that performance problems will not sink an otherwise brilliantly crafted and executed system.

Therefore:

Solution   **Indulge your performance worries by writing a short (e.g., two-page) performance assessment of the system. Identify critical resources outside of Smalltalk. Do the math to figure out how big and how fast the final system will be. Develop prototypes for areas of concern if absolutely necessary.**

Discussion   Some people call these "envelope calculations," after their tendency to be done on the back of an envelope. A typical performance assessment might conclude that only one mainframe access is allowable per user transaction.

Hard real-time systems have a long history of careful performance assessment. When you know you have to service an interrupt in 10 microseconds, well, that pretty much shapes at least one major subsystem. Most systems that are called real-time systems are in reality not nearly so restrictive.

Areas requiring a prototype might include any unique area of your system that you deem somewhat complex and whose responsiveness is critical to the success of your application. For example, you might have a map that needs to display hundreds of small labels and icons representing particular locations. You could throw together a prototype that pumps hundreds of random labels and icons to the screen in random spots. If it's too slow, you would then figure out what's taking all the time and tune the prototype. Once you were convinced it could (or couldn't) be done, you would throw out the prototype and start the real work (or revise your expectations).

Epilogue   The Performance Assessment will help you decide how to shape the Concise Design. You may be able to define your Performance Criteria directly from the assessment.

LAZY OPTIMIZATION

Prologue   Early Program quickly creates systems with the needed functionality. Concise Design refactors objects to improve clarity and flexibility.

Problem   **How do you achieve acceptable performance with the least short- and long-term cost?**

Forces   Users should have the experience of being in control of their computer, not the other way around. Even the best-designed user interface will frustrate and hinder a user if it does not respond with dispatch.

Some programs spend considerable time in Smalltalk. These programs will be efficient to the degree they leverage but do not stress Smalltalk resources such as message sending and the garbage collector.

Other programs are limited by factors out of the direct control of the programming language—available virtual memory, database access, graphics calls, and so on. Another measure of efficiency is how effectively a program uses available resources, how short the path is connecting a stimulus *from* the outside world to a stimulus *for* the outside world.

Almost every professional programmer has had the experience of writing a program, taking the heat because it is too slow, and (importantly) not being able to fix the performance problems in a timely fashion. Some programmers react to this rite of passage by insisting that performance is a legitimate concern throughout development. No request for functionality nor proposal for design refinement can be considered until it has passed the "can it run fast?" test.

This practice is the death of effective development. Progress slows to a crawl as every thought is forced to pass through the sieve of fear. Decisions are optimized for presumed performance impact rather than short- or long-term programming productivity and low risk. The result is large programs with limited functionality. They grow progressively more and more complex until they cease being valuable to the developing organization.

The irony is that such programs are virtually impossible to keep running fast. Their lack of clarity robs you of the ability to identify performance bottlenecks. Even if you could find a problem, chances are you could not address it without making widespread changes, exactly the sort of activity you must avoid late in development.

So, you have to worry about performance or your users won't be satisfied, but it doesn't help to worry about it all the time.

Therefore:

Solution   **Ignore efficiency through most of the development cycle. Tune performance once the program is running correctly and the design reflects your best understanding of how the code should be structured. The needed changes will be limited in scope or will illuminate opportunities for better design.**

Discussion   It is critical that this strategy be incorporated into your project plan. Plan on some optimization activities toward the end or at natural breaks, when functionality of a section is expected to be complete.

Not only will this strategy give you time to do the necessary optimization, but also it will appease early reviewers who deem your program to be too slow. You can always say, "Yes, we know it is too slow. You can see where, in our project plan, we plan on addressing this issue." Of course, if you don't give yourself enough time to actually do the tuning, you are still going to look bad. One rule of thumb is to assume 35 percent of development time will be required for tuning for those inexperienced at the process of tuning in Smalltalk, decreasing to 10 percent for experienced developers.

Epilogue   Agree with the client on the Performance Criteria the program will be measured against. Create a Performance Measurement that automatically runs that part of the program judged by users to be too slow.

PERFORMANCE CRITERIA

Prologue   The Performance Assessment may have discovered easily quantifiable criteria. Later, reviewers of your system, working after your Concise Design, may have identified some concerns.

Problem   **How do you know what is worth tuning and what is not?**

Forces   The naive view is that the whole program should be as fast as possible. This leads you either to commit to less functionality than you should implement or to muddle the design so badly that you can't get anything to work right, much less work fast.

   Many parts of your system will work without any complaints about performance, even if they are implemented in the simplest possible way. In addition, you cannot be sure in advance where performance bottlenecks will lie [Barry91]. You can't even be sure which bottlenecks will bother users and which won't.
   Therefore:

Solution   **Ask your client to give you ballpark response time or throughput criteria for your system. Be prepared to revise this list as the system matures.**

Discussion   At first you just want to know what the client is sure to notice. Typical Performance Criteria are

   ■ Interactive response time
   ■ Frame rate
   ■ Bits per second
   ■ Transactions per second

   As time goes on, your client (or you) may notice new things that just are not snappy enough. Make sure the particular complaints are specific and goals are explicitly stated.

Epilogue   Performance Criteria need a Threshold Switch to give you a concrete goal. Each Criterion should be accompanied by a set of Performance Measurements.

THRESHOLD SWITCH

Prologue   You have identified the performance criteria for your system. You have begun to improve the problem areas.

Problem   **How fast is fast enough?**

Forces   You might think that once you have settled on a Performance Criterion, you must comfortably exceed that criterion. This is almost never true.

Programs that are to be used by people are both constrained by and can take advantage of the quirks of human perception. In particular, actual performance and perceived performance are not linearly related.

Once you get past a perceptual threshold, substantial further measured performance improvement will result in little or no perceived improvement. Therefore:

Solution   **Agree that as soon as you meet the Performance Criteria, you will stop tuning. If you've beaten the pants off it (e.g., a subsecond response criterion now performs in 0.2 seconds) with the first Experiment, great. However, don't make a new goal of seeing how much you can beat the Criteria. When you hit the threshold of what is needed, stop tuning!**

Discussion   Always remember that the major cost of software is in maintenance. Most techniques used to improve performance sacrifice a bit of maintainability. Avoid them at all costs.

Epilogue   Once you've agreed to the concept of a Threshold Switch, you are ready to begin the actual process of tuning. However, before you do, you must gather Performance Measurements to make the Switches real.

PERFORMANCE MEASUREMENT

Prologue   You've established Performance Criteria and agreed to Threshold Switches.

Problem   **How do you consistently measure performance and ensure that the system keeps running while you are tuning, and how do you know when you have triggered your Threshold Switches?**

Forces As already noted, programmers typically aren't very good at identifying bottle-necks. Experienced programmers (those who have made more mistakes than you have ever dreamed of making) may be able to make a good guess at what's causing these bottlenecks. If you've got one of these people around, getting him or her to guess would be a great improvement over guessing yourself.

If you have a good list of efficiency hacks (e.g., "when you see A, do B instead"), you could look for all occurrences of the "slow" ways of doing things (e.g., the *A*s) and replace them with their faster counterparts (the *B*s). The odds are good that you'll end up with a much faster program, but it will take an awfully long time to find all of the potentially slow things you've done. Also, there may be so many places you have to change that you might wonder why you didn't just write your code like that in the first place. Then you'll look at the probably unreadable result and remember why. Chances are you will have replaced a lot of code that would have run "fast enough" if you had just left it alone.

Even if you've done this exhaustive search-and-destroy, you may have missed some bottlenecks that were not in your catalog of efficiency tricks. You might even have missed the one or two key bottlenecks that, if corrected first, would have made all the other efficiency hacks unnecessary.

Therefore:

Solution **Always write a routine that tests and times apparent performance problems in such a way that it does not rely on human intervention. Use a profiler to identify the biggest bottlenecks in the area in question.**

Discussion A VisualWorks customer was very concerned about the performance of his system. He was concerned that all the horror stories he had heard about Smalltalk's being too slow for real systems were true. It seemed that the fundamental section of his system was taking minutes to do anything, and he needed it to take seconds. He couldn't figure out what was taking so long, no matter how hard he tried.

In a last-ditch effort to figure out whether the customer's work could be salvaged, Dave Leibs, a Smalltalk performance guru from ParcPlace Systems, Inc., was called in for a day of consulting. The customer quickly described an overview of what he was trying to do. Nothing stood out to Dave as anything that would bring Smalltalk to its knees, so he asked, "Where did the Profiler indicate most of the time was being spent?"

"What's the Profiler?"

So Dave spent the next 30 minutes or so explaining what the Profiler was and helping the customer install it.

He then ran the Profiler on the section of code in question and found it was spending more than 98 percent of its time in Date>>printOn:. Dave thought for a second what might be so slow about Date>>printOn:. He felt it should not cause so great a problem, so he looked a little higher up the profile tree and examined the containing method.

He noticed the expression Date today printString inside of a loop, so he chose an experiment and pulled the expression out of the loop, storing the value in a temporary variable he then used inside the loop. Ten minutes after running the Profiler for the first time, he ran the code again. This critical section of code, which was central to the client's system, now took less than a second.

Dave then turned to his host and said, "So, what are we going to do for the rest of the day?"

Epilogue   After addressing the bottleneck (see Hot Spot) run the Performance Measurement again to verify whether you actually improved performance and whether you've brought it down to meet the Performance Criteria. If you have not, continue to use Hot Spot until you have met the Criteria or reached a point where you have to either give up or use Rethink Approach. Before moving on to the next bottleneck, verify that it still exists—well-factored methods, once tuned, often spark performance increases in other areas that rely on the method. You may have killed two or more birds with one stone.

HOT SPOT

Prologue   You've identified several areas of your system that don't meet your Performance Criteria.

Problem   **Where do you actually begin tuning?**

Forces   You could just list the problem areas and assign them as tasks on a queue, knocking them off one at a time. Individuals working on your project could just tackle the next problem on the list. The order in which they are addressed doesn't really matter as long as you insist that all of them must be addressed. You should probably prioritize them, however, as some might be nastier than others, and you don't want to spend your time fixing the simple ones if the critical ones are the real showstoppers. If an individual finishes his or her task before others, he or she can just move on to the next available task. Pretty simple, isn't it?

Dividing the work this way precludes collaboration and the benefit of finding commonality among problems, however. On the other hand, if you have everybody standing around analyzing the best way to go about solving your problems, they won't ever get addressed.

Solution   **Profile most or all performance problems before putting a lot of energy into prioritizing, assigning, and fixing them. At a more micro level, identify where the majority of time is being spent for each problem. These are the Hot Spots on which you should focus your tuning efforts. You may be surprised to find that multiple performance problems are due to a particular approach that spans multiple areas. The best approach to addressing these hot spots may be very different when you take into account several contexts in which the problems occur—priority items will become more apparent. If performance problems persist after these items have been addressed, repeat this pattern to identify the next set of hot spots.**

Discussion   If you are working on a large system, you may want to categorize problems first and then run the Profiler on a particular category of problems. You want to avoid waiting to begin your profiling efforts until after everyone else is waiting to tune. Again, find natural breaking points in the project (see Lazy Optimization) where a developer is available to work on areas where Concise Design has been completed.

Epilogue   In addressing Hot Spots, look through the remaining patterns to see whether the corresponding code matches the symptoms and then apply the suggested solutions.

EXPERIMENT

Prologue   You have identified an apparent Hot Spot but are not certain you have the solution that will get you to your Threshold Switch.

Problem   **How do I find the best performance solution?**

Forces   The mindset at this point in time is, "I need to make this thing faster, or I'm dead meat." However, we must remember the points made in Threshold Switch with respect to efficiency hacks' sacrificing later maintainability.
    Therefore:

Solution   **Treat each application of an efficiency hack as an experiment. If it didn't get you to the desired Criteria (e.g., you needed 10x improvement and it gave you 0.1x), make a note of what it did give you and undo it. Keep only the experiments that actually get you to your criteria. You may have to combine several to get you there, but concentrate on the big bang experiments rather than the little improvements.**

Discussion   In the discussion of Performance Measurement, we presented a problem that may have indicated that we needed to tune Date>>printOn:. Suppose Dave Liebs took some time ripping apart the Date>>printOn: method and putting it back together so that it was 40 percent faster (albeit less concise and in danger of blowing up in the fourth leap year in the 21st century). He then conducted the Experiment (Caching Temporary Variable) in the higher-level method that gave him the big bang. Leaving the faster printOn: method would now have the critical section run in 0.92 seconds instead of 0.93.

   Not only is it not worth leaving the new printOn: method in now, but for performance reasons you must also think about the future ramifications of leaving it in. Some poor maintenance programmer will have the thankless job of upgrading the system to the next release of VisualWorks. First she will try to find all the base image changes her company made that need to be carried forward. Then she will discover this change (which may or may not include a comment explaining what was done to it). She will notice that the new version of VisualWorks has a different version of the method than the previous version (before the hacked change). People will start noticing the amount of time spent trying to figure out what to do at this point much more than they ever noticed the 0.01 seconds it bought them in the first release of the product.

Epilogue   You should be getting closer to your desired Performance Criteria, with little impact to Concise Design.

CACHEABLE EXPRESSION

Prologue   The Profiler has identified a particular expression as a significant contributor to execution time. An expression is executed many times, often with the same result.

Problem   **How do we reduce the overhead of this repeated expression with the least impact on the integrity of the system?**

Forces   As in previous patterns, we would rather not compromise the design of the system in removing bottlenecks. We would also prefer to minimize the overhead of objects. Additional variables (e.g., instance variables) often propagate side effects of additional supporting methods, not to mention the memory required to hold the corresponding value. A variable cache eliminates design possibilities and offers opportunities to break encapsulation.

On the other hand, the result of an expression takes up memory somewhere (e.g., the execution stack), no matter what. We shouldn't get too carried away with avoiding memory usage.

Solution   **If you find an expression that often returns the same result, find the lowest-overhead type of variable that will alleviate the redundancy. This will cause a performance improvement while minimizing design compromises [Auer95].**

Discussion   Several years ago, a major portion of a Process Modeling System with which we were involved was devoted to rerouting and redrawing diagrams.

After a redesign of a prototype (Concise Design), performance improved significantly (three to five times). Even though performance was not a primary goal, this level was still deemed unacceptable. Therefore, Performance Criteria were established.

In a period of one week, system response time was improved by roughly one order of magnitude [White91]. Due to the Concise Design there was little to overhaul. Most of these performance improvements were due to our finding common expressions and speeding them up by Caching Expressions.

On the other hand, keeping caches may force other methods to be aware of caches. For example, if a Rectangle caches its area in an instance variable, all methods that allow changes to the Rectangle's coordinates must do something to make sure the cached area is reset.

Caching variables can also threaten the integrity of the object containing the cache itself. For example, before the area-cached instance variable is added, the following expression (although bad practice) would not threaten the integrity of the object:

aRectangle origin y: 25

For a variety of reasons, the implementor of Rectangle chose to take the risk of exposing its instance variable, knowing that, as the implementation stood, such an expression as this would not break anything.

As soon as the Cached Instance Variable is added, such an expression would result in a problem, as there would be no way to trigger a cache reset without additional mechanisms.

Epilogue Overhead and risk are typically lowest for Caching Temporary Variable, followed by Caching Argument, Caching Class Variable, Caching Class Instance Variable, and Caching Instance Variable.

CACHING TEMPORARY VARIABLE

Prologue A Cacheable Expression is causing a Hot Spot, most likely because it occurs in a loop.

Problem **How do you increase the performance of the loop?**

Forces Sacrificing good design will cost you during maintenance. Introducing a cache introduces the possibility that its value will become incorrect during the life of the method. Often, seemingly harmless expressions inside a loop return the same result each time.

Solution **For each expensive expression in the loop that returns the same value each time through, add a temporary variable that is set to the result of the expression before the loop begins, and replace all occurrences of the expression with the corresponding temporary variable.**

Discussion For example, if you wanted to collect a subset of a table based on selected column names, your code may look something like this:

```
collectColumns: anArrayOfColumnNames
    ^self rows collect:
        [:row |
        anArrayOfColumnNames collect: [:name | row at: (self columnIndexFor: name)]]

columnIndexFor: aColumnName
        ^self columnNameMaps at: aColumnName
```

Realizing that the column indices of interest are going to be the same each time through the loop, you could greatly reduce the amount of times #columnIndexFor: is sent as follows:

```
collectColumns: anArrayOfColumnNames
    | columnIndices |
    columnIndices := anArrayOfColumnNames collect: [:name |
self columnIndexFor: name].
    ^self rows collect:
        [:row |
        columnIndices collect: [:index | row at: index]]
```

Epilogue Although this may fix many problems, it is possible that the expression might still be repeated many times due to pervasiveness of a containing method. Therefore, the program may still not meet the Performance Criteria. If so, look for caching with a larger scope, such as Caching Instance Variable.

CACHING ARGUMENT

Prologue Multiple objects are creating similar transient objects to create pieces of the desired end result.

Problem **How can we reduce the number of transient objects?**

Forces Keeping "collector" objects in instance, class, class instance, or global variables (depending on scope) has undesirable costs. Although it does increase performance, it also adds a lot of overhead and tends to hold on to objects that are not needed past the completion of an operation.
  Therefore:

Solution **Keep a single transient object that can be used by multiple objects that contribute to the final result, and pass the object around as an argument to all the objects that can put it to use.**

Discussion Here is an example of an algorithm that uses collection concatenation, which causes lots of transient objects to be created:

```
printList
    | list |
    self isEmpty ifTrue: [^String new].
    list := self first printString.
    2 to: self size do:
        [:index |
        list := list, ', ', (self at: index) printString].
    ^list
```

Objects convert themselves into strings by creating a Stream on an empty string and sending themselves the printOn: message with the Stream as an argument. We could instead create a single Stream that all objects would write to:

```
printList
    | stream |
    stream := WriteStream on: String new.
    self do:
        [:each |
        each printOn: stream.
```

```
        stream nextPutAll: ', '].
    self isEmpty ifFalse: [stream skip: -2].
    ^stream contents
```

Another example would be to pass a collection into which all objects that had something to contribute would add to:

```
allFemaleChildren := Set new.
self people do: [:each | each addFemaleChildrenInto: allFemaleChildren]
```

The addFemaleChildrenInto: method would do nothing but add to the passed collection, or it would do nothing at all if there were no female children. It could be used instead of

```
allFemaleChildren := Set new.
self people do: [:each | allFemaleChildren addAll: each allFemaleChildren]
```

which would create an intermediate collection, maybe even an empty one.

Epilogue   Applying this pattern may result in modifications to multiple parts of the system if protocol must be changed to use the Caching Argument. Typically this can be avoided by adopting the old protocol (still to be supported using the new protocol) with the Caching Argument as its foundation. However, this may potentially hurt the performance of systems using the original protocol. Use Performance Measurement and Performance Criteria to determine if this is a problem.

CACHING STATE VARIABLE

Prologue   A Cacheable Expression is causing a Hot Spot, but because it is necessary in varied contexts, it cannot simply be cached in an argument or a temporary variable.

Problem   **How do you increase the performance of expressions that are needed in a variety of contexts?**

Forces   You never want to limit design possibilities. No one can tell what new requirements will develop later, and you would like to be able to easily map these requirements into simple methods in existing classes. Every time you add a state variable, a burden is placed on the developer to make sure every method that may have an effect on that state is aware of it. A method can no longer be concerned with simply giving an answer; you need to be concerned with side effects.

Nevertheless, ignoring the implied side effects of an operation is sometimes exactly what causes performance problems. Everything must be calculated dynamically, because you never can be sure whether the environment has changed since the last time the result of the expression was needed.

In the context of a single method or a chain of methods, knowledge of a local environment (temps, arguments, and so on) can be exploited via Caching Temporary Variables or Caching Arguments. The decisions to use these types of Cacheable Expressions affect no one but the execution stack, which is pretty well secure from the rest of the system. Unfortunately, the system encompasses much more than this local environment, and such techniques cannot solve all performance problems.

Yet we still want to avoid caching expressions at a level that exposes the cache to the entire system and therefore limits design possibilities and exposes integrity problems on a wide scale. For instance, if we kept the results of an expression for anyone to use in a global variable, all methods that wanted to benefit from the results of the cache would have to know about its existence by name. Additionally, any actions anywhere in the system that would invalidate its value would have to explicitly reset it.

You will want to encapsulate Cacheable Expression in as low a level as possible that will affect all of the contexts that would like to exploit the cache. Classes, MetaClasses, and Class hierarchies all define an environment narrower than the system level but broader than the execution stack. Each defines its own behavioral environment.

Therefore:

Solution   **Identify the behavioral environment (Class, Class hierarchy, or MetaClass) that encapsulates all of the contexts in which the Cached Expression can be shared before the probability of resetting the value would be expected. Add a corresponding state variable (instance, class, or class instance). Give it the name of the message to be cached. Rename the message to be cached by prepending "compute" to the corresponding selector. Use lazy initialization to compute the value of the variable. Modify other parts of the behavioral environment to make sure this value is reset whenever some event occurs that could possibly make this result obsolete.**

Discussion   If you needed a solid dot icon, you can recompute it every time:

```
dot
    ^"build the icon"
```

But the icon will be the same for all instances of all classes in the hierarchy. So:

```
dot
    Dot == nil
        ifTrue: [Dot := self computeDot].
    ^Dot
```

If the dot size needs to change based on user preferences changing, a hook would have to be inserted to flush the Dot whenever the user preferences changed.

Similarly, an instance method

```
fullName
    ^last, ', ', first, ' ', middle
```

could become

```
computeFullName
    ^last, ', ', first, ' ', middle
```

```
fullName
    fullName == nil
        ifTrue: [fullName := self computeFullName].
    ^fullName
```

and methods that set the parts of fullName would be modified to reset fullName, as this example shows:

```
last: aString
    last := aString.
    self fullName: nil.
```

If you need an icon to represent the *on* state for a particular class of button but the icons are different for different classes of buttons in the hierarchy, you could implement this:

```
onIcon
    ^"build the icon"
```

Realizing that the icon will be the same for all instances of all classes in the hierarchy, you rewrite it as:

```
onIcon
    ^self class onIcon
```

```
class>>onIcon
    onIcon == nil
        ifTrue: [onIcon := "build the icon"].
    ^onIcon
```

Clearing the cache of class instance variables may require some awkward code in the root class to ensure that all caches are cleared simultaneously:

```
class>>resetClassCache
    self withAllSubclassesDo: [:each | each cacheVar: nil].
```

Epilogue   With any Cached State Variable, there is the potential to eliminate design possibilities or to invalidate the previous class design assumptions. Be careful to adjust your Concise Design if the implications warrant.

SIMPLIFICATION

Prologue   You notice several methods are Hot Spots in a certain context that cannot be simplified while still maintaining the integrity of the system for all instances of the same class.

Problem   **How do we improve the Hot Spots for the context in question without causing undesirable side effects in other contexts where instances of the same class are used?**

Forces   Changing a method in such a way as to enable unadvertised side effects under certain conditions, no matter how remote, is inviting trouble.

Case statements could be inserted to detect a particular context. However, such statements are ugly and often slow down execution for the more general cases, due to the overhead involved in case checking.

Therefore:

Solution   **Examine the features of a class that are actually being used by a particular instance or group of instances. Determine if there is another existing class or a simplified version of the class being used that could provide the desired features more efficiently.**

Discussion   There are many examples of existing classes that act functionally similar for many operations yet offer distinct performance advantages.

Arrays are generally more efficient than Ordered Collections. They take up less space, they don't have extra instance variables to denote the beginning and end of a collection, and they avoid a level of indirection in accessing their indexed instance variables.

Symbols, once created, are much faster to compare than Strings, as they are merely comparing object pointers as opposed to comparing each individual element contained by the String.

Additionally, one can often create classes that are simplifications of more flexible classes, if such flexibility is not needed. For example, ComposedText in VisualWorks will handle various composition features of text (word wrapping, tabs, changes of fonts, and so on). If you simply want to display a simple ASCII String in a single font with no special characters or composition considerations, you could create a simple class such as VisualString, which simply calls the primitive for displaying a string using the particular font, without any intermediate effort.

Epilogue   After Simplification you may often find that other areas of your system are using more complex classes than they need to. You may wish to revisit Concise Design to delete classes that are redundant.

TRANSIENT REDUCTION

Prologue   You have some set of objects, A, and want some set of objects, B.

Problem   **How do I get from A to B in the most efficient manner?**

Forces   Objects are wonderful, and they can do wonderful things for us very elegantly. Encapsulation helps us hide the complexity of what's happening behind the scenes when we want some particular result. There may be tens of thousands or hundreds of thousands of objects that are created in helping to determine the desired result that we never even see. These objects give their life for our result, and we don't even know they exist. Some thanks they get.

  Ah, but their dirty little secret is that they don't like going unnoticed, so they leave their mark by gobbling up CPU cycles. Creation here, a few messages sent there, a little garbage collection to clean up the mess, and eventually someone might notice that more time has gone by than was planned.

Solution   **Reduce the number of transient objects in a given operation.**

Discussion   A client of ours complained about Smalltalk and how the garbage collector was constantly interrupting and taking up too much time during many of his graphical programming operations. After analyzing the situation, we found that moving a particular object from one place to another was causing tens of thousands of other objects to be created that were all short-lived and mostly unnecessary. The problem wasn't the efficiency of garbage collection but the constant garbage creation.

Epilogue   This can be accomplished using several other patterns, such as Object Transformation, Caching Argument, Pre-allocated Collection, and Concatenating Stream.

OBJECT TRANSFORMATION

Prologue   I have some set of objects, A, and I want another set of objects, B, of the same classes. Once I have B, I no longer need A.

Problem   **How do I get from A to B in the most efficient manner?**

Forces   There is overhead involved in creating the new object and garbage collecting the old one. We want to minimize such overhead while preserving encapsulation.

Solution   **Instead of creating new objects to replace the old objects, transform the old objects into the objects you desire.**

Discussion   For example, if you have a Rectangle of a particular shape and position, and you want to replace it with a new Rectangle with a similar shape but different position, you could simply send it the message translatedBy: with the appropriate argument to get the resulting Rectangle. However, this creates a new Rectangle and two new Points, causing the old Rectangle and its two points to be garbage collected. Instead, you could send the message moveBy:

```
moveBy: aPoint
    origin := origin + aPoint.
    corner := corner + aPoint.
```

which results in the old Rectangle's being transformed into the new, creating one less object and adding one less object to the garbage heap. If you really wanted to throw caution to the wind and were sure the original Rectangle was the only object referring to the Points held by its origin and corner variables, you could write a method (and send the corresponding message) that reused the same Points and therefore created no new objects nor added any objects to the garbage heap. For example:

```
transformBy: aPoint
    origin x: origin x + aPoint x.
    origin y: origin y + aPoint y.
    corner x: corner x + aPoint x.
    corner y: corner y + aPoint y
```

Epilogue   None.

HYPOTH-A-SIZED COLLECTION

Prologue   A Hot Spot involves spending time adding objects to a collection.

Problem   **How can I make this more efficient?**

Forces   Collections are designed in such a way that the details of how they manage to hold all the objects one places into them is hidden. Most collections start out with relatively few slots to place objects into, to avoid wasting space. When a collection needs more space, it simply allocates a bigger chunk of it, copies the objects previously held to the new space, and no one is the wiser . . . except the Profiler.

   When adding many objects to a relatively small collection, much of the programmer's time is spent growing incrementally larger buffers and copying objects from the old to the new buffer.

Solution   **When you realize an operation is bound to add a significant number of objects to a collection, make sure the collection is big enough, based on a hypothesis, to hold the results without growing, or at least with minimal growing.**

Discussion   Instead of something like this, for example,

```
nonBaseClasses
    | collection |
    collection := Set new.
    Smalltalk allClassesDo:
        [:each |
        each superclass == nil
            ifFalse: [collection add: each]].
    ^collection
```

allocate enough space in the collection to avoid growth:

```
nonBaseClasses
    | collection |
    collection := Set new: Smalltalk classNames size.
    Smalltalk allClassesDo:
        [:each |
        each superclass == nil
            ifFalse: [collection add: each]].
    ^collection
```

Epilogue   None.

CONCATENATING STREAM

Prologue   You may be collecting results in a Collecting Temporary Variable. You may be collecting results over several methods in a Collecting Parameter.

Problem   **How do you concatenate several Collections efficiently?**

Forces   Concatenation (,) is a simple way to join several Collections. When you have lots of Collections, though, your program can be slowed down because the objects in the first Collection are copied once for each Collection that is concatenated.

   Streams provide a way out of this dilemma. Streams are careful not to copy their contents many times.

Solution   **Use a Stream to concatenate many Collections.**

Discussion   We ran a quick benchmark to see how significant the difference was between Collection concatenation and Streams. We ran the following code, which concatenates one thousand Strings:

```
100 timesRepeat:
    [result := String new.
    1000 timesRepeat: [result := result , 'abcdefg']]
```

It took 53 seconds to run. Then we ran the Stream version:

```
100 timesRepeat:
    [writer := WriteStream on: String new.
    1000 timesRepeat: [writer nextPutAll: 'abcdefg'].
    writer contents]]
```

It took 0.9 seconds to run. The difference is a factor of almost 60.

   Sometimes you will use Concatenating Stream not because it is your choice but because you have to work with other code that already uses it. The most common example is specializing object printing by overriding printOn:.

   Note that this pattern can also be combined with Hypoth-a-sized Collection to create a Stream whose collection can avoid growing.

Epilogue   None.

REFERENCES

[Auer95] K. Auer. "Reusability through Self-Encapsulation." In J. Coplien and D. Schmidt (eds.), *Pattern Languages of Program Design.* Reading, MA: Addison-Wesley, 1995, pp. 505–516.

[Barry91] B. Barry. "Real-Time Object-Oriented Programming Systems." *American Programmer* (October 1991).

[White91] B. Whitefield and K. Auer. "You Can't Do That in Smalltalk! Or Can You?" *Object 1,1 (May/June 1991).*

Ken Auer can be reached at Knowledge Systems Corporation, 4001 Weston Parkway, Cary, NC 27513; kauer@ksccary.com. Kent Beck can be reached at First Class Software, 14525 Big Basin Highway, Boulder Creek, CA 95006-0226; 70761.1216@compuserve.com.

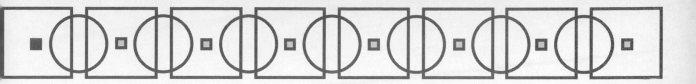

Partitioning Smalltalk Code into ENVY/Developer Components

3

Bobby Woolf

OVERVIEW

ENVY/Developer[1] is the most widely used source code and configuration management system for Smalltalk development. Unfortunately, many people find ENVY very difficult to apply. The difficulty is not that ENVY does not work well but that few people really understand how to use it. Thus this chapter explains the philosophy behind ENVY and demonstrates the best way to partition source code using it. The practices discussed below make ENVY much easier to employ and produce an improved software development and maintenance process.

This chapter describes a series of "patterns" that together form a "pattern language." Each pattern is discussed in a separate section. Some readers, accustomed to reading papers that unfold linearly from beginning to end, may find this format unusual and may not be prepared to let the patterns show them their own path. However, the format used here greatly reduces the effort required both to present and to understand the principles involved. Readers should find that patterns help convey difficult material clearly.

---

[1] ENVY/Developer by Object Technology International, Inc., Ottawa, Ontario, Canada.

What Is a Pattern?

A *pattern* is a format, originally developed by Christopher Alexander [Alexander+77], that documents the solution to a common problem in a context. An expert in a field can use patterns to document the techniques he has learned that make him an expert. The pattern format helps the author document a technique completely yet concisely [Woolf95b, pp. 13–14]. Thus one can read these patterns to quickly learn directly from the expert.

A pattern has four main parts:

- Title—The name of the pattern, describing *who* it is.
- Problem—*What* the pattern is designed to solve.
- Context—The forces and constraints that show *why* the problem is difficult to solve.
- Solution—*How* to solve the problem within the given context.

How to Read a Pattern

You do not necessarily have to read all of the sections in a pattern to gain its benefit. These steps show how to read a pattern quickly and still learn from it:

1. First, read the problem statement. If it does not sound interesting to you, skip this pattern.
2. Next, read the solution. If the solution makes sense, you need not read the rest of the pattern.
3. For illustrations of the solution, read the examples.
4. For an explanation of why the solution is appropriate for the problem, read the context.

What Is a Pattern Language?

"A *pattern language* is a collection of patterns that reinforce each other to solve an entire domain of problems" [Woolf95b, p. 14]. A pattern language combines patterns in a way that guides the reader through an entire solution process. When done well, a pattern language combines its patterns in such a way that its combined whole produces a greater benefit than the sum of its parts.

How to Read a Pattern Language

You do not necessarily have to read the patterns in a language in order, nor do you have to read all of them to learn from the language. These steps show how to read a pattern language quickly and learn from it:

1. Scan the problem statements of the language's patterns for one that sounds interesting.
2. When you find an interesting-sounding pattern, read it (as described in "How to Read a Pattern").
3. If the pattern refers to any others, read them next.
4. Scan for any more interesting patterns and read them. Keep reading interesting patterns until you understand the language.

THE PATTERN LANGUAGE: ENVY PARTITIONING

I often mentor Smalltalk programmers about how to use ENVY/Developer to manage the configuration of their code. The two most common questions they ask are, "How many applications should I use?" and "How many subapplications should I use?" The goal of this pattern language is to answer these two questions.

However, before I can answer them, I need to answer some more fundamental questions. If you read these patterns in the order presented, the answers to these two questions will make more sense. But if you can't wait to read about these particular questions, read those patterns first, then read the more fundamental patterns they reference.

To answer this question:	Read this section:
How should I design my (sub)system to help make my development team more productive?	1. Layered and Sectioned Architecture
How should I organize a (sub)system so that the components are fairly independent from one another?	1.1 Separate Layers
How should I organize a layer into sets of functionality?	1.2 Separate Sections

To answer this question:	Read this section:
How should I store my layers in ENVY so that I can manage them as encapsulated layers of code?	2. Layer in an Application
How should I store my sections in ENVY so that I can manage them as encapsulated sections of code?	3. Section in a Subapplication
How many applications should I divide my (sub)system into?	4. Two Applications
How many subapplications should I divide my application into?	5. No Subapplications

1. LAYERED AND SECTIONED ARCHITECTURE

Problem How should I design my (sub)system to help make my development team more productive?

Context References in code produce code dependencies. A code component that references another becomes dependent on that other component. If the other component does not work properly, the dependent one probably will not work either. A code reference can take many forms, but in Smalltalk a reference is usually a class reference. Thus, whenever a component uses a global variable that is a class, it is creating a dependency on that class and its code.

Dependencies between components make code difficult to implement, maintain, and reuse. A developer cannot finish implementing a component until the components it depends on have been implemented. Changes to a component with many dependents can adversely affect those dependents. A component cannot be reused if the components it depends on are not available. Thus, minimizing and simplifying the dependencies between components makes code better.

Dependencies between components become paths of communication between developers. Code structures reflect the organizational structures that create them [Coplien95, p. 204]. Numerous complex dependencies in the code require similarly complicated paths of communication within the team. Code dependencies and team communication paths become one and the same.

A team that must devote greater amounts of its resources to communication loses its effectiveness. In the worst case, a team of n people requires n^2

paths of communication. Each new team member adds n new paths, so coordination overhead goes up and productivity per team member goes down. Figure 1 sketches the relationship between a team's size and the productivity of its members. A team must simplify its communication, or it cannot grow effectively.

Dependencies within code are necessary, but the system architecture should minimize and simplify them; this will make the code better and the team more productive.

Solution Develop a system with a Layered and Sectioned Architecture to reduce dependencies between components and help make the developers more productive.

A complex system implemented with a large amount of code will be difficult to develop and manage as one huge chunk of code. Code should be designed and implemented with components that have high cohesion and low adhesion. Divide the system into components, each with a relatively simple and well-defined interface. Make the dependencies between these components as simple as possible by reducing the references between components. When references are necessary, make them one-way references if possible.

Two components can be related in one of three ways. Their relationship tells you how to design them:

1. Two components with no dependencies between them: These belong in peer layers, neither built on top of the other.

FIGURE 1 The productivity of each team member declines as a team gets larger.

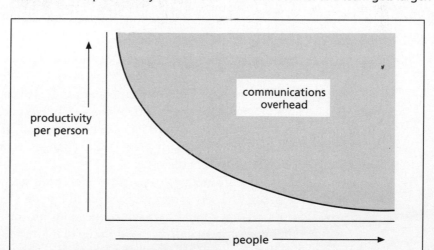

2. Two components where one depends on the other but not vice versa: These belong in separate layers, with one layer built on top of the other.

3. Two components that depend on each other: These belong in separate sections within the same layer.

A system designed with a Layered and Sectioned Architecture will produce these well-encapsulated components. To learn how to create such an architecture, read patterns 1.1, Separate Layers, and 1.2, Separate Sections.

Example Teams of 3 to 10 people tend to be highly productive, but larger teams do not [Coplien95, p. 204]. Some systems are so large and require so much code that they may seem to require 20 to 50 (or more) people to develop them.

The answer is not to develop a system with a team of 20 to 50 people, however. The effort required to coordinate all those people will cause the process to grind to a standstill. Instead, divide the system into well-encapsulated subsystems that can each be developed by a team of 3 to 10 people. Also, create an architecture and infrastructure team to define the subsystems and their interfaces and to enforce compliance.

If the subsystems are well encapsulated, this means that the dependencies between them will be few and simple. Similarly, the process to develop them will only require a small number of simple paths of communication between the teams. This will help keep the teams productive, reducing the project's risk.

1.1 SEPARATE LAYERS

Problem How should I organize a (sub)system so that the components are fairly independent from one another?

Context Code designed with a Layered and Sectioned Architecture is easier to maintain and reuse.

Reducing the references to code components helps to encapsulate the code. If two components refer to each other, changes in either can affect the other. Thus the two components will be easier to maintain if only one of them refers to the other, not both. This way, changes to the one that isn't referenced will not affect the other.

As components are grouped to separate referenced sets from the sets doing the referencing, the sets form layers, stacked one on top of the other. Like the floors of an office building, each set depends on the ones beneath it for support but does not depend on those on top of it (or in the office tower next door). Similarly, a layer of code will reference those below it but not those above it or at the same level.

Each layer should be simple enough that one team can be responsible for implementing and maintaining it. If two teams are required to develop a layer, they will need to coordinate their activities, which will increase communication overhead within and between teams.

Smalltalk code is a hyper-linked system, like hypertext, in which all of the code appears to refer to all of the rest of the code. Dividing such a system into loosely coupled components is difficult because it requires that the code in some components not refer to that in other components. The Smalltalk development environment allows—indeed, encourages—any code to refer to any other code, so it actually hampers the development of loosely coupled components. System developers must exercise discipline in order to design these loosely coupled components and implement code that will obey their boundaries.

Solution   Divide a (sub)system into Separate Layers to separate its components.

Design the (sub)system using a layered architecture. Each layer will depend on the ones below it but not those above it or at the same level. Each layer will be simple enough to be developed by one team. This way the code in the lower layers will be better encapsulated, because it will not depend on any of the code in the rest of the system. Each team will be better "encapsulated" as well, because it will only be responsible for its own layer(s) and not for miscellaneous parts of the entire system.

To separate code into layers, diagram (mentally or on paper) how the classes refer to each other. If two classes refer to each other, either directly or indirectly, they will have to go in the same layer. If one class (call it Class A) references another (Class B) but not vice versa, Class B can go in a layer that is lower than the one Class A is in. Repeat this process until all of the classes in each layer refer to each other or to classes in lower layers. A class should never refer to a class in a higher layer.

Sometimes when diagramming classes a developer will find that a large number of classes all reference one another eventually. This is spaghetti code that will be difficult to maintain and reuse. It should be redesigned and refactored in such a way that it can be divided into layers.

Example   The graphics system in VisualWorks[2] is layered. Here are some of those layers:

1. Kernel—Defines what a Smalltalk object is and how its code executes; includes fundamental classes like Object and UndefinedObject and hierarchies like Magnitude, Collection, Boolean, and so forth.

---

[2] VisualWorks, a dialect of Smalltalk, was developed by ParcPlace-Digitalk, Inc., Sunnyvale, CA.

2. Graphics System—Defines a system for describing graphical figures and drawings as objects.

3. Windowing System—Defines overlapping windows and standard widgets like buttons and scrollbars.

Each of these layers requires the one before it, but none of them uses those that come after it.

The layers help keep changes in one layer from affecting the other layers. For example, if you wanted to redesign the windowing system, you would need to rewrite the third layer. However, these changes to the third layer would hardly affect the first two, if at all. On the other hand, if you wanted to rewrite the graphics system, that wouldn't affect the first layer, but it would probably require rewriting the windowing system as well. Changes to a layer affect the layers above it but not those below it.

VisualWorks has another layer, File System, that implements streams to read from and write to the operating system's files. Since it's implemented using objects (as is all of VisualWorks), File System is built on top of Kernel. However, since File System doesn't do anything graphical, it's not built on top of Graphics System. File System and Graphics System are peers, so changes to one cannot affect the other. Thus, changes to one of those layers only affect part of the system, not the entire system. The only changes that can affect the entire system are those made to Kernel. Such a layered system is much safer than one where all code affects all other code.

1.2 SEPARATE SECTIONS

Problem   How should I organize a layer into sets of functionality?

Context   Code designed with Layered and Sectioned Architecture is easier to maintain and reuse.

If one component of code references another but not vice versa, they can be divided into Separate Layers. However, this can still leave a large number of components that all reference one another and must therefore be stored within the same layer.

Reducing the references between components helps encapsulate them. The components may all have to reference one another eventually, since they're in the same layer, but it's better to have relatively few references than too many. Components that have many references between them will be more dependent on one another than will those with few references between them.

Changes can often be made to one low-dependence component without requiring corresponding changes to components that depend on it very little.

As components are grouped into highly dependent sets that are fairly independent of one another, these sets form sections of code with high cohesion and low adhesion. Like multiple businesses on the same floor of an office building, each component depends on its own activities much more than it depends on those of other components. Similarly, a section of code will reference other sections some but will mostly reference itself.

Each section should be simple enough that one developer can be responsible for implementing and maintaining it. Otherwise, two developers implementing a section will need to coordinate their activities, coordination that increases communication overhead within the team.

Developing Smalltalk code into sections that are both highly cohesive and have low adhesion is difficult. Since the Smalltalk development environment allows and even encourages heavy referencing between code in various sections, discipline is required on the part of Smalltalk developers to design code that obeys those sections' boundaries.

Solution Divide each layer into Separate Sections, to partition its functionality.

Design each layer with a Sectioned Architecture. Each section should be highly cohesive but have low adhesion with the other sections. Each section should be simple enough to be developed by one person. This way, each component will be better encapsulated, as its connections to other components will be minimal. Similarly, each developer will be better "encapsulated," because he or she will only be responsible for his or her own section(s), not miscellaneous parts of the entire system.

To separate code into sections, diagram (mentally or on paper) how the classes refer to one another. If one class references another one a lot, and/or vice versa, put them in the same section. If two classes reference each other relatively little, put them in separate sections. If a resulting section contains numerous classes, repeat the process to divide it into sections. Repeat this process until all of the classes in a section refer to one another a lot and have fewer references to classes in other sections.

Sometimes when diagramming classes a developer will find that a large number of classes all reference one another heavily. This is spaghetti code that will be difficult to maintain and reuse. It should be redesigned and refactored in such a way that only a few classes reference one another heavily at a time.

Example VisualWorks contains a feature called BOSS (the Binary Object Streaming System) for writing an object to disk and reading it back into an image. Because it can be applied to any object, it is one of the most basic features of the VisualWorks system; thus it is part of the bottom layer (Kernel). Although it requires a number of classes to implement, only one of those classes (BinaryObjectStorage) is referenced by the rest of VisualWorks.[3] Thus BOSS is a section of code. The classes reference one another heavily, but they reference the rest of the system little. All of the references to the BOSS classes are channeled through one class with a relatively simple interface.

2. LAYER IN AN APPLICATION

Problem How should I store my layers in ENVY so that I can manage them as encapsulated layers of code?

Context Code designed with a Layered and Sectioned Architecture is easier to maintain and reuse. However, developing Smalltalk code with Separate Layers goes against the hyperlinked nature of that code.

Even if Smalltalk code has a Layered and Sectioned Architecture, these layers are difficult to recognize. A large set of code contains numerous classes, all of which seem to reference one another. A developer learning such a library of code often feels that he or she must learn all of it to understand any of it. The code may be in layers, but the developer cannot see those layers.

Actions are often applied to an entire layer of code at a time. A layer should be simple enough that one team can be responsible for implementing and maintaining it. When filing out a class, one often wishes to file out its associated classes without filing out the other classes in the system. This means that one should file out the layer as a whole.

As maintenance is performed on code, the layers must be preserved so that the advantages of the Layered and Sectioned Architecture are preserved. This is difficult to accomplish when the layers are not apparent.

Smalltalk needs a mechanism for distinguishing separate layers of code. ENVY adds such a mechanism to Smalltalk, a type of component called an *application*. Just as a layer contains tightly coupled classes, so does an application. A layer must know what layers come immediately before it, so an application records this information.

Although developing Smalltalk code with a Layered and Sectioned Architecture is difficult, it is necessary in order to partition the code into ENVY applications. ENVY allows each application to be loaded by itself, as long as

---

[3] BOSS is an example of the Facade pattern, in which BinaryObjectStorage is the Facade class. See [GHJV95, p. 185].

its prerequisite applications are loaded. This requires that the code in the application not attempt to collaborate with or reference any other code except that in its application's prerequisites. Therefore, a layered and sectioned architecture is required for effective use of ENVY.

Solution Store each Layer in an Application in such a way that you can manage it as such (that is, as a layer).

Design a system using a Layered and Sectioned Architecture, then give each layer a name. Implement the code using ENVY, creating an application for each layer and giving it the same name as its corresponding layer. Make each application's prerequisites the applications of the layers immediately beneath the layer being defined.

Example VisualWorks is implemented using a Layered and Sectioned Architecture, but this is very difficult to see in the base VisualWorks image (without ENVY). Base VisualWorks looks like a thousand classes that all seem to use one another to implement themselves.

ENVY clearly shows the Layered and Sectioned Architecture of VisualWorks. The main applications and the architecture they embody are shown in Figure 2. Each of the ten blocks in the figure is an application/layer. Two applications located along the same horizontal line (such as Compiler and FileSystem) are peer applications, which means that they do not depend on each other but do depend on the same foundation. Each vertical slice shows a column of layers with direct dependencies (there are six of them at most). The simplest column is the one with VisualWorksDevelopment on top. It is structured as follows:

1. Kernel—Defines what an object is and how code executes
2. Graphics—Defines how pixels are drawn on the screen

FIGURE 2 Applications show the layered architecture of VisualWorks.

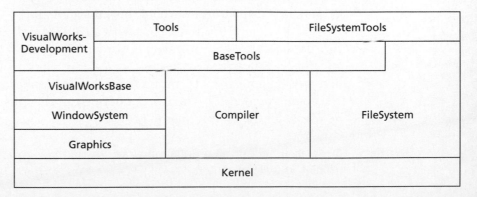

3. WindowSystem—Organizes those pixels into overlapping windows and standard widgets

4. VisualWorksBase—Introduces a window builder for creating windows from specifications

5. VisualWorksDevelopment—Introduces a window painter for producing window specifications

3. SECTION IN A SUBAPPLICATION

Problem   How should I store my sections in ENVY so that I can manage them as encapsulated sections of code?

Context   Code designed with a Layered and Sectioned Architecture is easier to maintain and reuse. However, designing code with Separate Layers and Separate Sections goes against the hyper-linked nature of Smalltalk code.

Even if Smalltalk code has a sectioned architecture, the sections are difficult to recognize. A developer learning a set of classes may not realize that some of the classes collaborate much more closely than others.

Actions are often applied to an entire section of code at a time. A section should be simple enough that one developer can be responsible for implementing and maintaining it. When filing out a class, one needs to also file out its close collaborators, which can easily be done by filing out the section as a whole.

As maintenance is performed on code, the sections must be preserved; but to do so, the sections must be apparent.

Smalltalk needs a mechanism for distinguishing separate sections of code. ENVY adds such a mechanism to Smalltalk, a type of component called a *subapplication*. Just as a section contains classes that collaborate a lot, so does a subapplication. And because a section must know what layer it belongs in, subapplications record this information.

While developing Smalltalk code with a Layered and Sectioned Architecture is difficult, it is necessary in order to use ENVY subapplications effectively. Subapplications show logical divisions in the code. If such divisions do not exist, separating them into subapplications is misleading and counterproductive. Therefore, a Layered and Sectioned Architecture is necessary for the effective use of ENVY.

Solution   Store each Section in a Subapplication so that you can manage it as such (that is, as a section).

VisualWorksBase									
UIBasics		UIBuilderBase			UILooks				VisualWorks-BaseExtensions
UIBasics-Datasets	UIBasics-Notebook	UIBuilder Fmwk	UIBuilder Specs	UIBuilder Support	Mac-UILooks	Motif-UILooks	OS2CUA UILooks	Win3-UILooks	

FIGURE 3 Subapplications show the sections of the VisualWorksBase application.

Design a system using a Layered and Sectioned Architecture, then give each section a name. Implement the code using ENVY, creating a subapplication for each section and giving it the same name as its corresponding section. Since the section is part of a particular layer, create the subapplication to be part of the application for that layer. If the section is located within a larger section, create its subapplication within the larger section's corresponding subapplication.

Example   The VisualWorksBase application contains the fundamental window builder code, a complex framework that combines many sets of functionality. To make this code easier to manage, ENVY divides it into sections:

- UIBasics—Additional visual widgets that are only available for windows developed using the builder
- UIBuilderBase—The builder classes themselves and associated code
- UILooks—Code to emulate various platforms' look and feel
- VisualWorksBaseExtensions—OTI code that enables ENVY to support the builder

Many of these sections are in turn divided into subsections.

ENVY clearly shows the sectioned architecture of VisualWorksBase, whose subapplications (and the architecture they embody) are shown in Figure 3.

4. TWO APPLICATIONS

Problem   How many applications should I divide my (sub)system into?

Context   When implementing Smalltalk code in an ENVY image, each piece of code must be stored in an application. Thus you will need at least one application to store your code in.

The base ENVY image already includes several applications that contain the vendor (ParcPlace and OTI) code. You could store your code in these, but this would introduce several problems, the primary one being the difficulty in distinguishing your code from the vendors'. Thus you should store your code in your own applications, not the vendors'.

You could store all of your code in one application. However, ENVY would then manage it all as one unit of code and would not be able to help you manage different sets of code independently. To manage these sets independently, design your subsystem with Separate Layers and store each Layer in an Application.

One layer is insufficient for managing most subsystems. Most can easily be broken into two distinct layers, however, one containing the domain models and the other containing the application models. As design and implementation progress, other layers may become apparent as well.

Solution   Start a (sub)system with Two Applications.

One of the applications will contain the domain model layer(s), and another will contain the application model layer(s).[4] As the need for other layers becomes apparent, create applications for those as well.

Example   A billing subsystem might contain domain objects such as Bill and Customer and application models for windows such as BillEditor and BillBrowser. Implement this using two ENVY applications:

- BillingDomain—Contains the Bill and Customer classes. Kernel would probably be the only prerequisite needed.

- BillingUI—Contains the BillEditor and BillBrowser classes. BillingDomain would be one of its prerequisites. It would also need some sort of windowing system code as a prerequisite.

Later, the subsystem might be expanded to contain some automated processing features. This would introduce a new layer and corresponding application:

- BillingProcessing—Contains classes like BillingProcessor. BillingDomain would be one of its prerequisites. Since it does not open any of the Billing windows, BillingUI would not be a prerequisite.

---

[4] Domain models and application models can be implemented in any object-oriented language. For a discussion of how to do this in VisualWorks, see [Woolf95a, pp. 17–18].

5. NO SUBAPPLICATIONS

Problem   How many subapplications should I divide my application into?

Context   When implementing Smalltalk code in an ENVY image, each piece of code must be stored in an application. Code does not have to be stored in a subapplication, however; it can be stored directly in an application.

You could store all of a layer's code in the application. However, ENVY would then manage it all as one unit of code and would not be able to help you manage different sets of code independently. To manage these sets independently, design your layer with Separate Sections and store each Section in a Subapplication.

Sections are often difficult to anticipate during design, and so they are often not discovered until implementation.

Solution   Start an application with No Subapplications.

Since a newly created application contains no subapplications, don't create any for it to begin with. As the need for sections becomes apparent, create subapplications to represent them.

Example   Let's say you're going to implement a number of user interface windows for your billing application. Create an application for them called BillingUI.

As you implement these windows, you may find that you have two main sets of windows. Perhaps you have one set of windows for reviewing large lists of data and another for entering and editing specific data elements. The windows in each group work together closely but interact little. Meanwhile, there is a main menu window that gives the user access to both sets of windows. When you discover this division, create subapplications to represent it:

- BillingReviewUI—Contains the reviewing window classes
- BillingEditingUI—Contains the editing window classes

The main menu window class is common to both sets, so it would go in the BillingUI application itself.

ACKNOWLEDGMENTS

I would like to thank Ward Cunningham and Ken Auer for their extensive help in revising this paper, Kent Beck for inspiring me to see the connection between coding processes and people's, and everyone at PLoP '95 and KSC who made suggestions for improving this paper.

REFERENCES

[Alexander+77] C. Alexander, S. Ishikawa, and M. Silverstein. *A Pattern Language*. New York: Oxford University Press, 1977.

[Coplien95] J. O. Coplien, "A Generative Development-Process Pattern Language." In J. O. Coplien and D. C. Schmidt (eds.), *Pattern Languages of Program Design*. Reading, MA: Addison-Wesley, 1995, pp. 183–237.

[Gamma+95] E. Gamma, R. Helm, R. Johnson, and J. Vlissides. *Design Patterns: Elements of Reusable Object-Oriented Software*. Reading, MA: Addison-Wesley, 1995.

[Woolf95a] B. Woolf. "Making MVC More Reusable." *The Smalltalk Report*, 4(4)(January 1995): 15–18.

[Woolf95b] B. Woolf. "A Sample Pattern Language—Concatenating with Streams." *The Smalltalk Report*, 4(5)(February 1995):13–17.

Bobby Woolf can be reached at Knowledge Systems Corporation, 4001 Weston Parkway, Cary, NC 27513-2303; bwoolf@ksccary.com.

GENERAL-PURPOSE PATTERNS

PART 2

Early work in software patterns focused on general-purpose patterns in object-oriented systems, as epitomized by Gamma et al.'s *Design Patterns: Elements of Reusable Object-Oriented Software* (nicknamed the "Gang of Four," or "GOF," book) [Gamma+95]. Of all the patterns in these pages, the six in this part are most similar in spirit to those in *Design Patterns*. In fact, half of them are extensions to patterns from that work.

The kinship between these patterns is their domain independence—they are as versatile as object-oriented programming itself. They offer solutions to problems that crop up at all levels, from system software such as compilers and operating systems, through middleware such as collection class libraries and user interface toolkits, and on up to domain-specific applications.

In Chapter 4, for example, Peter Sommerlad's Command Processor pattern expands on the Command pattern from *Design Patterns*. Command's intent is to promote a request to full object status, making it easier to manipulate and replace than a simple operation. Command Processor takes this a step further. It prescribes scaffolding for invoking Command objects and for undoing and redoing their effects—scaffolding that often attends the Command pattern. Command Processor addresses more of the application context than its progenitor, saving a designer considerable reinvention.

Jung Kim and Kevin Benner (Chapter 5) devote their energies to enhancing Observer, another pattern from *Design Patterns*. They found that Observer left many decisions to the designer. To make things easier, they boiled down their application experience into an extensive pattern language for implementing Observer. The bulk of their patterns have to do with transmitting update information from subject to observer, which says a lot about how deep those issues are. Another notable aspect of this work is the inclusion of a "negative" pattern, which details a common but undesirable design solution.

Much has been written about encapsulation in object-oriented programming, but nearly all of it has focused on instances. In "Patterns for Encapsulating Class Trees" (Chapter 6), Dirk Riehle considers encapsulation of class hierarchies (which he calls "class trees"). He argues that adherence to abstract interfaces is the key to evolvable software, and that the only way to ensure such adherence is by hiding concrete classes from clients. Any reference to concrete classes from outside the class hierarchy breaks its encapsulation.

A fundamental problem here is how a client obtains instances of concrete classes without referring to those classes. Dirk explains several reasons why Abstract Factory and Factory Method—two Gang of Four patterns that address this problem—are not ideal solutions. The most serious shortcoming is their lack of expressive power. They say little about how clients can control the classes that get instantiated; these patterns simply hard-wire the classes into the instance-generating operations. Dirk presents two alternative patterns: Class Retrieval and Late Creation. He shows how they subsume Abstract Factory and Factory Method and, further, how they give clients greater expressiveness and versatility in the instantiation process, all without disclosing details of the concrete class structure.

Hans Rohnert expands on another GOF pattern in "The Proxy Design Pattern: Revisited" (Chapter 7). The original pattern names and describes four common variants: remote, virtual, and protection proxies, and smart references. Hans introduces four more: cache, synchronization, counting, and firewall proxies. Moreover, he organizes all variants into a two-tiered structure. The first level describes the core design pattern, which is common to all variants. The second level presents the idiosyncrasies of each variant separately and then briefly relates how one might combine them. This chapter shows how far one can go beyond a seemingly comprehensive pattern like Proxy.

Most people in the pattern community accept the Alexandrian notion of a pattern as "a solution to a problem in a context." But when we look at Proxy and see so many variants, it's fair to ask why these aren't separate patterns. After all, each variant addresses a slightly different problem in the general proxy context.

Alexander Ran believes that lumping problems and solutions in a single pattern creates redundancy. Consequently, his chapter on "MOODS" (Chapter 8) departs a bit from conventional pattern forms. He calls his form a "Design Decision Tree," or "DDT." The idea is to avoid redundancy through what amounts to inheritance: the root node in his tree of design decisions captures the most general design decision, and subtrees share the forces, problems, and solutions of their ancestors. Interior nodes introduce new forces, problems, and solutions incrementally. Alexander applies this form to discuss state in object-oriented systems. His treatment goes well beyond the Gang of Four's State and similar patterns, expounding not just on state objects and transitions but also events, predicative classes, associations, and classifiers. As for the DDT form, it's highly reminiscent of a pattern language. See if you can spot how it differs from one.

The last chapter in Part 2 is by Jim Doble, who introduces us to the Shopper pattern. Shopper makes no pretense of being a pattern language; it is a design pattern in the Gang of Four vein. Shopper is kindred to the GOF Iterator design pattern: both entail traversal and its decoupling from what is traversed. But rather than providing sequential access to objects as Iterator does, a Shopper object *collects* references to objects during traversal. The collection criteria may vary by Shopper. Once traversal has ended, a client can access and operate on the collected objects to its heart's content. You might think of it as a "persistent traversal." Jim explains how to use the Iterator and Strategy patterns in Shopper's implementation—a good example of how patterns compose.

[Gamma+95] E. Gamma, R. Helm, R. Johnson, and J. Vlissides. *Design Patterns: Elements of Reusable Object-Oriented Software*, Reading, MA: Addison-Wesley, 1995.

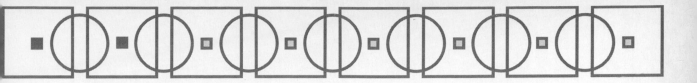

4 Command Processor

Peter Sommerlad

Many software systems today offer a graphical user interface. The components of such interfaces handle user input, control user functions, and provide different views into the program. The addition of more and more interactive features increases the complexity of the user interface structure—and its implementation.

The Command Processor design pattern separates a request for a service from its execution. A command processor component manages request objects, starts their execution, and provides additional services like storing the requests for scheduling or later undo.

Example   A text editor allows users to modify documents with change requests. The editor's user interface may provide several means for specifying these requests. For example, it may contain a text-based pull-down menu for novices, a row of iconographic push buttons for quicker access by advanced users, and even a noninteractive command language for batch-oriented text processing.

Providing a way to deal with mistakes is a desirable feature for a text editor. A simple method is to provide a request that undoes the most recent change. An undo mechanism must be implemented for every type of change request provided, however. A more attractive solution would allow the undoing of multiple requests. Let us call this text editor TEWUC (text editor with undoable commands).

The implementation's internal structure should fulfill these requirements in a flexible and extensible way. A rigid solution might include a direct call to a service procedure within the implementation of the push buttons (e.g., as a callback). Such a call would store the complete text before calling the service and restore it in case of an undo request. Unfortunately, this does not scale to multiple requests.

Context   You need to develop an application that is flexible and extensible in its control interface and implementation of services or provides an additional mechanism related to service execution—such as scheduling or undo.

Problem   An application that provides a large set of features should use a well-structured solution for mapping its interface onto its internal functionality. In addition, flexibility in the specification and implementation of service requests may be required. It should be possible to extend the functionality of the application by means of new service requests and service execution-related mechanisms. The following forces influence the solution:

- The user interface element for requesting a service may vary.
- Several user interface elements for the same request may exist.
- The number and implementation of available services may vary.
- Additional functionality related to service execution—like undo, redo, macros, logging, or service suspension and scheduling—should be implemented consistently.

Solution   The Command Processor pattern encapsulates service requests in command objects. The command processor component takes these command objects and causes their execution. In addition, it implements execution-related services such as storing the command object for undo.

The following components take part in the Command Processor pattern:

The controller represents the application interface. It accepts service requests ("paste text," for example) and creates the corresponding command objects. These are then delivered to the command processor for execution.

The abstract command component defines the interface of all commands. At a minimum this interface consists of a procedure to execute a service. TEWUC also provides undo and redo procedures for each command.

The command components implement the abstract command's interface for each individual kind of user request (such as "delete word"). For the undo procedure, the "delete word" command is responsible for storing enough state data to recover from its execution (i.e., the word deleted and its position in the text).

The supplier components represent the functional core of the application. They provide the services needed to execute concrete commands. Several related commands may share a single supplier. The component implementing the internal text representation is the main supplier in TEWUC.

The command processor component manages command objects and makes them execute the service they represent. It is the key component in implementing additional execution-related services. The TEWUC command processor implements the undo service with a stack of command objects that allows undoing them in reverse order.

The Command Processor pattern builds on the Command pattern described in Gamma, Helm, Johnson, and Vlissides' *Design Patterns: Elements of Reusable Object-Oriented Software* [Gamma+95]. It is likewise based on the idea of encapsulating service requests in command objects. The controller takes some of the responsibilities of the client and invoker roles in the Command pattern: it creates new command objects and decides which command to use. Activation of command execution is the responsibility of the command processor, however. This is the component that implements the additional execution-oriented services that are partially sketched in the Command pattern. The suppliers correspond to the receivers, but we do not require a one-to-one relationship between commands and suppliers.

Class Controller	*Collaborators* Command Command Processor
Responsibility • Accepts requests • Translates requests into commands • Transfers commands to the command processor	

Class Command Processor	*Collaborators* Abstract Command
Responsibility • Activates command execution • Maintains command objects • Provides additional mechanisms like a stack of undoable commands	

Class Abstract Command	*Collaborators*
Responsibility • Defines a uniform interface to execute commands • May provide additional interface for undo and redo	

Class Command	*Collaborators* Supplier
Responsibility • Encapsulates a service request • Implements interface of abstract command • Uses supplier to perform a request and its undo	

Class Supplier	*Collaborators*
Responsibility • Provides application-specific service(s) • May allow commands to retrieve and reset its state	

Structure   Since the controller creates the concrete command objects, it knows the concrete command classes. The command processor manages the command objects (e.g., by storing them for a later undo). However, the command processor remains independent of specific commands, by using only the abstract command interface. There is a command subclass for each service provided by the application. A command uses one or more application-specific suppliers during its execution, as shown in the accompanying figure.

Dynamics   The diagram on page 68 shows a typical scenario, in which a request comes in, is fulfilled, and is then undone:

- The controller accepts a service request within its event loop and creates a corresponding command object.

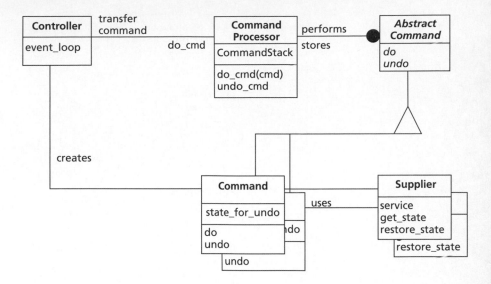

- The controller transfers the new command object to the command processor for execution and further handling. The command processor executes the command and stores it for later undo.

- The command object retrieves the current state from its supplier, stores it appropriately, and performs the requested service.

- After accepting an undo request, the controller transfers this request to the command processor. The command processor invokes the undo procedure for the most recent command.

- The command resets the supplier to the previous state.

- If no further undoing or redoing is possible, the command processor deletes the corresponding command object.

Implementation   To implement Command Processor, perform the following steps:

1. Define the interface of the abstract command. This interface will contain at least an abstract method to execute a command. Other abstract methods like undo are added to the interface as required by the application. For an undo mechanism, you should distinguish three types of commands:

   no change: This type characterizes commands that need no undo. Cursor movement in TEWUC falls into this category.

   normal: Normal commands can be undone. Substitution of a word in the text is an example of a normal command.

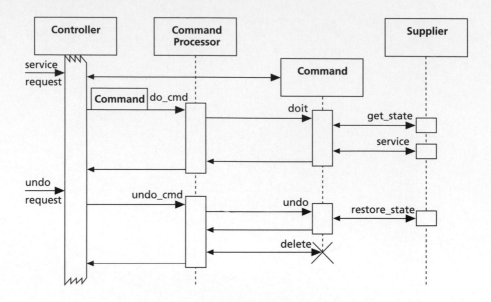

no undo: This command cannot be undone, and it prevents the undo of previously performed normal commands. An example is the loading of a new text file into TEWUC. Commands that would need an excessive amount of information for an undo typically fall into this category.

The TEWUC implementation adds a state machine to these command categories in its abstract command class. This state machine has the states "initialized," "done," "not done," and "finished." The TEWUC command processor will also keep the commands that are "undone" so that they can be redone later. The state machine will only allow redo on commands in the "not done" state and undo in the "done" state:

```
class Acommand{
public:
    enum CmdType { no_change, normal, no_undo };
    enum CmdState {initial, done, not_done, finished };
    virtual ~Acommand();
    virtual void doit(); // set state to done
    virtual void undo(); // set state to not_done
    virtual void redo(){ if(state==not_done) this->doit();}
    virtual void finish(); // set state to finished
    CmdType  getType() const { return type;}
    virtual String getName() const { return "NONAME";}
```

```
protected:
    CmdType type;
    CmdState state;
    ACommand(CmdType t=no_change)
            :type(t),state(initial){}
};
```

2. Implement each command component in such a way that it corresponds to each type of request the controller can accept. A command component is derived from the abstract command class and implements its interface. A command may rely on any number of supplier components, depending on the architecture of the application's functional core. A decision must be made about how to bind a command to the supplier(s) it needs. It may be hard-wired within the code of the command, or it may be provided by the controller when it creates the command object.

The "delete" command of TEWUC takes both the text representation and the specification of the range of characters to delete as parameters:

```
class DeleteCmd:public ACommand {
public:
    DeleteCmd(TEWUC_Text *t, int from, int to)
        : ACommand(normal),mytext(t){...}
    virtual ~DeleteCmd();
    virtual void doit(); // delete characters in mytext
    virtual void undo(); // insert delstr again
    virtual void finish(); // clean up info in delstr
    String getName() const { return "DELETE "+delstr;}
protected:
    TEWUC_Text *mytext; // plan for multiple text buffers
    int from,to;        // range of characters to delete
    String delstr;      // save deleted text for undo
};
```

A command object may also request further parameters needed for correct execution of the command. The TEWUC "load text file" command, for example, uses a dialog to ask the user for the file name.

For commands that need to store their supplier's state for later undo, use the Memento [Gamma+95] or Snapshot pattern to effect this storing without breaking the supplier's encapsulation.

3. To increase flexibility, provide macro commands that combine several commands in sequence. Apply the Composite and Iterator patterns to

implement the macro command component. In TEWUC, the macro command class interface looks like this:

```
class MacroCmd:public ACommand {
public:
    MacroCmd(String name,ACommand *first)
        : ACommand(first->getType()),macroname(name){...}
    virtual ~MacroCmd();
    virtual void doit();    // do every command in cmdlist
    virtual void undo(); // undo all commands in cmdlist
    virtual void finish(); // delete commands in cmdlist
    void add(ACommand *next) { commands.add(next); ... }
    String getName() const { return macroname;}
protected:
    String macroname;
    OrderedCollection<ACommand*> cmdlist;
};
```

The type of macro command to use depends on the type of commands added to the macro. For example, one command of type no_undo will prevent the undo of the complete macro command.

4. Implement the controller component. Depending on the implementation platform used, there may be more than one controller. For example, a single controller may hold the main event loop, or each user interface element may fulfill the responsibilities of the controller within its own, local event loop. The role of the controller is not restricted to a graphical user interface component. A script interpreter may provide a program-mable interface for an application. In this case you might use the Interpreter pattern [Gamma+95] and build the abstract syntax tree from command objects. The command processor then runs the interpretation and provides its context.

5. Connect the controller to the command processor to which it will transfer the created command objects. This may be a static binding, if there is only one command processor, or it may be a dynamic binding, if several command processors are available.

   TEWUC is implemented with dynamic flexibility in mind. Therefore, the controller contains the methods getCommandProcessor() and setCommandProcessor(), which are used to obtain the specific command processor.

6. Provide a means for the controller to create command objects. Additional flexibility may be obtained by exploiting the creational patterns Abstract Factory and Prototype [Gamma+95]. However, since the controller is already decoupled from the service components, this

additional decoupling of controller and commands is optional. Consider each user interaction in TEWUC as being handled by a callback procedure in the controller; the callback procedure then creates the corresponding command object and passes it to the command processor:

```
void TEWUC_controller::deleteButtonPressed(){
    ACommand *delcmd =
        new DeleteWordCommand(
            this->getCursorPos(),// pass cursor position
            this->getText());// pass text
    getCommandProcessor()->perform(delcmd);
}
```

An undo request is a special case for the controller. It can either start the command processor's corresponding procedure directly or instantiate an undo command class and pass the command object to the command processor. Such an undo command would use the command processor as its supplier.

TEWUC uses a separate UndoCommand class, which is instantiated by the controller. Implementation of this command more intimately cooperates with the internals of the command processor than with other commands, however:

```
class UndoCommand:public Acommand{
public:
    UndoCommand(CmdProcessor &cp)
        : Acommand(no_change),mycp(cp){}
    virtual ~UndoCommand();
// the control of the state machine is not shown here:
    virtual void doit() { mycp.undo_lastcmd(); }
    virtual void undo() { mycp.redo_lastcmd(); }
    virtual String getName() const { return "Undo";}
protected:
    CmdProcessor &mycp;
};
```

7. Implement the command processor component. The command processor receives command objects from the controller and takes responsibility for them. In C++ this means it must delete command objects that are no longer useful. For each command object, the command processor starts the execution (e.g., by calling its doit() method).

The quality of an undo mechanism may range from no undo to unlimited undo and redo facilities. An unlimited, multi-level undo/redo can be implemented with two stacks, one for the performed commands and one for the undone commands. For TEWUC, we would implement a class UnlimitedCommandProcessor:

```
class UnlimitedCommandProcessor:public CommandProcessor {
public:
    UnlimitedCommandProcessor();
    virtual ~UnlimitedCommandProcessor();
    virtual void do_cmd(ACommand *cmd);
        // do cmd and push it on donestack
    virtual void undo_lastcmd();
        // pop cmd from donestack,
        // undo it and push on undonestack
    virtual void redo_lastcmd();
        // pop cmd from undonestack and redo it
private:
    Stack<ACommand*> donestack,undonestack;
};
```

An advanced command processor may provide further mechanisms. It may log or store commands to a file for later examination or replay them if errors occur. The command processor may also include functionality to queue services and schedule them at a later time. This functionality may be used, for example, if commands should be executed at a specified time, if they should be handled according to their priority, or if they should execute in a separate thread of control. Another option is to implement transaction management with macro and undoable commands from separate sources.

Known Uses   ET++ [WGM88] exploits the Command Processor pattern. It provides different command processors supporting unlimited, bounded, and single undo and redo. The abstract class Command implements a state machine for the execution state of each command. The controller role is distributed among the event-handler hierarchy used by an ET++ application.

MacApp [Apple89] uses the Command Processor pattern to provide undoable operations.

InterViews [LCITV92] includes an abstract base class Action to provide the functionality of a command component.

ATM-P [ATM93] implements a simplified version of this pattern. It uses a hierarchy of command classes to pass command objects around, sometimes across process boundaries. The receiver of a command object decides how and when to execute it; thus the command processor role can be viewed as distributed.

Consequences   The Command Processor pattern provides the following benefits:

Flexibility in the number and functionality of requests: Since the controller and command processor are implemented independently of the functionality of individual commands, it is easy to change the implementation of a command or add new commands to an application.

Extensibility: It is possible using this pattern to build more complex commands from existing ones. Such compound commands, in addition to the macro mechanism, can be preprogrammed, and thus they easily extend the functionality of an application.

Execution-related services: Concentrating the command execution in the command processor makes it easier to add execution-related services. For example, a single command processor shared by several concurrent applications can provide a transaction control mechanism with logging and rollback of commands.

Concurrency: The Command Processor pattern allows commands to be executed in a separate thread of control (optionally in parallel with the controller). One effect is improved responsiveness, because the controller does not need to wait until the execution of a command has finished.

The Command Processor pattern also has some drawbacks:

Loss of some efficiency through indirection: As with all patterns that decouple components, the additional indirection may have costs in terms of storage and time. A controller that performs service requests directly will not suffer from this. However, extending such a controller with new commands, changing the implementation of single commands, and implementing an undo mechanism is usually much harder.

Potential for an excessive number of command classes: An application with rich functionality may lead to many command classes. A grouping of commands among abstractions may be needed. Another approach, for simple commands, is to parameterize them with service objects.

Complexity in obtaining and maintaining command parameters: Commands may need different means of getting additional parameters when they are created. For example, the user interface knows about the current selection in a text that needs to be passed; commands can then get closely bound to a specific controller, because they may actively ask for the additional parameters. This can restrict the flexibility of the solution. The command processor may be a good place to hold this context—such as the current cursor position—for commands.

REFERENCES

[Apple89] Apple Computer, Inc. *Macintosh Programmers Workshop Pascal 3.0 Reference.* Cupertino, CA, 1989.

[ATM93] Siemens AG. ATM-P, *Komplexspezifikation.* Internal document, 1993.

[Gamma+95] E. Gamma, R. Helm, R. Johnson, and J. Vlissides. *Design Patterns: Elements of Reusable Object-Oriented Software.* Reading, MA: Addison-Wesley, 1995.

[LCITV92] M. Linton, P. Calder, J. Interrante, S. Tang, and J. Vlissides. *InterViews Reference Manual* (3.1 ed.). Stanford, CA: CSL, Stanford University, 1992.

[WGM88] A. Weinand, E. Gamma, and R. Marty. "ET++: An Object-Oriented Application Framework in C++." In *Proceedings of Object-Oriented Programming Systems, Languages, and Applications Conference.* San Diego, CA, 1988, pp. 46–57.

Peter Sommerlad can be reached at Siemens AG, Dept. ZFE T SE 2, D-81730 Munich, Germany; peter.sommerlad@zfe.siemens.de.

Implementation Patterns for the Observer Pattern

5

Jung J. Kim and Kevin M. Benner

INTRODUCTION

We discovered the patterns presented in this chapter while we were design-ing and developing a set of reusable frameworks. One of them was a presentation subsystem framework intended for graphical object-oriented (OO) editors.

   When we set out to design the presentation subsystem framework, we decided to employ the Observer pattern [Gamma+95] in our design. We were surprised to find out just how much we had to decide on our own in order to complete the design. This experience led us to start thinking about comprehensive pattern languages that could be used for a wide spectrum of designs, from abstract, high-level designs to detailed, low-level designs, and ways to help designers make informed decisions about which patterns to use. Our goal became to create an intelligent, pattern-based OO design and development environment and guide the designer through it with a series of simple, cookbook-like steps.

We encountered many bad designs as well, which we present in this chapter as negative patterns. These patterns should be avoided *in most circumstances*. If we want to teach designers about the best pattern-based programming practices, it seems important that we alert them to the pitfalls they should avoid.

A substantial body of work on design patterns exists already, and some of it addresses issues similar to those addressed here [Beck+94, Buschmann+96, Coad+95, Coplien91, Coplien+95, Gamma+95, Johnson92, Pree95]. The patterns we describe here represent the starting point for a pattern language for graphical OO editors and our first attempt at interrelating patterns to form a rich and easily navigable design space.

PATTERN: CONDUIT OF SUBJECT CHANGE

Context   The designer is using the Observer pattern.

The Observer pattern describes how to establish a dependency among objects, via an abstract coupling, so that all objects are notified of any change in one object. The pattern does not supply sufficient detail on how the change information is actually conveyed to the dependent objects, however.

Problem   A design pattern is an abstract construct, requiring a substantial amount of decision making on the part of the designer before it becomes an actual design. Thus it is difficult for an inexperienced designer to come up with a good, detailed design of the observer update mechanism, even if she employs the Observer pattern. In fact, it is easy to spend a lot of time trying out many custom approaches, only to trip up against various intricacies of each and realize that none of them quite satisfy all the design requirements.

Solution   Therefore this pattern provides a uniform mechanism for sending state change information on a subject to the observer via a message. This requires very little customization as far as the underlying update mechanism is concerned (although an actual observer update, given a specific subject change, is obviously very application-specific).

An update message consists of four lists: Add list, Remove list, Modify list, and Container list. The subject simply includes all applicable change information in one or more update messages.

In Figure 1, gray indicates information already present in the Observer pattern; hence, the portion in black is the main focus of this discussion. The dotted line indicates the instance creation relation.

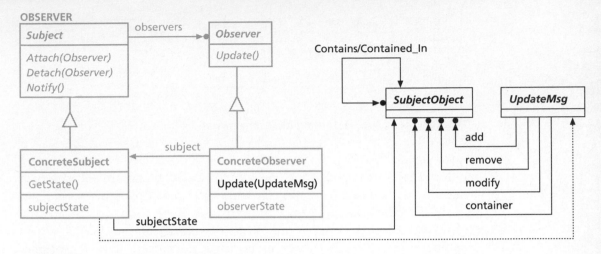

FIGURE 1 Conduit of Subject Change

In designs using this pattern, the subject usually consists of a number of objects. A state change in such a design is usually complex, involving multiple objects, and can be characterized by a series of new object creations (Add), old object deletions (Remove), and current object modifications (Modify) at certain locations. For more details on expressing a state change, see the Observer Update Message pattern.

Further, subject objects have a bidirectional containment relation, Contains/Contained_In (also known as parent-child and by some other domain-specific terms).

The containment relation does not have to be one explicit relation within the subject; instead it can consist of many, possibly indirect, relations whose names vary from class to class and from which the subject knows to infer the containment relationship. For example, suppose the subject represents a program. Figure 2 is a (simplified) language domain model class diagram. The relations consists_of, public_attrs, and public_ops are all containment relations. Therefore, an operation object is contained in a class object, which in turn is contained in a program object, and so on.

Discussion: Rationale

Close coupling between the subject and the observer is undesirable, because it makes it difficult to reuse them [Gamma+95, p. 298]. Complex subject changes tend to require it, however, because the observer needs to get detailed change information. Gamma et al. discuss two ways of forwarding change information to the observer, the push model and the

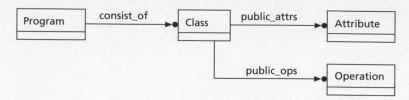

FIGURE 2 An example showing containment relations

pull model. In the pull model the observer usually has to work very hard querying the subject to figure out what changed; this can also happen multiple times for a change if there are more than one interested observer. Furthermore, it may even be nontrivial for the subject to compute the answer to a query, especially if the subject-observer interactions are complex and frequent. The push model tends to make the observer overly dependent on the subject.

The Conduit of Subject Change pattern is a variation of the push model. It has two important characteristics:

1. The update message has a universal fixed format that is generic and provides complete change information.

2. The observer "interprets" update messages.

Hence, the pattern eliminates the dependency of the regular push model and the inefficiency of the pull model.

Discussion: Message Object Creation

A message object can either be created by a change request initiator and passed to the subject or created by the subject upon its receiving a request. It is generally preferable that the message be created by the subject. For example, when multiple messages need to be created, the requester cannot predict how many messages will be required (see the One Message per Affected Object pattern).

Further Refinement
- If the simplest implementation is desired, use the One Message per Change Request pattern in order to further refine this pattern. A potential problem with the pattern is that a subject object may appear to be affected at a location where it does not belong (a "false hit"; see the One Message per Affected Object pattern for definition). For this pattern to be used, the subject typically needs to provide some sort of containment predicate method.

- If "false hits" are a problem (i.e., either the subject or the observer is incapable of dealing with them correctly), use the One Message per Affected Object pattern in order to further refine this pattern. A potential problem with it is that it may generate a very large number of update messages.

- If "false hits" are a problem and the number of messages must be controlled, consider using the Optimized Hybrid Message negative pattern. This pattern requires the greatest intelligence on the part of the subject. The designer must keep in mind that a large reduction in the number of messages is very difficult.

PATTERN: ONE MESSAGE PER CHANGE REQUEST

Context   The designer is using the Conduit of Subject Change pattern and wants to further refine the observer update mechanism.

Problem   The designer wants the simplest possible observer update design, in which the subject can simply store any and all state-change information into one message and not have to worry about much else.

Solution   When a change request is initiated, a message object is created (use the message class defined in the Observer Update Message pattern). When the subject changes its state, it stores the affected objects (which may have been created, deleted, or modified) in the appropriate list, depending on the nature of the change of those objects.

Discussion: Simple Remove versus Cascaded Remove

Note that a single change request can easily affect multiple objects. This frequently happens when an object is deleted, because the objects contained in the deleted object must then also be deleted. In general it is necessary to delete all the objects in the transitive closure of the Contains relation, starting from the original deleted object.

A consequence of storing all affected objects in one message is that sometimes there may be "false hits". A false remove, a particular type of false hit, occurs in the example in Figure 3.

Suppose P, M, C, and A stand for program, module, class, and attribute, respectively. The arrows indicate containment. When M1 is removed, the final resultant state of the update message will be Add={}, Remove={M1, C1, C2, A1, A2}, Modify={}, Container={P1, M1, C1, C2}. A false remove occurs

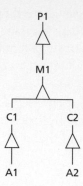

FIGURE 3 An example illustrating false remove

because the observer infers that A1 is also being removed from C2, and likewise, that A2 is being removed from C1.

As a result, the observer must be implemented in such a way that in case of a false remove, it simply ignores it. A typical way to deal with false hits is to provide a containment predicate method. To continue with the above example, Contains(C2, A1) would return False, thus enabling the observer to ignore this combination of objects, while Contains(C1, A1) would return True. If this kind of false remove is not desired, or if the observer simply cannot handle it, then use the One Message per Affected Object pattern.

Notice that a false add and false modify are also possible, depending on the functionality provided by the change request mechanism. A false modify can be handled in a manner similar to a false remove. A false add cannot be remedied so simply, however. Therefore, if false adds are a problem, use the One Message per Affected Object pattern.

PATTERN: ONE MESSAGE PER AFFECTED OBJECT

Context   The designer is using the Conduit of Subject Change pattern and wants to further refine the observer update mechanism.

Problem   The One Message per Change Request pattern can result in an incorrect interpretation of subject state-change information by the observer, because some objects in the subject may appear to be affected at a spurious location. This incorrect interpretation is termed a false hit. Some observers may not be able to handle false hits.

The designer wants a simple observer update design in which false hits do not occur, but the subject can still store any state-change information in update messages as simply as in the One Message per Change Request pattern.

Solution A single change request to the subject can easily result in multiple objects' being affected. For each affected object, generate an observer update message that communicates the object affected, its containers, and the nature of the change (either add, remove, or modify). Note that the message class defined in the Conduit of Subject Change pattern can be used without any modification. Alternatively, the three lists, Add, Remove, and Modify, can be replaced with an attribute to hold the affected object and another attribute indicating the operation (add, remove, or modify).

Discussion While the One Message per Affected Object pattern eliminates the false hit problem, it generates a potentially large number of messages. This may result in poor performance, or it may make it difficult for the observer to interpret the messages. In particular, there must be a special provision for signaling the beginning and end of a series of messages resulting from one change request. A suggestion for implementing this signal mechanism is to create two special messages indicating the beginning and the end, respectively. However, there will still be the problem of messages from different change requests' mixing with one another. To solve this problem, use the Message Packet pattern.

NEGATIVE PATTERN: OPTIMIZED MESSAGES PER CHANGE REQUEST

Context The designer is using the Conduit of Subject Change pattern and wants to further refine the observer update mechanism.

Problem The designer wants an observer update design in which a minimal number of update messages are generated without inducing the observer to infer spurious state-change information. The subject is prepared to perform some amount of extra reasoning to optimize the number of update messages. This pattern also assumes that the subject does not provide a containment relationship predicate.

Solution   This solution is effective only when the branching factor of the containment relation is high, and objects are usually contained in only one container object. When these conditions are met, the designer should perform a careful analysis of the overall savings, weighing the reduction of the number of messages against the added complexity to the subject.

Generate update messages according to the following rules as the state of the subject is changed:

1. Generate an update message for the current containing object. (Initially this is the top-level affected subject object.)

2. The same update message can be used to store the subject change information as the change is propagated in breadth-first fashion through the containment relation until one of the following two conditions holds:

   - The containment relation is traversed through more than one level. At this point, generate a new update message for each contained object affected. (In other words, new messages need to be generated at least at every other containment level, starting from the original affected object.)

   - You reach an object that has a set of container objects different from the set for the affected object for which the current update message was generated. At this point, generate a new message for the current object.

The Message class defined in the Conduit of Subject Change pattern can be used without any modification.

The same issues arise with respect to indicating and managing a sequence of messages from one change request, except of course that the total number of messages has been reduced. The Message Packet pattern can be used to package update messages. In fact, the designer should do some analysis to estimate the reduction in message numbers in comparison to the One Message per Affected Object pattern, in order to determine whether this more complicated pattern is worthwhile. If not, use the One Message per Affected Object pattern instead.

Discussion: More Optimization of the Number of Messages

Consider the example in Figure 4. Assume that A is being deleted; the contained objects, B's and C's, also need to be deleted.

If the subject generates new messages after A, B, and C are deleted as the optimization algorithm instructs, then $1+m+n$ messages are generated. If, on the other hand, the subject looks ahead and chooses to generate a new

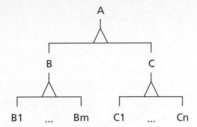

FIGURE 4 An example illustrating message optimization

message for B and C, then only 1+1+1 messages are generated. So, the payoff can be substantial. (In comparison, the One Message per Change Request pattern would generate 1 message, and the One Message per Affected Object pattern would generate 3+m+n messages.)

For yet another example of the kind of optimizations possible, we can introduce another rule: whenever multiple messages are generated for multiple objects that all share the same set of container objects, then those messages can be combined into one. Therefore, in the above example the subject only needs to generate 1+1+1 messages: one message for A, B, and C; one message for B1 through Bm, since they share the same container object, B; and one message for C1 through Cn, since they share C.

However, notice that this kind of optimization can become arbitrarily hard.

Discussion: Recommendation of One Message per Change Request

Considering the assumed complex nature of the subject, it will almost certainly provide some sort of containment predicate. If this is the case, the false hit is not a problem, and the One Message per Change Request is probably the right choice.

Discussion: Failed Attempts to Optimize in Other Ways

A message cannot be shared by objects spanning more than two levels of the containment relation, because this necessarily causes the observer to infer an incorrect containment relationship. In the above example, suppose A is being deleted and one message is shared among A, B's, and C's. At some point, the (partial) state of the message will be Remove={A, B1, C1}, Container={A, B1}. This means an attempt to remove A from B1 will be made. Avoiding such a situation (due to the pattern's inability to deal with it) provides the main motivation to depart from the One Message per Change Request pattern.

PATTERN: MESSAGE PACKET

Context   A system generates multiple messages. Some of these messages belong to a group (as defined for each specific application); it is important for the message receiver to be able to identify the beginning and end of a series of messages belonging to the same group and possibly process the messages in a group before further processing other messages.

Problem   If individual messages are sent separately, it is difficult for the receiver to identify and process groups of messages in their entirety. Introducing special delimiter messages that signal the beginning and end of a group of messages is a possibility, but it still leaves a lot of decisions to the designer. It is difficult to design a robust scheme in any case, because messages belonging in multiple groups can arrive at a receiver at any time and in any order.

Solution   A message generator usually knows best when a group of messages are generated. Therefore, the generator simply packages the messages into a packet—a simple list is almost always adequate—and sends the packet instead of the individual messages. The receiver is then free to process the messages in the packet in any manner appropriate.

Discussion   If there are multiple sources of messages and all messages belong to the same group and must be processed together, then the receiver of the message packets must still do a substantial amount of message management. The situation is no worse than it is with individual messages, however.

FIGURE 5 Observer Update Message

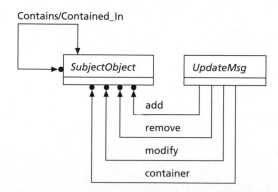

PATTERN: OBSERVER UPDATE MESSAGE

Context   The designer is using the Observer pattern or any of its refinements (e.g., the Conduit of Subject Change pattern). The subject consists of many objects with nested containment relationships among them.

Problem   The observer needs to be informed of the subject's state-change information in such a way that the observer is not overly dependent on the specifics of the subject.

Solution   Given the nature of the subject, any state change in the subject can be characterized by a series of new-object creations (Add), old-object deletions (Remove), and existing-object modifications (Modify) at certain locations. Accordingly, the subject update message will consist of four lists: Add list, Remove list, Modify list, and Container list. The contents of the Container list indicate the locations.

   As an example, suppose a message object is constructed as follows: the Add list includes an object, O1, and the Container list includes another object, O2. The interpretation of this message would then be that O1 has been created in O2.

Discussion: Multiple Inclusion of the Same Object

In light of the fact that one change request can affect multiple subject objects and one update message may contain all of those affected objects (e.g., a cascaded remove; see the One Message per Change Request pattern), it can be shown that a same-subject object may appear in more than one list in an update message. The question then is how that object should be processed. And, relatedly, in which order should the lists in the update message be processed? The following simple rules can be applied to an update message in order to process it correctly:

1. If an object appears in the Remove list and any other lists, it should be deleted from all other lists except the Remove list.

2. Process the lists in the following order: Remove list, Add list, and finally Modify list.

PATTERN: UPDATING OBSERVER

Once an observer receives an update message, it needs to interpret the contents of that message. There are many ways of doing this. We currently have an implementation that relies on runtime type information supplied by the subject objects in the message, but this implementation has yet to be fully described in pattern form.

REFERENCES

[Beck+94] K. Beck and R. Johnson. "Patterns Generate Architectures." *European Conference on Object-Oriented Programming.* Berlin: Springer-Verlag, 1994, pp. 139–149.

[Buschmann+96] F. Buschmann, R. Meunier, H. Rohnert, P. Sommerlad, and M. Stal. *Pattern-Oriented Software Architecture—A System of Patterns.* West Sussex, England: Wiley, 1996.

[Coad+95] P. Coad, D. North, and M. Mayfield. *Object Models: Strategies, Patterns, and Applications.* Englewood Cliffs, NJ: Prentice-Hall, 1995.

[Coplien92] J. O. Coplien. *Advanced C++ Programming Styles and Idioms.* Reading, MA: Addison-Wesley, 1992.

[Coplien+95] J. O. Coplien and D. C. Schmidt (eds.). *Pattern Languages of Program Design.* Reading, MA: Addison-Wesley, 1995.

[Gamma+95] E. Gamma, R. Helm, R. Johnson, and J. Vlissides. *Design Patterns: Elements of Reusable Object-Oriented Software.* Reading, MA: Addison-Wesley, 1995.

[Johnson92] R. E. Johnson. "Documenting Frameworks Using Patterns." Proceedings of OOPSLA '92. Vancouver, British Columbia:ACM Press, 1992, pp. 63–72.

[Pree95] W. Pree. *Design Patterns for Object-Oriented Software Development.* Reading, MA: Addison-Wesley, 1995.

Both Jung J. Kim and Kevin M. Benner can be reached at Andersen Consulting, 3773 Willow Road, Northbrook, IL 60062-6212; jkim@cstar.ac.com.

Patterns for Encapsulating Class Trees

Dirk Riehle

INTRODUCTION

Good object-oriented design relies heavily on abstract classes. Abstract classes define the interface used to work with the subclasses that implement them. If clients name these subclasses directly, they become dependent on them. This complicates both system configuration and evolution. The patterns presented in this chapter, Late Creation and Class Retrieval, overcome these problems by encapsulating class trees behind their root classes. Clients use class specifications to retrieve classes and create objects, so that classes can be removed and plugged into the class tree more easily. Thus, encapsulating class trees eases system evolution and configuration of system variants.

  The patterns discussed in this chapter are presented using a new variation of the pattern form. We start by outlining the overall background against which the patterns emerge. This background explains what the patterns are relevant for and what they achieve; it provides the overall pattern context and recursive closure of all subsequent pattern contexts.

After introducing the background, I present each pattern in a separate subsection. A subsection consists mainly of a pattern/context pair in which the actual pattern is presented separately from the embedding context. This is based on an understanding of a pattern as a *form* that emerges in specific contexts: the form is finite and can be described precisely, while the context is infinite and can be only partially described (that is, we extract what we think is relevant to understand the forces driving the pattern).

Section 2 introduces the presented patterns' background. Sections 3 and 4 present the patterns needed in order to encapsulate class trees. Section 5 compares the patterns with other patterns, most notably Factory Method and Abstract Factory [Gamma+95]. Section 6 discusses the pattern form and what we gain by using it. Section 7 summarizes the chapter and presents further conclusions.

BACKGROUND OF THE PATTERNS

Abstract classes represent the key design decisions that determine a system's macro structure. An abstract class represents an interface to an entire class tree. This interface is often sufficient for clients to work with the objects of classes within the class tree. Concrete subclasses of the abstract class have to be named only when selecting classes and creating objects of them. If this is done by clients of the abstract class, they become dependent on the class tree's internal structure: changes in class names or the class tree structure will force changes in these clients as well.

Therefore, the class tree behind an abstract class should be hidden from all clients of that class. If a client's knowledge is restricted to the abstract class only, all dependencies on subclasses are cut. This has several advantages. First, clients can focus on the relevant abstraction (that is, the abstract class); they don't have to bother with less important details like names of subclasses. Second, changes in the class tree have only local consequences, which makes system evolution easier. Third, plugging in and removing subclasses doesn't affect clients. Thus system variants can be configured easily.

The general idea behind encapsulating class trees is to let clients refer to abstract superclasses only. They can then retrieve classes and create objects by supplying class specifications. A specification describes the classes of interest to a client and makes up for the information loss in class names. A common meta facility maps these specifications onto classes. This task is conveniently carried out by a class tree's abstract superclasses. These superclasses, visible to clients, are called *interface classes* of the class tree. While working with encapsulated class trees, two different but related patterns emerged: Class Retrieval and Late Creation.

Class retrieval is the process of retrieving a set of classes (from an encapsulated class tree) that all adhere to a given specification. This set can be then used in making further decisions on how to proceed. For example, classes retrieved from an encapsulated Command class tree [Gamma+95] can be used in building a menu of possible commands.

Late creation is the process of creating a single instance of a class that matches a given specification. By this process, instances of hidden subclasses can be created using interface classes only. The most common example is object activation. A class id received from a stream is mapped to a class used to create a new object. Late creation lets clients not only perform object activation based on class ids but also create new objects based on all kinds of specifications. Such specifications might depend on existing objects and can therefore be used to create a set of objects in concert (from a behavioral pattern, for example).

Several ways of specifying classes can be thought of; interface definition languages and object request brokers are the most prominent examples. Here, however, additional forces are introduced: Class Retrieval and Late Creation have to be carried out quickly and in the same order of time as factory methods [Gamma+95]. Having achieved this, they can be incorporated into basic framework design and may be used as pervasively as factory methods.

The patterns Class Specification, Class Semantics, and Class Clause support Class Retrieval and Late Creation and achieve the desired order of speed. Class Specification is used to express requirements for classes to be retrieved and new objects to be created. Class Semantics is used to express the properties of a specific class so that it can be easily matched with a specification. Class Clause expresses an atomic property of a class as a first class object. Figure 1 shows an overview of the patterns and their dependencies.

The patterns have been implemented in two different frameworks, one in Smalltalk [Riehle+95a] and one in C++ [Riehle+95b]. A number of example designs from these frameworks are used here to discuss the patterns; these designs are

FIGURE 1 Overview of the patterns. An arrow illustrates a relationship in which the source pattern relies on the target pattern and therefore provides a possible context for this pattern's use.

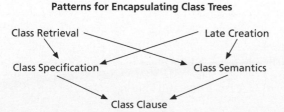

Patterns for Encapsulating Class Trees

based on a simple meta-level architecture that assumes some kind of representation of classes as objects, so that classes can be passed around. This is available in most major C++ application frameworks [Weinand+94, Gorlen+90, Campbell+93] as well as in CLOS [Steele90] and Smalltalk [Goldberg+83].

FRAMEWORK EXAMPLE

As an example, consider a system designed according to the Tools and Materials metaphor [Riehle+95b]. Users use tools to work on materials. Tools are the *means* of doing work, while materials are the intermediate or final *outcome* of work. A software desktop presents both tools and materials as icons to users. They start tools by clicking on the appropriate icon.

In this chapter I describe two tools used in a scheduling application: a calendar tool that works with an appointment book, and a planner tool that works with a timetable. Both the appointment book and the timetable are materials. The calendar is used to keep track of single appointments, while the planner is used to manage weekly dates like meetings and seminars.

Figures 2 and 3 show a simple software design. The classes `Calendar` and `Planner` are subclasses of the abstract superclass `Tool`. The classes `AppBook` and `TimeTable` are subclasses of the abstract superclass `Material`. In a running system, a single instance of class `Desktop` creates,

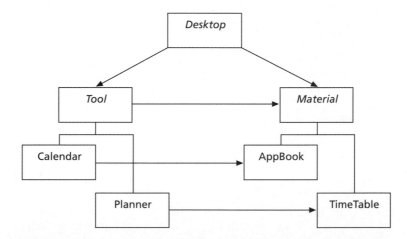

FIGURE 2 The software design used in the examples. Rectangles represent classes, arrows represent use, and lines represent inheritance relationships.

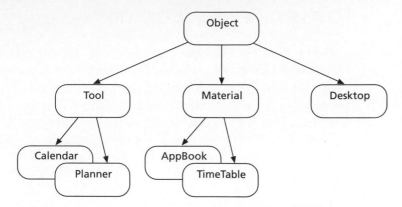

FIGURE 3 The class (object) tree described in the example. Each class holds a list of its subclasses. Objects are shown as rounded rectangles.

manages, and deletes all tools and materials. We can simplify the example by assuming that all classes are available in a single executable. To focus on the essentials, we will ignore issues of dynamically linked libraries and interprocess communication.

How would one encapsulate class trees in this example? Systems designed according to the Tools and Materials metaphor usually consist of a large and changing number of tools and materials supplied with a specific system variant. Therefore, the class `Desktop` should not know about specific tools but should use the abstract superclass `Tool` only. Thus, the class trees behind `Tool` and `Material` should be encapsulated for `Desktop`. In doing so, several tasks have to be reconsidered:

- Each tool in the system should be represented as an icon on the desktop. How can the desktop ensure that each represented tool is actually available in the current system variant?

- Assume that the user selects a tool icon or types in a tool name. How can the desktop determine the corresponding tool class and create an actual tool instance?

- Assume that the user double-clicks on a material icon to start it up. Usually a large number of tools can work on a material in more or less specific ways (see the pattern Tool and Material Coupling, described by Riehle and Züllighoven [Riehle+95]). How can the desktop find out which is the best-fitting tool class to work on the material?

These questions are answered in the example sections of the first two patterns described.

CLASS TREE ENCAPSULATION

Clients of an encapsulated class tree may not directly refer to the tree's internal classes. At runtime, however, they have to determine the available classes so that they can rely on them. Furthermore, they have to create objects from these hidden classes to actually make use of them. Class Retrieval shows how clients retrieve sets of classes that all adhere to a given specification. Late Creation shows how clients create objects from hidden classes (also using specifications).

Class Retrieval

Problem Clients of an encapsulated class tree need to retrieve classes from that tree. They delegate this task to the tree's interface class and provide it with a class specification. They receive a set of classes, all adhering to the specification. They can then use these classes for their specific purposes.

Context Several tasks require knowledge about the available classes in a class tree. For example, clients need to know the available classes in a Command [Gamma+95] class tree so they can build a list of menu items for them, and clients want to know all the classes in a Strategy [Gamma+95] class tree that perform with certain timing characteristics.

Clients of an encapsulated class tree may not know these classes by name; they only know the interface class of the class tree. However, they know the properties of those classes that they need for their task. Therefore:

Pattern Clients of an encapsulated class tree create a specification for those classes they are interested in. The specification is based on the properties that are relevant to the client. The client requests all classes from the class tree that adhere to the specification. This task is most conveniently delegated to the interface class of the class tree. The client receives a set of all classes in the class tree that match the specification.

All classes in the set are subclasses of the interface class and are therefore guaranteed to support its interface. The client can use this set according to its purposes (for example, to present each class as a possible choice in a graphical user interface). Specifications for Class Retrieval are usually ambiguous and denote a whole range of possible classes.

Example The desktop class has been written to work generically with tools; it doesn't know about specific tool classes. The tool classes vary with each system variant. Thus, during each system startup the desktop has to determine which tool classes are available. Icons should only be created for tool classes that are actually available.

Therefore, the desktop creates a specification for concrete tool classes. The specification consists of a single flag that indicates that the classes have to be concrete. It calls the `RetrieveClasses` operation of class `Tool`. A set of classes that fit the specification is returned (see the following code example). Among others, it contains the classes `Planner` and `Calendar`. The desktop can now safely create icons for these tool classes.

```
void Desktop::GetConcreteToolClasses( Set< Class* >* cset )
{
      // create simple specification for concrete classes
    IsAbstractClause spec( false );

      // request classes from interface class
    Tool::ClassObject()->RetrieveClasses( &spec, cset );
}
```

Design At least two possible implementations come to mind. The interface class can build the set by traversing the class tree from the top down. While traversing, it matches each class with the specification. If the specification fits, the corresponding class is put into the set that will be returned to the client. This is a slow implementation, but it introduces no additional memory overhead. Chapter 3 discusses how object-oriented specifications can be built easily.

If speed is more important, the specification can be used to compute the index for a table lookup. Each specification usually denotes a set of classes, which means that the index for the table lookup identifies the set of equivalent classes for a certain specification. These tables can be built in advance or on demand.

The execution time is now constant but requires some memory overhead for the tables. Our implementations use class-tree traversal for Class Retrieval and table lookup for Late Creation. It doesn't compute tables for all kinds of specifications (which would be impossible) but only for specifications built from a single clause (see pattern Class Clause).

Impact The code for retrieving classes can be written fully on the framework level. It usually consists of two lines: one creating a specification and one calling the `RetrieveClasses` operation. Retrieving classes requires additional functionality, which depends on the chosen implementation strategy. This is solved by the framework and shouldn't bother users. The only task left to users is to specify the semantics of the classes they introduce This is accomplished by writing an access operation for each property specified (see Late Creation).

Late Creation

Problem   Clients of an encapsulated class tree need to create objects for classes hidden in that tree. Again, clients create a specification for the objects to be created and delegate the task to the interface class. They receive either an instance of the class matching the specification or null.

Context   An encapsulated class tree is of no use unless objects of its internal classes can be created. Again, clients know only the interface class. In addition, they now have to know a property that unambiguously identifies the class they are interested in. For example, a class id received from an input stream has to be mapped to a class to activate an object.

Therefore:

Pattern   The client of a class creates a specification that unambiguously identifies a single class. It then requests a new instance of a class that fits the specification. Again, this task is conveniently delegated to the interface class. A returned object is guaranteed to adhere to both the interface of the interface class and the specification. If no matching class is found, no instance can be created, and null is returned.

The most widely known example of Late Creation is object activation. Class names or class identifiers received from a stream are mapped to a class that is then used to create an object. Late Creation is the generalization of several special-purpose solutions existing today [Grossman93, Gorlen+90]. Using table lookup, it can be carried out in constant time.

The name *Late Creation* has its roots in the notion of late binding. As with late binding, the class that is eventually referred to is determined at runtime.

Example   Tools should have unambiguous names like *Calendar* or *Planner*. Assume that the system can be started using aliases. The chosen alias indicates the first tool to be launched automatically. Thus, the desktop creates a specification for a tool class by using the alias string. Any unambiguous specification (class id, class name, tool name) will suffice.

The desktop calls the `CreateLate` operation of the abstract class `Tool`. `Tool` uses the specification to retrieve the corresponding subclass. `Tool` asks this class to create an instance of it, which is returned to the client. If no matching class is found, null is returned.

Design   Again, it is possible to either traverse the class tree or use table lookup to find a class. In this case, given an unambiguous specification, a table entry denotes a single class. Thus, the table can be built more easily. Developers should take care that during evolution the system stays free of ambiguities. We can solve this problem by carefully designing and inventing new classes; however, tool support is certainly desirable.

Ifclients are allowed to pass in ambiguous specifications, the class of the new instance can't be decided without further help. Thus, some means of handling ambiguities has to be introduced. Clients must supply additional hints, like "choose the most specialized" or "most general implementation," or they will just receive an instance of the first class that is retrieved.

Impact   Class Retrieval and Late Creation have similar impacts. Again, the execution speed depends on the chosen implementation strategy, and execution can be performed in constant time on the order of a factory method.

For certain classes, hiding the creation process from the client might turn out to be a problem. Inside the class tree, objects can be created only by using a standard initialization procedure. If a new object needs additional parameters, it must receive them from the client through an extra operation after creation. However, the protocol for this extra initialization operation has to be available in the interface class of the class tree, and no assumptions about class tree internal protocols should be made.

In very problematic cases, the specification can be enriched with the initialization parameters so that a special creation procedure or constructor can receive them during the early object-building process.

SPECIFICATION SUPPORT

This section discusses class specifications and class semantics. Both class specifications and class semantics are built from clauses. A clause is an atomic predicate about a class property. The semantics of a class are represented by a set of clauses. A class specification is an expression from propositional calculus, with clauses as its atomic constituents. Class specifications can be matched against class semantics in a straightforward fashion.

Class Clause

A class clause makes an atomic statement about a class property. It resolves to either true or false. It is represented by an object and can be compared to other clauses easily. Thus, it provides a basis for class specifications and first-class representations of class semantics.

Context Class Retrieval and Late Creation use specifications to describe classes of interest. Clients of an encapsulated class tree build specifications for one or more classes. Thus they need some basic means to express class properties. Furthermore, designers of a class will want to make its properties explicit as well. Thus they also need a basic means to express class properties. Finally, we have narrowed the context to the programmatic statement that specifications should be easy and need no further language or tool support.

Therefore:

Pattern Class properties are expressed as instances of clause classes. Each clause class picks on a specific aspect of a class's semantics and represents it as an object. Clients use clause class instances to build specifications. A single clause is a special case of a general class specification, and it can be used as such very well. Furthermore, classes use clauses to express their basic properties.

Several kinds of clause classes exist. Some express general properties (for example, whether a class is abstract or concrete). Others express performance or memory-consumption properties of instances of a class. Some clauses denote a class unambiguously (for example, clauses built from class ids, class names, or other identifiers). Clause classes are introduced as needed.

The class tree in Figure 4 shows some of the most convenient clause classes. All clause classes are subclasses of `Clause`. Those classes that offer an

FIGURE 4 Hierarchy of clause classes. Most clause classes are subclasses of `IdClause` and are thus capable of denoting a single class.

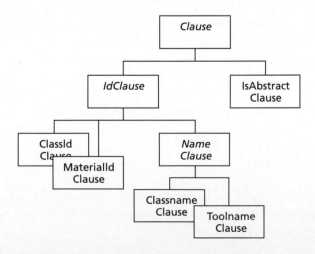

unambiguous id are subclasses of `IdClause`, which in turn is a subclass of `Clause`. Further clause classes are `IsAbstractClause` (a flag indicating abstract or concrete classes), `NameClause` (a string indicating a class), and several kinds of id clauses.

In addition to static properties of a class, clauses can express dependencies between several classes. A `MaterialIdClause` instance holds the id of a material class. It can be used as a simple specification for tool classes that can work with the indicated material. Such clauses are called *dependency clauses*.

When created, a clause instance receives its parameters from its creator. If the client is using the clause for a specification (see Class Specification), the client has to explicitly provide the class properties expressed through the clause. If the clause is instantiated to be part of a class's semantics, it might derive the properties from the class itself (see Class Semantics).

Example The specification for concrete tool and material classes is based on the clause class `IsAbstractClause`. It consists of a flag that indicates whether a class is abstract or not. The specification for object activation consists of a single `ClassIdClause` instance that holds the id for the class to be instantiated.

As another example, assume that the user activates a material instance of class `AppBook`. Now a tool has to be instantiated to work on the given material. The desktop creates a `MaterialIdClause` instance, which it provides with the class id retrieved from the appointment book. It calls `CreateLate` of class `Tool`. The `MaterialIdClause` instance is matched by the tool class `Calendar` as the most specialized class able to work on the indicated material. From the desktop's point of view, it has created a tool instance depending on a given material. Only the abstract superclasses `Tool` and `Material` were used. Thus the class trees are encapsulated.

As yet another example, consider a client that holds a `List` instance and wants to create an iterator for it. It calls the `CreateLate` operation of class `Iterator` and passes in a `ContainerIdClause`. This clause instance holds the class id of the container class (that is, the list class id). Each iterator class knows the container it has been designed for and can therefore decide whether it matches the specification. Using clauses this way avoids the usual factory methods of the container, thereby creating iterators and cursors of all flavors.

Design It remains to be proven that the execution time for class lookup can be similar to the time consumed by factory methods. Given a specification consisting of a single clause and a prebuilt table for looking up classes based on this clause class, the following steps have to be taken:

- Create a clause instance.
- Look up the right table based on the clause class.

- Look up the class based on the clause.
- Return it or call new on it.

These steps are usually performed in constant time.

The following code shows a simple C++ operation for `CreateLate`:

```
Object* Class::CreateLateByClause( IdClause* clause )
{
        // get clause instance table for the clause's class
    Table* cltab = ClauseTab->Lookup( clause->ClassObject() );

        // lookup class for given clause
    Class* classObject = cltab->Lookup( clause->Id() );

        // return new object of retrieved class
    if ( classObject != null ) return classObject->New();
    else return null;
}
```

Class Specification

A class specification is a formula from propositional calculus with clauses as its basic constituents. Clients build a specification by creating clauses and arranging them as a formula.

Context   Clients use specifications to retrieve classes from a class tree. They use clauses to express basic properties of these classes. Single properties are often not sufficient to give a precise specification for a class, however.

Therefore:

Pattern   As noted, a class specification is a formula from propositional calculus. Its atomic predicates are clauses that express simple class properties. A formula lets clients combine these clauses in a way sufficient for all the tasks we have encountered so far. The formula is built from clauses using the standard operators of propositional calculus (and, or, not).

An important case of class specification is a *dependency specification* built from dependency clauses. Consider an abstract design consisting of more than a single class. These classes are often subclassed in concert to take advantage of one another. Therefore, only specific subclasses work together. Only specific iterators match specific containers. A new object that is to participate in the design has to match the already existing objects. A specification for this object is a dependency specification consisting of a conjunction of id clauses, one for each existing object. Each class can check whether it can work with the classes indicated in the clauses. If so, it will match the specification.

Example Full specifications are often a combination of clauses. For example, the desktop might wish to retrieve all concrete tool classes that work with a certain material class. The resulting specification is a conjunction of an `IsAbstractClause` (indicating that the class has to be concrete) and a `MaterialIdClause` instance (indicating the material the tool has to work with). Asking class `Tool` for all concrete subclasses that can deal with a `TimeTable` material will result in quite a large set of tool classes. The set will include some general lister and browser tools as well as the more specialized planner tool.

Design A specification is an instance of `ClassSpec` that arranges the clause instances it receives as a formula from propositional calculus. Very often, however, a class specification consists of only a single clause. Therefore, interface classes should provide both `RetrieveClasses` and `CreateLate` operations for `ClassSpec` and `Clause` instances, respectively.

Impact The execution time required to evaluate a complex formula is still fast compared to interpretive approaches; however, it can't be compared with factory methods anymore. If this turns out to be problematic, a new clause class can be created that expresses the formula as a single clause. The logic has to be realized by program code, and thus it is as efficient as possible.

Class Semantics

For each class a set of clause instances is provided. Each clause makes a statement about the class for which it has been instantiated. The set of clauses is said to represent a class's semantics. A class can be matched against a specification, which is realized by comparing clauses and evaluating the formula.

Context Class specifications are built from clauses. Classes have to be matched against such specifications as described in Late Creation and Class Retrieval. The matching process should be simple and fast.
  Therefore:

Pattern For each class in the system, a set of clause instances is provided. Each clause instance makes a specific statement about a property of the class for which it is maintained. Thus each clause instance stands for a property of the class for which it has been designed and instantiated. It is sensible (though not necessary) to have a class maintain the set of clause instances describing its properties.

At least two rules based on the substitutability principle and deterministic semantics [Liskov88, Liskov+93] apply:

- If a class holds an instance of a specific clause class, then each subclass must also hold an instance of that clause class.

- If a clause instance makes a definitive statement about a class property, then this property cannot be changed in subclasses.

Clause classes should be designed with the substitutability principle in mind.

A specification is matched against a class by successive matching of clauses and by evaluating the formula. If a clause from a specification isn't found in the class's set of clauses, the formula evaluates to false. However, asking a class tree to evaluate clauses it doesn't know usually indicates a design flaw.

Example   The system's root class, `Object`, holds instances of `IsAbstractClause`, `ClassIdClause`, and `ClassnameClause`. Each subclass also holds instances of these classes. Class `Tool` holds an additional `ToolnameClause` and `MaterialIdClause` instance.

Design   Some managing facility has to be introduced to set up the structure described above. In the C++ framework we use the class `Metaclass` as a managing facility of its instances (i.e., the classes). In the Smalltalk framework we use an additional `ClassManager`. In C++ it is easy to introduce some kind of metaclass (though not full-blown, of course); in Smalltalk we don't want to interfere with the standard meta-level architecture.

This managing facility associates a set of clause classes with each class and creates instances of them. Each clause class is associated with a root class it can make a statement about; its instances are spread by the managing facility to the whole class tree of the root class.

Impact   A concrete design has to clarify where clause instances get their data for describing class properties. The data may be retrieved from external databases or held in some meta information provided by the class. The simplest approach (and the one we have used so far) is to make the class itself provide the data that clause instances rely on. This forces clients to write simple access methods for each class that return the data needed by the clauses. Each tool class, for example, has a `GetMaterialClass` operation that returns the material class for which the tool was originally written. This simple approach requires some discipline. It has worked well so far, however, mainly because not every new class requires a full set of access methods but can rely on those it inherited—they provide its "default semantics."

At first glance one might imagine that with hundreds or possibly thousands of classes, memory problems lie straight ahead. However, only a very small number of clause instances are held by each class (only `IsAbstractClause`, `ClassIdClause`, and `ClassnameClause`). `MaterialIdClause` instances, for example, are maintained only for tool classes, which is just a fraction of the overall number of classes in a system.

Moreover, clause instances usually aren't fat but consist of only 1 to 4 or 8 bytes. Memory consumption is fixed and can be calculated. (We haven't run into trouble with our applications.) In case of trouble, optimization strategies can easily be thought of (for example, using the Flyweight pattern [Gamma+95] to minimize the number of clauses).

RELATION TO OTHER PATTERNS

The patterns presented here are an alternative to two of the most important patterns known today: Factory Method and Abstract Factory [Gamma+95].

A factory method is an operation that creates an object that fits the current class. It is destined to be redefined in subclasses, where it creates an object that fits the subclass best. Using Late Creation and Class Retrieval, the factory method still exists; however, it needn't be redefined. The creation process is carried out on the abstract level using a specification for the new object. No redefinition of the operation is needed, which possibly avoids introducing a new subclass. Again, the desktop might serve as an example. In most designs, it might be subclassed to introduce the available tool and material classes by name. This isn't necessary, as has been shown.

An abstract factory encapsulates the process of creating instances of a family of classes. Some initial specification is used to choose among variants for different systems. The standard example is a window-system abstract factory. Based on the runtime environment, an abstract factory for either Motif, Macintosh, OS/2, or any other window system is chosen. The factory offers operations to create new windows, scrollbars, text fields, menus, and so on. This can easily be reinterpreted in terms of Late Creation. A client that wishes to create a new window uses a window system clause. This consists of a flag that indicates the current window system. The client directly asks the abstract class `Window` to create an instance late. It will receive an instance of a subclass that implements the window for the system indicated in the clause.

Gamma et al. [Gamma+95] list further creational patterns (Prototype and Builder). Although these patterns cannot be directly replaced by Late Creation and Class Retrieval, they do have some similarities to them. Prototype has classes as objects, and its usage resembles Class Retrieval. Builder does things that can be done using Late Creation as well.

I believe that Late Creation, like Factory Method, is a fundamental creational pattern that not only works alone but can also be used to implement the other patterns.

PATTERN FORM

In this chapter I have used a new presentation form based on an experience with patterns.

Each pattern is understood as a *form* within a specific, nonarbitrary context [Riehle95]. This form constitutes the actual pattern, and it is finite. Therefore, we can identify and describe all relevant parts of the pattern. The pattern's context is not finite, however. We can approach it only pragmatically, by describing what we perceive to be the relevant forces giving shape to the actual pattern (that is, the form that emerges within that context). Since understanding a pattern's context is crucial to understanding the pattern, and since pattern and context have to fit each other, we always describe them together. The result is a pattern/context pair, supplied for pragmatic reasons, with additional sections on examples and design or implementation issues.

Contexts overlap, and individual patterns often serve within a whole that is more than just the sum of its parts (i.e., the individual patterns). Therefore, we start describing a set of patterns by introducing their background. We describe the overall rationale (class tree encapsulation, in this case) and thus provide an embedding and a higher-level understanding of the patterns to follow. This background serves as the closure for what would otherwise be an infinite recursion of embedded pattern/context pairs.

As discussions at the 1995 PLoP conference showed, the entry point to a set of related patterns is still considered problematic. A "first-pattern approach" doesn't seem to work well, since it focuses subsequent patterns too narrowly on the base provided by the initial pattern. The notion of background presented above might be a better alternative.

We have experimented with different pattern forms, and we think that the best presentation form for a particular pattern depends on its intended use. The problem/context/solution form, for example, seems to be aimed at developing solutions for problems in design; it doesn't seem to work well when perceiving and identifying patterns in existing structures is more important (in legacy systems, for example). A pattern/context pair is more general, since it doesn't induce specific ways of using the pattern.

SUMMARY AND CONCLUSIONS

This chapter has presented patterns that enable developers to encapsulate class trees. A possible design can be based on a simple meta-level architecture that lets developers encapsulate class trees without too much overhead.

   Coplien's generic exemplar idiom [Coplien92] is a variant of Late Creation. Lortz and Shin report on concepts for Class Hiding as well [Lortz+94]. Berczuk presents similar patterns (see Chapter 12). ET++ [Weinand+94] uses a special-purpose variant of Late Creation to perform object activation. Several pattern relationships exist to interface definition languages and object request brokers. Thus, variants of the patterns presented here have been developed independently around the world. This gives the presented concepts real pattern status.

   The patterns will work alone; however, tool support for system variant configuration should be provided. Such a tool generates the makefiles used to build a specific system variant. The tool should provide support for specifying dependencies between classes so that no class participating in a design is forgotten. This will prevent runtime failures due to missing classes.

   The pattern form has been reduced to a pattern/context pair, thereby imposing less structure on the pattern description. This is still a time of experimentation, however, and future revisions of our understanding of the pattern form might lead to different and enhanced results.

ACKNOWLEDGMENTS

I wish to thank Steve Berczuk, Walter Bischofberger, Brad Edelman, and Kai-Uwe Mätzel for reviewing and/or discussing this chapter with me. I'd also like to thank the reading group at UBILAB, which discussed the chapter in a writer's workshop setting. Finally, the writers' workshop at PLoP '95 pointed out unclear issues and helped me improve the chapter further.

REFERENCES

[Campbell+93] R. H. Campbell, N. Islam, D. Raila, and P. Madany. "Designing and Implementing Choices: An Object-Oriented System in C++." *Communications of the ACM, 36*(9), (1993):117–126.

[Coplien92] J. O. Coplien. *Advanced C++ Programming Styles and Idioms.* Reading, MA: Addison-Wesley, 1992.

[Gamma+95] E. Gamma, R. Helm, R. Johnson, and J. Vlissides. *Design Patterns: Elements of Reusable Object-Oriented Software.* Reading, MA: Addison-Wesley, 1995.

[Goldberg+83] A. Goldberg and D. Robson. *Smalltalk-80: The Language and Its Implementation.* Reading, MA: Addison-Wesley, 1983.

[Gorlen+90] K. E. Gorlen, S. M. Orlow, and P. S. Plexiko. *Data Abstraction and Object-Oriented Programming in C++.* New York: Wiley, 1990.

[Grossman93] M. Grossman. "Object I/O and Runtime Type Information via Automatic Code Generation in C++." *Journal of Object-Oriented Programming, 6*(4) (1993): 34–42.

[Liskov88] B. Liskov. "Data Abstraction and Hierarchy. " (OOPSLA '87 Addendum.) *ACM SIGPLAN Notices, 23*(5) (1988):17–34.

[Liskov+93] B. Liskov and J. Wing. "A New Definition of the Subtype Relation." *ECOOP '93 Conference Proceedings.* Berlin: Springer-Verlag, 1993, pp. 118–141.

[Lortz+94] V. B. Lortz and K. G. Shin. "Combining Contracts and Exemplar-Based Programming for Class Hiding and Customization." (OOPSLA '94). *ACM SIGPLAN Notices, 29*(10) (1994):453–467.

[Riehle95] D. Riehle. *Patterns—Exemplified through the Tools and Materials Metaphor.* (Master's thesis written in German.) (UBILAB Technical Report 95.6.1.) Zürich: Union Bank of Switzerland, 1995.

[Riehle+95a] D. Riehle and M. Schnyder. *Design and Implementation of a Smalltalk Framework for the Tools and Materials Metaphor.* (UBILAB Technical Report 95.7.1.) Zürich: Union Bank of Switzerland, 1995.

[Riehle+95b] D. Riehle and H. Züllighoven. "A Pattern Language for Tool Construction and Integration Based on the Tools and Materials Metaphor." In J. O. Coplien and D. C. Schmidt (eds.), *Pattern Languages of Program Design.* Reading, MA: Addison-Wesley, 1995, pp. 9–42.

[Steele90] G. L. Steele. *Common Lisp: The Language* (2nd ed.). Burlington, MA: Digital Press, 1990.

[Weinand+94] A. Weinand and E. Gamma. "ET++ a Portable, Homogenous Class Library and Application Framework." In W. R. Bischofberger and H. P. Frei (eds.), *Computer Science Research at UBILAB.* Konstanz, Germany: Universitätsverlag Konstanz, 1994, pp. 66–92.

Dirk Riehle can be reached at UBILAB, Union Bank of Switzerland, Bahnhofstrasse 45, CH-8021 Zurich; reihle@ubilab.ubs.ch.

The Proxy Design Pattern Revisited

7

Hans Rohnert

ABSTRACT

The Proxy design pattern makes a component's clients communicate to a representative rather than to the component itself. The pattern consists of three participants: the client, the proxy, and the original. The original implements a service. The client invokes the functionality of the original indirectly, by accessing the proxy. The proxy ensures correct and efficient access to the original.

There are seven variants of this pattern: virtual proxy, cache proxy, remote proxy, protection proxy, synchronization proxy, counting proxy, and firewall proxy. To reconcile generality with specialization, I use a simple two-level pattern language. First I describe, in an abstract way, what these seven variants have in common. Then I describe the individual "subpatterns."

This paper revisits the Proxy pattern described by Gamma and his colleagues [Gamma+95]. The major contribution of this description is in that it adds new variants and restructures a multifaceted pattern into a two-level pattern language. More differences are investigated toward the end of this chapter.

EXAMPLE

Many in-house engineers regularly consult data stores for information on material providers, available parts, blueprints, and so on. Every remote access may be costly; many accesses are typical and happen again and again. Obviously, there is room for different optimizations concerning access times and cost. But we do not want to burden the engineer's application code with such optimizations. The presence and kind of optimizations should be largely transparent to the application's user and programmer.

THE GENERIC PATTERN

The Proxy design pattern makes a component's clients communicate to a representative rather than to the component itself. Introducing such a placeholder can serve many purposes, including enhanced efficiency, easier access, and protection.

CONTEXT

A client needs access to the services of another component. Direct access is technically possible but seems questionable.

PROBLEM

Often it is inappropriate to access a component directly. We do not want to hardwire its location into clients; direct and unmitigated access to the component may be inefficient or even insecure. Additional access-control mechanisms are needed. A solution to such a design problem has to balance some or all of the following forces:

1. Accessing the component should be runtime-efficient, cost-effective, and safe for both sides.

2. Access to the component should be transparent and simple for the client. In particular, the client should not have to (significantly) change its calling behavior and syntax from that used to call any other direct-access component.

3. The client should be well aware of possible performance or monetary penalties for accessing remote clients. Full transparency can be counter-productive.

SOLUTION

The Proxy design pattern consists of three participants: the client, the proxy, and the original:

- The original implements a particular service. Such a service may range from simple actions like returning or displaying data to complex data-retrieval functions or computations involving further components.

- The client is responsible for a specific task. To do its job, it invokes functionality of the original in an indirect way by accessing the proxy. The client does not have to change its calling behavior and syntax from the way it calls ordinary local components.

- Therefore, the proxy offers the same interface as the original. An abstract base class describes this common interface. Both the proxy and the original inherit from it. The proxy ensures correct access to the original. To this end, the proxy maintains a reference to the original it represents. Usually there is a one-to-one relationship between the proxy and the original, though there are exceptions to this rule for remote and firewall proxies.

The following CRC cards show a first cut at the classes involved.

Class Client	Collaborators Proxy
Responsibilities • Uses the interface provided by the proxy to request a particular service • Fulfills its own task	

Class *Abstract_Original*	Collaborators -
Responsibilities • Serves as an abstract base class for the proxy and the original	

Class Proxy	Collaborators Original
Responsibilities • Provides the original's interface to clients • Ensures a safe, efficient and correct access to the original	

Class Original	Collaborators -
Responsibilities • Implements a particular service	

STRUCTURE

The following OMT diagram graphically depicts the relationships between our classes.

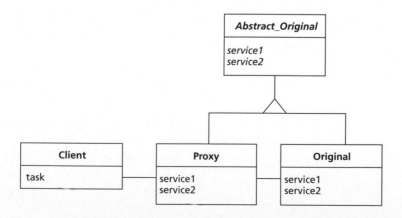

DYNAMICS

A typical dynamic scenario of a Proxy structure appears in the diagram below. Note that the actions performed in the proxy differ depending on its actual specialization (see next section):

- The client asks the proxy to carry out a service.

- The proxy receives the incoming service request and preprocesses it. This preprocessing involves actions like looking up the address of the original or checking in a local cache if the requested information is locally available.

- If the proxy has to consult the original for fulfilling the request, it forwards the request using the proper communication protocols and security measures, if any.

- The original takes the request and fulfills it. It sends the response back to the proxy.

- The proxy receives the answer. Before or after transferring the answer to the client, it may take additional post-processing actions like caching the result, calling the destructor of the original, or releasing a lock.

The following message sequence chart illustrates the fundamental use case of our pattern.

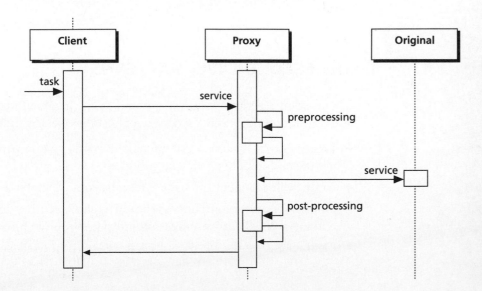

IMPLEMENTATION

1. Identify all responsibilities for dealing with access control to a component. Attach these responsibilities to a separate component, the proxy. The details of this step are deferred to the section describing the seven variants.

2. If possible, introduce an abstract base class that specifies the common parts of the interfaces of both the proxy and the original. Derive the proxy and the original from this abstract base. If identical interfaces for the proxy and the original are not feasible, you may use an adapter [Gamma+95] for interface adaptation. Adapting the proxy to the original's interface preserves the client's illusion of identical interfaces (and a common base class for the adapter and the original may be possible again).

3. Implement the proxy's functions (check the roles specified in the previous step).

4. Free the original and its clients from responsibilities that have migrated into the proxy.

5. Associate the proxy and the original by giving the proxy a handle to the original. This handle may be a pointer, a reference, an address, an identifier, a socket, a port, and so on.

6. Remove all direct relationships between the original and its clients. Replace them by analogous relationships to the proxy.

THE SECOND-LEVEL PATTERNS

This section describes the seven variants of the generic Proxy pattern. Let us start by summarizing the respective applicabilities of the individual variants:

- Processing or loading a component is costly, while partial information about the component may be sufficient (virtual proxy).

- Multiple local clients can share results from the outside (cache proxy).

- Clients of remote components should be shielded from network addresses and interprocess communication protocols (remote proxy).

- Components must be protected from unauthorized access (protection proxy).

- Multiple simultaneous accesses have to be synchronized (synchronization proxy).
- Accidental deletion of components must be prevented (counting proxy).
- Local clients should be protected from the outside world (firewall proxy).

Remote Proxy

A remote proxy encapsulates and maintains the physical location of the original. It also implements the IPC routines that perform the actual communication with the original. For every original, instantiate one proxy per address space in which the services of the original are needed. For complex IPC mechanisms, refine the proxy by shifting the communication with the original to a forwarder component (see the Forwarder-Receiver pattern [Buschmann+96]). Using the Whole-Part pattern [Buschmann+96], these two parts of the proxy can be reunited. Analogously, introduce a receiver into the original.

For reasons of efficiency, you may introduce shortcuts for local originals: if client and original live in the same address space or on the same machine, it may be appropriate or even mandatory to use different communication schemes from the remote case. Where should these three different possibilities (same process, same machine, different machine) be differentiated? I argue that this should usually not happen in the client. Rather, this is an inherent task of the proxy. See the section on Consequences for the rationale.

Protection Proxy

A protection proxy protects the original from unauthorized accesses. To this end the proxy checks the access rights of every client. Preferably, use the access-control mechanisms your platform offers. If appropriate and possible, give every client its own set of permissions to other components. Access-control lists are a common implementation of this concept.

Cache Proxy

To implement a cache proxy, extend the proxy with a data area to temporarily hold results. Develop a strategy to maintain and refresh the cache.

When the cache is full and you need space for new entries, there are several strategies you can use. For example, delete those cache entries that were used least frequently, or implement a move-to-front strategy. The latter is usually easier to implement and efficient enough. Whenever a client accesses a cache entry, it is moved to the front of, say, a doubly linked list. When new entries to the cache have to be incorporated, delete from the back of the list.

Also take care of the cache invalidation problem: when data in the original change, copies of these data cached elsewhere become invalid. If it is crucial for your application to always have up-to-date data, you may declare the whole cache invalid whenever the original copy of one of its entries gets changed. Alternatively, you may use a write-through strategy (from microprocessor cache design) for fine-grained control. If you can live with slightly outdated information, you may label individual cache entries with expiration dates. Examples of this strategy include Web browsers.

Synchronization Proxy

A synchronization proxy controls multiple simultaneous client accesses. If only one client at a time should access the original, the proxy implements mutual exclusion via semaphores [Dijkstra65], or it may use whatever means of synchronization your operating system offers. You may also differentiate between whether the access is read or write. In the former case, you may adopt more liberal policies (for instance, allowing arbitrarily many reads when no write is active or pending).

Counting Proxy

A well-known technique for automatically deleting obsolete objects is reference counting. The counting proxy maintains the number of references to the original and deletes the original when this number gets to zero. If you would like to use this mechanism, extend the synchronization proxy with a counter, and increment the counter with every new client. Whenever a client ceases to access the original, decrement the counter. When it reaches zero, delete the original, maybe by calling its destructor. But keep in mind that this scheme works only if there is exactly one proxy for an original and if every access to the original goes through its proxy. This alone does not address the problem of reclaiming isolated components that refer to each other.

Virtual Proxy

A virtual proxy, also known as lazy construction, assumes that an application will reference secondary storage (say, the hard disk). This proxy does not disclose whether the original is fully loaded or only skeletal information about it is available. Loading missing parts of the original is performed on demand. Let us assume that the proxy's reference to the original is implemented as a pointer. When a service request arrives and the information present in the proxy is not sufficient to handle the request, load the needed data from disk and forward the request to the freshly created or expanded original. If the original is already sufficiently loaded, just forward the request. This forwarding is done in a transparent way (i.e., the clients always use the same interface, independent of whether the original is in main memory or not). It is the responsibility of the client or an associated module to notify the proxy when the original or parts of it are no longer needed. Then the proxy frees the space allocated. When several clients reference the same original, it may be appropriate to add the capabilities of the synchronization and cache proxies.

Firewall Proxy

A firewall proxy subsumes the networking and protection code necessary to communicate with a potentially hostile environment. It is beyond the scope of this pattern to describe the design of such a proxy in detail. Indeed, the introduction of firewall proxies was meant to relieve application programmers from bulky, complicated, and error-prone networking code. So, we assume that a firewall proxy is given, say, as a daemon process. All clients with requests to the outside reference this proxy. Clients register once with the proxy. All succeeding communication is done in a transparent way; that is, clients work as if they have unhampered access to a comfortable communication protocol by which they in turn have access to outside components.

COMBINING THE VARIATIONS

Often you may need more than one of the above proxy variations. You may want the proxy to play several of the above roles and fulfill the corresponding responsibilities. Proceed as follows: pick the desired roles (e.g., virtual and cache); then think about combining these roles into one proxy with different roles.

If combining them bloats the resulting proxy too much, split it into smaller chunk-sized objects. An example of this is factoring out complicated networking code into a forwarder/receiver structure (see the Forwarder-Receiver pattern [Buschmann+96]; in this case the proxy is only left with the location information of the original and the local vs. remote decision).

SOLUTION TO EXAMPLE

The remote data access problem can be solved by hybrid proxies with the properties of remote and cache proxies. Implementing such a mixed-mode proxy can be accomplished by using the Whole-Part pattern [Buschmann+96].

- One part is the cache. It contains a storage area and strategies for updating and querying the cache. By using a least-frequently-used strategy and tuning the cache size, the cost of external accesses can be cut down. Invalidate individual cache entries upon modifying the corresponding original database entries. Each access to the cache of the combined proxy also has to check whether an entry found is still valid.

- The other part of the combined proxy maintains the name and address of the original and performs the actual IPC. If the original is a simple component, use the Forwarder-Receiver pattern. If it is, say, a relational database, translate the client request into SQL queries and transform back the results.

RELATED WORK

Gamma and his colleagues [Gamma+95] also describe the Proxy design pattern. Specifically, they describe four variants: the remote, virtual, and protection proxies, as well as the smart reference proxy (which is a combination of the counting, virtual, and synchronization proxies). Their proxy description is very much down-to-earth, with C++ and Smalltalk code samples sprinkled in between. Despite the many insights they deliver, their tendency to jump back and forth between different kinds of proxies and low-level programming tricks makes an otherwise excellent description somewhat hard to read.

In contrast, I have attempted to give a more abstract design view (which may have other problems, see the Open Problems section).

SELECTED KNOWN USES

- The Proxy pattern is used in the NeXTSTEP operating system to provide local stubs for objects that may be distributed. Proxies are created by a special server upon the first access to the remote original. The responsibilities of a proxy object within the NeXTSTEP operating system are to encode incoming requests (as well as their arguments) and forward them to their corresponding remote original.

- OMG-CORBA uses the Proxy pattern for two purposes. So-called client stubs or IDL stubs guard clients against the concrete implementation of their servers and the object request broker. IDL skeletons are used by the object request broker itself to forward requests to concrete remote server components [OMG92].

- Orbix [IONA95], a concrete OMG-CORBA implementation, uses remote proxies. A client can bind to an original by specifying its unique identifier. The bind call returns a C++ pointer, which the client can then use to invoke the possibly remote object, using normal C++ function invocation syntax.

- The Proxy pattern can be used to implement reference counting for shared resources. Here it is often useful to introduce a separate proxy for each client, in order to be explicitly independent of the existence of further clients.

- Another application for the Proxy pattern is the locking and unlocking of shared resources for read and write access.

- The Proxy pattern is often used in combination with the Forwarder-Receiver pattern [Buschmann+96] to implement the stub concept [Löhr+94].

- A World Wide Web proxy [Luotonen+94] is an HTTP server that typically runs on a firewall machine. It gives people inside the firewall concurrent access to the outside world. Efficiency is increased by caching recently transferred files.

CONSEQUENCES

The Proxy pattern entails the following benefits:

- *Enhanced efficiency and lower cost:* The virtual proxy helps implement a load-on-demand strategy. This way you avoid unnecessary loads and usually speed up your application. A similar argument holds for the cache proxy. But be aware that the additional overhead of going through a proxy may have the inverse effect, depending on the application (see drawbacks, next bulleted list).

- *Decoupling clients from the location of server components:* By putting all location information and addressing functionality into a remote proxy, clients will not be affected by the migration of servers or changes in the networking infrastructure. This way, client code becomes more stable and reusable. But note that a straightforward implementation of a remote proxy will still have the location of the original hardwired into its code. The advantage of this is usually better runtime performance. If the lack of flexibility is important here, you may think about introducing a dynamic lookup scheme in addition to the proxies described in the Client-Dispatcher-Server pattern (see Chapter 29).

- *Separation of housekeeping code from functionality:* In more general terms, this benefit applies to all proxy variants. A proxy relieves the client of burdens that do not inherently belong to the task the client is to perform.

Two drawbacks of the Proxy pattern can be identified:

- *Less efficiency due to indirection:* All proxies introduce an additional layer of indirection. This loss of efficiency is usually negligible compared to the gain of efficiency (for the virtual and cache variants) or the cleaner structure of the clients. Nevertheless, check this latter claim thoroughly for every single application of the Proxy pattern.

- *Overkill via sophisticated strategies:* Be careful with intricate strategies for caching or loading on demand. They do not always pay. For example, when originals are highly dynamic (like in airline reservations systems), complex caching with invalidating may introduce overhead that defeats the intended purpose. Also, many small entries in the cache may not be worth the cache maintenance effort.

SEE ALSO

- The Interface-Body design pattern [Buschmann+96] can be viewed as a special variant of the Proxy design pattern. The interface can be viewed as a proxy that represents the implementation of the original component, embodied in the body hierarchy. However, the main purpose of the Interface-Body pattern is to provide multiple implementations for components over their lifetime.

- The Counted Pointer idiom [Coplien94, Buschmann+96] describes a C++-specific implementation of the counting proxy. The original component is extended with reference-counting functionality (but note that we put the counter into the proxy instead, due to the more general nature of the proxy). For every client of the shared original, a separate proxy is introduced. Memory management is added to the proxy class, particularly to its implementation of the initialization, assignment, copying, and destruction of the original.

- The Decorator pattern [Gamma+95] is very similar in structure to Proxy. ConcreteComponent (the original) implements some behavior that is invoked via a Decorator (the proxy). Both classes inherit from a common base. The major difference is the intent: the decorator adds functionality or, more generally, gives options for dynamically choosing functionality in addition to the core functionality of ConcreteComponent. The proxy frees the original from very specific housekeeping code.

OPEN PROBLEMS

Having seven variants of this pattern creates problems in describing the pattern. I have tried to resolve this by describing the invariant parts in a general pattern first and putting the variants into their own sections. Other possibilities would have been to expand the Implementation section to include the details of the seven variants (this was the original solution). Or I could have broken the pattern into seven related but separate patterns. Another proposal was to first describe seven concrete patterns and then abstract out the commonalities.

Also, this pattern description is still very abstract. Does covering so much ground, as this pattern does, forbid inclusion of details like sample code?

One last problem with the Proxy pattern as it is described here is that not all forces are equally resolved. The traditional focus is on easy handling and getting a certain degree of efficiency automatically (forces one and two in the Problem section). But what happens when the user or programmer needs to keep explicit control for fine-tuning (force three)? One possibility is to mirror this on the level of source code by doing away with the abstract superclass. Then the programmer is always aware of the question of whether the object at hand is "the real thing" or just a surrogate. This again violates forces one and two.

ACKNOWLEDGMENTS

I would like to thank my shepherd, Ken Auer, for his help. The first version of this chapter had all seven variations jumbled up in the Implementation section. His most important advice was to refactor the chapter into a two-level pattern language.

I also thank the members of PLoP '95 Working Group 3 for their valuable criticism and suggestions for improvement.

REFERENCES

[Buschmann+96] F. Buschmann, R. Meunier, H. Rohnert, P. Sommerlad, and M. Stal. *Pattern-Oriented Software Architecture: A Pattern System*. West Sussex, England: Wiley, 1996.

[Coplien94] J. O. Coplien. *The Counted Pointer Idiom: Pattern Mailing Reflector*. February 1994.

[Dijkstra65] E. W. Dijkstra. "Solution of a Problem in Concurrent Program Control." *CACM*, 8(9) (1965):569.

[Gamma+95] E. Gamma, R. Helm, R. Johnson, and J. Vlissides. *Design Patterns: Elements of Reusable Object-Oriented Software*. Reading, MA: Addison-Wesley, 1995.

[IONA95] IONA Technologies, Ltd. *Orbix Distributed Object Technology: Programmer's Guide*. (Release 1.3.1). Dublin, Ireland, 1995.

[Löhr+94] K. P. Löhr, I. Piens, and T. Wolff. *Verteilungstransparenz bei der objektorientierten Entwicklung verteilter Applikationen, OBJEKTspektrum*, 5(1994):8–14.

[Luotonen+94] A. Luotonen and K. Altis. "World-Wide Web Proxies." Paper presented at the WWW94 Conference, 1994.

[OMG92] Object Management Group. *The Common Object Request Broker: Architecture and Specification*. (OMG Document No. 91.12.1, Revision 1.1.) Online document, 1992.

Hans Rohnert can be reached at hans.rohnert@zfe.siemens.de.

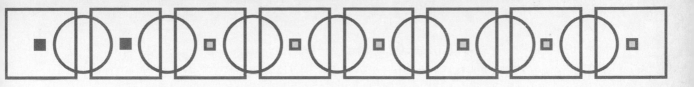

MOODS: Models for Object-Oriented Design of State

8

Alexander Ran

DESIGN DECISION TREES

Behavior of some objects depends significantly on their state and may thus be qualitatively different at different times. Such objects behave as if they had moods. Specification, design, and implementation of objects with moods may be very complex. MOODS is a family of design patterns that may be used to simplify the design and to implement objects with complex, state-dependent representation and behavior (i.e., moody objects).

MOODS is presented as a design decision tree (DDT). Design decisions are fine-grained elements of design. A typical design pattern includes a number of design decisions. Design decisions are made one at a time, based on the requirements of the problem at hand and on earlier decisions. A DDT explicitly exposes the sequence and dependence of the design decisions that constitute a particular pattern or design. A DDT may represent a family of patterns or a family of specific designs.

In the mathematical sense, a DDT is a directed graph. The "tree" is symbolic, conveying a sense of ordering, alternatives, and simplicity. (Also, in a lighter spirit, it helps make the acronym effective against bugs.)

Figure 1 shows the DDT described in this chapter. Each design decision is represented by a box with three parts: the decision, the specific context or requirements that it addresses, and its implications. Links between design decision (i.e., between boxes) are marked with the criteria used to select the appropriate path. Each path on a DDT corresponds to one member of the pattern family represented by the DDT.

A design pattern specifies a solution to a problem that recurs in a certain context; a solution that satisfies the explicit requirements of the problem and those implied by the context.

In different contexts the same problem may require different solutions. Even in the same context a number of solutions to the same problem may exist. If each variation in the problem-context-solution trinity is represented by independent patterns, essential information regarding their commonality and variability is lost and much information that is shared by these patterns is replicated.

Therefore:

Patterns that address similar problems and share important properties or decisions should be grouped into families. Families of patterns should be represented in a form that explicitly exposes their commonality and variability. DDT is one such form.

A DDT incrementally specializes the context, problem, and additional requirements on every path, from the root to the leaves. Each node corresponds to a design decision, the requirements it satisfies, and the consequences it implies. Each design decision is taken in the context of all the earlier design decisions. When alternatives exist, they form alternative branches of the DDT. All shared aspects of the alternative design decisions are represented on their shared path from the root of the DDT. Since a DDT supports incremental specification of the problem, the context, and the corresponding design decisions, it is suitable to represent a family of patterns.

Besides presenting some useful models for object-oriented (OO) design of systems with complex state-dependent behavior, the goal of this chapter is to demonstrate how architectural knowledge may be organized, explored, and gradually refined using DDTs. Note that the MOODS DDT is not complete. Not all of the relevant design decisions are explored with an equal degree of detail, and some are not explored at all. DDTs are rarely complete. Variations in context and requirements are endless, except for very simple problems. However, DDTs are useful at every stage of software development as an effective way to organize existing, incomplete, and evolving design knowledge.

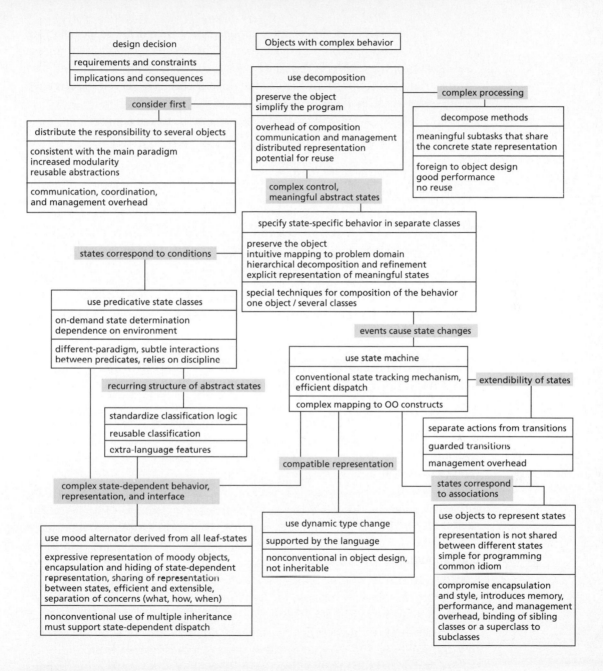

FIGURE 1 Design Decision Tree for Models of Object-Oriented Design of State

Most of the sections in this chapter explain one design decision per section. The names of these sections have two parts. The first part attempts to express the essence of the problem, the context, or the objective, and the second part summarizes the recommended decision. Either part may serve as a reference to the section in the rest of the text.

Here is the list of the design decisions presented in this chapter:

1. To SIMPLIFY COMPLEX BEHAVIOR use DECOMPOSITION.
2. For OBJECT WITH MOODS use STATE CLASSES.
3. When EVENTS CAUSE MOODS use STATE MACHINE.
4. For STATE MACHINE use TRANSITION METHODS.
5. When STATES ARE CONDITIONS use PREDICATIVE CLASSES.
6. When STATES ARE ASSOCIATIONS use STATE OBJECTS.
7. For COMPLEX MOODS use MOOD ALTERNATOR.
8. For OBJECT WITH MANY MOODS use MOOD CLASSIFIER.

DESIGN DECISION 1: TO SIMPLIFY COMPLEX BEHAVIOR, USE DECOMPOSITION

In OO design, we are first concerned with finding objects that model essential elements of the problem in the solution space (i.e., in the computer program). After finding the objects, we have to design their behavior—that is, the way the objects provide their services.

The behavior of some objects is relatively simple and may be expressed by short methods performing the same sequence of actions whenever the methods are called. These objects have few attributes, and these can always be assigned a meaningful value during the objects' lifetime.

Objects that correspond to entities in the problem domain, such as reactive objects, controllers, and managers, often have complex behavior that depends on the object's history and environment. The sequence of actions performed by the methods of these objects may depend on the values of their attributes or even on their environment. The attributes of such objects are often numerous, and they do not always have a meaningful value.

How can one make specification of complex behavior simpler? Use decomposition to reduce complexity. Consider these questions carefully:

- What principles should be used to find the components?
- What composition mechanism will be used to integrate the components?

The main elements of the OO paradigm are objects, classes, and methods. These provide the three main dimensions for decomposition:

- Try first to follow the main decomposition principle of the object paradigm: decompose each object with complex behavior by distributing its responsibilities among several simpler objects.

- When an object with complex behavior may not be naturally decomposed into a group of collaborating objects, when the complexity of its behavior is due to control, or when it is perceived as having a number of abstract states, decompose the class of the objects into a cluster of State Classes.

- When an object with complex behavior may not be naturally decomposed into a group of collaborating objects, and the complexity in its behavior is due not to control but to processing, decompose each complex method separately, following the conventions of structured programming.

DESIGN DECISION 2: FOR OBJECTS WITH MOODS, USE STATE CLASSES

Complexity in the behavior of some objects is due to various conditions that determine how the objects provide (or deny) their services. When the same conditions affect a number of services provided by an object, identifying these conditions with abstract states may help simplify specification of the object's behavior.

Consider a service point manager (SPM) that assigns requests to available servers, using possibly complex logic for scheduling and matching, to control the load, optimize service availability, maintain some degree of fairness, and avoid frustrating clients. It is an integral entity that centralizes control and maintains and monitors the relevant information. However, behavior of the SPM object may be very complex. Some information maintained by the SPM is meaningful only under specific conditions. For example, when the SPM is overloaded, it must notify its clients to prevent repeated requests. This notification should provide clients with information regarding when the service will be available. This kind of processing, and the associated representation, are only needed and meaningful when the SPM is overloaded.

Abstract states are conditions that guarantee more specific behavior of an object. When an object in an abstract state has complicated behavior that depends on additional conditions, substates of the abstract state may be identified that will guarantee more simple behavior of the object in each substate. This process of incremental specialization of conditions and the corresponding behavior will continue until sufficiently simple behavior characterizes each abstract state.[1]

How does one specify the representation and behavior of entities with a complex hierarchy of abstract states?

The OO paradigm does not provide a dedicated construct for representing abstract states. Thus, abstract states must be modeled using the basic building blocks of OO design: objects, methods, and classes.

Abstract states are often important concepts in the problem domain. The OO approach uses classes to model important concepts. Since abstract states are chosen to guarantee more specific behavior of objects, they specialize classes of behavior. Thus hierarchies of abstract states may be mapped onto generalization/specialization hierarchies of classes. Classes that model abstract states may be called state classes.

Therefore:

To simplify the modeling of objects with abstract states, use a cluster of state classes. The base class of the cluster specifies the interface and implements the state-independent representation and behavior. Each derived class represents an abstract state and implements state-specific representation and behavior. Substates are represented by the corresponding subclasses.

Note that clusters of state classes are tightly bound organizations. The principles for design of state classes differ from the general OO strategies used to design independent, reusable classes. In clusters of state classes, inheritance is used to establish a hierarchical scope that controls the applicability of its methods as well as visibility and sharing of the structure and values of its attributes.

A very simple SPM is similar to an assigner that assigns clerks to clients on a "first-come, first-served" basis. An assigner's public interface includes two messages: `ClientComes(Client &)` and `ClerkGetsFree(Clerk &)`. The behavior of the assigner in response to these messages depends on whether there are free clerks or not when a client comes and whether there are clients waiting or not when a clerk gets free. These conditions identify important abstract states of the system.

The class diagram in Figure 2 shows how an assigner's behavior may be specified by a cluster of state classes. Note that the queue of clients is only accessible and visible in the states in which this queue has a meaningful existence—when there are no free clerks. The same is true about the pool of clerks. The subclasses on this diagram are also true subtypes. This example demonstrates how state classes help to decompose and incrementally specify state-dependent representation and behavior.

[1] Where appropriate, I will use the word "mood" as a shorter alternative to "abstract state."

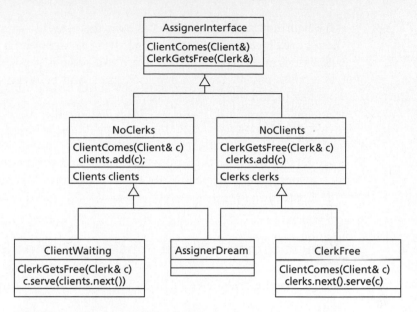

FIGURE 2 Assigner with State Classes

Modeling abstract states as classes achieves several important objectives:

- State Classes offers a powerful approach for decomposing complex, state-dependent representation and behavior.

- Abstract states that are important concepts of the problem domain are explicitly represented. This improves traceability between different stages of development and views of software.

- Each state class specifies only the behavior that is specific to the corresponding abstract state and is sufficiently easy to write and read.

- Visibility and access of state-specific attributes is properly controlled. Attributes shared in a number of abstract states are defined in their common superclass.

- It is possible to provide a state-specific interface by adding new services to state classes.

How to Keep Track of the Changing Mood of an Object

We have used State Classes to decompose and incrementally specify the complex behaviors of objects with moods. Now we have to make decisions regarding mood management.

How can one determine the current mood of a moody object?

The current mood of an object is a result of its history and, indirectly, the history of objects related to it. The history of an object is partly reflected by the values of its attributes. There are two possibilities:

1. When the current mood of the object can be unambiguously determined from the values of its attributes, this dependence should be explicitly expressed using Predicative State Classes.

2. When the current mood of the object cannot be unambiguously determined from the values of its attributes, the mood must be explicitly represented and specifically tracked by State Machine, possibly using Transition Methods.

How to Support Mood-Sensitive Method Selection

The actual methods selected by a moody object to perform a service request depend on its mood.

How can one program mood-sensitive method selection in common OO languages?

- If changing moods are seen as a result of changing an associated object, use State Objects.

- If the object has complex moods and your programming environment supports multiple inheritance, use Mood Alternator.

- If moods have identical representation and the object type is not intended for further derivation, use dynamic type change.[2]

- If you work with a meta-language system (such as the Common Lisp Object System), you may extend the mechanism of dynamic binding to use the object's mood when selecting the applicable methods.

DESIGN DECISION 3: WHEN EVENTS CAUSE MOODS, USE STATE MACHINE

When the current mood of an object cannot be unambiguously determined from the values of its attributes, the mood must be explicitly represented and specifically tracked.

---

[2] Dynamic type change, in general, has a bad reputation for a number of justified reasons. However, in the case of dynamically changing state classes, these reasons are not applicable.

Use a finite state machine (FSM) to specify the mood-tracking logic when the frequency of events is comparable to the frequency of mood changes and the change of mood depends only on the current mood and event. The FSM paradigm may be described as follows:

- An object is always in one of a finite set of states.
- In each state, one of a finite set of events may occur.
- In response to an event, the object may perform an action.
- In response to an event, the object may change its state.[3]

OO implementation of state machines requires design decisions regarding the mapping of states, events, actions, and transitions onto the constructs of OO programming. There is a wide range of choices for this mapping. Here I only address the choices compatible with our earlier decision to use State Classes for modeling abstract states. OO modeling of events requires a number of design decisions that are not discussed here.

DESIGN DECISION 4: FOR STATE MACHINES, USE TRANSITION METHODS

In response to events, event-dispatch mechanisms invoke event-response methods of reactive objects. It is common to assign response methods responsibility to perform the action of the response and to update the state of the reactive object. It is often an effective solution, since both actions and transitions are state-dependent. However, when action methods of a one-state class explicitly refer to sibling state classes for transitions, they are more difficult to reuse or extend.

How can one preserve the separation between the actions and the transitions? How can one track state transitions without introducing unnecessary binding between the state classes?

A transition is a function of the current state and an event. A guarded transition also depends on a special guarding condition. State classes are good for implementing actions because the actions of an object with moods are mood-dependent. State transitions depend on the mood as well, and it is possible to allocate transition logic to state classes. However, it should be

---

[3] The term "state transition" is often used to mean "response to an event." This practice requires you to talk about transitions to the same state in order to describe responses that only imply an action without changing the abstract state of the object. I find this counterintuitive and use the term "state transition" to mean a real change of the object's abstract state.

separated from the method implementing the actions. Dedicated transition methods can also implement the guarding condition.

Therefore:

To manage the complexity of state dependency and allow for independent refinement of actions and transitions, implement State Machine using dedicated transition methods of state classes.

Transition methods may be invoked independently of action methods (by the same mechanism that invokes action methods on an event), or they may be called by the corresponding action methods. If transition methods are directly called by action methods, separation of actions from transitions would further require dynamic binding of transition methods.

DESIGN DECISION 5: WHEN STATES ARE CONDITIONS, USE PREDICATIVE STATE CLASSES

Explicitly implementing state transitions may be inappropriate in a number of situations. Such is the case when events that cause transitions are significantly more frequent than events that cause state-dependent actions. Also, when objects need to adjust their behavior in correspondence with changes in their environment, explicit modeling of state transitions may not be a good choice. Though change notification may be used to make State Machine applicable in such situations, it may result in a rather inefficient model.

How can the object-to-state relation be maintained without explicitly modeling state transitions?

In many situations, the mood of an object may be determined from the values of its attributes or the state of its environment. Since an object's moods correspond to conditions for different types of behavior, these conditions may be explicitly specified by predicate functions.[4] This would make it possible to determine the abstract state of an object on demand.

Therefore:

Use Predicative State Classes to explicitly specify the conditions for the different moods of an object.

Predicative State Classes is a specialization of State Classes. Each predicative state class must include in its definition a predicate that ensures that the object is in the abstract state represented by the state class.

---

[4]   A predicate function returns a boolean value and does not have side effects.

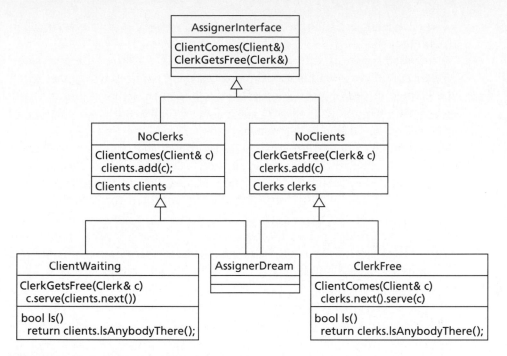

FIGURE 3 Predicative state classes for the assigner

Usually only the concrete state classes (i.e., the leaves of a state hierarchy) must be predicative. This is because an object is always in a concrete state. The superstates exist for factoring common features of their substates. Since leaf states are mutually exclusive, one of the leaf states may be left without a predicate. This state will become the default state of the object. The class diagram of the assigner with predicative state classes is shown in Figure 3.

The Predicative State Classes may serve the Mood Alternator to classify its instance into the appropriate state class. Generic implementation of dynamic state classification is explained in the State Classifier.

DESIGN DECISION 6: WHEN STATES ARE ASSOCIATIONS, USE STATE OBJECTS

After we have applied State Classes, the representation and behavior of the modeled entity is jointly specified by a cluster of classes. It is an unusual situation. Normally, each object is identified with one class that determines the representation and behavior of this object at all times.

How can an object follow the behavior specified by different classes when in different states?

One possible approach is for the object, while it is in the different states, to delegate the responsibility for the actual service to different objects. When the change in the object's state can be conceptualized as a change in its association to some collaborator object, State Objects offers a simple and effective solution [Beck+94, Gamma+95].

The State Objects pattern is based on a collaboration between the server object, which appears to provide all the services to the clients, and the state objects that are instances of the state classes. When the server object receives a service request from a client, it delegates the request to the appropriate state object. In a typical implementation of State Objects, the server object holds a pointer whose current value determines the current state of the object. When state transitions occur, the value of this pointer should be updated. Thus, behavior of the server object, as seen by the clients, depends on its state.

A number of further design decisions affect significantly the applicability and implications of State Objects. These decisions should address the following questions:

- How does one partition the attributes between the server and the state objects?
- How does one manage the attribute values consistency between the server and the different state objects?
- How does one control allocation and deallocation of state objects?
- How does one control visibility of attributes and access rights between the server and the state objects?
- How does one manage state transitions?

The class diagram in Figure 4 is for the assigner with state objects. In the last section of this chapter you will find C++ source code for this example. It is instructive to compare it with the source code for the Mood Alternator, also found in the last section.

In this example, the following design decisions were made:

- To allow access to the attributes shared in several states, they are allocated to the server object.
- To avoid object management overhead, state objects are designed as stateless Singletons [Gamma+95]. Thus the private attributes of all states also must be allocated to the server object.

When using State Objects, one must be aware of the following:

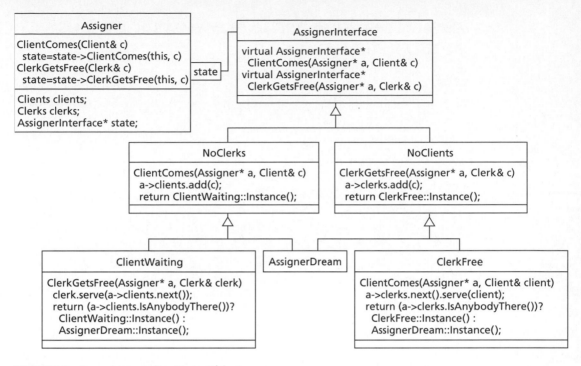

FIGURE 4 An assigner using State Objects

- Since each state is represented by an independent object, sharing an attribute in different states is not simple. Also, having an attribute of the object visible in some states and hidden in others is not possible. This limits the ability of State Classes to implement hierarchies of abstract states.

- State Objects relies on the mechanism for late binding of method calls built into the language. These mechanisms require maintenance of some meta structures in memory. When the program requires a few objects that have a large number of states, the memory overhead of the meta structures becomes significant.

- Creating, destroying, and managing multiple state objects implies additional overhead. Performance may be negatively affected indirectly due to communication between independent objects that represent one entity.

When modeling an object with a complex hierarchy of abstract states, or when having to tune the application for performance or memory usage, you may use an appropriate specialization of Mood Alternator.

DESIGN DECISION 7: FOR COMPLEX MOODS, USE A MOOD ALTERNATOR

After we have applied State Classes to simplify the design of a complex entity, its behavior and representation are specified by a cluster of classes. An integral entity is best modeled as one object.

How can one object, when it is in different states, follow the behavior and have the attributes specified by different state classes?

To follow the behavior and have the attributes specified by different state classes, the object must be an instance of all these classes. This is possible if it is an instance of a class derived from every state class in the cluster. This is the Mood Alternator class. Its instances include the attributes needed in all states; however, the visibility of an attribute is controlled by the state class that defines the attribute. Each method of the Mood Alternator calls the corresponding method of the state class, selected based on the mood of the alternator's instance.

Mood Alternator uses multiple inheritance in an unconventional way. Normally, classes used for multiple derivation provide *complementary* services and attributes, combined by the derived class. Alternator derives from classes that provide *alternative* services, and explicitly selects the right alternative at runtime.

A mood alternator may be designed as a state machine. In order to delegate the service request to the appropriate state class, the alternator object must know its mood. When delegating requests for actions, the Alternator can also implement the logic for tracking state transitions.

The assigner class diagram in Figure 5 is designed using Mood Alternator and Predicative State Classes. The last section of this chapter also contains the C++ source code for this example.

Since Mood Alternator is an alternative to State Objects, they may be compared in terms of their requirements and consequences. To be concrete, let us assume that implementation is done in C++. The following differences may be pointed out:

- Mood Alternator allows hierarchical decomposition of states with proper encapsulation of state-dependent attributes and sharing of common attributes between states.
- Mood Alternator uses less RAM, as it does not need virtual tables and multiple objects.
- State Objects requires memory management of multiple state objects.
- State Objects rely on the virtual function call mechanism. Virtual functions may not be inlined, preventing many possible compiler optimizations. Mood Alternator does not require functions of the state classes to be virtual.

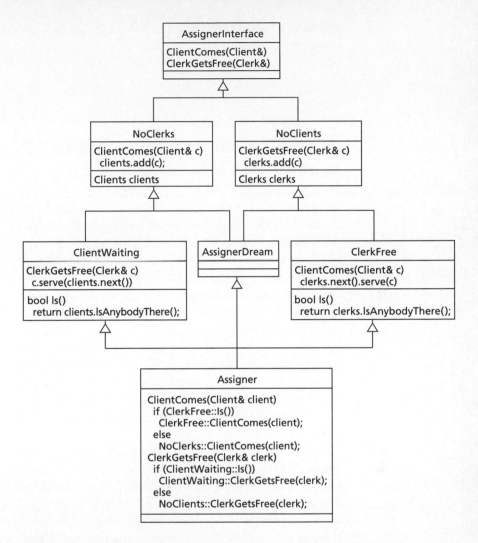

FIGURE 5 Assigner using Mood Alternator and Predicative State Classes

- Mood Alternator uses virtual multiple inheritance. State Objects uses only single inheritance.

In order to delegate a service request to the appropriate state class, an Alternator object must be able to determine the mood of its instance. A common way to track the abstract state is to explicitly program state transitions, as in State Machine. In State Machine, the object-to-state relation is represented by memory and is "eagerly" maintained. It is also possible to represent the object-to-state relation by computation and to use "lazy evaluation" on demand. This can be achieved by using a combination of Predicative State Classes and State Classifier. The code for classification of moods is often trivial and repetitive. For design of an object with many moods, consider using the generic mood classification mechanisms in Mood Classifier.

DESIGN DECISION 8: WHEN THERE ARE MANY MOODS, USE MOOD CLASSIFIER

While it is always possible to handcraft the mood classification logic in the methods of Mood Alternator, a generic classification mechanism offers some advantages with respect to reuse, readability, and ease of creation.

How can one create a generic classification mechanism that can be used with different, complex, and changing hierarchies of predicative state classes?

Generic classification mechanisms may be based on a set of standard meta structures that represent the lattice of predicative state classes, their methods, and state predicates.

Since an object is always in one leaf state, the classification may be performed by sequentially applying the predicates of the leaf states to the object. Use this scheme when predicates are only associated with leaf states; when the superstates do not have associated conditions and only exist to factor common actions, transitions, and attributes of their substates.

Therefore:

When conditions common to substates are explicitly factored as the conditions of their superstates, use the hierarchy of state classes and the corresponding predicates as a decision network. An object is classified as being in some abstract state if it is in all the superstates of this state and it satisfies the predicate of the state. Mood Classifier can traverse this decision network, testing the state of the classified object against the predicates, and eventually delegating the method to the most specific state class of the object.

Let us consider extending the simple Assigner with overload control. When clients are waiting, such an Assigner should consider the current processing load whenever new clients come or clerks get free. If the load does not exceed the preassigned maximum value, new clients are accepted and put on the queue. Otherwise, clients are politely denied the service and advised when to try again.

The class diagram in Figure 6 shows the hierarchy of moods for an assigner with overload control using Mood Classifier. The example demonstrates reuse of earlier defined moods and incremental specialization. Note that the methods of the assigner, and the corresponding meta structures (tables of

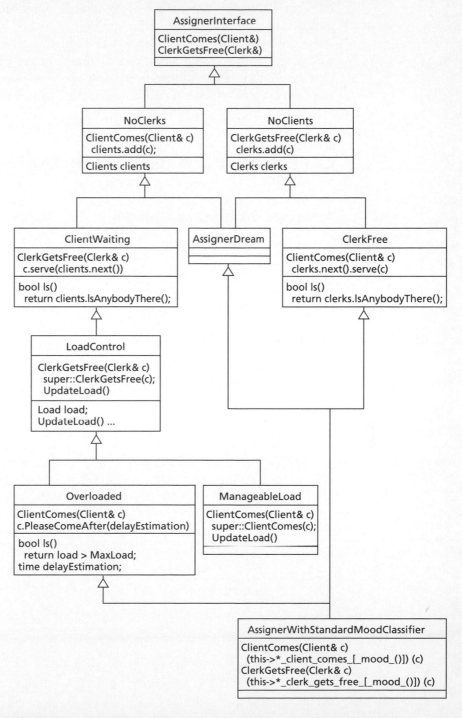

FIGURE 6 The hierarchy of moods for an assigner with overload control

member functions), may be trivially generated. C++ code for this example is included in the next section of this chapter.

Using mood classifiers is halfway between designing a program and designing a language. Further design decisions are required to make the mood classification mechanism easier to use, to make it applicable in a wider category of situations, and to improve its performance and memory requirements.

C++ SOURCE CODE USED IN THE EXAMPLES

Assigner with State Objects

```
class Assigner {
friend class AssignerInterface;
friend class NoClerks;
friend class NoClients;
friend class ClientWaiting;
friend class ClerkFree;
friend class AssignerDream;
public:
  Assigner();
  void ClientComes(Client& c);
  void ClerkGetsFree(Clerk& c);
private:
  Clients clients;
  Clerks clerks;
  AssignerInterface *state;
};


class AssignerInterface {
public:
  virtual AssignerInterface *ClientComes
         (Assigner * a, Client& c) = 0;
  virtual AssignerInterface *ClerkGetsFree
         (Assigner * a, Clerk& c) = 0;
};

class NoClerks : public virtual AssignerInterface {
public:
  virtual AssignerInterface *ClientComes
         (Assigner * a, Client& c);
};
```

```cpp
class NoClients : public virtual AssignerInterface {
public:
  virtual AssignerInterface *ClerkGetsFree
          (Assigner* a, Clerk& c);
};

class ClerkFree : public NoClients {
public:
  virtual AssignerInterface* ClientComes
          (Assigner* a, Client& c);
  static AssignerInterface* Instance();
};

class ClientWaiting : public virtual NoClerks {
public:
  virtual AssignerInterface *ClerkGetsFree
          (Assigner* a, Clerk& c);
  static AssignerInterface* Instance();
};

class AssignerDream : public NoClerks, public NoClients {
public:
  static AssignerInterface* Instance();
};

Assigner::Assigner() : state(AssignerDream::Instance()){
}

void Assigner::ClientComes(Client& c){
  state = state->ClientComes(this, c);
}

void Assigner::ClerkGetsFree(Clerk& c){
  state = state->ClerkGetsFree(this, c);
}

AssignerInterface* NoClients::ClerkGetsFree
          (Assigner* a, Clerk& c) {
  a->clerks.add(c);
  return ClerkFree::Instance();
}

AssignerInterface* NoClerks::ClientComes
          (Assigner* a, Client& c) {
  a->clients.add(c);
  return ClientWaiting::Instance();
}
```

```
AssignerInterface* ClientWaiting::ClerkGetsFree
        (Assigner* a, Clerk& clerk) {
  clerk.serve(a->clients.next());
  return (a->clients.IsAnybodyThere()) ?
ClientWaiting::Instance() :
        AssignerDream::Instance();
}

AssignerInterface* ClerkFree::ClientComes
        (Assigner* a, Client& client) {
  a->clerks.next().serve(client);
  return (a->clerks.IsAnybodyThere()) ?
        ClerkFree::Instance() :
        AssignerDream::Instance();
}

AssignerInterface * ClientWaiting::Instance() {
  static ClientWaiting instance;
  return &instance;
}

AssignerInterface * ClerkFree::Instance() {
  static ClerkFree instance;
  return &instance;
}

AssignerInterface * AssignerDream::Instance() {
  static AssignerDream instance;
  return &instance;
}
```

Assigner as Alternator with Predicative State Classes

```
class AssignerInterface {
public:
  void ClientComes(Client& c);
  void ClerkGetsFree(Clerk& c);
};

class NoClerks : public virtual AssignerInterface {
public:
  void ClientComes(Client& c);
protected:
  Clients clients;
};

class NoClients : public virtual AssignerInterface {
```

```cpp
public:
  void ClerkGetsFree(Clerk& c);
protected:
  Clerks clerks;
};

class ClerkFree : public virtual NoClients {
public:
  void ClientComes(Client& c);
protected:
  bool Is() { return clerks.IsAnybodyThere(); }
};

class ClientWaiting : public virtual NoClerks {
public:
  void ClerkGetsFree(Clerk& c);
protected:
  bool Is() { return clients.IsAnybodyThere(); }
};

class AssignerDream : public virtual NoClerks,
                      public virtual NoClients {
};

class Assigner :  private ClerkFree,
                  private ClientWaiting,
                  private AssignerDream {
public:
  Assigner () {}
  void ClientComes(Client& c);
  void ClerkGetsFree(Clerk& c);
};

void NoClients::ClerkGetsFree(Clerk& c) {
  clerks.add(c);
}

void NoClerks::ClientComes(Client& c) {
  clients.add(c);
}

void ClientWaiting::ClerkGetsFree(Clerk& clerk) {
  clerk.serve(clients.next());
}

void ClerkFree::ClientComes(Client& client) {
  clerks.next().serve(client);
}
```

```
void Assigner::ClientComes(Client& client){
  if (ClerkFree::Is()){
    ClerkFree::ClientComes(client);
  }
  else {
    NoClerks::ClientComes(client);
  }
}

void Assigner::ClerkGetsFree(Clerk& clerk) {
  if (ClientWaiting::Is()) {
    ClientWaiting::ClerkGetsFree(clerk);
  }
  else {
    NoClients::ClerkGetsFree(clerk);
  }
}
```

Assigner as Mood Classifier

```
// classes AssignerInterface, NoClerks, NoClients,
// ClientWaiting, AssignerDream, ClerkFree as in
// the example 2.

class LoadControl : public virtual ClientWaiting {
public:
  void ClerkGetsFree(Clerk& c);
protected:
  static const int MaxLoad;
  LoadControl() : load(0) {}
  void UpdateLoad(Client&) { load++; }
  void UpdateLoad(Clerk&) { load--; }
  int load;
};

const int LoadControl::MaxLoad = 1;

class Overloaded : public virtual LoadControl {
public:
  void ClientComes(Client& c);
protected:
  bool Is() { return load > MaxLoad; }
};
```

```
class ManageableLoad : public virtual LoadControl {
public:
  void ClientComes(Client& c);
};

void LoadControl::ClerkGetsFree(Clerk& clerk) {
  ClientWaiting::ClerkGetsFree(clerk);
  UpdateLoad(clerk);
}

void Overloaded::ClientComes(Client& client) {
  client.ComeLater();
}

void ManageableLoad::ClientComes(Client& client) {
  ClientWaiting::ClientComes(client);
  UpdateLoad(client);
}

// the rest is trivially generated

class Assigner :  private ClerkFree,
                  private Overloaded,
                  private ManageableLoad,
                  private AssignerDream {
public:
  Assigner () {}
  void ClientComes(Client& c) {
    (this->*_client_comes_[_mood_()])(c); }
  void ClerkGetsFree(Clerk& c) {
    (this->*_clerk_gets_free_[_mood_()])(c); }
private:
  int _mood_();
  typedef void (Assigner::*_ClientComes_)(Client&);
  typedef void (Assigner::*_ClerkGetsFree_)(Clerk&);
  static _ClientComes_ _client_comes_[];
  static _ClerkGetsFree_ _clerk_gets_free_[];
};

Assigner::_ClientComes_ Assigner::_client_comes_[] = {
  &ClerkFree::ClientComes,
  &Overloaded::ClientComes,
  &ManageableLoad::ClientComes,
  &AssignerDream::ClientComes
};

Assigner::_ClerkGetsFree_ Assigner::_clerk_gets_free_[] = {
  &ClerkFree::ClerkGetsFree,
  &Overloaded::ClerkGetsFree,
```

```
  &ManageableLoad::ClerkGetsFree,
  &AssignerDream::ClerkGetsFree
};

int Assigner::_mood_() {
  enum {
_ClerkFree=0, _Overloaded, _ManageableLoad, _AssignerDream
  };
  if (ClerkFree::Is()) return _ClerkFree;
  else if (ClientWaiting::Is()) {
    if (Overloaded::Is()) return _Overloaded;
    else return _ManageableLoad;
  }
  else return _AssignerDream;
}
```

REFERENCES

[Beck+94] K. Beck and R. Johnson. "Patterns Generate Architectures." In *Proceedings of ECOOP '94*, New York: Springer-Verlag, 1994.

[Gamma+95] E. Gamma, R. Helm, R. Johnson, and J. Vlissides. *Design Patterns: Elements of Reusable Object-Oriented Software*. Reading, MA: Addison-Wesley, 1995.

Alexander Ran can be reached at Nokia Research Center, P.O. Box 45, 00211 Helsinki, Finland; ran@research.nokia.com.

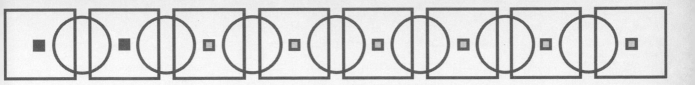

9 Shopper

Jim Doble

INTRODUCTION

The intent of the Shopper pattern is to provide a means for a "consumer" object to obtain an arbitrary collection of items from a set of "provider" objects without introducing coupling between the shopper and the providers.

MOTIVATION

Consider any application that can be subdivided as follows (see Figure 1):

- A set (potentially distributed) of collaborating application objects that implement the basic functionality of the application.

- A set of report/view generator objects, each generating a report or view consisting of a collection of application information items that may be distributed among the application objects.

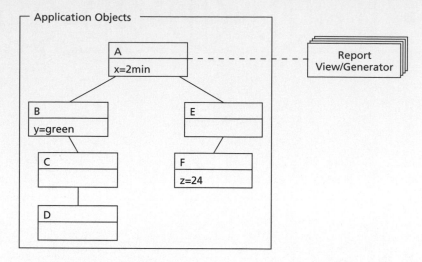

FIGURE 1 Example application configuration for the Shopper pattern

The overall application should be able to support a variety of report/view generators, each of which may have different information collection needs. Some report/view generators may require many information items, while others may require only a few. Some information items may always be present, while others may or may not be present, depending on the state of the application. Information items required by a report/view generator may be mandatory (always required) or optional (required only if present).

The application objects should not be aware of specific report/view generators and their particular information needs. Moreover, the report/view generators should not need to know how to navigate the arrangement of application objects from which the required information items will be obtained.

One approach to solving this problem would be to arrange the application objects in a group and repeatedly apply the Iterator pattern [Gamma+95], iterating across the entire group once for each required information item. However, depending on the arrangement of the application objects and the number of information items required, it may be more efficient (particularly in the case of distributed applications) to pass a composite request through the application objects once, rather than requesting information items one at a time. The composite request can be implemented in the form of a Shopper object, which contains a list of information item requests and a bag that can be used to collect the information items. The shopper obtains the information items from the application objects, as illustrated in Figure 2.

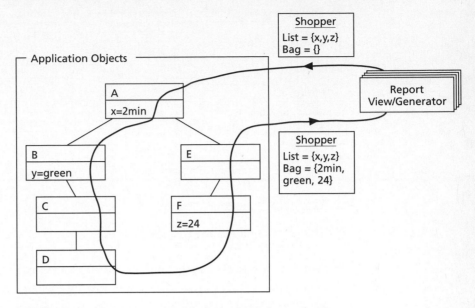

FIGURE 2 How the Shopper object obtains information items

The essence of the Shopper pattern is that an object playing the role of a "consumer" (in the example, a report/view generator) creates a Shopper object with a list of information item requests and an empty bag. The shopper traverses a set of objects playing the role of "provider" (in the example, application objects), collects the requested items in the bag, then returns to the consumer.

STRUCTURE

The general structure of the pattern is illustrated in Figure 3.

Note that different consumers create different lists according to their specific needs. In addition, different providers provide different items based on their role in the application.

APPLICABILITY

The Shopper pattern can be used in situations where

- An object (a consumer) needs information from a set of other objects (providers), and it is desirable to avoid coupling between the consumer

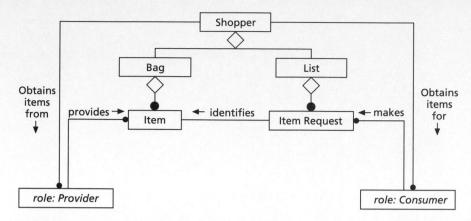

FIGURE 3 Structure of the Shopper pattern

and the providers. The providers should not need to have prior knowledge of the needs of the consumer, and the consumer should not need to have detailed knowledge of the nature, location, or arrangement of the providers.

- Multiple consumers may be supported with different information needs, and it is inefficient to provide a superset of information to all requesters.

- The variation, complexity, and/or distribution of the provider objects makes it inefficient for the consumer to request items one at a time.

PARTICIPANTS

The Shopper pattern involves the following participants:

- **Consumer (role).** Passes a "shopping list" of item requests to the shopper, then requests the shopper to obtain the specified items; processes the items in the "shopping bag" when the shopper returns; may provide the shopper with information necessary to locate/traverse the providers, depending on implementation choices.

- **Shopper.** Takes the shopping list provided by the consumer and "visits" various providers, obtaining requested items and placing them in a shopping bag; may select items based on a selection strategy ("first found," "last found," "all found," "best found," or "cheapest found") and/or may know how to locate/traverse the providers, depending on implementation choices.

- **Provider (role).** Contains (or is associated with) one or more items and makes these items available to shoppers; may assist shoppers with locating/traversing other providers, depending on implementation choices.
- **Item Request.** Identifies a specific item (or type of item) required by a consumer.
- **Item.** Anything owned by (or associated with) a provider, described by an item request, requested by a consumer, and obtained by a shopper.

COLLABORATIONS

The basic collaborations for the Shopper pattern are illustrated in Figure 4. More detailed collaborations are dependent on implementation choices, as discussed in the Implementation section.

Figure 4 The basic collaborations for the Shopper pattern

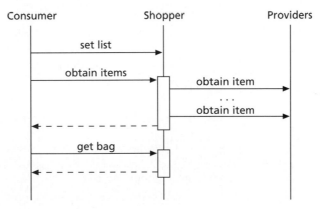

CONSEQUENCES

The Shopper pattern has the following consequences:

1. It decouples the requesting (or "consumer") object from the objects that provide the requested items.
2. A variety of requesting applications can be supported with differing information needs. New requesting applications can be introduced without needing to modify the providing objects.

3. Responsibility for providing items can be moved between provider objects (at compile time or runtime) without the need to modify the requesting application.

4. The arrangement of the provider objects can be modified without the need to modify the requesting application.

5. Handling of optional items can be optimized so that additional processor execution time is incurred only when the optional item is present (see Implementation).

IMPLEMENTATION

The Shopper pattern supports a wide variety of application variations and implementation alternatives. Two key implementation issues for the Shopper pattern are

1. Traversing the set of providers
2. Obtaining/selecting requested items at a provider

These issues will be discussed in the following sections.

Traversing the Set of Providers

The Shopper pattern can be used in a variety of situations, including the following:

1. Providers grouped into an aggregate object; aggregate known by the consumer or stored as a global variable

2. Providers arranged in a simple list; first provider known by the consumer or stored as a global variable

3. Providers arranged in an arbitrary graph topology; one or more providers known by the consumer or stored as a global variable

4. A combination of the above

A useful approach to accommodating these variations is to apply the Strategy pattern [Gamma+95], configuring the Shopper object with a traversing Strategy object that "knows" how to locate and traverse the set of providers. Depending on the application, the traversing Strategy object may have implicit knowledge of some or all of the providers (one or more providers or provider aggregates stored as globals), or it may need to obtain this information from the consumer.

Having located the set of providers, the shopper (or traversing strategy) may employ an iterator to traverse the providers. A provider (or provider aggregate) can be used as a factory to create an iterator object that "knows" how to traverse the providers and provides a simple interface (first, next, current, done) to the shopper. This approach is illustrated in the Sample Code.

In cases where the providers are arranged in a linked topology such as a list or graph, it is useful for each provider to support a generic means for the shopper (or traversing strategy or iterator) to request the list of adjacent providers. Note that care must be taken in order to prevent infinite looping in the case of cyclic graphs.

If the strategy for selecting items at a provider is "first found," it is possible for the shopper to terminate as soon as all of the item requests have been satisfied, without necessarily having visited all of the provider objects. In other cases ("last found," "all found," "best found," etc.) it may be necessary for the shopper to visit all of the providers.

Obtaining and Selecting Requested Items at a Provider

Implementation approaches for obtaining and selecting requested items at a provider should be based on the following principles:

1. The shopper knows the set of items it needs to obtain but should not know what items can be provided by a given provider.[1]

2. The provider knows which set of items it can provide but should not know what items a given shopper needs.

In keeping with these principles, processing of the shopping list at a provider can be implemented by having the shopper perform the following steps:

1. Ask the provider for a list of items it can provide.

2. Compute a list that is the intersection of the shopping list and the list of items the provider can provide.

3. Ask the provider for each of the items in the intersection list.

---

[1] Note that this principle is key to differentiating between the Shopper and Visitor patterns: Visitor is able to perform specific actions based on the class of object being visited, while Shopper performs the same actions for all providers.

Computing the intersection list can be made extremely efficient in cases where both lists can be represented in the form of bitmapped structures. As a consequence of this approach, optional items that were requested but were not present incur no additional processor execution time (they never show up in an intersection list, because they do not occur in any of the providers' lists). In addition, optional/not-present items incur no additional processor execution time during processing of the bag, assuming that the consumer simply processes the contents of the bag without checking for specific requested items.

In cases where items satisfying the same item request may be found at multiple providers, it is useful to apply the Strategy pattern, configuring the shopper with a selecting Strategy object that "knows" how to select appropriate items for a given application. Possible selection strategies include "first found," "last found," "all found," "best found," and "cheapest found."

SAMPLE CODE

The Smalltalk sample code in this section is intended to illustrate one possible implementation of the Shopper pattern. In the interest of brevity, instance creation and accessing methods are not shown. The implementation example is based on the following assumptions:

1. Providers are linked together in a graph structure. Each provider keeps a list of associated providers and supports methods to return a list of associated providers, return a list of provided items, and return specific requested items. In addition, each provider can be used as a factory to create an iterator for the provider graph.

2. The consumer creates the shopper, configuring it with a list of item requests and a factory object (in this case, an arbitrary provider for which the consumer has a reference), which the shopper can use to create an iterator for the provider graph.

3. The shopper uses the supplied factory to create an iterator and uses this iterator to traverse the provider graph. The shopper implements a "first found" selecting strategy: when a requested item is found, its corresponding item request is removed from the shopping list; when the shopping list becomes empty, traversal of the provider graph is terminated, even if all providers have not yet been visited.

The Consumer class can be implemented as follows:

```
Object subclass: #Consumer
    instanceVariableNames: 'provider'
obtainItems1
    | list shopper |
    list := List
            with: HammerItemRequest
            with: CerealItemRequest
            with: SocksItemRequest.
    "create/configure the shopper"
    shopper := Shopper
            list: list
            iteratorFactory: self provider.
    "ask the shopper to obtain the requested items"
    shopper obtainItems.
    "inspect the contents of the bag"
    shopper bag do:
        [:each | Transcript show: each; cr].
```

The Shopper class can be implemented as follows.

```
Object subclass: #Shopper
    instanceVariableNames: 'list bag iteratorFactory'
obtainItems
    | iterator |
    "use the factory to create an iterator for the
provider graph"
    iterator := self iteratorFactory iterator.
    "use the iterator to visit to traverse the
provider graph until all requested items have
been obtained"
    iterator first.
    [iterator isDone] whileFalse:
        [(self visit: iterator current) ifTrue:
        [^self].
        iterator next].
visit: a Provider
    | intersectionList providedList |
    "Calculate the intersection between the
shopper's list and the provider's list"
    providedList:= aProvider providedList.
    intersectionList :=
        self list select:
            [:each |
                providedList includes: each].
    "continued..."
```

```
"obtain all requested items which the provider is able
to provide"
intersectionList do: [:each |
    each obtainFrom: aProvider into: self bag.
    self list remove: each].
"test if all requested items have been obtained"
^self list isEmpty.
```

The GraphIterator subclass can be implemented as follows. Note that the instance creation method (not shown) is used to initialize the "nodes" instance variable with a list containing a reference to the provider that created the graph iterator. Also note that the graph iterator keeps track of nodes (i.e., providers) that have already been visited in order to prevent infinite looping in the event of cyclic graphs.

```
Object subclass: #GraphIterator
instanceVariableNames: 'nodes current visited'
current
    ^current.
first
    self nodes isEmpty ifTrue:
        [self current: nil]
    ifFalse:
        [self current: nodes first.
        self visited: Set new.
        self addNewAssociates].
isDone
    ^self current = nil.
next
    current = nodes last ifTrue:
    [self current: nil]
    ifFalse:
        [self current: (nodes after: current).
        self addNewAssociates].
addNewAssociates
    self current associates do:
        [:each |
            (visited includes: each) ifFalse:
            [(nodes includes: each) ifFalse:
            [nodes add: each]]
```

A Provider object can be implemented as follows:

```
Object subclass: #GroceryStore
    instanceVariableNames: 'associatedStores'
```

<u>associates</u>
  ^self associatedStores.
<u>iterator</u>
  "create an iterator for the provider graph"
  ^GraphIterator with: (List with: self).
<u>providedList</u>
  "note that soda is not present (optional/not-present)"
  ^List with: CerealItemRequest
      with: CookiesItemRequest
      with: HammerItemRequest.

<u>getCereal</u>
    ^#RiceKrispies.
<u>getCookies</u>
    ^#ChocolateChipCookies.
<u>getHammer</u>
    ^#CheapHammer.
<u>getSoda</u>
    ^#CocaCola.

Item requests can be implemented as follows:

Object subclass: **#CerealItemRequest**
<u>obtainFrom: aProvider into: aBag</u>
  aBag add: aProvider getCereal.

RELATED PATTERNS

The Strategy pattern can be used to allow mixing and matching of provider traversal and item selection strategies. Provider traversal can be implemented using the Iterator pattern.

Shopper is somewhat similar to Chain of Responsibility, with the providers acting as "handlers" and the shopping list acting as a composite "request." The composite nature of the request results in a number of significant differences, however:

- Multiple handlers may contribute to the handling of the request.
- Some selection strategies allow traversal to terminate once the request has been handled (i.e., once all requested items have been obtained); others (for example, "best found") require traversal to continue until all handlers have been visited.
- Handlers may have multiple successors; the selection of an initial handler may be arbitrary, and the traversal order for handlers is not necessarily fixed.

ACKNOWLEDGMENTS

The author would like to thank Gerard Meszaros (BNR), Allen Hopley (BNR), and my PLoP workshop group for their useful comments and suggestions, which have resulted in considerable refinements and improvements in this description of the Shopper pattern.

REFERENCE

[Gamma+95] E. Gamma, R. Helm, R. Johnson, and J. Vlissides. *Design Patterns: Elements of Reusable Object-Oriented Software.* Reading, MA: Addison-Wesley, 1995.

Jim Doble can be reached at `jdoble@bnr.ca`.

SPECIAL-PURPOSE PATTERNS

P A R T 3

The preceding part is titled "General-Purpose Patterns," so you might expect a corresponding part on "Special-Purpose Patterns." And here it is: a potpourri of domain-specific patterns and pattern languages. These chapters are a sampling of the diverse domains to which people are applying the pattern form.

Rather than search for a unifying theme, this part gives us an opportunity to explore the dimensions of variability in pattern form and content. Such exploration helps us understand the pattern "space." That's important, because as the world's repertoire of patterns grows, we quickly reach a point where people can't find the patterns they need. Viable indexing schemes presuppose a system of pattern classification, but neither will emerge until we understand how patterns vary and where the boundaries of that variance are.

One dimension of variance is how interdependent a set of patterns is. At one extreme we have a pattern that stands alone; at the other we have an integrated set of patterns forming a pattern language. Here we have representatives from both ends of the spectrum.

At the single-pattern end, Aamod Sane and Roy Campbell present Detachable Inspector (Chapter 10). This pattern generates a separation of design concerns in programming environment tools such as debuggers and inspectors. The pattern follows the Gang of Four (GOF) structure [Gamma+95], putting it unequivocally at one end of the spectrum.

Another single-pattern contribution comes in Chapter 13, from Satish Subramanian and Wei-Tek Tsai. Their Backup pattern focuses on imparting fault tolerance and reliability to object-oriented systems. They combine ideas from several GOF patterns—including Command, State, Proxy, and Chain of Responsibility—to create a mechanism for handling client requests in a fail-safe manner. While most of their pattern appears in classic GOF style, they extend that style with Alexander-like sections describing fault tolerance in general and its attainment through redundancy. So while the pattern belongs at the same end of the spectrum as Detachable Inspector, it is poised for integration into a larger pattern language on fault tolerance.

Gustavo Rossi, Alejandra Garrido, and Sergio Carvalho's contribution (Chapter 11) moves us further along the spectrum. Their chapter on patterns for hypermedia applications contains two GOF-style patterns that describe flexible mechanisms for navigation and for managing the navigation history. The authors intend to develop this work into a pattern language eventually— these are patterns in motion along the spectrum.

Now compare the preceding chapters to Crossing Chasms, a quintessential pattern language (Chapter 14). Authors Kyle Brown and Bruce Whitenack address one of the most commonly recurring design problems in object-oriented system development: how to tie a relational database to an object-oriented system. Notice how their pattern language decomposes the problem into separate but interdependent patterns, each with its own statements of problem, context, forces, and force resolution. The patterns have finer granularity than their single-pattern relatives, and they are much shorter on average.

Despite the differences among these four chapters, they present comparable amounts of information. It's likely that each could be recast in pattern or pattern language form with reasonable success. As you read these chapters, think about how to transform the single patterns into pattern languages and vice versa. Try also to ascertain which end of the spectrum works best for you.

A second dimension of variance is the scope of the pattern or pattern language. In his original work on pattern languages in building architecture [Alexander77], Christopher Alexander partitioned his patterns into three levels: *towns*, *buildings*, and *construction*. This defined a progression from broad to narrow scope. The patterns in these chapters reflect an analogous progression. Detachable Inspector, the Backup pattern, the two hypermedia patterns, and Crossing Chasms are narrow in scope. They address day-to-day software design and implementation problems. Moving to the middle of this dimension we find Ralph Johnson's Transactions and Accounts (Chapter 15).

We could compare this pattern language to Alexander's *building* level: its focus is business accounting systems—a domain considerably broader than any of the earlier patterns. Businesses, like buildings, are complex, multidisciplinary systems. Ralph reduces the problem of modeling businesses to a concise, symbiotic set of patterns. Half the language is devoted to transaction processing, suggesting that the language could well be bigger.

Continuing toward the broad-scope end of the spectrum, we find Organizational Multiplexing, by Steven Berczuk (Chapter 12). This pattern language shows you how to design an architecture for a satellite telemetry system. What makes this language broad is its allowance for *organizational* constraints, not just technical ones. Steven does a good job of weaving together technical and organizational considerations without producing an unwieldy beast of a pattern language. His secret lies in leveraging existing patterns. He builds on Jim Coplien's organizational patterns [Coplien+95], various GOF patterns, some unpublished patterns, and even Crossing Chasms and others from this book. The result is a pattern language of consummate breadth, one comparable in scope to Alexander's town-level patterns.

We've discussed two dimensions: single pattern versus pattern language, and scope. Many other dimensions could prove relevant. We might contrast the form and format of each pattern. The patterns here adopt a variety of popular approaches. Note the (absence of) section headings and the way a pattern is explained. Is the context discussed before the problem or after it? Are the forces part of the context, or are they separate? Do you prefer a prosey style or a more structured one? All of these questions add up to the definitive question: Which form communicates most effectively in which circumstances?

Another possible dimension measures the quantity and quality of drawings. Alexander insists on a drawing in every pattern. In the software field, many patterns have no drawings, though some might illustrate a point with source code. Object-oriented patterns often include diagrams that use notations from standard design methodologies. Most people schooled in object technology can read such diagrams, but their notations were not designed with patterns in mind. Alexander rarely used standard architectural notation in explaining his patterns. Perhaps there are different and better ways to illustrate pattern concepts, ways that take the unique properties of patterns into account.

Positioning these diverse patterns along different dimensions is a useful thought exercise because it helps you abstract common properties of patterns. The "patterns of patterns" that begin forming in your mind give you a better basis for understanding, applying, and writing new patterns. It's an exercise you couldn't do just a short time ago; it became possible only after a critical mass of patterns had accumulated. It's an ongoing exercise too, as people expand the pattern space by developing new patterns and reworking old ones.

REFERENCES

[Alexander77] C. Alexander, S. Ishikawa, and M. Silverstein, with M. Jacobson, I. Fiksdahl-King, and S. Angel. *A Pattern Language.* New York: Oxford University Press, 1977.

[Coplien+95] J. Coplien, and D. Schmidt, eds. *Pattern Languages of Program Design.* Reading, MA: Addison-Wesley, 1995.

[Gamma+95] E. Gamma, R. Helm, R. Johnson, and J. Vlissides. *Design Patterns: Elements of Reusable Object-Oriented Software.* Reading, MA: Addison-Wesley, 1995.

Detachable Inspector/Removable cout: A Structural Pattern for Designing Transparent Layered Services

10

Aamod Sane and Roy Campbell

ABSTRACT

Facilities for instrumentation or runtime "printf" debugging are commonly implemented by instrumentation or debugging statements interspersed within program code. Such hardwiring makes the programs dependent on assumptions about the implementations of these services (meta facilities) that are used by almost every program module. As a result, program modules become difficult to reuse in contexts where the meta services may be absent or have different implementations. This pattern shows how to organize the meta-level code so that it can be changed with minimal effects on the original program.

Intent Decouple and segregate development and runtime meta facilities such as instrumentation, debuggers, and object marshallers so that they can be changed or removed without affecting the program.

Aliases Out-of-Band, Removable Meta, Invited Visitor

MOTIVATION

Meta-level[1] facilities are useful for various features, including controlling debugging at runtime, instrumentation, persistence, and marshalling. A common example is "printf" debugging, which is typically implemented by interspersed "printf" (or, in C++, `cout <<`) statements throughout the code. Since the desired debugging depends on the inputs and the program control flow, it is necessary to interleave the debugging commands in the program. Such interleaving leads to several problems, however:

- Since the debugging facility is global, changing the formats or names of the printing routines may require global recompilation.

- It becomes difficult to reuse modules with different formats or names for the printing routines.

- Program behavior may become dependent on unstated assumptions about the debugging infrastructure, such as initialization, buffer allocation, buffer flushing, and so on.

- Fine-grained runtime control of the debugging facilities becomes difficult, since it is hard to name the relevant places in the program code that should be affected.

A partial solution to these problems integrates access to the debugging facilities with the class hierarchy.[2] For example, class hierarchies are designed with a common ancestor class, such as `Object`, which has a method `Object::inspect()`. The `inspect()` method prints the object on the standard output. Now, subclasses can refine `inspect()` on a per-class basis for subclass-specific printing. Classes also allow us to name relevant pieces of a program during debugging. For instance, one may use class-specific variables such as a boolean `shouldInspect`, which we can change at runtime to control the printing behavior of the instances of that class (or even those of its children). But this scheme also has drawbacks:

- The method `inspect()` might be inadvertently specialized in arbitrary ways. It requires a tedious and error-prone process to ensure that inspection operations do not have unwanted side effects.

---

[1] Meta-level facilities are facilities used to manipulate the program itself. They are in some sense incidental to the actual computation implemented by the program.

[2] This technique is also used for meta facilities like object marshallers.

- Since the behavior of `Object::inspect()` depends on input-output classes (which are themselves descendants of the class Object), any changes to the input-output classes could affect all the children of class Object. Thus, we introduce inadvertent couplings among classes and dependencies on the behavior of the debugging infrastructure.

- The scheme is intrusive and fragile, because it uses a common Object class and forces all classes to be related to each other as children of Object. It is difficult to reuse children of Object without replicating the services provided by Object, and it may require analysis of the effects of redefining methods like `inspect()`.

Generalizing from this example, we can observe that meta facilities define a global infrastructure that affects all code. Therefore, unless the interaction of program modules with the infrastructure is carefully demarcated, it becomes difficult to reuse the modules. A designer of meta services must resolve the following forces:

- It must be easy to decouple the meta-service implementation from the program classes (or collections of classes).

- It must be possible to specialize the service on a per-class basis.

- A programmer should not be forced to derive one class from another solely for the purpose of inheriting a meta-service specialization.

- It must be possible to use classes that use different meta services in the same program.

- The service must be easy to use.

There are several solutions that resolve these forces, to varying degrees:

- Assume standard, generic[3] meta facilities, such as in Smalltalk or CLOS, that can be used to program other meta services. But this means that the "runtime" infrastructure that supports the general meta service is always required. Although there are tools that can analyze the source code and strip unused runtime support, a programmer may inadvertently create unnecessary dependencies that defeat these tools.

- Rely on programmer discipline to separate the meta and ground[4] code. This is a tedious, error-prone process, and it may make meta services difficult to use.

---

[3] Languages like Smalltalk and CLOS expose most language facilities at the meta level. This meta information can be used to implement many different meta facilities.

[4] The terms *ground* and *meta* originated in philosophy and mathematics. *Ground* refers to an entity being described, and the description itself is a *meta*-level entity.

- Design a meta-ground interface so that the meta facilities can be easily attached to the ground code or detached from it.

With a carefully designed meta-ground interface, most of the forces can be resolved as shown below. The resulting solution is useful in avoiding unnecessary program dependencies on global facilities such as I/O, debugging, instrumentation, and marshalling.

SOLUTION

To implement detachable meta facilities, make sure that information flows from the ground level to the meta level but not the other way. We can identify program constructions that may reverse the flow and forbid their use:

1. Ground-level objects do not directly invoke meta-level methods. Thus, we forbid methods like `Object::inspect()`, but meta-level objects like `Inspector` have meta-level methods like `Inspector::inspect()`. Ground objects invoke meta-level methods indirectly, through well-known instances of meta-level classes such as `GlobalInspector`.
2. Ground-level classes may not inherit from meta-level classes.
3. Ground-level objects should not query meta-level objects, and they should not change ground-level behavior based on the return values (ground-level objects can `set()` but not `get()` meta data).

These three restrictions decouple the meta-service implementations from the rest of the program. Figure 1 shows a possible implementation. The other forces are resolved as follows:

1. To specialize meta services, we specialize meta-level objects like GlobalInspector and ensure that classes that desire specialized services will access specialized inspectors when they request it.
2. The association between a class and its desired meta server can be implemented via some name service.[5] Thus, the association is independent of the class hierarchy.
3. Similarly, as long as classes use meta services indirectly, classes using different services or the same service with different names can easily coexist.
4. Classes always access the meta facility through default servers like GlobalInspector. Thus, meta facilities like inspection are invoked with

[5] A simple hash table will do.

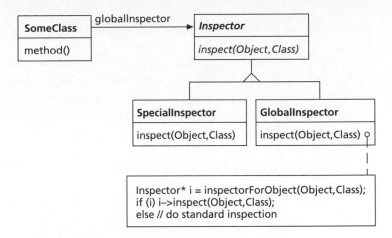

FIGURE 1 Implementing the inspection meta service

A simple, *uniform* syntax. Calls to `GlobalInspector->inspect()` may be inserted in the code. So the meta service is easy to use.

Note that because of the decoupling it is easy to detach the inspector—simply substitute a do-nothing global inspector. Similarly, we can attach new meta services by rebinding the inspector accessed by a class.

APPLICABILITY

Use Detachable Inspector when you have to implement infrastructure services like I/O, instrumentation, debugging, or persistence that will be used by almost every program module. The pattern is applicable when:

- Ground-level behavior is relatively independent of meta-level behavior.
- Ground-level and meta-level operations can be clearly separated.
- Ground-level classes may be used in situations where the meta level may not exist.
- Ground-level objects with different expectations about meta services must coexist.

The pattern is not directly applicable when ground-level behavior depends on meta-level behavior (ground-level objects need to `set` and `get` meta-level data). However, in the Variations section, we discuss how this pattern can mitigate ground-meta coupling even when ground behavior depends on meta behavior.

STATIC AND DYNAMIC STRUCTURE

Figure 2 generalizes the structure from the simple implementation of Figure 1. The `inspectorForObject()` function used in `GlobalInspector::inspect` is generalized to a ground-meta association class, GroundMetaAssoc. (Note that a different implementation of GroundMetaAssoc is used in the Implementation section.)

Classes, Responsibilities, and Collaborators

- GroundClass (SomeClass). GroundClass is a ground-level class in the system.

Responsibilities:

- Includes a `method()` that has code that invokes `metaop()`.
- Registers itself with class GroundMetaAssoc and declares the required service.

Collaborators: MetaService, GroundMetaAssoc.

- GroundMetaAssoc (`inspectorForObject()`). Maintains the association between ground and meta objects.

Responsibilities:

- Exports a registry to be used by ground and meta classes.

FIGURE 2   Static structure of detachable inspector

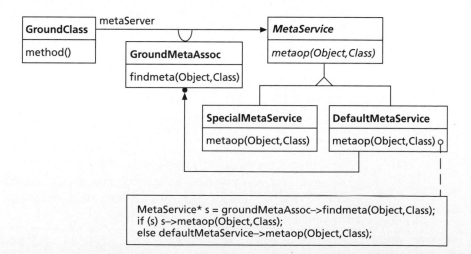

Collaborators: DefaultMetaService, GroundClass.

- MetaService (Inspector). An abstract class that declares the meta-service interface `metaop()`.
- DefaultMetaService (GlobalInspector). The default version of the meta service used when objects do not specify their own specialized meta services.

Responsibilities:

- Implements the default meta functionality.
- Helps ground classes select the appropriate SpecialMetaService by interacting with GroundMetaAssoc.
- Dispatches meta operations to SpecialMetaService, if one exists.

Collaborators: GroundMetaAssoc, SpecialMetaService, GroundClass.

- SpecialMetaService (SpecialInspector) Different meta service implementations that must conform to the MetaService interface.

Responsibilities:

- Implements a specialized `metaop()`.
- May examine GroundClass for meta information.

Collaborators: GroundClass.

Dynamic Collaborations

Figure 3 shows the dynamic interactions that occur when a ground object uses a specialized meta service. If the default service is used, there is no interaction between the default and special meta servers.

CONSEQUENCES

To explain the consequences of using this pattern, we first note that meta levels are transparent to varying degrees:

1. The capabilities provided by the meta level are "not essential." For example, in principle you could do without inspection.
2. The capabilities are essential but transparent. For example, in a distributed object system you usually need RPCs (remote method calls

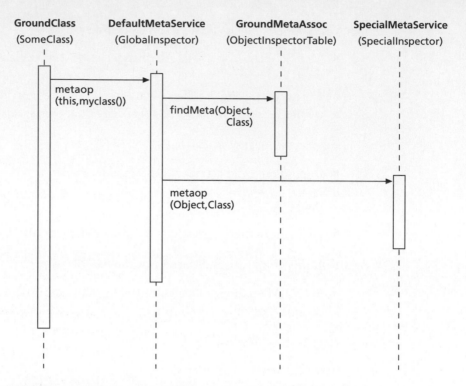

| GroundClass | DefaultMetaService | GroundMetaAssoc | SpecialMetaService |
| (SomeClass) | (GlobalInspector) | (ObjectInspectorTable) | (SpecialInspector) |

FIGURE 3 Dynamic collaborations

via stubs), but if you happen to have all your objects on one machine, you don't need the meta level.

3. The capabilities are not essential, but they are not totally transparent either. For example, consider instrumentation—the ground level has to explicitly manipulate the meta level to turn instruments on and off at the right places.

4. The capabilities are essential and not transparent. For example, consider persistence—the ground level has to explicitly manipulate the meta level.

All four categories converge to some extent, however. As soon as you start putting inspect statements in your code, the inspection level is not totally transparent. Detachable Inspector caters to the first three degrees of transparency. In these cases, the pattern has several benefits:

- *Understandability.* The primary behavior of the program can be understood independent of the behavior of the meta level. The programmer is forced to separate the meta and non-meta levels so that the design intent becomes obvious.

- *Explicit assumptions.* Assumptions about the meta levels (such as initialization of meta objects) are made explicit, since the meta objects are clearly identified.

- *Improved cohesion.* Code for meta facilities become segregated instead of being scattered throughout the program and mixed indelibly with non-meta behavior.

- *Explicit ground-meta interface.* Since meta facilities are invoked with uniform syntax and interact with the program through controlled interfaces, it is easier to detect the use of meta facilities in programs.

- *Compositionality.* Meta facilities become compositional. For example, message objects can be marshalled using a marshaller, which can be inspected by an inspector.

- *Reusability.* Any implementation of a meta service that conforms to the meta interface can be used. Therefore, ground classes using meta services become more modular and reusable.

- *Fine-grained control.* Since the association between a class and its meta server can be modulated through the name service, it is easy to control meta-service invocations at runtime or compile time.

- *Uniform syntax.* The meta services are invoked with a uniform syntax. Therefore, if necessary we can use text-manipulation tools like `awk` or `perl` to mechanically detect, add, remove, or change the use of meta facilities.

The liabilities are as follows:

- *Tedious customization.* Calls such as `object->inspect()` can be customized in arbitrary ways. In contrast, Detachable Inspector requires the programmer to design a custom inspector to achieve the same effect. In the worst case, one may have to design a separate inspector inheritance hierarchy.

- *Care in initialization.* Special object creation methods may be required to instantiate an object with the proper inspector.

- *Necessary meta facilities.* Detachable Inspector presupposes that programs should be understandable without meta facilities. There are situations, such as explicit use of object types (Run Time Type Identification (RTTI) in C++ [Stroustrup+92]) where the facilities for typing should probably not be considered meta facilities. Note, however, that most programming guidelines suggest spare or stylized use of such meta information.

- *Indirection overhead.* Indirect access to meta facilities adds runtime overhead.

Using Detachable Inspector alone cannot guarantee modularity or detachability of subsystems, as there are other sources of dependencies than meta-level dependencies:

- Objects in a subsystem may inherit from objects outside the subsystem.
- Objects in a subsystem use objects from other systems—especially objects from data structure libraries.
- Subsystems interact via "hidden" channels, such as storage management.

A truly detachable subsystem must be designed to minimize and explicitly *document* these assumptions.

IMPLEMENTATION

In an implementation, we must observe the restrictions set by the pattern (e.g., no set(), as mentioned in the Solution section). If the implementation language has modules, they should be used to separate the ground and meta levels so that only the meta-service interface is known to the ground level. Then the ground level cannot inherit from the meta level, and it cannot define methods accessing the meta level. Also, ground classes are forced to use the uniform meta-level interface.
   In addition, we must observe other hygienic practices:

- Ground-level classes should not inherit from meta-level classes. By the same token, it would be confusing for a meta-level class M to inherit from a ground-level class G, because by the usual typing rules, M *is* a G. So does M belong to the meta level or the ground level? Such inheritance need not be prohibited, though, since if M is used entirely in the meta level, the ground level is still independent of the meta level.

- As a matter of design, just as the ground level must be independent of the meta level, so should the meta level be independent of the ground level. The meta-level classes should access data in ground-level classes only through well-known interfaces.

The other principle implementation concern is the implementation of the association between the ground- and meta-level classes:

- *Intrusive.* An intrusive implementation uses a global ancestor, such as Object, to maintain pointers to meta-level classes for each ground-level class or instance. In this case it is easy to determine the meta-level class corresponding to a given ground-level object. But this approach creates dependencies on a global class, so changes to the global class affect the entire system.

- *External.* An external implementation creates an explicit table of associations between ground- and meta-level classes. With an external interface, one must be careful to initialize the meta services before they are used by ground objects. One easy approach is to contact the GroundMetaAssoc class during ground-object creation and request creation or initializion of the required meta service.

One other concern is the management of *meta data*, the information required by the meta level from the ground level. For example, a debugger may request values of variables, information about when to start and stop debugging, and so on. Again, we have either intrusive or external implementations:

- *Intrusive.* An intrusive implementation uses a global ancestor, such as Object, to maintain meta data such as debugging control masks. Values of instance variables and other data are explicitly communicated to the meta level by code interspersed within the program. In this case it is easy to determinc the meta information for a ground-level object. Also, it is easy to initialize the meta information. But the difficulty in this is that it leads to unwanted coupling between the meta and ground levels.

- *External.* An external implementation creates an explicit meta-to-ground access interface that is used by the meta level to access ground-level objects. In C++ this might be implemented using `friend` classes that can access protected or private instance variables. The meta-level control information, like debugging flags, can be maintained in external tables. The meta interface is extended to set the data (using `set()`) in the external table.

SAMPLE CODE AND USAGE

Consider adding inspection to a C++ class hierarchy. For simplicity, we consider an intrusive implementation here (see Figure 4) and do not present any specialized inspectors. Referring to Figure 2, we see that there is no explicit GroundMetaAssoc and no inspector hierarchy. In the intrusive implementation, the ground-meta association is implicitly implemented by keeping an `_inspector` variable in the class Object, and each subclass SomeClass can set its inspector to the desired inspector (i.e., the associated meta-level class). Class Object maintains meta data, here just an _inspectMask, which contains a mask setting an inspection level. It also refers to an inspector, which is normally null, indicating that the global inspector is to be used:

```
class Object {
    friend class Inspector;
public:
    Object() :
        inspectMask(0),
        inspector(0) {};
    virtual ~Object() {};
private:
    int inspectMask;
    Inspector * inspector;
};
```

Class Inspector defines the masks and operations that manipulate the mask. For example, the mask CtorDtor will enable inspection statements only within constructors and destructors. It is the programmer's responsibility to use the proper masks in inspection statements:

```
class Inspector {
public:
    // mask
    enum {
        CtorDtor = 1,
        PublicMethod = 2,
        OtherMethod = 4,
        Detail = 8,
        Error = 16
    };
    void setMask(Object& o, int code);
    int getMask(char * className);
    ostream& Stream(Object& o);
    bool shouldInspect(Object& o, int code);
    static Inspector * instance();
};
```

Figure 4 shows the structure; the "method" shown is really the expanded version of the following macro. The macro defines the standard way of using the inspection facilities:

```
#define Inspect(code) \
    if ( Inspector::instance()-> \
        shouldInspect(*this,Inspector::##code)) \
            Inspector::Stream(*this)
```

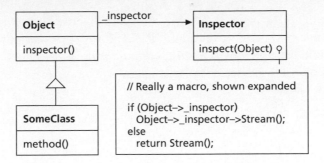

FIGURE 4 Intrusive implementation of Inspector

```
#define InspectorMask(class) \
    Inspector::instance()->setMask(*this, \
        Inspector::instance()->getMask(#class))
```

The method `shouldInspect()` decides if there is a specialized inspector and if the inspect mask setting demands inspection:

```
bool
Inspector::shouldInspect(Object& o, int code)
{
    if (o.inspector)
        return o.inspector->shouldInspect(o,code);
    else
        return (o.inspectMask & code);
}
```

Similary, `Inspector::Stream` will return the specialized inspector, if necessary, or simply return the default stream. Now, given some class SomeClass, the inspector is used as follows:

```
class SomeClass : public Object {
public:
    SomeClass() {
        InspectorMask( SomeClass );
        Inspect( CtorDtor )
            << "SomeClass created" << endl;
    };
    void method() {
        Inspect( PublicMethod )
            << "SomeClass::method()" << endl;
    };
};
```

Notice that we need some runtime support to actually change or set the masks on a per-class basis.

Detaching is easy: return a null inspector that returns false for all `shouldInspect()` calls and does nothing for `setmask()`. This can even be done at runtime. If done at compile time, a clever optimizer would elide the inspection code. Similarly, changing the `_inspector` variable attaches an inspector.

KNOWN USES

While designing a distributed virtual memory system [Sane+90, Sane+95], an attempt was made to separate out the virtual memory subsystem from the rest of the operating system for porting. Two problems surfaced during this effort. First, the inspection facility was provided in the usual way, by defining a method `Object::inspect()`. On occasion, that method had been tailored for specific I/O devices and formats. Further, the use of I/O in inspection meant that constructors for Object, the common ancestor, depended on the I/O classes, which themselves were descendants of Object. Removing these circularities, by observing that I/O and inspection could be treated as meta facilities and that they should not depend on the class hierarchy, led to this pattern. Later, we used the pattern to build a message marshaller, an instrumentation controller, and a debugging inspector. This effort evolved into an inspection subsystem capable of adding runtime debugging, marshalling, and instrumentation[6] to C++ classes with little effort.

Smalltalk provides meta information through methods such as `FooObject inheritsFrom:`. Kent Beck[7] suggests separating meta information into a meta object returned by the method `meta`. This would deter beginners from indiscriminate use of meta information, since having to say `FooObject meta inheritsFrom:` warns the programmer that a meta-level operation is being used (and it is also more inconvenient than a straightforward `FooObject inheritsFrom:`).

Concerns about confusion between the ground level and meta-level have also prompted a meta architecture based on a meta helix [Chiba+, n.d.].

---

[6]   And even error handling, for systems built before C++ compilers supported exceptions.

[7]   K. Beck. Meta object in Smalltalk. Personal communication, August 1995.

RELATED PATTERNS

Decorator

Detachable Inspector is like Decorator [Gamma+95] in that it adds responsibilities and can withdraw them. Decorator, however, alters object behavior by rebinding methods to execute the decorations; Detachable Inspector does not. Instead it supports new "Out-of-band" (or meta) behavior, to which the object is oblivious.

Visitor

Visitor [Gamma+95] bears some similarities to Detachable Inspector. A visitor visits objects, and the objects call the visitor back with operations specific to the object. Thus, different visitors can interpret the callbacks in different ways, and they can thus effectively "add" new methods to those objects without spreading the code among all the visited classes. While Detachable Inspector has a similar goal for segregating code for meta services, the difference is that in this pattern the ground-level code directly invokes the meta-level code, as opposed to having a visitor visit objects. Detachable Inspector inverts the flow: it is as though the objects ask the visitor to visit *them*. Further, the interface an object exports to the meta level often exposes representation and other details.

Singleton

The global inspector is implemented as a singleton [Gamma+95].

COMMENTS

There seems to be an interesting duality between layers and inheritance. For instance, it is commonly held that abstract classes should not have data members but may abstractly define behavior. Detachable Inspector suggests that ground-level objects may set data intended for meta levels but may not have meta-level behavior. Thus, various meta levels are seen as different abstractions of the ground level.

VARIATIONS

These variations arise due to increasing dependencies between the ground and meta levels:

- *Wide and direct interfaces:* Detachable Inspector defines a narrow interface for the interaction between the ground and meta levels. Further, the meta level is accessible indirectly, through the global meta server. These two constraints may lead to some overhead, which is undesirable in applications such as instrumentation. Thus, we allow direct write-only access from the ground level to meta-level objects. For instance, instrumentation facilities avoid indirection for speed. So we allow the ground-level objects to say `instr.on()` and `instr.off()` but not `if (instr.value() == 10) then { // do something ...}`. Now, detaching is a little harder: we have to fabricate null instruments that have the same `set()` interface.

- *Explicit dependencies on meta-information.* If the ground-level behavior depends on meta-level behavior, then the meta level cannot be totally detached. One has to substitute semantically equivalent meta facilities in their place. For example, consider a situation in which persistent objects are implemented using a file system and the program explicitly freezes and thaws those objects. If you want to detach the persistent meta level without affecting the program, you need some "fake" file system. To minimize dependencies, our only recourse is to keep the `get()` interface as small as possible.

Another variation is a subpattern:

- *Avoid inheritance-reference cycles:* As we saw in the Motivation section, if I/O facilities are used in class Object and I/O classes are children of Object, then the behavior of Object becomes dependent on its children. Thus, changes to the I/O classes may affect Object and all of its descendants. We call this an inheritance-reference cycle. Since inheritance-reference cycles introduce subtle and undesirable coupling, we must avoid them unless we are certain that the referred objects will not change significantly.

ACKNOWLEDGMENTS

M. Sefika suffered through discussions of earlier versions of the pattern. Ken Auer suggested runtime stripping tools as another possible solution. Discussions with Ralph Johnson prompted thoughts about "degrees of transparency."

Ellard Roush, Willy Liao, Amitabh Dave, and John Coomes helped with the presentation. We would also like to thank our shepherd, Grady Booch, and the PLoP '95 Writers' Workshop "Group One" for its many improvements.

REFERENCES

[Chiba+, n.d.] S. Chiba, G. Kiczales, and J. Lamping. "Avoiding Metacircularity: The Meta-Helix." Unpublished manuscript.

[Gamma+95] E. Gamma, R. Helm, R. Johnson, and J. Vlissides. *Design Patterns: Elements of Reusable Object-Oriented Software.* Reading, MA: Addison-Wesley, 1995.

[Sane+90] A. Sane, K. MacGregor, and R. Campbell. "Distributed Virtual Memory Consistency Protocols: Design and Performance." In *Second IEEE Workshop on Experimental Distributed Systems*, Huntsville, AL, 1990.

[Sane+95] A. Sane and R. Campbell. *Coordinated Memory: A Distributed Memory Model and Its Implementation on Gigabit Networks.* (Technical Report No. UIUCDCS-R-95-1773.) Urbana-Champaign: University of Illinois, Department of Computer Science, 1995.

[Stroustrup+92] B. Stroustrup and D. Lenkov. "Run-Time Type Identification for C++." *Proceedings of the USENIX C++ Conference*, 313–337, 1992.

Aamod Sane can be reached at sane@cs.uiuc.edu; Roy Campbell can be reached at rhc@uiuc.edu.

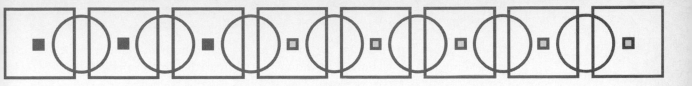

11

Design Patterns for Object-Oriented Hypermedia Applications

Gustavo Rossi, Alejandra Garrido, and Sergio Carvalho

ABSTRACT

This chapter proposes design patterns for object-oriented (OO) applications enhanced with hypermedia functionality. It briefly discusses problems encountered in building a software architecture that seamlessly unites OO applications with a hypermedia interface and a navigational style. Two new design patterns, NavigationStrategy and NavigationObserver, are presented, and ways to use them to design flexible and extensible navigational structures are examined.

INTRODUCTION

Hypermedia applications are characterized by the representation of unstructured information chunked in a collection of nodes related through links. These links are navigated by the user with or without a predefined order, drawing the user's desired path. Many features of hypermedia applications may be included in information systems to increase their utility and usability, leading to a new concept in the hypermedia arena: "hypermedia functionality" [Oinas-Kukkonen94]. These features include the following:

- The representation of unstructured information, allowing the program to relate any piece of information to any other or define annotations.
- The ability to link large numbers of information units to be shared by collaborative groups [Balasubramanian+94].
- The enhancement of graphical user interfaces, providing each user with information that suits his or her needs when navigating and using maps and browsers to view and explore the application's database from different viewpoints and abstraction levels.

Hypermedia functionality is particularly helpful in software engineering environments and decision support systems [Kerola92, IEEE92], where it is necessary to combine formal with informal knowledge (e.g., coupling the formal definition of a software component to its design rationale).

Some commercial applications, such as Microsoft Windows (in its standard Help feature) and Lotus-123 (in its self-teaching guide), let the user explore an information base stored in a stand-alone hypermedia subsystem of the application that retains control. Link servers, like Microcosm [Davis+92], represent a different approach—interapplication linking. We are interested in a richer use of hypermedia, however: as a way of improving access to the information resources in an OO application and combining that information with the application's specific behavior.

A key problem in designing these hybrid applications is how to factor out the hypermedia structure from the application-specific behavior and still allow different views of application objects (represented as hypermedia nodes) and navigation among them without affecting their semantics (in a passive mode) or triggering their methods (in an active mode). For example, in CASE environments we can explore relationships among design documents, but we may or may not be able to affect them (depending on our role in the project).

In this context, we decided to build an OO framework that would allow us to combine navigational features with the functionality of an OO application. While constructing the framework, different design patterns were applied, and others were created; we are now aimed at designing a pattern language in the hypermedia domain.

The hypermedia framework has been used in different application domains, such as learning environments [Leonardi+94], sophisticated CASE tools [Alvarez+95], and a design environment for the Object-Oriented Hypermedia Design Model [Schwabe+95a; Schwabe+95b].

The next section briefly outlines the architecture and use of the hypermedia framework. Then two design patterns are presented that we found while we were trying to apply existing patterns and needed some variations. Finally, some concluding remarks are presented. Patterns referenced in the chapter can be found in Gamma et al. [Gamma+95] unless otherwise indicated.

AN OBJECT-ORIENTED FRAMEWORK FOR HYPERMEDIA

We have already designed and implemented an OO framework that defines an abstract design for applications combining rich navigational and interface styles with usual object behavior and semantics [Rossi+94]. Users of this framework will be able to add hypermedia functionality to an OO application or create a hypermedia application from scratch.

The application's architecture as induced by the framework is divided into three levels: the object level, the hypermedia level, and the interface level. Different implementations may further divide the interface component (using, for example, an extension of the Model-View-Controller framework [Krasner+88]). As mentioned above, the hypermedia framework allows mapping of different views of application-level objects to hypermedia-level nodes. An object's view in this context can be regarded as the "face" the object shows, with a subset of its data and behavior, for a specific user role or profile. Moreover, hypermedia nodes may be built by just "observing" single application objects or as sophisticated views on sets of related objects. Thus, the user will have to define a node class for each different application class (or set of classes) in such a way that its instances will be displayed in hypermedia nodes. Navigation is supported by links that may be either statically defined or computed online during navigation.

Design patterns play a significant role in the framework architecture because they help us improve the design and communicate with a common vocabulary of design artifacts. Many patterns described by Gamma et al. [Gamma+95] were applied, such as Observer, to define the connections among objects and nodes and those among nodes and their interfaces; Composite, in order to aggregate nodes; and Mediator and Adapter, while implementing the framework using Tool [Carvalho92], a strong typed OO language. We are now working on defining a pattern language in the hypermedia domain; such a language will not only deal with aspects related to the association of objects with nodes and links, but also (mainly) with the navigational structure of the application. In this context, new and specific design patterns will arise.

The following sections show an outline of two design patterns that, although they are specializations of existing patterns, have their own motivation and applicability. The first one, NavigationStrategy, addresses the computation of link endpoints while navigating. The second, NavigationObserver, deals with the process of recording visited nodes and links in a navigation history. It also defines a separated hierarchy of viewers for that history.

Though these patterns were developed specifically for the hypermedia domain, we have found that they can be easily generalized for use in other domains (as mentioned in the Applicability section for each pattern).

NAVIGATIONSTRATEGY

Intent   The intent of this pattern is to define a family of algorithms that decouples the activation of hypermedia links from the computation of their endpoints, thus allowing different means of obtaining the endpoints, and their lazy creation.

Motivation   In conventional hypermedia applications (Microsoft's Art Gallery, for example), links are hard-coded from the source node to the target. But when the endpoint of a link depends not only on the target node but also on context information, or if it must be computed dynamically, it is necessary to perform some testing in the source node (or anchor). This situation is more complex in applications such as CASE tools or in decision-support environments that allow navigation across design documents, because the target of the link might be created on demand or just remain unspecified for later definition. Suppose, for example, that we want to navigate from the CRC card of a class to the class browser, showing its current version. It may be necessary to query the version manager to obtain the link's target. Moreover, if there is no implementation for that class, traversing that link may mean creating the target node by opening the browser in editing mode.

Our first approach to solving this problem was to use the Strategy pattern, which models the encapsulation of different algorithms in a separated hierarchy, letting them vary independently from clients that use them. In this way, each link would be configured with the needed algorithm. But as we also wanted to support lazy creation of link endpoints, we extended the pattern with a subhierarchy of abstract factories. With this approach, the strategy algorithm encapsulated in each factory class becomes a Factory Method. The concrete factory classes are associated with each different

Endpoint class (node class) and with another concrete strategy class, which will hold the endpoint computation once it is created. We called this new pattern NavigationStrategy.

Figure 1 shows an example of the NavigationStrategy pattern using Object Modeling Technique notation. The diagram shows the different Concrete-NavigationStrategy classes (subclasses of EndpointSolver) that were defined in the hypermedia framework. The only concrete Endpoint-Factory subclass shown (for simplicity) is related to the creation of endpoints for those nodes stored in a database. The dashed lines mean that the Factory Method (`getEndpoint`) will create an endpoint and a Fixed-Endpoint solver that will contain it once created. The Link class is also subclassified with the class of links that display some information when they are navigated.

Applicability   Use the NavigationStrategy pattern in the hypermedia domain when

- You need different variants of the algorithm that computes the endpoint of a link.
- You need lazy creation of endpoints (e.g., in order to improve memory requirements).

In a general context, the NavigationStrategy pattern may be used when there is a need to establish a relation between two or more objects at different

FIGURE 1 EndpointSolver hierarchy and its relation to the Link class

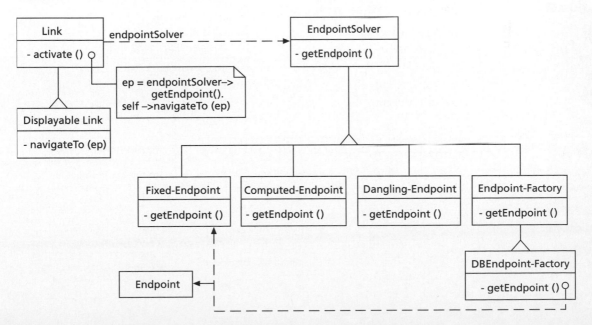

times (i.e., statically or dynamically, where the latter can also lead to the lazy creation of the related object). It may also be useful when some objects are stored in a database and you want to retrieve them in memory only when a related object needs them.

Structure The structure of NavigationStrategy is shown in Figure 2.

Participants

1. Link maintains a reference to a NavigationStrategy and defines a Template Method to perform its activation, which will get the endpoint from its NavigationStrategy and then navigate to it.

2. ConcreteLink implements the `navigateTo` method. It may define different ways of performing navigation (e.g., displaying link attributes).

3. NavigationStrategy declares an interface common to all supported algorithms that compute the link endpoint.

4. ConcreteNavigationStrategy implements the algorithm that obtains the link endpoint. (For example, it may be a fixed or computed endpoint.)

5. AbstractStrategyFactory is the algorithm that obtains the link endpoint; it acts as a Factory Method that creates an endpoint and another instance of ConcreteNavigationStrategy.

6. ConcreteStrategyFactory is the endpoint factory for nodes of certain types and instances of ConcreteNavigationStrategy, which it is related

FIGURE 2 Structure of the NavigationStrategy pattern

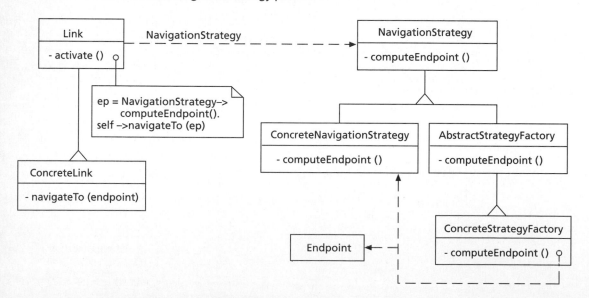

to. This relationship between product and factory is shown in Figure 2 by a dashed line from the Factory Method.

Collaborations
1. Link and NavigationStrategy interact to implement the navigation through the web of nodes. When activated, the link asks NavigationStrategy to get its endpoint (by passing the necessary arguments) and later performs the navigation process with the obtained endpoint.

2. Link's anchors (in source nodes) are the clients that activate links. They are not responsible for ConcreteNavigationStrategy instance creation or selection, however; they are just a means of accessing and activating the link.

3. ConcreteStrategyFactory creates both an endpoint and another ConcreteNavigationStrategy instance for later access.

Consequences
1. NavigationStrategy offers the same benefits as the Strategy pattern, providing an alternative to conditional statements or subclassing, and it also allows the dynamic creation and linking of nodes in an active hypermedia environment.

2. This separation in the navigation process allows us to define different kinds of links (such as those that display themselves while navigating) and different types of endpoints as single or multiple.

3. NavigationStrategyFactory may also improve memory requirements by deferring the retrieval of the target node (for example, when it is stored in a database), creating the associated endpoint in memory only when needed.

4. Finally, the same drawbacks found in Strategy can be found here: an increased number of objects and communication overhead between Link and NavigationStrategy (in cases where the anchor is not needed). Also, the subhierarchy of AbstractStrategyFactory can lead to class proliferation (as discussed under Abstract Factory), but this can be solved by using the Prototype pattern instead of Abstract Factory.

Implementation
The implementation issues described by Gamma et al. for the Strategy pattern [Gamma+95] also apply to this pattern, and other considerations must be stated as well:

1. *Data exchange between Link and Strategy:* The only information that is normally exchanged between a link and its strategy is the link's anchor (from Link) and the endpoint (from NavigationStrategy). This information

is necessary when a link server is used or when the node has been dynamically computed or created.

2. *Endpoint and Node classes:* The Endpoint class may be further subclassified with SingleEndpoint (for one target node) and MultipleEndpoint (for a set of target nodes), so each link will be associated by way of NavigationStrategy, with only one endpoint. Moreover, each endpoint may contain some context and representation information through which the target node will be reached.

   Node classes will be further subclassified by the user for each different application class that he or she decides to observe in the hypermedia, as discussed above. This implies a further subclassification of the AbstractStrategyFactory, associating each different ConcreteStrategyFactory with a different Node class. As discussed earlier, a different approach could be to use prototypes for node creation, following the Prototype pattern.

3. When nodes are extracted from a database, other considerations must be taken into account, such as storage and update of nodes. These are beyond the scope of this chapter, however.

Known Uses   NavigationStrategy is widely used in modern hypermedia environments. For example, in Microcosm [Davis+92], an open hypermedia system that provides linking mechanisms between third-party applications (like Microsoft Word, Assimetrix's Toolbook, etc.), links are always dynamically extracted from a link database that contains information about the anchors' offsets and types.

In some proposed extensions to Netscape, for example [Hill+96], it is possible to define new (private) links by using a mechanism similar to the one presented here. Moreover, the separation of links from documents allows the implementation of "generic" links (i.e., those defined in terms of content rather than location), which can greatly ease the authoring of common links and reader-led navigation.

Some implementations of the Dexter Hypermedia Model [Halasz+94] (as discussed by Grønbæk, for example [Grønbæk94]) propose different alternatives for obtaining link endpoints, similar to those presented here.

NavigationStrategy may be used to improve the design of existing hypermedia applications. For example, in World Wide Web (WWW) browsers, the process of locating the endpoint of a link is often a nonatomic transaction (which may even be unsuccessful) and must be clearly separated from the activation process.

In the CASE environment presented by Alvarez et al. [Alvarez+95], NavigationStrategy allows the designer to link design documents with dynamically computed animations of those documents. The link endpoint may be fixed to another document, trigger the creation of a document, or be created on demand.

Related Patterns   NavigationStrategy is similar to Strategy in that it allows the designer to define a family of algorithms for computing endpoints, making them interchangeable and allowing the Link class to be extended independently of those algorithms. However, it differs from Strategy in that the former includes a subhierarchy of factories in which the strategy algorithm acts as a Factory Method, thus allowing the lazy creation of endpoints and navigation strategies. AbstractStrategyFactory is also similar to the Acceptor pattern [Schmidt95] in that both use lazy connection establishment; however, the former is similar to Abstract Factory, whereas Acceptor is not.

NavigationStrategy also uses Template Method in Link for defining the abstract algorithm for performing navigation.

NAVIGATIONOBSERVER

Intent   The intent of this pattern is to decouple the navigation process from the perceivable record of the process. NavigationObserver simplifies the construction of navigation history viewers by separating the hypermedia components (nodes and links) from the objects that implement both the record of navigation and its appearance.

Motivation   Hypermedia applications should record the state of the navigation in a user-perceptible way. As navigation progresses, this record must be updated automatically. For example, suppose a hypermedia application shows European cities, and we are navigating through them using different indices and links. We may reach the same city through different navigation paths and may want to know the cities we have already visited. This can be achieved by having a map of Europe always visible in some part of the screen. Whenever we visit a city, it is highlighted on this map, so we can instantly know which cities have been visited during the navigation. We could visualize which paths have been followed by displaying not only nodes (cities) but also links (roads). In some commercial hypermedia environments there is a predefined way to show the history of a navigation. For example, Hypercard provides a list of small pictures representing each card that has been accessed.

We could implement this behavior by requiring that objects representing cities (nodes in the hypermedia application) communicate with the object representing the map with the message `highlight(self)`. This solution makes the existence of different perceivable records difficult, however, by adding a strong dependence among nodes and viewers, and it requires modifying the hypermedia components for each new type of viewer that is defined.

The most convenient way to implement this type of history viewers is to use the NavigationObserver pattern. NavigationObserver provides a useful, perceivable record of the nodes and links visited while navigating the hypermedia space. Further, it makes this record independent of the nodes and links, changing its style according to user needs and preferences so that the same design and interface style can be reused in different applications.

Applicability   Use the NavigationObserver pattern in the hypermedia domain when

- You need to maintain the navigation history.
- You want not only nodes but also links or access structures to be recorded in the history.
- You need different viewers for the history.
- You need to support backtracking in the path made while navigating.

In a general context, the NavigationObserver pattern may be applied when you need to register the occurrence of some event in a "log" and you also want to configure the log with one of several different viewers.

Structure   Figure 3 shows the structure of the NavigationObserver pattern.

FIGURE 3 Structure of the NavigationObserver pattern

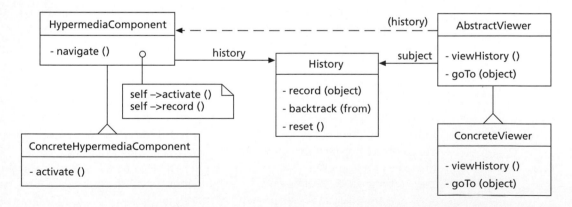

Participants

1. HypermediaComponent uses Template Method in such a way that each time an instance of a subclass is visited, it will notify the History object.

2. ConcreteHypermediaComponent (Node, Link, Index) implements the `activate` method.

3. History records the history of navigation; is configured with the ConcreteHypermediaComponent(s) to be recorded, or with predicates to be tested against; and implements the `backtrack` method.

4. AbstractViewer defines an abstract interface for clients that need to display the history of navigation and perform navigational operations such as `goTo` (a hypermedia component in the history). This is shown with a dashed line in Figure 3, illustrating how the viewer can activate the hypermedia component, getting it from the history.

5. ConcreteViewer (List, Map, Graph) implements the `viewHistory` and `goTo` methods.

Collaborations

1. Each time a hypermedia component is accessed, it sends the message `record` to the history, sending itself as the argument, and the history registers it when corresponding.

2. When the user wants a perceivable view of navigation, the message `viewHistory` is sent to an instance of the corresponding Concrete-Viewer, which in turn makes the current history perceivable.

3. Concrete viewers interact with hypermedia components to perform `goTo` operations.

4. The message `reset` is sent to the history each time the user wishes to "reset" the navigation history.

Consequences

NavigationObserver offers the following benefits:

- It decouples navigation from its history and the history from a particular way of displaying it.

- This decoupling allows the separation of the application-specific style of viewing the history from the application-independent functionality (that of activating nodes and traversing links).

Some overhead can arise when the viewer is only interested in certain types of nodes (e.g., a map of visited cities in a hypermedia application that also includes tourist attractions such as monuments and museums). The viewer will have to interpret the history to filter out the cities, or type of nodes, it is interested in.

Implementation

Several issues related to the implementation of NavigationObserver are discussed below.

1. *History configurations.* The history object may be configured with a predicate to be tested against hypermedia components, if it is necessary to filter some of them. However, if the predicate becomes too complicated, a subclassification of the History class may be more appropriate.

2. *Different algorithms for defining the history.* Though histories may be regarded as simple stacks that record each visit to a hypermedia component, it might sometimes be necessary to provide viewers with a "condensed" history. This may happen either when the same object is visited more than once or when complex backtracking in a multiple windows environment occurs. One possible approach is to define a different method in History that returns the record of navigation, discarding duplicates and cycles. Another approach is to add this responsibility to viewer objects that will analyze the stack when needed.

3. *Mapping viewers to a history.* This issue is similar to the one that affects the Observer pattern [Gamma+95] as viewers observe the history. It could be implemented either by using an associative lookup to maintain the history-to-viewer mapping (which does not incur storage overhead but increases the cost of accessing viewers) or by storing references to viewers in each History object (although this may be too expensive when there are many histories and few observers).

4. *When to update viewers.* Viewers may request information from a history each time they need to be displayed. Also, one may want to update the view each time a new hypermedia component is visited. These two options may be used together, as discussed by Gamma et al. [Gamma+95].

5. *Having two or more histories.* If multiple users can access the hypermedia application concurrently, different History objects are needed to record the different navigation sessions (this is common in some hypermedia environments, like Trellis [Stotts+89]). This possibility complicates the implementation, because the same hypermedia component may be visited in different contexts. In such cases, hypermedia components must be aware of the "current" History object, or we may use a Mediator among hypermedia components and the history.

Known Uses   Different hypermedia products provide different ways of visualizing navigation history. For example, the Microsoft Windows help feature shows the history of a help session as a list of visited topics. Similarly, in some (WWW) viewers, like Netscape, it is also possible to select a location from the navigation history. Though in Netscape only a text-based list is presented, the underlying structure of the application (running as a client of the WWW server) allows the use of NavigationObserver to build new types of viewers, such as those discussed by Das Neves [DasNeves94], Wood et al. [Wood+94], and Chi [Chi94].

Another example, not related to hypermedia applications, arises in OO environments that provide ways to access and manipulate the execution history. In Smalltalk, for example, different types of debuggers (ConcreteViewers) can be implemented by accessing the execution stack (History). Alvarez et al. [Alvarez+95] discuss how to build animations that show the way objects interact with one another; in their example the history "filters" objects and methods according to user choice, and those objects are later animated. Decoupling objects, histories, and viewers helped in achieving a more flexible and extensible architecture for building animations.

Related Patterns   The relationship between viewers and history resembles the Observer pattern. In turn, History may be implemented as a Singleton, or Mediator may be used to decouple hypermedia components from a particular history when dealing with multiple browsing sessions.

CONCLUDING REMARKS

This chapter has analyzed the role of design patterns in the process of building OO hypermedia applications (i.e., applications in which we can navigate through objects' views by following links that mimic the relationships between objects). We have presented two new design patterns, NavigationObserver and NavigationStrategy, that solve recurrent design problems in hypermedia applications. Other, similar patterns for structuring, controlling, or monitoring navigation must be discovered once we gain understanding about the kind of navigation structures found in hypermedia applications. Designing a pattern language for building these kinds of applications will then be a feasible and fruitful approach to simplifying construction tasks in this domain.

ACKNOWLEDGMENTS

We would like to thank John Vlissides for shepherding our work through the approval process and helping us improve this chapter with his careful review. The writers' workshop participants also made many useful comments.

REFERENCES

[Alvarez+95] X. Alvarez, G. Dombiak, A. Garrido, M. Prieto, and G. Rossi. "Objects on Stage. Animating and Visualizing Object-Oriented Architectures in CASE Environments." *Proceedings of the International Workshop on Next Generation CASE Tools, CASE '95.* Paris: University of Paris Press, 1995.

[Balasubramanian+94] V. Balasubramanian and M. Turoff. "Incorporating Hypertext Functionality into Software Systems." Paper presented at the 1994 ACM, ECHT workshop on incorporating hypertext functionality into software systems, Edinburgh, Scotland, September 1994.

[Carvalho92] S. Carvalho. "Tool. The Language." Technical report, PUC-Rio. Rio de Janeiro, Brazil, 1992.

[Chi94] H. Chi (Ed.). "Webspace Visualization." Article available on WWW: http: //www.geom.umn.edu/docs/weboogl/weboogl.html.

[DasNeves94] F. Das Neves. "Pictures from an Exhibition: A Spatial Metaphor for the Concrete Narrative in Hypermedia." Paper presented at the 1994 ECHT workshop on spatial metaphors in information systems, Edinburgh, Scotland, September 1994.

[Davis+92] H. Davis, W. Hall, I. Heath, G. Hill, and R. Wilkins. "Towards an Integrated Environment with Open Hypermedia Systems." *Proceedings of the ACM Conference on Hypertext, ECHT '92.* December 1992.

[Gamma+95] E. Gamma, R. Helm, R. Johnson, and J. Vlissides. *Design Patterns: Elements of Reusable Object-Oriented Software.* Reading, MA: Addison-Wesley, 1995.

[Grønbæk94] K. Grønbæk. "Composites in a Dexter-Based Hypermedia Framework." *ECHT '94 Proceedings.* New York: ACM Press, 1994.

[Halasz+94] F. Halasz and M. Schwartz. "The Dexter Hypertext Reference Model." *Communications of the ACM, 37*(2)(1994).

[Hill+96] G. Hill, W. Hall, D. DeRoure, L. Carr. "Applying Open Hypertext Principles to the WWW." *Proceedings of the International Workshop on Hypermedia Design,* Montpellier, France, June 1995. Berlin: Springer-Verlag, forthcoming.

[IEEE92] *IEEE Software.* "Special Issue on Integrated CASE", March 1992.

[Kerola92] P. Kerola and H. Oinas-Kukkonen. "Hypertext System as an Intermediary Agent in CASE Environments." *The Impact of Computer Supported Technologies on Information Systems Development.* K. E. Kendall, K. Lyytinen and J. I. DeGross (eds.). North Holland, New York, 1992.

[Krasner+88] G. Krasner and S. Pope. "A Cookbook for Using the MVC Interface Paradigm in Smalltalk-80." *Journal of Object-Oriented Programming, 1*(3)(1988).

[Leonardi+94] C. Leonardi, M. Prieto, G. Rossi, and R. Gonzalez Maciel. "Microworlds: A Tool for Learning Object-Oriented Modeling and Problem Solving." *Proceedings of the Educator's Symposium. ACM Conference on Object-Oriented Programming Systems Languages and Applications. OOPSLA'94.*

[Oinas-Kukkonen94] H. Oinas-Kukkonen. "Hypertext Functionality Approach Defined." Paper presented at the September 1994 ACM, ECHT workshop on incorporating hypertext functionality into software systems, Edinburgh, Scotland, September 1994.

[Rossi+94] G. Rossi, A. Garrido, and A. Amandi. "Extending Object-Oriented Applications with Hypermedia Functionality." Paper presented at the September 1994 ACM, ECHT workshop on incorporating hypertext functionality into software systems, Edinburgh, Scotland, September 1994.

[Rumbaugh+91] J. Rumbaugh, M. Blaha, W. Premerlani, F. Eddy, and W. Lorensen. *Object-Oriented Modeling and Design.* Englewood Cliffs, NJ: Prentice-Hall, 1991.

[Schmidt95] D. C. Schmidt. "Acceptor and Connector: Design Patterns for Active and Passive Establishment of Network Connections." Paper presented at the August 1995 ECOOP workshop on pattern languages of object-oriented programs, Aarthus, Denmark, August 1995.

[Schwabe95a] D. Schwabe and G. Rossi. "Building Hypermedia Applications as Navigational Views of an Information Base." *Proceedings of the IEEE Hawaii International Conference on System Science,* 1995.

[Schwabe95b] D. Schwabe and G. Rossi. "The Object-Oriented Hypermedia Design Method." *Communications of the ACM* (August 1995).

[Stotts+89] P. D. Stotts and R. Furuta. "Petri-Net-Based Hypertext: Document Structure with Browsing Semantics." *ACM Transactions on Information Systems,* 7(1)(1989): 3–29.

[Wood+94] A. Wood, N. Drew, R. Beale, and R. Hendley. "HyperSpace: Web Browsing with Visualisation." Available on WWW: http://www.cs.bham.ac.uk/~nsd/research.html.

Both Gustavo Rossi and Alejandra Garrido can be reached at LIFIA: Laboratorio de Investigación y Formación en Informática Avanzada, Dpto. de Informática, Fac. de Cs. Exactas, Universidad Nacional de La Plata, C.C. 11, (1900) La Plata, Buenos Aires, Argentina; garrido@sol.info.unlp.edu.ar, grossi@ada.info.unlp.edu.ar.

Sergio Carvalho can be reached at Departamento de Informática, Pontificia Universidade Catolica, R. M. de S. Vicente, 225, Rio de Janeiro, RJ 22453-900, Brazil; sergio@inf.puc-rio.br.

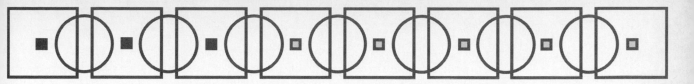

Organizational Multiplexing: Patterns for Processing Satellite Telemetry with Distributed Teams

12

Stephen P. Berczuk

ABSTRACT

Organizational issues play a significant role in many software architectures, though often more as a side effect than by design. This chapter presents a pattern language for developing ground software for satellite telemetry systems. The language demonstrates how to take organization into account in the architecture. In particular, the chapter addresses the following:

- Extending a pattern from the 1994 PLoP conference [Berczuk95] into a pattern language
- Assembling patterns from other pattern languages into a domain-specific pattern language
- Recognizing social context as a context force for a pattern

Since satellite systems are often developed at academic institutions, where similarities between ongoing projects exist only at the architectural level (i.e., code typically cannot be reused), documenting architectural insights such as these in a pattern form can be a very practical way to achieve reuse. Since assembly of telemetry involves (re)creation of objects from a serial stream, these patterns are relevant to designers of any systems that create objects from a serial stream.

INTRODUCTION

Organizational issues have an impact on the development of software systems. For example, it is important to design software architectures so that they fit well with existing social and organizational constraints.

As an example of how these issues can be addressed, this chapter presents a pattern language to guide the development of a ground-based system that will process telemetry data from an earth-orbiting astronomical observatory. Systems of this type involve many diverse and often geographically distributed groups of people; thus such a system is challenging to design from a social as well as a technical perspective. The patterns in this language are applicable to other systems with similar organizational constraints. Since telemetry can be considered a form of persistence (objects are serialized into a stream and transmitted), some of these patterns will also be of interest to developers building systems that use parsing and reconstruction of objects from a serial data stream.

This pattern language uses Coplien's patterns of organization [Coplien95][1] as its context. It also shows how to effect some of these patterns in the context of a ground-based scientific telemetry processing system.

After a description of the relevant organizational and structural elements of a typical project, patterns that address some of the issues raised by these elements will be described.

PROJECT ORGANIZATION

Most of the projects under way at the Center for Space Research at MIT share an organization similar to the one illustrated in Figure 1:

---

[1] To facilitate understanding of this chapter, the Summary at the end of the chapter summarizes referenced patterns from James Coplien [Coplien95], Erich Gamma and his colleagues [Gamma+95], and Kent Beck [Beck94].

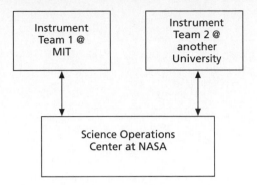

FIGURE 1 Typical project organization

This particular structure is based on that of the X-Ray Timing Explorer project (XTE), currently in progress at the MIT Center for Space Research. It includes the following structural elements:

- A number of *instrument teams,* each with primary responsibility for deployment and analysis of the data from a single scientific instrument that will be on the satellite. Often these teams are at geographically separate locations.

- A central organization (the *Science Operations Center*) that performs a coordination function. Personnel at the operations center may not have the expertise to understand the scientific objectives of the instrument teams; rather, the central organization is focused on the operational aspects of the system (processing so many bytes of telemetry per second, archiving data, and so on).

- A small base of shared knowledge between the instrument teams and the operations center.

- Small work groups, particularly at the instrument team locations. At each team site, many of the subsystems fulfill the context of Solo Virtuoso [Coplien95].

The architecture of the data analysis system takes the general form illustrated in Figure 2.

The operations center depends on the instrument teams for details about telemetry specific to each instrument.

The teams have very different motivations: the instrument teams are focused on getting the best science from "their" instruments, and the operations team is focused on getting the system assembled (with science

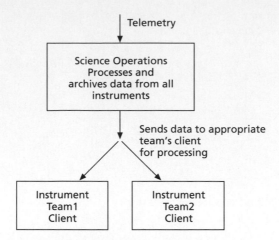

FIGURE 2 Typical system architecture

often being a secondary consideration). The teams have a large degree of autonomy, but they must agree on certain interfaces. As a result, a minimal amount of coupling is best.[2] A major challenge in designing an architecture for such a system is to handle the organizational and political issues that arise in such a way that individual organizations are not overly affected by external forces.

The general organizational forces involved in scientific satellite telemetry processing systems can be summarized as follows:

- Distributed experience
- Small teams, geographically distributed
- Little carryover of personnel from one project to the next

This chapter focuses on the process of classifying and interpreting telemetry packets received from the spacecraft and dispatching the resulting data objects for further processing. Other patterns can be developed to guide the development of other aspects of the system, such as commanding the instrument and data analysis.

While this chapter discusses patterns found in a specific scientific application, the patterns have applications to other domains as well.

---

[2] It can be argued that minimizing coupling is an important consideration in building any system. Because of the degree of decentralization and nonlocality in the projects discussed here, it is especially important.

THE PATTERNS

The architectural goals of the language, and the patterns that accomplish them, are as follows:

- *Facilitate autonomous development:* Loose Interfaces
- *Interpret a data stream:* Parser/Builder
- *Divide responsibilities for interpretation:* Hierarchy of Factories
- *Connect systems:* Handlers

Pattern 1: Loose Interfaces

Context   To help the development of a system with many teams procccding at a reasonable pace, it is important to keep interfaces between systems loose. This is particularly important in situations in which teams of developers are geographically distributed or rapid turnaround times for design and development are important.

Problem   Communication is difficult. If requirements are changing and teams are located in a variety of places, poor communications can stall a project. This can be particularly problematic when an organization does not have an architectural center, as specified in Architect Controls Product [Coplien95].

This is particularly true of many scientific research efforts (such as satellite projects), where teams are small, requirements are changing, and the potential for gridlock is great if dependencies are too high. Although the operations center is the organizational center of the architecture, it does not always have the capability to design a complete system. To avoid development bottlenecks, we need to be able to limit the effect that one team's work will have on another's.

Therefore:

Solution   Limit the number of explicit, static interfaces. Use loose interfaces like Callback, Parser/Builder, and Hierarchy of Factories to achieve this.

Decoupling interfaces in this way will also simplify implementation of Early Programs [Beck94], since it provides a mechanism for building incremental systems. It can also facilitate implementation of Developer Controls Process [Coplien95], by making it easy to define features that can be controlled by a developer or group.

Pattern 2: Parser/Builder

Context Many systems need to read data from a stream and classify elements in the stream as objects. Thus developers need a way to create arbitrary objects based on tokens in the data stream.

Problem Given a data stream, we want to interpret it, classifying the elements within it by class. The data stream contains tags that can be used to identify the raw data; we want to convert the stream into object form so we can process that data.

Consider the problem of reading raw UNIX files and classifying them into types of files based on their "magic number"—as in the tags in the /etc/magic file. You could create the appropriate subclass of File and then invoke its virtual edit() method, bringing up the appropriate editor.

In a telemetry processing system, each telemetry packet has identifying information in its header. The design of a telemetry processing system requires that an object, once created, knows how to process itself (i.e., we will not use a dispatch table or a switch on type, in order to satisfy the Organization Follows Location pattern [Coplien95]). At the lowest level, objects are created using a Factory Method [Gamma+95]. Each class of packets is processed differently; some assemble themselves into larger units, others issue messages. Consider the hierarchy in Figure 3 for a spacecraft requiring two subclasses of Packet: APacket and BPacket.

We want each packet, once created, to process itself using a virtual method, process(). If we pass a data stream into a factory, we want to return a pointer to a packet that has the appropriate type. To summarize the forces:

- There is a need to interpret a raw data stream.
- There is a generic way to process the packets once they are returned from the factory.

FIGURE 3 Sample packet hierarchy

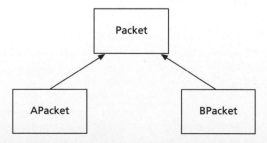

- The raw data contain tags that can be used for classification.

Therefore:

Solution   To resolve these forces, use a parser/builder that reads the identifying information from the header of the packet and creates an object of the appropriate type, removing only one object's worth of data from the stream.
An example of a client interface is as follows:

```
while (!dataStream.empty()) {
    PacketFactory f;
    Packet* p = f.make(dataStream);
    if(p) p->process()
}
```

This is a variant of Abstract Factory [Gamma+95], but the object to be created is defined in the data stream rather than by the client. Factories and parser/builders can be used to partially implement Loose Interfaces by providing a means of separating clients from producers of data (assuming that data producers also define the factories).

Other Uses   In some object-persistence mechanisms, objects are assigned class ids placed in the storage stream. These ids are restored first to allow the system to decide what class of object to make from the restored stream.
Parser/Builder is used in the pattern Query Objects[3] (see Chapter 14) to convert SQL statements to QUERY objects. In Chapter 6, Dirk Riehle discusses similar issues, such as building objects on a desktop using specifications.
The distinction between this pattern and Builder and Factory Method [Gamma+95] is that in this pattern the factory reads from a stream, and the client does not know which type of object will be returned. For text interpretation, Parser/Builder can be the front end to the Interpreter pattern [Gamma+95].

Pattern 3: Hierarchy of Factories

Alias   Composite Factory

Context   Once we decide that using Parser/Builder is the right way to create objects, we need to partition the details of how to construct objects of various classes into the various groups responsible for this construction. In other words, we

---

[3] Query Objects addresses the problem of handling the generation and execution of SQL statements in an object-oriented way when you are trying to use a relational database to store objects.

need to have loose interfaces. We want to complete Form Follows Function [Coplien95] or Organization Follows Location [Coplien95]. On a lower level, we want to implement Developer Controls Process [Coplien95] for a system that creates objects of various types.

Problem   In a distributed work group, it is important to divide responsibilities as cleanly as possible and to reduce coupling. There should be a way to do this in a creational system.

Sometimes the secrets of classifying elements in a data stream are divided among various groups. The reasons for this partitioning can involve company politics or simply the fact that knowledge of telemetry formats is distributed among the groups and there is a strong desire to reduce coupling. We need a way to partition the responsibilities for classifying telemetry packets while maintaining a centralized client interface.

In a telemetry application, various instruments can generate telemetry data, which is then fed into one stream. The instruments are developed by different teams (sometimes at different institutions), and these teams have control over the format of the telemetry data they generate (after taking some standard headers into account).

We want a way to isolate the details of identifying each team's objects while allowing the objects to be identified and created in a single application. The scheme we develop should be layered so that the main factory needs to know only of the existence of a class of objects but not how deep the hierarchy below that class is. Packets created from the hierarchy are processed in a generic way, perhaps using virtual functions.

One way to address this classification problem is to put all the classification/dispatch logic into a single parser/builder (combining the Interpreter pattern with a builder [Gamma+95])—perhaps by using a big switch statement—and rely on the communications methods between the groups to ensure that the details make it into the master code. This solution is error-prone and subject to delays, however. We could also divide the processing into a number of factories and have the client call each one in turn. This violates our requirement of transparency, however, and in any case the client needs to know when a new class of object is added.

It would be useful to discover a way to have the client interface emulate a single factory but hide the details of the construction hierarchy.

To summarize the forces:

- There is a division of responsibilities (Organization Follows Location).
- There is a need for a central interface for parsing data streams and building objects.

- There is a need to add objects to the construction hierarchy in a manner transparent to clients.
- The system has the ability (or requirement) to process entities by virtual functions.
- Each class of object can know about its immediate derived classes.

Therefore:

Solution   Use a hierarchy of factories in which each factory understands the criteria for making a packet of its type and knows about the immediate subtypes. The client invokes the `make` method with the base class factory method. That factory object checks to see that there is indeed an object of class Packet in the stream, based on some attributes. The factory then passes the data stream to the factories of each of its immediate subclasses, which check the appropriate data fields in the manner of the Parser/Builder pattern. Figure 4 illustrates this pattern.

The Singleton pattern [Gamma+95] can be used to access the factories for the derived classes, or the members of the hierarchy can be registered with the master factory at runtime.

Although this pattern violates encapsulation to some extent by requiring a base class to know about its immediate subclasses, it can be made acceptable by agreeing on generic interface classes (say, one per team) and allowing each team free reign to subclass these interface classes. Also, for this application this requirement is not terribly limiting, since the top-level operations team knows about the basic instrument-team interfaces and the number of instrument teams is fixed by contract when the project begins.

An example implementation is as follows:

```
//base class factory method
Packet* PacketFactory::make(Stream* dataStream){
   Packet* pkt=0;
   if(isAPacket(dataStream))
     if(!pkt = APacket::factory()->make(dataStream))
```

FIGURE 4 Hierarchy of factories

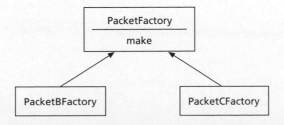

```
        if(!pkt = BPacket::factory()->make(dataStream))
          pkt = new Packet(dataStream);
    return pkt;
}
```

The result of applying this pattern is that each class needs to know only

- the criteria for what constitutes a member of that class in terms of elements in the data stream
- the immediate subclasses

It is possible to use a registration mechanism[4] to inform the base class of what the subclasses are, rather than hard-coding the relationship. It is also possible to implement this pattern using containment rather than inheritance.

Other Uses   This pattern is also useful for isolating the definition of packets for which a single team is responsible (so the information can be encapsulated, making it easier to work on a project with large or widely distributed teams).

Related Patterns   This pattern is similar to the Builder pattern [Gamma+95] in that it has a hierarchy of "factories." It is different from that pattern in that the data stream defines what is made rather than the application's explicitly specifying what objects to construct by sending arguments to the factory.

This pattern helps us realize the patterns Organization Follows Location and Code Ownership [Coplien95].

Pattern 4: Handlers[5]

Context   This pattern provides the decoupling needed to implement Organization Follows Location [Coplien95]. It also allows for the products of a creational system. After we assemble packets from the telemetry data stream, we process them, generating data products. We need a way to direct the processing of these new data products.

---

[4] The Registration pattern is not yet written, but it would specify a mechanism for notifying a base class factory that a derived class factory has been created. The basic idea would be similar to the View/Model connection in a Model/View/Controller mechanism, but it would also address issues of uniqueness (only one instance of each derived class can notify a base class) and guaranteed notification (the construction of any object/factory of the derived classes would automatically generate a registration event).

[5] Adapted from PLoP '94 paper. See [Berczuk95] for details.

Problem   In an environment in which components developed by separate teams with different specific goals must interoperate, it is necessary to partition responsibilities in such a way that dependencies are reduced but interoperability maintained. In particular, well-defined portions of the system should be isolated from the to-be-specified pieces. This may be particularly important if the teams are geographically distributed.

To summarize the forces at work:

- Requirements for the end-to-end system are not completely specified.

- Requirements for one component of a system need to be available before downstream processing is defined.

- Upstream and downstream components will be demonstrated and tested at different times.

- Upstream components should know nothing of downstream processing.

Therefore:

Solution   Use a callback mechanism to define connections between the assembly process and the processing process. Provide a mechanism (registration) for assigning a Handler object to which a completed entity will be forwarded. Figure 5 illustrates this pattern.

One implementation uses a static Handler object for class Unit. Whenever a Unit class object is completed, it hands itself to the Handler object for processing.

The question of when to subclass and when to differentiate objects by an attribute can be confusing. It can only be resolved by examining the specific

FIGURE 5 Callback pattern

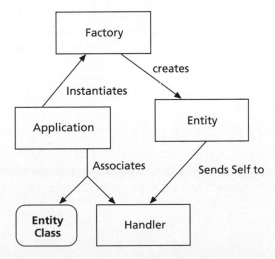

details of entities to be modeled, such as the number of classes and the type of behavior.

This pattern is similar to Observer [Gamma+95], but it differs in that the "observer" is the class of object being created, and the event that triggers the notification is the creation of an object of a given class.

CONCLUSION

Organizational issues play a significant role in determining the direction a software system can take. They affect the context in which a system is developed. It is necessary to design a system to minimize the negative effects of organizational issues. When organizational patterns such as those described by Coplien [Coplien95] exist, there should be ways to design a system that promotes good organizational patterns. This chapter has illustrated ways to reflect organizational issues in the context of other patterns and implement good organizational patterns in a software architecture.

Although there is a common structure to satellite applications, there also tends to be little carryover of personnel between projects; thus many of the lessons learned in one project must be rediscovered in new ones. Since there are different hardware and software platforms from one project to the next and the details of each project vary greatly, *code* reuse is not really feasible. *Design elements* can be reused, however. This application domain, and others that share similar forces, could benefit greatly from documentation of common architectural principles as patterns.

While the patterns described here explicitly address satellite telemetry, the ideas in this chapter are applicable to any system that has a number of distinct teams. Some of the patterns, such as Parser/Builder, are also applicable in other creational systems.

PATTERNS REFERENCED IN TEXT

This section briefly describes the intent of the referenced patterns. These summaries are quite brief, and the original patterns should be consulted to fully understand them.

Patterns from "A Generative Development-Process Pattern Language" [Coplien95]

These summaries are an adaptation of the work of the IM Pei group at PLoP '95.

Architect Controls Product. Describes how a central architect in a controlling role can help build a cohesive product.

Code Ownership. Modules are assigned to developers, who control them and typically make all changes. This simplifies the task of keeping up with the details of the entire system.

Developer Controls Process. Use a developer as a focal point for project communications and process for the development of a given feature.

Form Follows Function. In a project lacking well-defined roles, group closely related activities (those coupled either by implementation, manipulation of artifacts, or domain) together.

Organization Follows Location. When assigning tasks across a geographically distributed work force, assign architectural responsibilities so that decisions can be made locally.

Solo Virtuoso. Design and implementation of a small software product required in a short time should be done by one or two people.

Patterns from *Design Patterns* [Gamma+95]

These summaries are taken from the intent summaries on the inside cover of Gamma et al.'s book [Gamma+95]. They are repeated here for reference.

Abstract Factory. Provide an interface for creating families of related or dependent objects without specifying their concrete classes.

Builder. Separate the construction of a complex object from its representation so that the same construction process can create different representations.

Factory Method. Define an interface for creating an object, but let subclasses decide which classes to instantiate.

Interpreter. Given a language, define a representation for its grammar along with an interpreter that uses the representation to interpret sentences in the language.

Singleton. Make sure that a class has only one instance, and provide a global point of access to it.

Patterns from *Early Development Patterns* [Beck94]

Early Program. Build concrete software early on that shows how the system works and fulfills specified scenarios.

ACKNOWLEDGMENTS

Thanks to Dirk Riehle, Doug Lea, and Lena Davis for reviewing early and final drafts, and thanks to the members of my PLoP '95 working group for making many useful suggestions. The IM Pei home group at PLoP '95 made helpful suggestions on how to reference other patterns, and the Summary is based on their ideas. This work was supported in part by NASA/GSFC contract number NAS5-30612.

REFERENCES

[Beck94] K. Beck. *Early Development Patterns.* Portland, OR: Portland Patterns Repository (URL: `http://c2.com/ppr/early.html`), 1994.

[Berczuk95] S. Berczuk. "Handlers for Separating Assembly and Processing." In J. O. Coplien and D. C. Schmidt (eds.), *Pattern Languages of Program Design.* Reading, MA: Addison-Wesley, 1995, pp. 521–528.

[Coplien95] J. Coplien. "A Generative Development-Process Pattern Language." In J. O. Coplien and D. C. Schmidt (eds.), *Pattern Languages of Program Design.* Reading, MA: Addison-Wesley, 1995, pp. 183–238.

[Gamma+95] E. Gamma, R. Johnson, R. Helm, and J. Vlissides. *Design Patterns: Elements of Reusable Object-Oriented Software.* Reading, MA: Addison-Wesley, 1995.

Stephen P. Berczuk can be reached at `berczuk@optimax.com`.

13

Backup Pattern: Designing Redundancy in Object-Oriented Software

Satish Subramanian and Wei-Tek Tsai

ABSTRACT

Designing redundancies in software has provided developers with a mechanism for enhancing the reliability of software systems. In this chapter a pattern is discussed, Backup, that captures the essence of designing redundancy in software. The Backup pattern can be used when one wants to provide various alternates for a given function and switch among these alternates dynamically during execution. An object-oriented (OO) design of the Backup pattern is discussed, which provides developers with the flexibility to decide the number and order of the alternates for a given function. The pattern is described in a form similar to that used by Gamma and his colleagues in *Design Patterns* [Gamma+95].

INTENT

The pattern's goal is to provide different alternatives for a given function and allow the developer to switch among these alternatives dynamically.

ALIASES

Standby, Recovery Block

PROBLEM AND CONTEXT

Most systems are prone to faults that may lead to failures. They require some kind of mechanism to counter these faults and keep the system operational. The faults can occur due to wrong implementations or unknown operational conditions.

One way of increasing the reliability of a system is to add redundancy. In most hardware systems, when a fault occurs in a component the system switches to a backup mode of operation. Backup components take over the functions of the original (primary) component, avoiding termination or failure of the entire system's operations. Usually, backup components are designed with less sophistication than the primary component. They have minimal but time-tested and reliable features that will keep a system operational until a fix or repair can be performed. For example, an automobile with a sophisticated braking mechanism usually falls back on simple braking mechanisms when undesirable road or environmental conditions affect breaking operations. In software systems, too, such backup mechanisms are required to provide reliable operations and avoid failures during execution.

FORCES

Some of the forces that need to be resolved in developing fault-tolerant software systems are as follows:

Reliability and availability requirements. Most systems need to avoid operations failures—they must be able to remain operational for a prolonged period of time. The software system needs to be continuously available to support user requests.

Nonuniform reliability requirements. Sometimes the reliability requirements of a system are not uniform, which means that some operations have higher reliability requirements than others.

Program modifications. When software is enhanced or modified using different algorithms or data structures, the new version sometimes contains bugs. It would thus be convenient to retain the older working version in the code, rather than replacing it entirely with the new version. Then the program can choose whatever version works at runtime.

Cost and scheduling. Cost and scheduling are always a concern during software development, so reliability requirements are sometimes compromised.

Size of the software. Some software systems cannot afford to have a large size due to performance or system constraints.

FORCE RESOLUTION

In the Backup pattern, there is a trade-off between the forces of reliability and the cost and size of the software. In order to maximize reliability, there might be an increase in the cost of development. The pattern also tries to provide adequate flexibility for systems with nonuniform reliability requirements. The Backup pattern provides a mechanism for dynamically switching between working versions of a module when one version fails to satisfy certain *acceptance tests*. The backup version is designed to be simple and less complicated than the primary version, in order to pass the acceptance tests the primary failed to pass. Backups can consist of earlier working versions of the module that take over when there is a fault in the primary module at runtime.

MOTIVATION

A sort program can be implemented using many different algorithms with different complexities in terms of execution time and implementation effort. For example, a quick-sort algorithm is faster but more complex to implement than an insertion-sort algorithm, as it needs to use a relatively sophisticated recursion mechanism [Cormen+90]. The buffer requirements for the recursive operation of a quick sort is known only at runtime; therefore there could be failures at runtime if the program runs out of stack space. An insertion sort, on the other hand, is simpler and can be implemented using normal loop iteration constructs. Thus, in this case the primary module for the sort can be the quick-sort algorithm, and the backup can be the insertion-sort algorithm. One way of implementing this would be to use nested `if` conditions:

```
sort(list){
 qsort(list);                       // first try quick sort
 if (check(list) == FAIL) {         // check quick sort's result
  isort(list);                      // try insertion sort
  if (check(list) == FAIL){         // check insertion sort's results
     // try some more alternates, if available, or give up
  }
 }
}
```

Even though the above code provides alternates for the sort function and the ability to switch between them, it does not have enough flexibility—all the clients using the sort procedure must use the redundancy mechanism provided. One way to avoid this is to allow different clients to choose the number of alternates, depending on their reliability requirement. One such design is shown in Figure 1.

The sorter gets sort requests from the client and delegates them to the sort handler. SortHandler is an abstract class that provides the interface for sets of objects that can perform sort operations. In Figure 1, three subclasses are shown for sortHandler; these are the concrete implementors of sortHandler's interface. InsertionSort and QuickSort implement the appropriate sorting algorithms, respectively. The ReliableSort object is slightly different from these two, however. It consists of an aggregate of sort algorithms (like

FIGURE 1 Sort program modules with QuickSort as primary and InsertionSort as backup

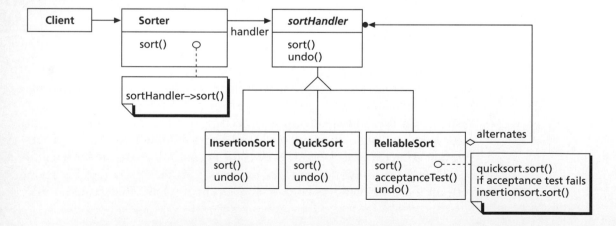

quick-sort and insertion-sort algorithms), which are ordered based on reliability considerations. ReliableSort does the sorting by trying different algorithms, in order, until it gets one that works without faults. For example, if ReliableSort had a quick sort as its primary function and an insertion sort as its backup, then at runtime it would first try the QuickSort (primary) object's `sort()` and then switch to the InsertionSort (backup) object's `sort()` if the quick sort failed to satisfy certain acceptance tests.

In the case of a sorting function, the acceptance test can be designed in different ways. One way could be to check that the list after the sort is in nondecreasing order. Another way could be to see if any data was lost during sorting. The criteria for acceptance can vary a lot depending on the application. The ReliableSort object needs to undo the operations of one alternate if it fails the acceptance test, before trying another. The choice, number, and order of alternates, as well as the selection of acceptance tests, can be decided dynamically in this pattern (discussed below), thus providing the required flexibility.

APPLICABILITY

Some of the situations in which the Backup pattern can be applied are as follows:

- When you want to build a reliable system that tolerates faults. Backup lets you add backups to a software component which will take over when there is a failure or unacceptable operation of the component.

- When you want to add alternatives for a given function and switch among them at runtime.

- When you want to perform remedial actions after faults have been discovered by runtime checks for unforeseen or residual design faults in the code.

STRUCTURE

The notations used in Figure 2 for inheritance, delegation, aggregation, and classes are the same as those found in *Design Patterns* [Gamma+95]. The object diagram in Figure 3 shows one scenario, in which the receiver is using the services of a ReliableHandler object. The ReliableHandler instance has two alternates, aPrimary and aBackup.

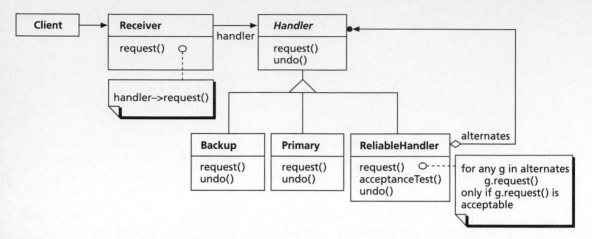

FIGURE 2 The Backup pattern's structure

There can be other scenarios too, one of which is shown in Figure 4. In this case the receiver does not use a reliable handler but instead uses just one primary. Thus the pattern provides the flexibility to create scenarios that do not require redundancy for reliability.

Participants

The Backup pattern consists of a client, a receiver, a handler, and at least three concrete handlers: ReliableHandler, Primary, and Backup. The roles of each of these are described below:

Client

- Sends requests to the receiver

FIGURE 3 Object instance diagram for the Backup pattern

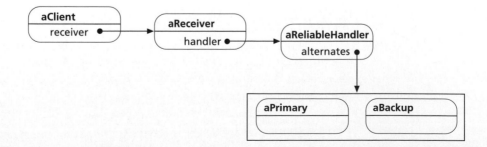

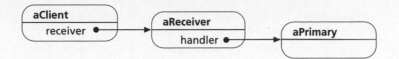

FIGURE 4 Another possible scenario, which does not use redundancy

Receiver

- Receives requests from the client
- Delegates the request to a ReliableHandler object

Handler

- Declares the interface for objects that handle the request for the receiver

Primary

- Implements the operations in the handler's interface
- Can undo the effects of its own execution and restore its original state

Backup

- Carries out the same function as the primary for the handler
- Has less functionality than the primary in order to be less susceptible to failures
- Can undo the effects of its own execution and restore its original state

ReliableHandler

- Stores an ordered set of alternates for handling the request and switches among them dynamically to recover from the failure of any one of them
- Runs the acceptance tests on the functions performed by the alternates to test the acceptability of the results
- Can undo the effects of the execution of its alternates

COLLABORATIONS

The participants collaborate among themselves in the following manner:

- The receiver gets requests from the client and delegates them to a concrete ReliableHandler object. The instances of the ReliableHandler object satisfy the request by employing appropriate multiple implementations, like Primary and Backup.
- The ReliableHandler object carries out the functions of the receiver by first using the services of the Primary object. In case the Primary object

produces unacceptable results, ReliableHandler object switches over to the Backup object for performing the same function. Before doing the switch, the ReliableHandler object asks the Primary object to undo the side effects, if any, of its execution.

The interaction diagram in Figure 5 shows the forwarding of the request from the receiver to a ReliableHandler object. The ReliableHandler instance tries the request with the aPrimary object and then runs an acceptance test on it. In the example shown in the figure, the aPrimary object fails the acceptance test and thus is asked to undo its operations; the request is then forwarded to the aBackup object.

FIGURE 5 Interaction diagram for the Backup pattern

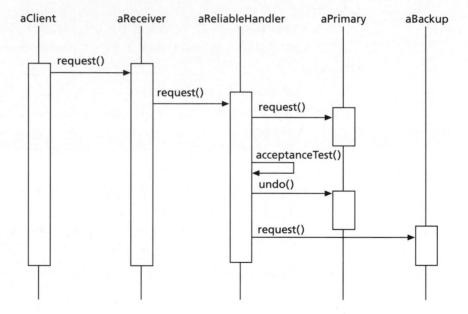

CONSEQUENCES

Some of the advantages and disadvantages of using the Backup pattern are as follows:

1. *Increased availability.* The ability of the ReliableHandler object to switch from the primary mode to the backup mode prevents a failure at one location in the program at runtime from affecting or halting the entire

system's operation. The increase in availability through redundancy increases the reliability of the program.

2. *Error-handling mechanism.* Backup provides a clean mechanism for designing error detection and handling in OO software. Graceful exits and transitions can be designed using the Backup pattern, as the ReliableHandler object performs the error detection and the backup mode provides an alternate solution or remedy.

3. *Coupling.* The ReliableHandler object is tightly coupled to its Receiver class. The ReliableHandler object's method has to be specific to some function that it is handling for the Receiver object. But the reason for not merging them both (thereby making the Primary, Backup, and ReliableHandler objects inherit directly from the receiver) is to allow the receiver to have more than one handler. The receiver might perform different kinds of operations for the client, and for each kind of operation it can have a different handler. But if the receiver and handler are the same, then if one operation's primary fails, the receiver will have to switch from primary to backup for *all* of its operations. However, if the receiver has different handlers for each operation, then it can switch to backup mode only for operations for which the primaries have failed, not for all operations. This means that the receiver can have redundancies in its different functions independent of one another.

4. *Client transparency.* The client requesting the operations is not aware of the switches between the primary and backup objects; thus it perceives a smooth operation for its requests from the receiver.

5. *Flexibility.* As the receiver has a reference to the abstract base class Handler but not directly to ReliableHandler, it can decide to use the redundancy mechanism only when it requires it. All the concrete handlers are type-compatible with the Handler class, so different Receiver instances can have different redundancies by choosing the appropriate concrete handler for their operations. The choice, number, and order of the alternates in the ReliableHandler can also be decided dynamically in this pattern (see the Implementation section).

6. *Execution and development overheads.* There is runtime overhead involved in performing the acceptance tests, switching to backup mode, and performing the same functions again in backup mode. The development overhead occurs because of the creation of different alternates (backup and primary) of the same function. Designers need to develop at least two different implementations of the Receiver function in order

to use the Backup pattern. So use of the Backup pattern can be justified only in systems that have very high reliability and availability requirements.

7. *Size overhead.* Because there are two alternate modes for any given function, the size of the software increases. If a system has size constraints, it may not be possible to include alternate implementations in the code for each function. Also, to support the undo operations, the system state needs to be stored before executing each alternate operation (see Implementation). Thus, runtime storage requirements increase when this pattern is used.

IMPLEMENTATION

Some issues that need to be considered in implementing this pattern are as follows:

Creating the Alternates

To perform the switch between the various alternates for a given function, the ReliableHandler object needs to create and store a list of concrete objects belonging to its sibling classes (the various alternates) so that they can handle the requested function. The creation can be done in different ways.

Receiver Creates the Objects One way to create the various alternates in the ReliableHandler object is to make the Receiver object itself decide the number of alternates it requires, and then add them to the ReliableHandler object. The abstract class Handler then needs to support the operation add() (similar to the Composite pattern [Gamma+95]), which will allow the receiver to add the primary and backup alternates to its handler. This is shown in the following code:

```
class Receiver {
public:
 Receiver() {
  // constructor for receiver.
  createHandler();
 }
private:
 Handler *handler;
 void createHandler();// creates and initializes the handler
};
```

```
void Receiver::createHandler() {
  handler=new ReliableHandler;// choose reliable handling
  handler.add(new Primary);// add primary as first alternate
  handler.add(new Backup);// add the backup also.
  // order of addition determines the order
  // in which alternates are tried
}
```

In this case, the Handler class's interface must have a method add() that will be defined in the concrete handler classes. The simple handlers (primary and backup) will not support additions, whereas the reliable handlers should. This is similar to what the Leaf and Composite objects do in the Composite pattern [Gamma+95].

ReliableHandler Creates the Objects

Another way to create alternates is to make the ReliableHandler object itself explicitly know about the alternates and initialize them when an instance of ReliableHandler is created. Also, in this case the add() method will be private to the ReliableHandler object, and the number of simple handlers it will contain as alternates is also determined by the ReliableHandler object. This means that the receivers using a particular ReliableHandler object will get the same amount of redundancy. The example in the Sample Code and Usage section uses this approach.

Independence of the Alternates

The Backup and Primary classes have to be developed independently in order to reduce the possibility of them both having the same fault. Otherwise, switching from primary to backup mode for a failure-free operation will not work.

Maintaining the State of the Current Alternate

Because the alternates are tried only when their predecessors fail, there is a need to maintain information about which alternates have failed and which should be tried next. This can be done by maintaining the state of the alternate currently being tried. Since the alternates are ordered by the pattern, once the current alternate fails, the next in line can be chosen. The current alternate can be considered the current operational mode (for example, primary or backup), and the switches that occur when it fails are then considered the mode changes. The sample code shows a ReliableSort object with a variable called `currAlternate`, which is included to let the object remember the alternate currently being used for sorting.

Determining the Correct Functionality

In some situations, the primary and backup modes provide the same functions but differ in the degree of complexity or efficiency available [Anderson+81]. The backup system may consist of an older version of the primary system and thus not be affected by faults introduced during functional upgrades to the primary system. Also, the backup system can be deliberately designed to be less efficient in order to pass the acceptance tests. For example, in a real-time system the backup module can be simple and small so that it can satisfy execution timing constraints when the complex primary module appears to violate them. Another example is when the backup system is slow but can handle all possible input cases, whereas the primary system, although fast, cannot handle all cases.

Undoing the Effects of the Primary Module's Execution

Switching from the primary to the backup module may not be straightforward because the execution of the primary module may cause permanent changes in the state of the system (e.g., by modifying values of variables). These changes must be undone before switching over to the backup module. Implementations of `undo()` can make use of the Memento pattern [Gamma+95], along with Backup, to save and restore the original state of the objects affected by the execution of the primary module. This is called *checkpointing* [Tonik75]. But if the operations performed by the primary module are not reversible, then the implementation of the backup module and the ReliableHandler classes will be greatly affected. The applicability of the Backup pattern is questionable in these cases.

Acceptance Tests

Another important part of the implementation of the ReliableHandler class is the implementation of the acceptance tests on the operations or outputs of the primary module. Acceptance tests can range from checking the primary module's output values to monitoring the execution times of its operations. The design of these tests depends on what kinds of errors need to be captured at runtime.

Errors can be either input-related (i.e., errors in data values) or output-related. Output-related errors can be detected by running the acceptance test after the primary module executes. Faults related to execution times cannot, in general, be captured after this time, because the timing constraint might be violated even before the primary module can complete executing. Examples of such faults include infinite loops, indefinite Wait statements, and modules' taking a longer time to execute than is allocated. In these cases, the acceptance checks need to be designed such that the ReliableHandler object can execute concurrently with the primary module, allowing it to monitor the primary module's execution time. Another alternative is to include a timeout mechanism that schedules a timeout event concurrently with the Primary object's execution of the function. So, for such execution time-related errors, some form of concurrency or detached execution is required. Another kind of error that can occur at runtime are internal exceptions, such as divide-by-zero. These faulty events raise internal exceptions that can be considered to indicate acceptance test failures. Also, when the ReliableHandler object exhausts all of its alternates, then the acceptance test is assumed to have failed, and the receiver needs to be notified of the failure.

Acceptance checks can also be implemented using exception handling mechanisms, if the programming language allows it (for example, the `try` and `catch` mechanism in C++ [Stroustrup91]). In this case, failure to pass the acceptance test can be designed to raise an exception, and the exception handler can do the switching to the backup module. Such mechanisms are not a must for implementing the Backup pattern, but they certainly can be used if they are available.

Refining Acceptance Tests

Acceptance tests need not be the same for all situations. In fact, they need to be modified or refined depending on the situation. This can be done through inheritance. The classes deriving from the class ReliableHandler will have different acceptance tests. The receiver can then choose the appropriate ReliableHandler class with the required acceptance test.

Organizing Acceptance Tests

Some acceptance tests have several subparts; in these cases, combining all the acceptance checks into one reliable handler will not work. For example, if the primary module for sorting uses an algorithm located in a remotely located server using a remote procedure call, then the acceptance tests will have several parts to them, such as

- Check to see if the sort results have come from an authentic server.
- Check to see if there is no data loss.
- Check to see if the data is actually sorted.

All these checks cannot go into one reliable handler's acceptance test, because the authentic-server check is not needed for a local sort algorithm. So there needs to be a hierarchy of acceptance tests in this situation, but the Backup pattern does allow this (see Figure 6). The different reliable handlers have different acceptance tests, as shown. The bigger the hierarchy, the stricter the acceptance criteria (and thus the more reliable the results).

FIGURE 6 Hierarchical acceptance tests

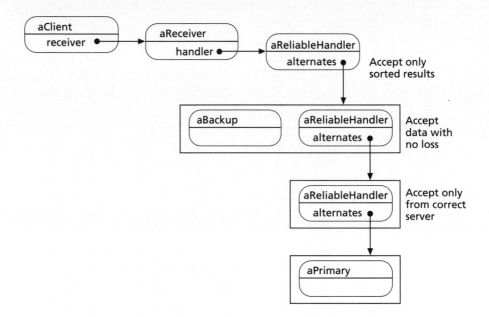

SAMPLE CODE AND USAGE

This is a sample C++ sorting code that declares and defines the participants of the Backup pattern and their behavior. In this example, the acceptance test is run after the primary module terminates. Only two alternates (quick sort and insertion sort) are shown in this example. There can be many alternates for a given primary module. Also, neither the C++ exception handling mechanism nor any form of concurrency is used in this example. First, the Sorter class is shown.

```
class Sorter{
public:
 Sorter();
 int sort(intArray A){
  handler->sort(A); // delegate to sort handler
```

```
  }
private:
 SortHandler *handler;
};
```

The Sorter class has a `sort()` method that is available to the client for sorting a list of integers. Also, it has a private `handler` instance variable that handles the requests for it. The Sorter class has to initialize its `handler` per the reliability requirements. If it wants a reliable handling of the sort, it will initialize its `handler` to an instance of `ReliableSort`; otherwise, it can use `Qsort` or `Isort` instances.

```
handler = new ReliableSort; // for reliable sorting
 or
handler = new Qsort; // for using just quick sort
                     // with no redundancy
```

`ReliableSort` and `Qsort` are subclasses of the abstract class SortHandler, which is declared as

```
class SortHandler {
public:
 virtual int sort(intArray);
 virtual void undo();
};
```

The classes Qsort, Isort, and ReliableSort all inherit from this SortHandler class. The classes Qsort and Isort are similar in their declaration but differ in their definition of the methods `sort()` and `undo()`.

```
class Isort: public SortHandler {
public:
 int sort(intArray A) {
  insertionSort(A); // do insertion sort on the array
 }
 void undo(); // undo side effects of the execution
              // of insertionSort()
};
class Qsort: public SortHandler {
public:
 int sort(intArray A) {
  quickSort(A); // perform quick sort on the array
 }
 void undo(); // undo side effects of the execution
              // of quickSort()
};
```

The class ReliableSort differs greatly in its declaration and definition from the above two sort classes.

```
class ReliableSort: public SortHandler {
public:
 ReliableSort();              // initializes alternates
 void undo();                 // will undo side effects of sort()
 int sort(intArray);          // handles the sort operation
private:
 int acceptanceTest();        // makes the decision to switch
                              // to Backup
 void add(SortHandler*);      // adds alternates
 List<SortHandler*> alternates; // list of alternates
 SortHandler* currAlternate;// the current alternate being used
};
```

The ReliableSort class has a `sort()` method that is called from the Sorter class. The private methods `add()` and `acceptanceTest()` are used to add alternates and switch among them. The ReliableSort class has to initialize its list of alternates first when it is created. (The initialization can also be done by the Sorter class. See the Implementation section for more discussion on this.)

```
ReliableSort::ReliableSort() {
 // create instance member alternates
 // create and add the alternate sort objects in order
 add(new Qsort); // qsort becomes the primary
 add(new Isort); // isort is the backup.
 // initialize the current alternate pointer.
 currAlternate = alternates->first();
}
```

The `add()` method will look like this:

```
ReliableSort::add(SortHandler* s) {
 alternates->append(s);  // append the alternates to
                         // the alternates list
}
```

The ReliableSort object maintains a pointer to the alternate that is currently being used to handle requests. Initially this will point to the first member of the list (as shown in the code for the constructor, above). When sort requests are delegated from the Sorter object to the ReliableSort object, the list of alternates is traversed in order to get the first alternate that executes the `sort()` and also passes the acceptance test. One way to implement the method `sort()` in ReliableSort class is as follows:

```
int ReliableSort::sort(){
 // iterate through the alternate list
 while(acceptanceTest(currAlternate->sort())==ERROR){
   // unacceptable operation
   undo();// restore initial state
   currAlternate=alternate->next(); // try next alternate
```

```
    // ...
  }
}
```

Code for detecting the end of the alternates list has to be added in the above method. The ReliableSort class uses the `undo()` method to undo the operations of its alternate, which can be written as follows:

```
ReliableSort::undo() {
 currAlternate->undo();  // undo the operation of
                         // the current alternate
}
```

As the `undo()` method is a virtual function, it is bound to the correct alternate's `undo()` method.

KNOWN USES

One popular scheme for adding redundancies is the recovery block [Randell75]. The Backup pattern mimics this scheme. Blocks have been used in avionics systems (e.g., in Airbus A310 and A320) and for nuclear reactor safety systems (e.g., in PODS) [Voges88].

RELATED PATTERNS

The patterns State, Proxy, and Chain of Responsibility, presented by Gamma and his colleagues [Gamma+95], are related to the Backup pattern.

The ReliableHandler object in the Backup pattern can be considered a proxy, but with an ordered set of alternate real subjects. Also, the Backup pattern uses the idea of forwarding requests, like Chain of Responsibility; but here the forwarding is handled centrally, in the ReliableHandler object.

Even though both the State and Backup patterns have a dynamic switching mechanism, they are different. The Backup pattern switches between different modes of operation, whereas the State pattern switches between different states. The switches in the State pattern change the behavior of the object, but the switches in the Backup pattern do not. Also, with the Backup pattern a state can have many different modes of operation. An airplane provides an illustrative analogy. An airplane can exist in various different states (taking off, flying, landing); for each of these states, there can be both a normal (primary) and a standby (backup) mode of operation. The same thing applies in the Backup pattern.

Redundancy in a system can be active or passive. In active redundancy, all the alternates are executed in parallel, and output is selected from them using a voting scheme. This active redundancy scheme was presented in the Master-Slave pattern [Buschmann95]. On the other hand, the Backup pattern is based on a passive redundancy scheme, in which the alternates are tried sequentially.

CONCLUSION

The Backup pattern provides a design solution that captures undesirable events in a system and dynamically switches to a backup mode of operation that is time-tested, simple, and reliable. It implements the principle of temporal or passive redundancy in software, as there is a specific *time order* in which the various alternates are tried during execution. It gives developers a way to include error detection and redundancy in OO software. To increase the applicability of this pattern to many different types of failures and faults, the acceptance tests should be designed using sophisticated mechanisms like concurrency and exception handling.

ACKNOWLEDGMENTS

We would like to thank Gerard Meszaros for reviewing this chapter and bringing it to its present form. We thank the various participants of PLoP '95 for providing valuable feedback and suggestions for improvement. Thanks are also due to our colleague Ramakrishna Vishnuvajjala for his comments and discussions on earlier versions of this pattern.

REFERENCES

[Anderson+81] T. Anderson and P. A. Lee. *Fault Tolerance: Principles and Practice.* Englewood Cliffs, NJ: Prentice-Hall, 1981.

[Buschmann95] F. Buschmann. "The Master-Slave Pattern." In J. O. Coplien and D. C. Schmidt (eds.), *Pattern Languages of Program Design.* Reading, MA: Addison-Wesley, 1995, pp. 183–238.

[Cormen+90] T. H. Cormen, C. E. Leiserson, and R. L. Rivest. *Introduction to Algorithms.* New York: McGraw-Hill, 1990.

[Gamma+95] E. Gamma, R. Helm, R. Johnson, and J. Vlissides. *Design Patterns: Elements of Reusable Object-Oriented Software.* Reading, MA: Addison-Wesley, 1995.

[Randell75] B. Randell. "System Structure for Software Fault Tolerance." *IEEE Transactions on Software Engineering, SE, 1*(2), 1975:220–232.

[Stroustrup91] B. Stroustrup. *The C++ Programming Language* (2nd ed.). Reading, MA: Addison-Wesley, 1991.

[Tonik75] A. B. Tonik. "Checkpoint, Restart and Recovery: Selected Annotated Bibliography." *SIGMOD FDT Bulletin, 7*(3–4), 1975:72–76.

[Voges88] V. Voges (ed.). *Software Diversity in Computerized Control Systems.* Berlin: Springer-Verlag, 1988.

Satish Subramanian can be reached at subraman@cs.umn.edu. Wei-Tek Tsai can be reached at *tsai@cs.umn.edu.*

Crossing Chasms: A Pattern Language for Object-RDBMS Integration

14 The Static Patterns

Kyle Brown and Bruce G. Whitenack

ABSTRACT

Crossing Chasms is a growing pattern language created to help design and build object-oriented (OO) applications that use a relational database for persistent storage. Crossing Chasm's patterns are categorized into three groups: static, dynamic, and client-server. The static patterns deal with the definition of the relational schema and the object model. This discussion of Crossing Chasms is limited to these static issues.

INTRODUCTION

Just as patterns can be used to express the rationale behind a given architectural design. Crossing Chasms can be used as a foundation in constructing a relational database for an OO application architecture. It was created to help designers build OO applications that use a relational persistent store. Building such a system requires difficult design decisions involving maintainability, performance, simplicity, and interoperability between the client and server systems. Any database architecture, framework, or tool used in OO applications of this type should support these patterns.

Relational databases are commonly used for applications (even those that are developed in an OO language) for the following reasons:

- They exist in legacy systems that must be used by new systems.
- It is a technology that has been used and tested for a number of years and is consequently well understood.
- The table model is a simple model with a sound mathematical foundation.

The drawbacks in using a relational database with an object system are

- Limited modeling capabilities (object instantiation, behavior, and inheritance are not easy to define when compared to an object database).
- Poor performance for complex applications. Multiple table joins may be required to represent a complex object. This is much less efficient than directly referencing an object.
- There is a semantic mismatch with OO languages. There are a limited set of data types in a relational database, while there are potentially an infinite number of classes.

It is important to keep these strengths and weaknesses in mind as the patterns are described. Crossing Chasms patterns are categorized into three groups: static, dynamic, and client-server. Static patterns describe how to define the structural relationships of the entities (objects and tables) as well as their properties.

STATIC PATTERNS (RELATIONAL SIDE)

The static patterns for the relational side deal with when and how to define a database schema to support an object model. The identity of the objects, their relationships (inheritance, aggregation, semantic associations), and their state must be preserved in the tables of a relational database. The Table Design Time pattern deals with selecting the best time during development to actually design the relational schema. The patterns Representing Objects as Tables, Representing Object Relationships as Tables, Representing Inheritance in a Relational Database, Representing Collections in a Relational Database, and Foreign-Key Reference deal with defining the relationships between objects and defining each object's state.

The pattern Object Identifier (OID) defines how to establish object identity in a relational database.

Table Design Time

Problem   When is the best time to design a relational database during OO development?

Forces   Assume that no legacy database exists prior to development, or if one does exist, it is extremely flexible (i.e., it can be changed according to application needs). When the database design is kept foremost in mind during development, the object model will tend to be data-driven. Thus, the behavior and responsibilities of the objects will be deprived of the thought and energy they deserve. Consequently, the object model will tend to have separate data objects and controller objects. This leads to a design that has heavy-duty controller objects and stupid data objects, rather than a better, more-distributed, less-centralized design [Wirfs-Brock95]. If the database design is completely ignored until the application is completed, the project may suffer. Since often 25 to 50 percent of the code in such applications deals with object-database integration, the design of the database is crucial and should be considered early in development.

Therefore:

Solution   Design the tables based on your object model, after you have implemented the model in an architectural prototype but before the application is in full-stage production.

Discussion   Defining domain object behavior and properties represents a first pass at database design. A stopgap approach to persistence (perhaps using flat ASCII files) is often "good enough" for an architectural prototype. A benefit of this approach is that legacy data can be quickly exported from existing databases to an ASCII file. The prototype can then be easily demonstrated on stand-alone workstations that may not have a relational database and still show "real" data that is familiar to customers.

Related Patterns   Representing Objects as Tables

Representing Object Relationships as Tables

Representing Inheritance in a Relational Database

Representing Collections in a Relational Database

Architectural Prototype (Kent Beck's Smalltalk Best Practices patterns)

Representing Objects as Tables

Problem   How do you map an object structure into a relational database schema?

Forces   Objects do not map neatly into tables. For instance, object classes do not have keys. Tables do not have the same identity property as objects. The data types of tables in a relational database do not match the classes in the object model. Complex objects can reference other complex objects and collections of objects.

Solution   Begin by creating a table for each persistent object in your object model. Determine what type of object each instance variable is likely to contain. For each object that is representable in a database as a base data type (i.e., String, Character, Integer, Float, Date, Time), create a column in the table corresponding to that instance variable, naming it the same as the instance variable. If an instance variable contains a Collection subclass, use Representing Collections in a Relational Database. If an instance variable contains any other value, use Foreign-Key Reference.

Finally, create a column to contain this object's OID (see Object Identifier [OID]).

Discussion   The database design may need modification (for instance, denormalization), depending on the access patterns required for particular scenarios. Remember that constructing this design is an iterative process.

There are several variations of mappings between classes and tables:

- One Object class maps to one table.
- One Object class maps to multiple tables.
- Multiple Object classes map to one table.
- Collections of the same class map to one table.
- Multiple Object classes map to multiple tables.

The database access architecture must handle each of these variations.

Sources   Ramez Elmasri and Shamkent Navathe [Elmasri+94] and James Rumbaugh et al. [Rumbaugh+91] discuss these issues.

Representing Object Relationships as Tables

Problem   How do you represent object relationships in a relational database schema?

Forces   A variety of relationships exist between classes in an object model. These relationships may be

- One-to-one (husband-wife)
- One-to-many (mother-child)
- Many-to-many (ancestor-child)
- Ternary (or *n*-ary) associations (student-class-professor)
- Qualified associations (company-office-person)

In a qualified association, the association between two objects is constrained or identified in some way. For example, a person can be associated with a company through a position held by that person with that company. The position qualifies the association between the company and the person.

An association between objects may represent containment, it may reflect associated properties of those objects, or it may possess some special semantic meaning on its own, independent of the particular objects involved (e.g., marriage represents a special relationship between [any] man and [any] woman).

The choice for one-to-one and one-to-many relationships is to either merge the association into a class or create a class based on the association.

It is important to remember that the semantics of relationships between objects can be significant. It is often useful to create classes to represent associations, especially if a relationship between objects has values of its own. These classes will be represented as tables in the relational database. For many-to-many, one-to-many, and one-to-one associations with a meaningful existence in the problem domain, create a class for the association. A meaningful existence is when the relationship itself can have value (for example, when it possesses properties such as duration, quality, or type, like a marriage).

Therefore:

Solution   Merge a one-to-one association with no special meaning into one of the tables. If it has special meaning, create a table based on the class derived from the association. For a one-to-many association, create a relationship table (see Representing Collections in a Database).

A many-to-many relationship always maps to a table that contains columns referenced by the foreign keys of the two objects. Ternary and *n*-ary associations should have their own table that references the participating classes by foreign key.

A qualified association should also have its own table.

Discussion   A consideration of the forces in this pattern will often result in changes to a first-pass object model. This is desirable, since it will often generate a more general and flexible solution.

Sources   James Rumbaugh [Rumbaugh+91] discusses this pattern.

Related Patterns   Representing Inheritance in a Relational Database
Representing Collections in a Relational Database

Representing Inheritance in a Relational Database

Problem   How do you represent a set of classes in an inheritance hierarchy within a relational database?

Forces   Relational databases do not provide support for attribute inheritance. It is impossible to do a true one-to-one mapping between a relational table and a class when that class inherits attributes from another class or other classes inherit from it.

   Two possible contexts may be considered for this pattern, depending on what is more important to your particular application, the speed of your queries, or the maintainability and flexibility of your relational schema.

Solution   When ease of schema modification is paramount, create one table for each class in your hierarchy that has attributes. (This will include both concrete and abstract classes.) The tables will contain a column for each attribute defined in that class, plus an additional column that represents the common key shared between all subclass tables. An instance of a concrete subclass is retrieved by performing a relational JOIN of all the tables in a path to the root, with the common key as the join parameter.

Discussion   This is a direct mapping, which makes it easy to change if a class anywhere in the hierarchy changes. If a class changes, you must change at most one table. Unfortunately, the overhead of doing multitable joins can become a problem if you have even a moderately deep hierarchy.

Solution   When query speed is more important, create one table for each concrete subclass in your hierarchy that contains *all* of the attributes defined in that subclass or inherited from its superclasses. An instance is retrieved by querying that table.

Discussion   This avoids the joins of the previous solution, making queries more efficient. This is also a simple mapping, but it has a drawback: if a superclass is changed, many tables must be modified. It is also difficult to infer the object design from the relational schema.

There is a third solution, which may be more appropriate in a multiple-inheritance environment but does not have much to recommend itself beyond that. It is possible to create a single table that represents *all* of the superclass's and subclasses' attributes, with SELECT statements picking out only those that are appropriate for each class. Unfortunately, this can lead to a large number of NULLs in your database, wasting space.

Sources   Ramez Elmasri and Shamkent Navathe [Elmasri+94] discuss how this problem is dealt with in the Extended ER (EER) model. Both Ivar Jacobson et al. [Jacobson+92] and James Rumbaugh et al. [Rumbaugh+91] discuss this problem and present this solution.

Related Patterns   Object Identifier (OID)

Representing Collections in a Relational Database

Problem   How do you represent Collection subclasses in a relational database?

Forces   The first normal form rule of relational databases prevents a relation from containing a "Multivalued" attribute, or what we would normally think of in OO terms as a collection. The kind of 1-N relationships represented in OO languages by collection classes are represented in a very different form in a relational database.

Collection classes in Smalltalk often convey additional information besides the object that contains the collection and the relationship between the objects contained. Order, sorting methods, and type of contained objects arc all problems that must be addressed.

Solution   Represent each collection in your object model (where one object class is related to another object class by a 1-N has a relationship) by a relationship table. The table may also contain additional attributes that address the other issues.

The basic solution involves creating a table that consists of at least two columns. The first column represents the primary key (usually the OID) of the containing object (the object that holds the collection), and the second represents the primary key of the contained objects (the objects held in the collection). Each entry in the table shows a relationship between the contained object and the containing object. The primary key of the relationship table is composed of both columns. A third column may be needed to indicate either the class of the object or the table in which the object is located. Collections may contain objects of various classes.

Discussion   There are other possible representations of the 1-N relationships, including back pointers. Back pointers have a drawback, however: it is difficult to have an object contained in more than one collection at the same time when two collections are contained in different instances of the same class.

The simplest (and most common) additional information to include in a relationship table is a column that indicates the type of the contained object. This is necessary when a Collection is heterogeneous. If an OrderedCollection is utilized and the order is significant, the position of the object in the collection may be stored in an additional column.

It must be noted that unless a distinguishing column indicating a position or an OID is added to a relationship table and made part of its primary key, then the basic solution represents a Set. This is because the key constraint of relational databases prevents a tuple from occurring more than once in the same table.

Sources   Ramez Elmasri and Shamkent Navathe [Elmasri+94] prcscnt this as the primary solution for handling 1-N relationships in the E-R model. Bob Beck and Steve Hartley [Beck+94] and Mary E. S. Loomis [Loomis94] present additional information about constraints on these relationships when mapping Smalltalk collections to relational tables.

Related Patterns   Object Identifier (OID)

Object Identifier (OID)

Problem   How do you represent an object's individuality in a relational database?

Forces   In OO languages, objects are uniquely identifiable. In Smalltalk, an equivalence comparison (==) determines if two objects are exactly identical. This is accomplished through the comparison of their object pointers (OOPs), which are uniquely assigned to each object when it is instantiated.

In an environment where objects may become persistent, some way of identifying what particular persistent structure corresponds to that object has to be added to the mix. OOPs are reassigned and reclaimed by the system, precluding their use as object identifiers.

Solution   Assign an identifier (i.e., an OID) to each object that is guaranteed to be unique across image invocations. This identifier will be part of the object and will be used to identify it during query operations and update operations.

Discussion   OIDs can be generated either internally or externally. Some relational databases include a sequence number generator that can be used to generate OIDs, and it is preferable to use that option when available. OIDs only need be unique within a class, as long as some other way of identifying the class of an object is provided by the persistence scheme. OIDs are customarily long integers.

If an OID is generated within the application, it is often common to have a table that represents the latest available OID for each class. The table will be locked, queried, updated, and unlocked whenever a new OID is required. To improve performance, sometimes an entire block of OID numbers can be acquired at once.

OIDs can include type information encoded into the identifier. In this case, it may be more appropriate to use a char or varchar column rather than an integer.

Sources   Ivar Jacobson et al. [Jacobson+92] and James Rumbaugh et al. [Rumbaugh+91] discuss the use of OIDs. Many papers on OODBMSs also discuss the use of OIDs in their implementation.

Related Patterns   Foreign-Key Reference

Foreign-Key Reference

Problem   How do you represent the fact that in an object model an object can contain not only "base datatypes" like Strings, Characters, Integers and Dates but also other objects?

Forces   The first normal form (1-NF) rule of relational databases specifically precludes a tuple from containing another tuple. Therefore, you must use another representation of an object, one that can be represented by a legal value that a column can contain.

Solution   Assign each object in your object model a unique OID. (See pattern OID.) Add a column for each instance variable that contains an object that is not either

- A collection object or
- A "base data type"

In this column, store the OID of the object contained in the previous object. If your database supports it, declare the column to be a foreign key to the table that represents the class of object whose OID is stored in that column.

Discussion   This restriction (the 1-NF rule) is both a strength and the Achilles' heel of the relational model. When this pattern is used in self-similar objects (e.g., a Person has children, who are also Persons) it is exceedingly difficult in a single SQL query to retrieve a tree of connected objects rooted on a single object.

If you find that the vast majority of columns in your database schema arise from this pattern, you may wish to reconsider the decision to use a relational database as a persistent object store. This is a sign that these objects have a significant number of complex relationships, requiring a number of time-consuming joins for full instantiation.

Sources   James Rumbaugh et al. [Rumbaugh+91] discusses the use of foreign key references.

Related Patterns   Object Identifier (OID)

Representing Collections in a Relational Database

STATIC PATTERNS (OBJECT SIDE)

The preceding section discussed the definition of class properties and their relationships within a relational database schema. We must also consider the definition of the object model on the client, however. The pattern Foreign Key versus Direct Reference addresses how to best define the relationships of complex objects to be instantiated in the object image.

Foreign Key versus Direct Reference

Problem   In the domain object model, when should you reference objects with a "foreign key," and when should you have direct reference with pointers?

Forces   In general, the object model should closely reflect the problem domain and its behavior. The network of objects that support this model can be complex and large, however. Modeling a large corporation with its numerous organizations and branches may require hundreds of thousands of objects and multiple levels of objects of different classes.

In object models, objects usually reference one another directly. This makes navigation among the object network direct and easier than via foreign-key reference.

Objects can reference other objects by using their foreign keys, however. When this is the case, the objects must also have methods to dereference their foreign key to get the referenced object. This makes maintaining the object relationships in the object model more complex. If foreign keys are used to reference the objects, then more searches and more caches are required to support the accessing methods. However, using foreign keys makes it easier to map the domain objects to the database tables during their instantiation and passivation. Relying on foreign keys alone with the object model can result in recursive relations and may also result in extremely poor performance problems, as large collections of objects are needed to represent a complex object.

In many cases, the application simply requires a list of names to peruse in order to locate the object of interest. The number of objects in such a list may be in the millions, however. This puts a heavy strain on the requirements of such a system. In the great majority of cases, the application requires a foreign key only for display and selection purposes. This means you should keep the supporting application domain models "light," making sure they contain only those attributes necessary for display purposes.

Solution   An object model should use direct reference as much as possible. This permits fast navigation over the object structures. Build the object network piece by piece, as required, using Proxy objects to minimize storage. Make the associations only as complex as necessary. When dealing with large collections or a set of complex objects, use foreign keys and names to represent the objects for user interface display and selection. After selection is made, instantiate the complex object, depending on memory constraints and performance.

Discussion   If each domain object maps to a single table, then there is probably a table model in the domain object layer. You may be adding complexity to the whole system. If the domain objects have no behavior other than their being information holders, you may consider getting them out of the way. Instead, have the application model refer directly to broker objects. This way you do not have an object cache that must be kept in sync with the relational tables. If domain behavior is required (it probably will be), then you can add domain objects as required. Make the domain objects "prove" themselves. In reference to using foreign keys instead of direct references within the object model, one developer learning Smalltalk said, "What the hell good is objects if you do not hold real objects? You might as well use PowerBuilder."

Related Patterns   Foreign-Key Reference

REFERENCES

[Beck+94] B. Beck and S. Hartley. "Persistent Storage in a Workflow Tool Implemented in Smalltalk." *OOPSLA '94 Proceedings*, 1994, pp. 373–387.

[Elmasri+94] R. Elmasri and S. Navathe. *Fundamentals of Database Systems*. Redwood City, CA: Benjamin Cummings, 1994.

[Jacobson+92] I. Jacobson et al. *Object-Oriented Software Engineering: A Use-Case Driven Approach*. Reading, MA: Addison-Wesley, 1992.

[Loomis94] M. E. S. Loomis. "Hitting the Relational Wall." *Journal of Object-Oriented Programming* (January 1994): 56–59.

[Rumbaugh+91] J. Rumbaugh et al. *Object-Oriented Modeling and Design*. Englewood Cliffs, NJ: Prentice-Hall, 1991 (5), 8.

[Wirfs-Brock95] R. Wirfs-Brock. "Characterizing Your Application's Control Style." In *Smalltalk Solutions '95*. New York: SIGS Publications, 1995.

Kyle Brown can be reached at kbrown@ksccary.com.
Bruce G. Whitenack can be reached at bwhitenack@ksccary.com.

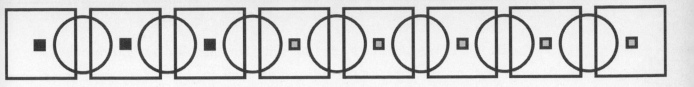

15 Transactions and Accounts

Ralph E. Johnson

ABSTRACT

Transactions and Accounts is a pattern language for the kinds of transaction processing systems common in business, in which transactions cause master files of accounts to be updated. This includes accounting systems, inventory systems, and payroll systems (in other words, most traditional business software). The pattern language describes both the way most business transaction processing systems work and how to improve them. This gives it the potential to make business transaction processing systems easier to construct and maintain.

INTRODUCTION

Suppose you are modeling the current state of a business. The business buys and sell things and has to keep track of how much it owes, how much others owe it, how much business it has done, and how much money it is making and can expect to make.

Whether you are using a computer or doing everything by hand, you will probably follow the same patterns. (Well, maybe not. You could pay your workers each day, count inventory periodically, reorder when items run low, and find out how much money you have by asking your bank. But this only works for small businesses.) You will

1. Record all changes to the state of the business, using Business Transactions.

2. Model the state of the business, using Business Accounts.

3. Structure transactions, using Composite Transactions.

4. Fix mistakes by Adjusting Transactions (rather than redoing them).

5. Catch and resolve errors using Month End Closing.

I believe this is an accurate description of the patterns commonly used in systems based on transactions and accounts. I think life can be better, however. Month End Closing is the real problem, though business people have lived with it for so long that they often think it is inevitable. It is a pattern that resolves many forces, so it is hard to change.

One of the reasons people use Month End Closing today is that they implement their business rules by embedding them in software that processes transactions. *Business rules* describe how a business operates. In a business transaction processing system, they determine

- When and how to create new transactions
- When and how to create new accounts
- Which accounts a transaction should be posted to
- How to calculate the value of an account from the transactions posted to it

Traditionally, each business transaction is a record in a file. Each account is also a record (or set of records) in a file. A business transaction is processed by a program that reads the transaction file and updates the account file (or "master file"). This "update" program checks whether the transactions are valid, finds the accounts that the transaction should be posted to, and updates those accounts, calculating the new value of the account from its old value and the value of the transaction.

To replace Month End Closing with another pattern, you have to figure out another way to resolve its forces. One of the key alternative patterns is Explicit Business Rules. This pattern eliminates the need to change software only at the end of a month. It also makes it easier to change business rules.

Systems that embed business rules in code usually require you to embed a single rule in several places, forcing you to find and change each place to change a business rule. If business rules are explicit, then you only have to make one change.

You can eliminate the need to fix bad transactions at the end of the month by continuously making the checks that would be performed at Month End Closing; this way, errors are corrected when they occur instead of piling up. (This pattern is Continuous Processing.) If you represent business rules explicitly, then the system can check the rules automatically as well as use them to process transactions.

Another reason for representing your business rules explicitly is that it allows you to keep track of how they change over time. You can therefore process (or undo) transactions based on the rules in effect at the time the transaction took place rather than the time the transaction was processed by the computer. This means you don't have to process transactions in any particular order but can process them whenever all the data is available (i.e., you can permit continuous processing).

Making business rules explicit has many advantages. It will make month-end closings simpler and easier. It will let you design your systems at a higher level, just like GUI builders and DBMSs let us design our systems at a higher level.

Making business rules explicit also has disadvantages. In particular, many systems must handle huge volumes of transactions, and systems that make business rules explicit tend to be less efficient. This is partly because we have less experience building business transaction processing systems this way, and partly because of the overhead caused by interpreting rules.

Recall that an account's attributes are functions of the transactions that have been posted to it. When an account stores its attributes locally, they are cached results of these functions. For example, "Sales, Year-to-Date" on an inventory account is the sum of the "amount" field on all sales transactions posted to the account that year. You could encode this rule in the program that posts sales transactions to an inventory account, as well as in a program (if there is one) that backs them out and programs that post other kinds of transactions to the inventory account and so must avoid this field. But the system will be easier to understand if you only define the meaning of this attribute once, in terms of the transactions.

Accounts[1] is a system I've been building based on these principles.

---

[1] *Accounts* home page: http://st-www.cs.uiuc.edu/users/johnson/Account.html

BUSINESS TRANSACTIONS

Problem   As much as possible, businesses need to leave a paper trail. That is, they need to be able to prove to auditors (or their customers) that things are as they say they are. Thus, they must turn everything into a transaction that they can then record. The current state of a business should be apparent from this aggregate record.

Creating this trail is not always a natural process, since some things (like depreciation and shrinkage) happen continuously, not at discrete points in time like a transaction model implies. Nevertheless, this is standard business practice, and there are ways to work around the problems that occur.

Therefore:

Solution   Represent a business's activity by means of a set of transactions that correspond to the paper documents (or their electronic analogues) the business has exchanged with other people.

For example, an inventory system has transactions like purchases, sales, and shrinkage. A payroll system has transactions like time cards, paychecks, and salary changes. A bank has transactions like deposits, withdrawals, and interest payments.

You should then use Separate Transaction Processing from Archival Processing.

SEPARATE TRANSACTION PROCESSING FROM ARCHIVAL

Problem   Business Transactions provides a focus during transaction processing for complicated events, processing activities, and policy decisions. The sequence of transactions forms the historical record of the organization.

In theory, transactions "last forever," as part of the permanent record of the organization. But they can't be stored in the same way forever (and some may be lost). Eventually they have to be moved to some less expensive form of storage. Much of the data needed in processing a transaction (such as which processing steps have already been performed) are not needed for posterity. On the other hand, you may need to keep certain information in an archive (not necessarily one associated with a specific transaction) during processing. For example, you may need to archive information about the effect a transaction had on a customer relationship (e.g., "before" and "after" values for key pieces of information).

Therefore:

Solution Use different representations of transactions during processing than those used for archival purposes. Don't archive transactions until you have finished all processing related to a given business event, including rerunning it and generating management information.

BUSINESS ACCOUNTS

Problem Business accounts are duals of business transactions. Transactions show the flow of money, goods and services, and even commitments. Accounts show the state of a business (i.e., the amount of money available, the goods available, and the outstanding commitments). Sometimes an attribute of an account seems concrete and tangible, such as on-hand quantity in an inventory account. Other attributes, such as quantity sold this year, seem much less tangible. However, all of them are part of the user's model.

A given account's attributes change over time; they are functions of all the transactions that have occurred to date. The amount of inventory today is different from what it was yesterday, depending on how much was bought or sold.

It is theoretically possible to define an account as a set of functions, one for each of its attributes. You could then determine the value of an account attribute at a particular point in time by applying this function to all transactions recorded up to that point. However, this is too expensive if there are a lot of transactions.

What is "a lot" clearly depends on the context. If you are running your business with paper and ink, then 10 transactions per day is a lot by the end of the month. If you are running it using a RDBMS, then 10 transactions per day is very little, and you could calculate almost anything you wanted to in a few seconds using SQL queries. But if you have enough data to computerize, you probably also have enough that it is too expensive to repeatedly compute the state of your business. So, you need to cache the state at various points in time.

Therefore:

Solution Keep a set of accounts that keep track of the current state of the business. The state variables are attributes of the accounts.

In a payroll system, there is an account for each employee. An employee's attributes include hours worked this pay period, accrued vacation, and taxes withdrawn for the year. In an inventory system, there is an account for each item in inventory. An inventory account's attributes include the on-hand amount, month-to-date sales, and cost of goods sold. In an accounts payable system, there is an account for each vendor. A vendor's attributes include how much you owe it and how much you've bought from it this year.

COMPOSITE TRANSACTIONS

Problem   When bookkeeping was first invented, each account was a page in a book (or a set of pages), on which the bookkeeper would record transactions that changed the account. Each transaction became a line on the page. In double-entry bookkeeping, each transaction is recorded in two accounts, to help detect arithmetic errors and prevent fraud.

Any bookkeeping system will sometimes require posting a transaction to several accounts. For example, a sales transaction might involve several kinds of inventory, so it would require changing several inventory accounts.

Therefore:

Solution   Some transactions are composite transactions; these can be posted to many accounts simultaneously.

A sales transaction might need to be posted to both a sales system and an inventory system, or even to an accounts receivable system. Furthermore, it might involve many kinds of inventory and so need to be posted to more than one inventory system.

ADJUSTING TRANSACTIONS

Problem   Even bookkeepers make mistakes. In the old days, each account had a list of transactions, with running totals. A new transaction was added to the end of the list, and the running total was updated. It was easy to go back to any day and see what the running totals were then, and it was easy to add a new transaction.

However, it was hard to undo a transaction or post a transaction out of order. Deleting or changing a transaction required updating all the running totals after that transaction, which was very tedious if they were written in ink. Correcting arithmetic mistakes was bad enough, but changing the transactions themselves would destroy the audit trail that the transactions were originally designed for.

Therefore:

Solution Never change a transaction once it has been posted; instead, post a new "adjustment" transaction to carry out the change.

The result is that most accounts will include three kinds of transactions: those that make them get bigger, those that make them get smaller, and adjustments. Ideally there will be few adjustment transactions, but they always seem to be necessary.

MONTH END CLOSING

Problem There seem to be a lot more ways to make errors in a computerized accounting system than in a manual one. There are bugs in programs, people often enter data when they really don't know what they are doing, and there is often so much data to enter that it is hard to check it for accuracy. This implies that it is more important to be able to back out or correct transactions in computerized accounting systems than it is for paper-based systems.

Another problem with computerized systems is that the rules for processing transactions are often built into the software. This makes it hard to change the rules, because you might have to process transactions under both the old and the new rules. Even when the rules for processing transactions are stored in a database, the rules might not be time-dependent. For example, an employee's salary might be represented by a number rather than a function that converts time to numbers, so when you process an old transaction (or reprocess one) you'll be using the current value rather than the one that was correct at that time.

Also, accounting systems are often built out of several separately developed modules, but data has to flow from one to the other. This is usually done by having one module produce transactions that feed into the other.

Finally, transactions accumulate quickly and take up a lot of space. Thus they must be purged periodically.

Therefore:

Solution Finalize all transactions at month-end closings. If accounts are out of balance, then the transactions can be adjusted to fix these problems. Once a month-end closing is over, transactions for that month cannot be changed. They can be changed beforehand, however. All transactions for a given month will use the same rules, but a new month can bring new versions of programs. Month-end closings will cause each subsystem to create the transactions that flow into the next subsystem. Finally, the month-end closing is a good time to purge old transactions, because that is when account information for a particular month becomes immutable.

Note that the pattern works the same whether you close monthly, weekly, quarterly, or yearly. Many businesses use both month-end closings and year-end closings.

I first learned about the Month End Closing pattern when I worked on the RATEX system at the Cornell Campus Bookstore. Every night the computer would download sales transactions from the cash registers and use this information to update the sales system, the inventory system, the accounts receivable system, and the textbook and trade book systems. The sales system kept detailed day-by-day accounts, but the other systems just kept data on a month-by-month basis. At month-end closings, the program redesignated current data as last month's data and then cleared the current-month's data files. The data from each subsystems was then posted to the general ledger, which only kept data on a month-by-month basis.

Month-end closings were the only times when data from all the different subsystems were compared. If the total sales in the inventory system didn't match up with the total sales in the sales system, then something was wrong.

The business manager often tore his hair out at the end of the month. It often took several days to finish a month-end closing, and the accounting system wouldn't work to full capacity until it was over. The main problem was that errors would accumulate until the end of the month, but they were not visible until the month-end closing, when the system tried to balance the accounts. I spent a lot of time trying to eliminate errors in the system so month-end closing would run more smoothly.

Some companies make Month End Closing run smoothly, but I think most do not. It often takes several days to carry out a month-end closing, because a lot of problems with the data only become apparent at month's-end closing. In the simplest systems, business transactions cannot be processed until the month-end closing is complete, so there is a lot of pressure to finish it. More sophisticated accounting systems (most of them) will let you start work on the next month while you try to finish up the last. This relieves the pressure on the people closing the month, unless it takes more than a month to finish! However, it makes it easy to draw out month-end closings, making it even harder to get timely data.

EXPLICIT BUSINESS RULES

Problem   Although the rules for processing transactions don't change every day, it sometimes seems like it! Rules that are embedded in programs are hard to change. Worse, many business rules are not implemented in a single place but are spread among a set of programs. Any program that changes files might have to know all the rules. Worst of all, it is common to need to process a transaction using last week's rules, or even last month's.

Making business rules explicit means you can store them in a database instead of in program logic. This has several advantages:

- You can keep track of how the rules change over time.

- You can process (or undo) a transaction based on the rules in effect when the transaction took place, rather than the rules in effect when the transaction is processed.

- If you make a mistake in installing the rules, you can back out the effected transactions, change the rules, and try again.

- You can add rules that will take effect in the future, and they will be automatically installed at the proper time.

- Each rule is defined in one place, making it easier to change the system.

- You can change the rules without knowing a traditional programming language. Therefore, business people can customize their own systems.

On the other hand, it takes hard work to figure out what the business rules are and how you can represent them in a database. Any database system will be limited; if it weren't, it would be just like a conventional programming language.

Therefore:

Solution   Separate the business rules from the transaction-processing software and store them in a database. Each rule must have a specified time during which it is valid.

Every program that is table-driven follows this rule pattern to a certain extent, but most of them still implement a lot of business rules in code. Moreover, few programs keep track of how tables change over time.

This pattern is easier to follow in completely object-oriented languages, since they allow you to make objects that represent the business rules. (It's still not easy, though.)

Note that making your business rules explicit lets you stop programming in terms of the implementation language and start programming in the language of the rules themselves. You are then programming at a higher level, with all the advantages that entails, but you are still programming. Although the language is better suited to the problem, the people who use it are likely to be inexperienced programmers; thus you might still have plenty of problems with it.

Lots of people advocate this pattern, but few programs using it are documented. I know of at least one insurance program and several accounting programs like this. The only documented program I know that follows this pattern is *Accounts*, and it is only a research prototype my students and I built. *Accounts* lets you define functions for computing account attributes using a simple language like that found in spreadsheets. I'm sure there are other programs, and I'd appreciate hearing about them.

CONTINUOUS PROCESSING

Problem   Month End Closing makes it hard to get up-to-date data, since the available data tends to be a month old. It tends to hide mistaken transactions until the end of the month, when they are even harder to find because they are buried under so much data. Also, one mistake can mask the effects of another.

Most businesses use several different programs for month-end closing to check the consistency of the data. We could run these programs every day to catch errors early, possibly by simulating month-end closing every day. Even better, we could change Month End Closing.

Therefore:

Solution   Process all transactions completely as soon as they are entered into the system. This amounts to posting them to accounts, updating the attributes of the accounts they were posted to, and then checking for any dependencies or actions that depend on the updated attributes.

I wrote some programs for the Cornell Campus Store that simulated the checks of Month End Closing, and they had a dramatic effect. Problems would be spotted and solved long before the end of the month. This made month-end closings go much smoother than they had before. It also helped me find some problems in my own code and made me a lot more bold about installing fixes, since I knew that any errors I made would probably be caught by the checks we were running nightly.

Unfortunately, this duplicated a lot of checking code. *Accounts* avoids duplicating code by processing all transactions right away. It only uses Month End Closing as a way of keeping people from changing data.

ACKNOWLEDGMENTS

A lot of these ideas came from discussions with Larry Best (and from his book [Best90]), Ward Cunningham, and the students who implemented *Accounts,* especially Paul Keefer. Larry Best and Grady Booch gave helpful comments on earlier versions of this paper.

REFERENCE

[Best90] L. J. Best. *Application Architecture: Modern Large-Scale Information Processing.* New York: Wiley, 1990.

Ralph E. Johnson can be reached at `johnson@cs.uiuc.edu`.

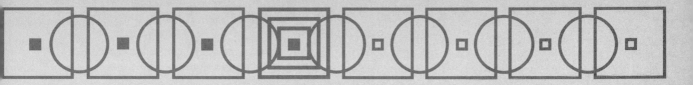

ARCHITECTURAL PATTERNS

PART 4

Architecture. The word conjures up images of flying-buttressed cathedrals and Doric columns, even among computer cognoscenti. Yet more than 20 years have passed since computer science appropriated the term for a new meaning. Back then most people thought "software development" meant "writing code," but some in the software development community knew better. They observed people attempting ever-larger software systems, and they saw how traditional *ad hoc* development approaches were failing them with alarming regularity.

 "Large" systems are inherently larger than one person can build. So to build them, developers had to foster discipline and cooperation. They had to scope out their system ahead of time and break it up into manageable pieces. They needed ways of specifying what the pieces did and how they communicated with other pieces. They had to define abstractions that gave programmers and maintainers insight into the system's workings. They had to be creative in the large, not just clever in the small. In short, they needed a notion of overall design apart from implementation—*software architecture.*

Effective software architecture, like all creative exploits, takes talent and experience. There are far fewer examples of good software architecture than good building architecture, but there are some. And these are enough to reveal patterns.

Software architectural patterns are distinct from the design patterns and idioms that predate them. Idioms are language-specific, and design patterns capture relationships at the class and object level. Architectural patterns are a further step up in granularity, capturing relationships at the *subsystem* level. Consequently, architectural patterns tend to be more ambitious than design patterns and idioms, both in scope and detail. They are strategic to your design; their cousins are tactical.

This part presents three contributions to the architectural pattern inventory. The first, "Some Patterns for Software Architecture" (Chapter 16), is by Mary Shaw, who provides a set of simple yet fundamental architectural patterns. Anyone who has dealt with a large software system will recognize most of them. In fact, a typical undergraduate in computer science can appreciate patterns such as Pipeline, Data Abstraction, and Main Program and Subroutines. Undergraduates and graduates alike will value Mary's prodigious bibliography, which references a good cross-section of literature in the field.

Software architecture's *raison d'être* may be building large systems, but that would mean little if it didn't also abet *change* in those systems. One seldom has the luxury of redesigning a nontrivial system from scratch. That's why changeability is so important in software architecture. Software and classical building architecture diverge in this regard, but modern building architecture has paid increasing attention to changeability in recent years. The forces there are much the same as those propelling change in software: the need for nimbleness in the face of changing requirements, faulty specifications, and variability due to unforeseen fabrication (*viz.* implementation) exigencies. The remaining chapters in this part offer architectural insights into changeable software.

Traditionally, people have associated changeability in software with programming language mechanisms. Consider extensible programming languages. Work in the area began in the fifties, almost immediately after programming languages themselves were invented. Initially the goals of such extension were many and varied, if they were understood at all. But in the last decade or so, changeability has emerged as the primary goal.

The LISP community has been at the forefront of what is now termed "reflective programming" or "metaprogramming"—programming the programming language. True, Smalltalk systems have supported metaclasses since the late seventies. But it was dialects of LISP, starting with Common-Loops and ObjVlisp, that pushed metaprogramming toward the mainstream

[Bobrow+86, Cointe87]. The early work laid the foundation for the Metaobject Protocol [Kiczales+91], which has done much to popularize metaprogramming. Commercial systems have begun exploiting metaprogramming too, particularly IBM's SOM platform.

Two impediments to more widespread adoption of metaprogramming have been its complexity and general misunderstanding of how best to apply it. Frank Buschmann's Reflection pattern (Chapter 17) combines principles of architecture and metaprogramming into a practical guide to general-purpose changeability. Notably, the pattern manages to avoid getting bogged down in esoterica, a common sticking point of metaprogramming literature. Indeed, the pattern makes a fine tutorial on the topic. But most important, the Reflection pattern articulates the applicability, pitfalls, benefits, and costs of reflection at the architectural level.

The third and last chapter in this part is "Evolution, Architecture, and Metamorphosis" (Chapter 18), by Brian Foote and Joseph Yoder. Like Buschmann, these authors contemplate reflection in software architecture. But where Frank concentrates on nuts and bolts in a single pattern, Brian and Joseph offer a pattern language on a more philosophical level. The two chapters thus complement each other nicely.

Brian and Joseph's three-pattern language is hierarchical, in the Alexandrian tradition. At the top of the hierarchy is Software Tectonics. Appealing to geology, this pattern argues for continual small-scale evolution as a way to avert major disruption in the software lifecycle. Flexible Foundations resolves some of the forces in Software Tectonics using metaprogramming facilities, specifically by casting traditional development tools (language, compiler, debugger, and code repository) as first-class objects. Such facilities build flexibility into a system, making it much more amenable to static modification than systems in which meta-information is compiled away. Metamorphosis resolves the remaining forces by calling for metaprogramming facilities that let one modify the system at runtime, not just compile-time. Throughout the pattern language, the authors back up their claims with allusions to a reflective architecture from an industrial application. The result is a colorful and thought-provoking treatise on architecture for change.

REFERENCES

[Bobrow+86] D. G. Bobrow, K. Kahn, G. Kiczales, L. Masinter, M. Stefik, and F. Zdybel. "CommonLoops: Merging LISP and Object-Oriented Programming." OOPSLA '86 Proceedings, Portland, OR. New York: ACM Press, 1986.

[Cointe87] P. Cointe. "Metaclasses Are First Class: The ObjVlisp Model," OOPSLA '87 Proceedings, Orlando, FL. New York: ACM Press, 1987.

[Kiczales+91] G. Kiczales, J. des Rivières, and D. G. Bobrow. *The Art of the Metaobject Protocol.* Cambridge, MA: MIT Press, 1991.

16

Some Patterns for Software Architectures

Mary Shaw

ABSTRACT

Software designers rely on informal patterns, or idioms, to describe the architecctures of software systems—the configurations of components that make up the systems. At the first PLoP conference in August 1994, I identified seven patterns that guide high-level system design and discussed the way they influence the composition of systems from particular types of components [Shaw95]. This chapter extends the descriptions of those patterns (and adds one) in response to discussions at the conference. Most significantly, it adds information on the kinds of problems each pattern handles best.

DESIGN PATTERNS FOR SOFTWARE ARCHITECTURES

Software designers describe system architectures using a rich vocabulary of abstractions. Although their descriptions and the underlying terminology are imprecise and informal, designers nevertheless communicate with some success. They depict the architectural abstractions both in pictures and words.

"Box-and-line" diagrams often illustrate system structures. These diagrams use different shapes to suggest structural differences among components, but they make little discrimination among the lines that depict different kinds of interactions. Further, architectural diagrams are often highly specific to the particular systems they describe, especially in their labeling of components.

The diagrams are supported by prose descriptions. This prose uses terms with common, if informal, definitions:

> *Camelot is based on the client-server model and uses remote procedure calls both locally and remotely to provide communication among applications and servers [Spector+87].*

> *Abstraction layering and system decomposition provide the appearance of system uniformity to clients, yet allow Helix to accommodate a diversity of autonomous devices. The architecture encourages a client-server model for the structuring of applications [Fridrich+85].*

> *We have chosen a distributed, object-oriented approach to managing information [Linton87].*

> *The easiest way to make the canonical sequential compiler into a concurrent compiler is to pipeline the execution of the compiler phases over a number of processors. . . . A more effective way [is to] split the source code into many segments, which are concurrently processed through the various phases of compilation [by multiple compiler processes] before a final, merging pass recombines the object code into a single program [Seshadri+88].*

> *The ARC network [follows] the general network architecture specified by the ISO in the Open Systems Interconnection Reference Model. It consists of physical and data layers, a network layer, and transport, session, and presentation layers [Paulk85].*

I studied sets of such descriptions and found a number of abstractions that govern the overall organization of the components, and their interactions. A few of the patterns (e.g., Object Organizations [Booch86] and Blackboards [Nii86]) have been carefully refined, but others are still used quite informally, even unconsciously. Nevertheless, architectural patterns are widely recognized. System designs often appeal to several of these patterns, combining them in various ways.

Garlan and Shaw [Garlan+93] describe several common patterns for architectures. Ours is not, of course, an exhaustive list; it offers rich opportunities for both elaboration and structure. These idiomatic patterns differ in four major respects: the underlying intuition behind the pattern, or the system model; the kinds of components that are used in developing a system according to the pattern; the connectors, or kinds of interactions among the components; and the control structure, or execution discipline. By using the same descriptive scheme, we can improve our ability to identify significant differences among the patterns. Once the informal pattern is clear, the details can be formalized [Allen+94]. Further, the process of choosing the architecture for a system should include matching the characteristics of the architecture to the properties of the problem [Jackson94, Lane90]; having uniform descriptions of the available architectures should simplify this task.

  Systems are composed from identifiable *components* of various distinct types. The components interact in identifiable, distinct ways. Components roughly correspond to the compilation units of conventional programming languages and other user-level objects, such as files. Connectors mediate interactions among components; that is, they establish the rules that govern component interaction and specify any auxiliary implementation mechanisms required. Connectors do not, in general, correspond to individual compilation units; they manifest themselves as table entries, instructions to a linker, dynamic data structures, system calls, initialization parameters, servers that support multiple independent connections, and the like. A pattern is based on selected types of components and connectors, together with a *control structure* that governs their execution. An overall *system model* captures the developer's intuition about how these are integrated [Shaw+95].

ARCHITECTURAL PATTERNS

We turn now to patterns for some of the major architectural abstractions. The purpose of each of these patterns is to impose an overall structure for a software system or subsystem that

- Is appropriate to the problem the system or subsystem is required to solve
- Clarifies the designer's intentions about the organization of the system or subsystem
- Provides a paradigm that will help establish and maintain internal consistency
- Allows for appropriate checking and analysis
- Preserves information about the structure for reference during later maintenance tasks

In practice, a designer adopts one or more patterns to shape a design. Patterns may be used in combination. They might, for example, provide complementary views during the initial design, as in a system that may be viewed either as a repository or an interpreter [Garlan+93]. Alternatively, a component of one pattern might be elaborated using another pattern, as in a layered system in which some layers are elaborated as pipelines and others as data abstractions. Such progressive elaboration can be continued repeatedly until the architectural issues are resolved, at which point conventional programming techniques take over.

The description of each pattern discussed here includes notes on

- *The problem the pattern addresses.* What in the application requirements leads the designer to select this pattern?
- *The pattern's context.* What aspects of the setting (the computation environment or other constraints on implementation) constrain the designer in the use of this pattern?
- *A solution.* The system model captured by the pattern, together with the components, connectors, and control structure that make up the pattern.
- *A diagram.* A figure showing a typical pattern, annotated to show the components and connectors.
- *Significant variants.* For some patterns, major variants of the basic pattern are noted.
- *Examples.* References to examples or more extensive overviews of systems that apply this pattern.

Pipeline

Problem   This pattern is suitable for applications that require a defined series of independent computations to be performed on ordered data. It is particularly useful when each of the computations can be performed incrementally on a data stream. In such cases the computations can, at least in principle, proceed in parallel, and when this is possible it can reduce the latency of the system.

Context   The pattern relies on being able to decompose the problem into a set of computations, or *filters*, that transform one or more input streams *incrementally* to one or more output streams. The usual implementation embeds each transformation in a separate process and relies on operating system operations, or *pipes*, to stream the data from one process to another. The analysis is simplest if the filters do not interact except via explicitly defined pipes.

Solution   **System model** Data flow between components, with components that incrementally map data streams to data streams

Components Filters (purely computational, local processing, asynchronous)

Connectors Data streams (ASCII data streams for Unix pipelines)

Control structure Data flow

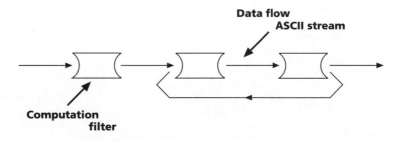

Data flow
ASCII stream

Computation
filter

Significant Variants   This pattern is commonly mentioned by Unix programmers, who often use it for prototyping. Note that the pattern calls for "pure" filters, with local processing and little state. Unix "filters" often consume the entire input stream before producing output, however. This still works for systems without loops, but it interrupts the smooth flow of information through the system and can cause starvation if the data flow topology includes loops.

Examples   Allen+94, Bach86, Barbacci+88, Delisle+90, Seshadri+88, Kahn74.

Data Abstraction

Problem   This pattern is suitable for applications in which a central issue is the identification and protection of related bodies of information, especially representation information. When the solution is decomposed to match the natural structure of the data in the problem domain, the components of the solution can encapsulate the data, the essential operations on the data, and the integrity constraints, or *invariants*, of the data and operations.

Context   Numerous design methods provide strategies for identifying natural objects. Newer programming languages support various variations on this theme, so if the language choice or the methodology is fixed, it will strongly influence the flavor of the decomposition.

Solution   **System model**   Localized state maintenance

Components   Managers (e.g., servers, objects, abstract data types)

Connectors   Procedure call

Control structure   Decentralized, usually single thread

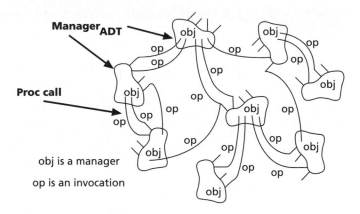

obj is a manager

op is an invocation

Significant Variants   Classical objects (nonconcurrent, interacting via procedurelike methods) are closely related. They differ largely in their use of inheritance to manage collections of related definitions and in their use of runtime binding for procedure calls (method invocation is essentially a procedure call with dynamic binding).

Examples   Booch86, Gamma+95, Linton87, Parnas72.

Communicating Processes

Problem This pattern is suitable for applications that involve a collection of distinct, largely independent computations whose execution should proceed independently. The computations involve coordinating data or control at discrete points in time. As a result, correctness of the system requires attention to the routing and synchronization of the messages. Note that this pattern should be distinguished from data flow, which is generally taken to be of smaller granularity, higher regularity, and unidirectional flow. Although many other patterns may be *implemented* with message passing, the Communicating Processes pattern is intended to apply when the essential character of the abstraction involves communication.

Context The selection of a communication strategy is often dictated by the communications support provided by the available operating system.

Solution **System model** Independent communications processes

Components Processes that send and receive messages to and from explicitly selected recipients

Connectors Discrete messages (no shared data) with known communication partners

Control structure A separate thread of control for each process which may either suspend or continue at communication points

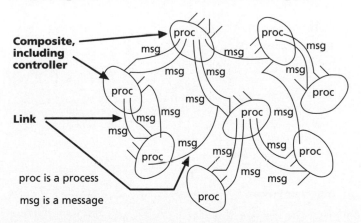

proc is a process

msg is a message

Significant Variants Specific patterns of communication have proven useful in specific situations. The major points of variance include the topology of the communication network, its requirements on delivery, synchronization, and the number of recipients of each message (e.g., simple messages, broadcast, multicast).

Examples Andrews91, Paulk85.

Implicit Invocation

Problem   This pattern is suitable for applications that involve a loosely coupled collection of components in which each component carries out some operation and may in the process enable other operations. These are often *reactive* systems. The pattern is particularly useful for applications that must be reconfigurable on the fly (either by changing a service provider or by enabling and disabling capabilities).

Context   Implicit invocation systems usually require an event handler that registers components' interest in receiving events and notifies them when events are raised. They differ in the kind and amount of information that accompanies events, so it's important to choose a design that fits the problem at hand. Reasoning about the correctness of the system depends very heavily on accurate reasoning about the kinds of events it will handle, the collection of components it will contain, and the collective effect of these elements; this reasoning is trickier than reasoning about correctness when the execution order is known.

Solution   **System model**   Independent reactive processes

Components   Processes that signal significant events without knowing the recipients of those signals

Connectors   Automatic invocation of processes that have registered interest in events

Control structure   Decentralized; individual components not aware of signal recipients

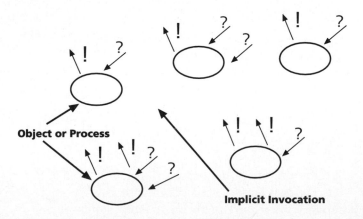

Examples   Balzer86, Garlan+92, Gerety89, Habermann+86, Hewitt69, Krasner+88, Reiss90, Shaw+83.

Repository

Problem   This pattern is suitable for applications in which the central issue is establishing, augmenting, and maintaining a complex central body of information. Typically the information must be manipulated in a wide variety of ways. Often, long-term persistence may also be required. Different variants support radically different control strategies.

Context   Repositories often require considerable support, either from an augmented runtime system (such as a database) or a framework or generator that processes the data definitions.

Solution   **System model**   Centralized data, usually richly structured

Components   One memory, many purcly computational processes

Connectors   Interaction between computational units and memory by direct data access or procedure calls

Control structure   Varies with type of repository—may be external (depends on input data stream, as for databases), predetermined (as for compilers), or internal (depends on state of computation, as for blackboards)

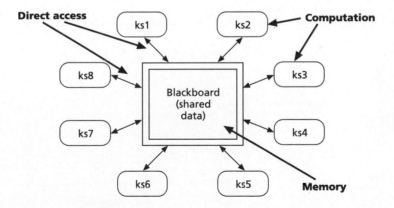

Significant Variants   Repository covers large, centralized, transaction-oriented databases; the blackboard systems used for some AI applications; and systems with predetermined execution patterns in which different phases add information to a single complex data structures (e.g., compilers). These variants differ chiefly in their control structure.

Examples   Ambriola+90, Nii86, Barstow+84.

Interpreter

Problem This pattern is suitable for applications in which the most appropriate language or machine for executing the solution is not directly available. It is also suitable for applications in which the core problem is to define a notation for expressing solutions (for example, as scripts). Interpreters are sometimes used in chains, translating from the desired language or machine to an available one in a series of stages.

Context The interpreter is most often designed to bridge the gap between the desired machine or language and some (possibly virtual) machine or language already supported by the execution environment.

Solution **System model** Virtual machine

Components One state machine (the execution engine) and three memories (current state of execution engine, program being interpreted, current state of program being interpreted)

Connectors Data access and procedure calls

Control structure Usually state-transition for execution engine and input-driven for selecting what to interpret

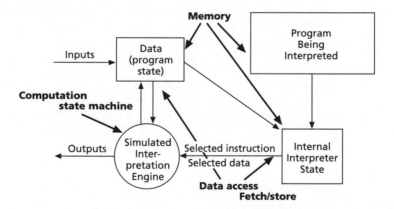

Significant Variants Expert systems are often implemented as interpreters for the collection of rules, or productions, that represent the expertise. Because the productions require a complex selection rule, specialized forms of interpreters have evolved.

Examples Hayes-Roth85.

Main Program and Subroutines

Problem This pattern is suitable for applications in which the computation can appropriately be defined via a hierarchy of procedure definitions. It is usually used with a single thread of control.

Context Many programming languages provide natural support for defining nested collections of procedures and calling them hierarchically. These languages often allow collections of procedures to be grouped into modules, thereby introducing name-space locality. The execution environment usually provides a single thread of control in a single name space.

Solution **System model** Call and definition hierarchy; subsystems often defined via modularity

Components Procedures and explicitly visible data

Connectors Procedure calls and explicit data sharing

Control structure Single thread

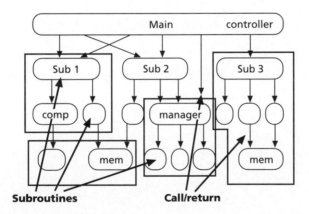

Significant Variants The extension of the procedure call model to concurrent components is achieved through the remote procedure call (RPC). Although the RPC is typically implemented by communications messages, the abstraction it presents is of single-threaded procedure calls.

Examples Parnas72, Spector87.

Layered Architecture

Problem   This pattern is suitable for applications that involve distinct classes of services that can be arranged hierarchically. Often there are layers for basic system-level services, utilities appropriate to many applications, and specific application tasks.

Context   Frequently, each class of service is assigned to a layer, and several different patterns are used to refine the various layers. Layers are most often used at the higher levels of design, using different patterns to refine them.

Solution   **System model** Hierarchy of opaque layers

    Components Usually composites; composites most often collections of procedures

    Connectors Depends on structure of components: often procedure calls, under restricted visibility; might also be client-server

    Control structure Single thread

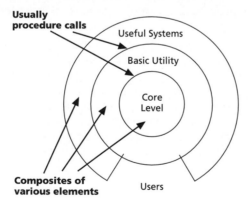

Significant Variants   (a) Layers may be transparent (i.e., the interfaces from lower layers show through) or opaque (i.e., only the interface defined by a given layer may be used by the next layer up). (b) Layered systems are often organized as chains of virtual machines or interpreters.

Examples   Batory+91, Fridrich+85, Lauer+79, Paulk85.

ACKNOWLEDGMENTS

The technical results reported here were developed jointly with various coauthors, especially David Garlan. A good share of the motivation for this effort came from sources outside computer science, most notably Alexander's work on pattern languages [Alexander+77] and some conversations with Vic Vyssotsky on urban planning. Discussions of this chapter at the 1994 and 1995 PLoP workshops showed me a number of ways to improve the content and presentation.

This research was supported by the Carnegie Mellon University School of Computer Science; by a grant from Siemens Corporate Research; and by the Wright Laboratory, Aeronautical Systems Center, Air Force Materiel Command, USAF, and the Advanced Research Projects Agency (ARPA) under grant F33615-93-1-1330. Views and conclusions contained in this chapter are those of the author and should not be interpreted as representing the official policies, either expressed or implied, of any of her sponsors.

REFERENCES

[Alexander+77] C. Alexander, S. Ishikawa, M. Silverstein, et al. *A Pattern Language.* New York: Oxford University Press, 1977.

[Allen+94] R. Allen and D. Garlan. "Formalizing Architectural Connection." In *Proceedings of the 16th International Conference on Software Engineering.* IEEE, 1994.

[Ambriola+90] V. Ambriola, P. Ciancarini, and C. Montangero. "Software Process Enactment in Oikos." Proceedings of the Fourth ACM SIGSOFT Symposium on Software Development Environments. *SIGSOFT Software Engineering Notes,* December 1990.

[Andrews91] G. R. Andrews. "Paradigms for Process Interaction in Distributed Programs." *ACM Computing Surveys,* 23, 1 (March 1991): 49–90.

[Bach86] M. J. Bach. *The Design of the UNIX Operating System.* Englewood Cliffs, NJ: Prentice-Hall, 1986, pp. 111–119.

[Balzer86] R. M. Balzer. "Living with the Next-Generation Operating System." *Proceedings of the 4th World Computer Conference,* September 1986.

[Barbacci+88] M. R. Barbacci, C. B. Weinstock, and J. M. Wing. "Programming at the Processor-Memory-Switch Level." *Proceedings of the 10th International Conference on Software Engineering,* April 1988.

[Barstow+84] D. R. Barstow, H. E. Shrobe, and E. Sandewall (eds.). *Interactive Programming Environments.* New York: McGraw-Hill, 1984.

[Batory+91] D. Batory and S. O'Malley. *The Design and Implementation of Hierarchical Software Systems Using Reusable Components.* TR 91-22. Austin: Department of Computer Science, University of Texas, June 1991.

[Booch86] G. Booch. "Object-Oriented Development." In *IEEE Transactions on Software Engineering* (February 1986): 211–221.

[Delisle+90] N. Delisle and D. Garlan. "Applying Formal Specification to Industrial Problems: A Specification of an Oscilloscope." *IEEE Software*, (September 1990).

[Fridrich+85] M. Fridrich and W. Older. "Helix: The Architecture of the XMS Distributed File System." *IEEE Software*, 2(3) (May 1985): 21–29.

[Gamma+95] E. Gamma, R. Helm., R. Johnson, and J. Vlissides. *Design Patterns: Elements of Reusable Object-Oriented Software*. Reading, MA: Addison-Wesley, 1995.

[Garlan+92] D. Garlan, G. E. Kaiser, and D. Notkin. "Using Tool Abstraction to Compose Systems." *IEEE Computer*, 25 (June 1992).

[Garlan+93] D. Garlan and M. Shaw. "An Introduction to Software Architecture." In V. Ambriola and G. Tortora (eds.). *Advances in Software Engineering and Knowledge Engineering*, Vol. 2. Singapore: World Scientific Publishing Co., 1993, pp. 1–39.

[Gerety89] C. Gerety. *HP Softbench: A New Generation of Software Development Tools*. TR SESD-89-25. Fort Collins, CO: Hewlett-Packard Software Engineering System Division, November 1989.

[Habermann+86] N. Habermann and D. Notkin. "Gandalf: Software Development Environments." *IEEE Transactions on Software Engineering*, Vol. SE-12 (December 1986).

[Hayes-Roth85] F. Hayes-Roth. "Rule-Based Systems." *Communications of the ACM*, 28 (September 1985).

[Hewitt69] C. Hewitt. "Planner: A Language for Proving Theorems in Robots." *Proceedings of the First International Joint Conference in Artificial Intelligence*, 1969.

[Jackson94] M. Jackson. "Problems, Methods, and Specializations." *IEE Software Engineering Journal* (November 1994).

[Kahn74] G. Kahn. "The Semantics of a Simple Language for Parallel Programming." *Information Processing* (1974).

[Krasner+88] G. Krasner and S. Pope. "A Cookbook for Using the Model-View-Controller User Interface Paradigm in Smalltalk-80." *Journal of Object-Oriented Programming*, 1 (August/September 1988).

[Lane90] T. G. Lane. *Studying Software Architecture Through Design Spaces and Rules*. Technical Report No. CMU-CS-90-175. Pittsburgh, PA: Carnegie Mellon University, Department of Computer Science, September 1990.

[Lauer+79] H. C. Lauer and E. H. Satterthwaite. "Impact of MESA on System Design." *Proceedings of the Third International Conference on Software Engineering*, 1979.

[Linton87] Mark A. Linton. "Distributed Management of a Software Database." *IEEE Software*, 4(6) (November 1987).

[Nii86] H. P. Nii. "Blackboard Systems." *AI Magazine* 7(3) (1986): 38–53; 7(4) (1986): 82–107.

[Parnas72] D. L. Parnas. "On the Criteria to Be Used in Decomposing Systems into Modules." *Communications of the ACM*, 15(12) (December 1972): 1053–1058.

[Paulk85] M. C. Paulk. "The ARC Network: A Case Study." *IEEE Software*, 2(3) (May 1985): 62–69.

[Reiss90] S. P. Reiss. "Connecting Tools Using Message Passing in the Field Program Development Environment." *IEEE Software*, 7(4) (July 1990): 57–66.

[Seshadri+88] V. Seshadri. "Semantic Analysis in a Concurrent Compiler." *Proceedings of ACM SIGPLAN '88 Conference on Programming Language Design and Implementation*, 1988.

[Shaw95] M. Shaw. "Patterns for Software Architectures." In J. Coplien and D. Schmidt (eds.). *Pattern Languages of Program Design.* Reading, MA: Addison-Wesley, 1995, pp. 453–462.

[Shaw+83] M. Shaw, E. Borison, M. Horowitz, T. Lane, D. Nichols, and R. Pausch. "Descartes: A Programming-Language Approach to Interactive Display Interfaces." *ACM SIGPLAN Notices 18* (June 1983).

[Shaw+95] M. Shaw, R. DeLine, D. V. Klein, T. L. Ross, D. M. Young, and G. Zelesnik. "Abstractions for Software Architecture and Tools to Support Them." *IEEE Transactions on Software Engineering,* 21(4) (May 1995): 314–335.

[Spector+87] A. Z. Spector et al. *Camelot: A Distributed Transaction Facility for Mach and the Internet—An Interim Report.* Technical Report No. CMU-CS-87-129. Pittsburgh, PA: Carnegie Mellon University, Computer Science Department, June 1987.

Mary Shaw can be reached at `mary.shaw@cs.cmu.edu`.

17 Reflection

Frank Buschmann

INTRODUCTION

The Reflection architectural pattern helps developers design for change and evolution. It divides an application into two parts: a base level and a meta level. The base level includes the software's functional core and user interface. The meta level provides information about the software itself and encapsulates selected system aspects that might be subject to change. Changes in the meta level affect the subsequent behavior of the base level.

Aliases This pattern is also known as Open Implementation, Meta-Level Architecture.

EXAMPLE

Consider a C++ application that includes a persistence component. Its implementation must explicitly specify how to store and read every individual type used in the application: persistence is not a built-in feature of C++. Many solutions to this problem, such as hard-coding type-specific Store and Read methods into the persistence component, are expensive and error-prone. Whenever we change or extend the type system of the application, we must modify the persistence component. This is especially tedious when developing for reuse or when adding persistence to the application after its original development. The same problem arises when we provide a special base class for persistent objects from which application classes are derived with particular methods overridden.

We want to develop a persistence component that is independent of the specific type structure of our application: changes or extensions to the type structure should not affect the persistence component's implementation.

Context   You are building a software system that supports change and extension without needing to modify existing source code explicitly.

Problem   Large-scale software systems often evolve over their lifespan. They must respond to changing technology, environments, and user requirements. For example, during system development (and after), customers make sudden, urgent "add-this-feature-immediately" requests. To satisfy these customers, you need software that supports its own modification. In other words, you need to design for change and evolution. A similar problem occurs when developing for reuse. When you want to reuse a particular piece of software, you usually have to modify it. An artifact must be adaptable to new contexts if real benefit is to be gained by reusing it.

There are several forces associated with this problem:

- You need to change and extend the software without modifying the existing code. There are three reasons for this. First, sensitive parts of a system must sometimes be changed dynamically. For example, in warehouse management systems it must be possible, at runtime, to integrate new strategies for searching for free storage locations [Knischewski+94].

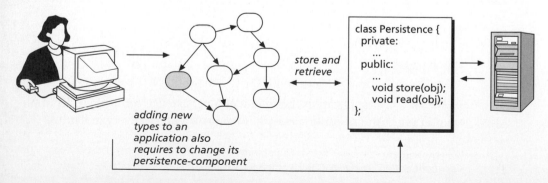

Second, parts of the system whose code is inaccessible may sometimes need tuning. Third-party components and the window system [Kiczales92] are examples of this. Third, sometimes you want particular changes performed by the customers (for example, in order to adapt the software to a specific look and feel guideline [Eisenhauer+94]).

- Integrating changes and extensions into an application should be easy and, if possible, based on a uniform mechanism. If every kind of change requires its own integration technique, modifying an application becomes awkward, and the system may end up being less modifiable.

- Integration of changes and extensions into an application should be safe. Modification should not affect the software's overall semantics. For example, changing a particular type declaration should not affect components that do not use this type.

- Since almost everything can change in a software system, you want to be able to modify both its structure and its behavior. For example, you may want to change the location of the components in a distributed software system, or the implementation underlying a particular component.

- You want to be able to integrate changes that cannot be foreseen today. For example, in business applications some change will be caused by tax law changes (like Germany's recently introduced reunification tax). Such changes do not generally follow a predictable logic; they just happen, and you must respond to them.

Most available techniques for adapting and changing software provide inadequate solutions to the problem. First, they usually require explicit modification of existing code. Even design patterns that support change-ability, such as the Subject-Policy pattern or the Abstract Factory pattern, require explicit code modification for software extensions. Second, many techniques—such as parameterization—only support changes that can be foreseen. However, you often do not know what will change. Therefore, you want to "anticipate the unanticipated," such as the need to add a new function.

Solution   Divide your application into two parts: a base level and a meta level.

The base level should be responsible for computation in the problem domain. It should include the software's user interface and those parts of the functional core that will remain stable throughout the product's lifetime.

The meta level should ease changes and extensions to the software. It should include selected behavioral aspects of the application that might be subject to change, such as algorithms used by particular application services and structural information about the system (for example, runtime type information). Encapsulate these aspects into special components, so-called meta objects.

Specify an interface to the services and information the meta level provides, the *meta object protocol* (MOP). Use the MOP to build a changeable and extensible base level.[1] The result should be independent of particular system details such as the application's specific type system.

Provide the meta object protocol with additional functions that allow clients to modify specific meta objects. Changing such meta objects may alter the subsequent behavior of the software. Implement these functions so that clients need only specify a desired change—the meta object protocol is responsible for checking its correctness and also for performing its execution.

Building a generic persistence component mainly requires some means of achieving structural reflection. We specify a meta level with meta objects providing runtime type information about the application and a meta object protocol for accessing these meta objects. For example, to store an object we must know its type and also the types of all its data members. With this information available, we can recursively iterate over any given object structure. We can break it down into a sequence of built-in types. The persistence component "knows" how to store these. Following similar strategies for every function, we can construct a persistence component at the base level of the application that is able to read and store arbitrary data structures. We can also reuse it in every other application that provides runtime type information.

Class Base Level	Collaborators Meta Level
Responsibility • Does computation about the problem domain. • Includes the user interface, if existent. • Uses the meta level to stay flexible.	

Class Meta Level	Collaborators Base Level
Responsibility • Encapsulates system internals that may change. • Provides an interface to facilitate modifications to the meta level. • Controls base level behavior.	

---

[1] When the base level uses meta objects that encapsulate behavioral aspects of the system, we refer to it as "behavioral reflection" or "procedural reflection." When the base level uses meta objects that provide structural information about the software, we refer to it as "structural reflection."

STRUCTURE

This section describes the detailed structure of the Reflection architectural pattern. The base-level subsystem models and implements the software's external problem domain. Its components represent the various application services, as well as their underlying data model. Furthermore, the base level specifies the fundamental collaboration and structural relationships among all the components it includes. The user interface, which is also part of the base level, specifies the perceivable input and output behavior of the application. It allows users to make productive use of the base-level functionality. Ideally, the base-level implementation stays stable over the whole lifetime of the software: implementation of those aspects of the software that are likely to vary over the software's lifetime is factored out into the meta level.

As already mentioned, we implement the persistence component as part of the base level. Its interface provides functions for storing and reading arbitrary C++ data structures. We keep the body of the component independent of the concrete type-structure of our application. For example, the store procedure only implements the general algorithm for recursively breaking down a given object's structure into a sequence of built-in types. It does not hard-code any information about specific user-defined types, namely the type, size, and order of their data members. The software's user interface provides the menu entries for storing and reading objects, as well as dialog boxes for selecting data files and presenting status and error messages.

The meta level contains a model of selected aspects of the software (the distribution of the software's components, for example). It includes a set of meta objects, each capturing a particular aspect of the structure, behavior, or state of the base level. Meta objects make information that would otherwise be only implicitly available explicitly accessible and modifiable by the application. (This process is often referred to as reification.) More generally, the meta objects maintain aspects of the software that may vary or change or that are customer-specific. Meta objects help to build a flexible and changeable base level.

For the persistence component, we specify meta objects that provide information about every type available in the application: what types exist, how they are related to one another, and what their inner structure is.

The meta object protocol (MOP) is the meta level's interface; it allows clients to access specific system details and modify certain meta objects or their relationships. MOP clients include the base level, other applications, and (privileged) human users.

Every MOP function falls into one of the following three categories:

1. *Introspection.* Clients can access information about the software itself, such as runtime type information.

2. *Explicit invocation.* Clients get access to basic system operations that would otherwise be only indirectly triggered through base-level activity (for example, LRU and LFU page swapping).

3. *Intercession.* Clients can change or exchange meta objects and their connection with the base level, or they can integrate new meta objects with the meta level (creating, for example, a new sorting algorithm).

The MOP for our persistence component example provides introspective access to the type structure of the application. We can obtain information about the name, size, data members, function members, and superclasses of a given type or object. We can also provide a function to explicitly instantiate raw objects of an arbitrary type. We would use this function when reading the content of a data file to restore the original data structure. We can further provide the MOP with functions that allow us to specify how to store and read a given type (for example, catering for cases where not every data member is persistent). Changing this specification directly impacts the behavior of our persistence component.

Several kinds of connections between the base level and the meta level are possible. They keep the levels coordinated:

- If meta objects encapsulate particular behavioral aspects of the software, they are usually directly connected with specific base-level components. For example, if a meta object specifies the method dispatch mechanism to be used by the base level, it is directly consulted whenever a base-level component calls a function of another base-level component. The MOP needs access to the internal structure of all base-level components affected by the change if it is to modify such connections. An example is switching the method dispatch from single dispatching to double dispatching.

- To modify base-level behavior, such as the method dispatching mechanism, clients use the MOP. Changes are performed by modifying particular meta objects or specific relationships between base-level components and meta objects. The results of these changes affect the subsequent behavior of the base level.

To obtain information about the software (for example, information about the currently used implementation of a particular component), the base level also uses the MOP.

A rough sketch of a possible structure of a system that includes a persistence component is given in the following diagram:

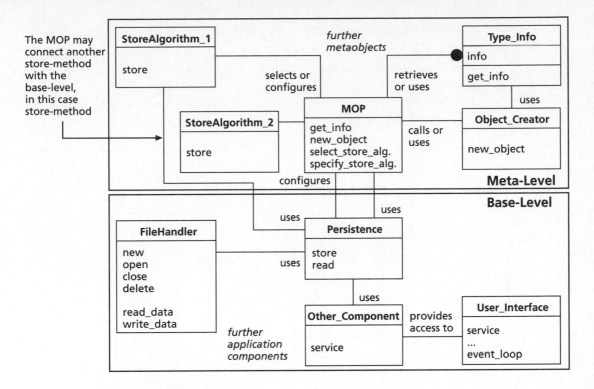

The MOP may connect another store-method with the base-level, in this case store-method

DYNAMICS

We can illustrate the three kinds of collaborations between the base level and the meta level of the Reflection architectural pattern with the help of two scenarios. Both are based on the persistence component example.

First, we show how the base level inspects the meta level and how it invokes basic system services when reading persistent objects. The scenario can be divided into five phases:

1. The user wants to read an externally stored object structure. He selects the appropriate menu entry and specifies a data file. The user interface forwards the request to the read procedure of the persistence component.

2. The persistence component must know the type of an object read from a data file. It also needs to know the types, names, order, and size of all data members of that object. The base level calls the MOP to obtain this information (introspection).

3. The MOP retrieves the meta object providing the requested type information and returns it to the persistence component.

4. To transform the stored data into a C++ object, the read method first invokes the MOP to create a raw object of the previously determined

type (explicit invocation). The MOP returns a handle to this object to the persistence component.

5. The read method iterates over the data members of the created object to assign the data file content. If a data member is a built-in type, it directly assigns the currently read data item to the data member. Otherwise, the read method calls itself recursively.

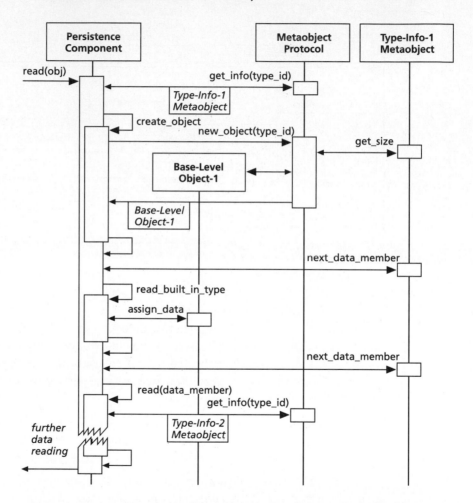

The second scenario illustrates the way the meta level controls base-level behavior and how changes to the meta level affect base-level computations. The scenario is based on storing an object structure. It too is divided into five phases:

1. The user wants to store an object structure and selects the appropriate menu entry. The user interface invokes the Store method of the persistence component.

2. The Store method first determines the type of the object to be stored (introspection).

3. Second, the Store method calls the MOP to provide the storage algorithm for the object (intercession).

4. The MOP selects the appropriate algorithm, which determines how the object should be stored. It connects the algorithm with the Store method of the persistence component.

5. The Store method resumes execution and uses the selected algorithm to iterate over the data members of the object being stored. If a data member is a built-in type, the Store method directly stores its content. Otherwise, the store method calls itself recursively.

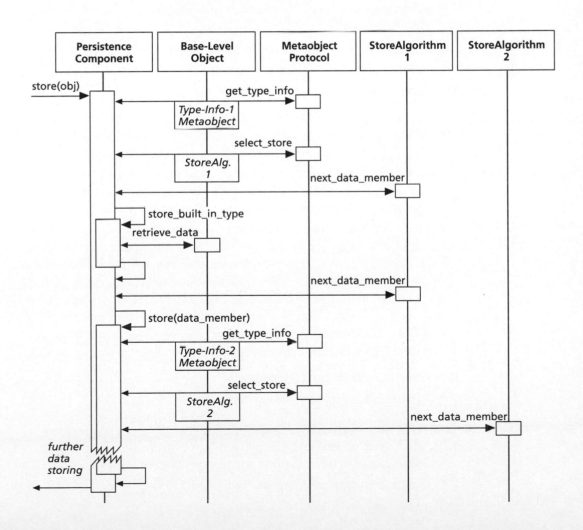

IMPLEMENTATION

The following guidelines will help with implementing a reflective architecture. If necessary, iterate through any subsequences of these steps.

1. *Define a model of the application.* Analyze the problem domain and map it onto an appropriate software structure. Do not focus on changeability and extensibility. In this step, find a proper decomposition, representation, and organization of domain-specific system functionality. Basically, answer the following questions:

   ▪ What services should the software provide?

   ▪ To what components should these services be attached?

   ▪ What are the structural and communications relationships between the components?

   ▪ How do the components cooperate or collaborate?

   ▪ What data do the components operate on?

   ▪ How will the user interact with the software?

   Follow an appropriate analysis method when specifying the model. You may also use suitable domain-specific patterns, if any are available.

   We need two components for our example. A persistence component provides the functionality for storing and reading objects. It uses a second component, a file handler, that is responsible for locking, opening, closing, unlocking, and deleting files as well as for writing and reading data.

2. *Identify variable behavioral aspects.* Analyze the model developed in Step 1 to determine which of the services may vary and which are stable. Note that there are no general rules for specifying what can be altered in a system. Whether a certain aspect varies depends on many factors, such as the application's domain, its environment, and its customers and users. An aspect that is likely to vary in one system may be stable in others. Techniques like communality/variability analysis help with this step. The following are examples of system aspects that often vary:

   ▪ Real-time constraints [Honda+92]

   ▪ Transaction protocols [Stroud+95]

   ▪ Interprocess communication mechanisms [Chiba+93]

   ▪ Exceptional behavior [Eisenhauer+94, Honda+92]

   ▪ Algorithms for application services [Eisenhauer+94]

   ▪ Component implementations [Eisenhauer+94]

One aspect of the persistence component may vary. Its implementation must support application-specific ways of storing and reading objects that contain data members that are not persistent. For simplicity, we have not considered the need for the file handler to support several data formats (such as ASCII, XDR, and binary).

3. *Identify structural information.* Determine which information that is only implicitly available should not affect the application. Examples include the type structure of an application [Buschmann+92], its object model [McAffer95], and component distribution [McAffer95].

In addition, for those aspects identified in this and the previous step, specify what other structural information about the software is needed to support changeability. For example, to change the distribution of components, you need information about their physical location.

Both the persistence component and the file handler should be reusable for all applications that need persistence. We must design and implement them independent of application-specific types. To achieve this goal, we need access to runtime type information: the name, size, inheritance relationships, and internal layout of each type, as well as the types, order, and names of their data members.

4. *Identify system services.* Determine which system services are needed to support both variation of the application services identified in Step 2 and independence from the system details identified in Step 3. For example, to keep the persistence component independent of the application's type structure, you must be able to create new components of arbitrary types. Other examples of basic system services that you may need access to are

- Resource allocation
- Garbage collection
- Page swapping
- Exception handling

In the persistence component example, we must be able to create objects of arbitrary classes. These objects are used to read object structures from an external repository.

5. *Define the boundary between the base level and the meta level.* Separate all services and system aspects that you want to be able to vary, or which the software should be independent of, from the system model developed in Step 1. These will form the meta level of the application. The remaining system model will form the base level.

In our example, the runtime type information as well as the facility for providing variants of the persistence component are part of the meta level. All other parts of the system form its base level.

6. *Specify the meta objects.* For each service and information item provided by the meta level, define appropriate meta objects.

Encapsulating behavior is supported by several domain-independent design patterns, such as Objectifier [Zimmer94], Subject-Policy, Interface-Body, and Abstract Factory. Sometimes you may find appropriate domain-specific patterns that support this step, for example the Acceptor and Connector patterns for developing distributed systems [Schmidt95]. Encapsulating structural information is supported by design patterns like Objectifier and State [Gamma+95].

In our example we encapsulate algorithms that specify how a particular type is read and stored into separate objects. The meta objects that provide type information are organized as follows:

The C++ standard library class `type_info` is used to identify and compare types [Konig/Ed.95]:

```
class type_info {
    // ...
private:
    type_info(const type_info& rhs);
    type_info& operator=(const type_info& rhs);
public:
    virtual        ~type_info();
    int            operator==(const type_info& rhs) const;
    int            operator!=(const type_info& rhs) const;
    int            before(const type_info& rhs) const;
    const char*    name() const;
};
```

The class `ext_type_info` provides access to information about the size, superclasses, and data members of a class:

```
class ext_type_info {
    // ...
public:
    size_t        size() const;
    base_iter*    bases(int direct = 0) const;
    data_iter*    data(int direct = 0) const;
};
```

The class `base_info` offers functions for accessing the `type_info` object about a base class as well as for calculating its offset in the class layout:

```
class base_info {
    // ...
public:
    type_info&      typeOf() const;
    long            offset() const;
};
```

The class `data_info` includes functions that return the name of a data member, its offset, and its associated `type_info` object:

```
class data_info {
    // ...
public:
    const char*        name() const;
    const type_info&   typeOf() const;
    long               offset() const;
};
```

It would certainly be possible to integrate the functions that specify how to store and read a type into the class `type_info`. However, not every user of runtime type information needs persistence, and they should not pay for overhead they do not need.

7. *Specify the meta object protocol.* The MOP should include functions that allow the base level or other clients of the software to

- Inspect information that meta objects provide about the system
- Explicitly invoke the services identified in Step 4
- Get access to behavior encapsulated in meta objects
- Modify existing meta objects or extend the meta level with new meta objects

The MOP should also shield meta objects and the internal structure of the meta level from unauthorized access and modification. Design patterns like Facade [Gamma+95] or Whole-Part will help with this.

With the MOP in our example, standard type information is accessible by two functions:

```
const type_info* get_info() const;
const type_info* find_info(char* type_name) const;
```

The first function allows an object to access type information about itself; the second function allows the object to access type information about an arbitrary type. A third function allows clients to access extended type information:

```
const ext_type_info* get_ext_info() const;
```

All other type information, such as base class information, is accessible through the returned `ext_type_info` object. New objects can be created with the following function:

```
void* new_object(type_info* info) const;
```

The MOP includes two functions for specifying how to store and read particular types:

```
void specify_store(type_info* info,
        char* alg_name, char* members) const;
void specify_read(type_info* info,
        char* alg_name, char* members) const;
```

The `alg_name` parameter allows users to define a name for the algorithm they specify. This supports the persistence component providing several store or read algorithms for the same type. The members parameter is basically a string containing the names of the data members to store or read. Two functions help in selecting a particular store or read algorithm:

```
select_store(type_info* info, char* alg_name) const;
select_read(type_info* info, char* alg_name) const;
```

To secure access to persistent data members, we provide two other functions:

```
data_iter*      store_data(type_info* info) const;
data_iter*      read_data(type_info* info) const;
```

8. *Implement the base level.* Use the MOP to develop a flexible and changeable base level.

   Implementation of the Read and Store methods of the persistence component follows the scenarios depicted in the Dynamics section, with one exception. Like the Store method, the Read method consults the meta level to determine whether there are application-specific ways to read a particular object.

9. *Connect the base level with the meta level.* Specify how the base level and meta level will cooperate. When inspecting the meta level, the MOP may either return meta objects that provide the desired information or retrieve the information from the meta objects and return it to the base level. In the persistence component example, the meta object protocol returns `type_info` meta objects rather than the information they include.

   When the base level consults the meta level to determine a specific behavior, the MOP often needs system information to decide what to do (for example, when selecting a particular algorithm). This information may be passed as a parameter to the MOP, the MOP may retrieve it from other meta objects, or it may retrieve it from an appropriate base-level component. For example, to determine an appropriate type-specific store algorithm for the persistence component, the MOP needs to know what type to store.

If meta objects represent behavioral aspects of base-level components, they should be directly connected with the base level. This allows base-level components to use the services these meta objects provide efficiently, avoiding an additional level of indirection. Otherwise, the meta object protocol must retrieve the appropriate meta object, call the service it provides, and return the results it computes back to the base level. In our example, the meta level directly connects selected type-specific store and read algorithms to the persistence component.

Those functions that can modify behavioral aspects of base-level components need access to their internal structure. An example of such a modification is to change a connection of a base-level component to a meta object representing a particular algorithm implementation. To perform such changes, the MOP either needs direct access to the inner structure of base-level components or the base-level components must provide appropriate configuration functions. The Subject-Policy and Interface-Body patterns will help with implementing such connections. In the persistence component example, we decided to provide the base level with specific configuration functions that are only accessible by the meta level.

We must specify how many base-level components are connected to a particular meta object, and we must distinguish between per-object reflection and groupwide reflection. Per-object reflection means that a meta object is connected to only one base-level component (when representing parts of its behavior, for example). Modifying or exchanging the meta object only affects this one base-level component (for example, when connecting a type-specific store algorithm to the persistence component).

Groupwide reflection means that a meta object is connected to several base-level components (for example, when representing systemwide behavior-modifying objects such as a method-dispatching mechanism). Modifications to this meta object, or its replacement, affect the subsequent behavior of all the base-level components connected to it. The Proxy-Original design pattern (or, for C++ implementations, the Counted-Pointer and Envelope-Letter idioms) helps avoid any need for updating more than one connection when replacing a meta object.

In our persistence component example, every application-specific class is directly connected to its corresponding `type_info` object. This allows objects of that class to access type information about themselves. All other meta-level services and information can be obtained by using the MOP or the meta objects it returns.

10. *Implement the meta object protocol.* Always consider the following aspects [Kiczales92]:

Scope control. When programmers use the MOP to customize a reflective application, they should be given control over the scope of this specialization. Any modification should only affect those parts of the meta level and base level that are the subject of the change. For example, if we replace a meta object encapsulating an algorithm, only this meta object and those base-level components that use it should be affected; other parts of the software should not be.

Conceptual separation. It should be possible to use the MOP without understanding all the functions it offers. For example, functions for modifying method dispatching should be separated from functions for introspecting the type system of the application.

Incrementality. A client should not take total responsibility for integrating changes and extensions to the meta level. Ideally, a client should only specify a change or extension, and the MOP should be responsible for its integration. Incrementality helps us avoid direct manipulation of source code.

For example, suppose you want to add a new sort algorithm to your software. First you must provide its implementation. To integrate it into the meta level, call the appropriate function of the MOP. Implementation of the algorithm as well as information about when to use it are included as parameters. The MOP integrates the change as follows: it generates a class that includes the algorithm's implementation and adds it to the hierarchy with other versions of the sort algorithm. Furthermore, it extends the function that decides what version of the sort algorithm base-level components should use. If the application is a compiled program, the MOP dynamically recompiles all changed parts of the meta level and links them to the running application.

Robustness. Probably the most important considerations when implementing a MOP are safety, reliability, and security.

First, a MOP must be safe. Errors in change specifications should be detected whenever possible. For the sort algorithm from above, we would check, for example, the correct specification of its interface.

Every change or extension to the meta level must be reliable. We need to check, and eventually restore, its consistency with other parts of the meta level. For example, consider a software system in which you can change the distribution of its components. If we reorganize the structure of this system, we must update meta objects containing information about the physical location of their components. We must also change some connections of base-level components to meta objects that specify their communications mechanism, switching them, for example, from a standard message call mechanism to one for remote procedure calls. While restoring consistency, we must also prevent the base level from accessing inconsistent information.

Security means that clients cannot modify the meta level directly—they must use the MOP. This allows the meta level to keep control of changes. Unauthorized access is impossible, especially for clients outside the system. As already mentioned, the Subject-Policy pattern and Interface-Body pattern can help with this.

However, it is not always possible to detect all the errors and inconsistencies that may occur when changing or extending the meta level. Therefore, every modification should have an appropriately limited effect on the rest of the software system. However, the more robust a MOP is, the more restricted is its power.

Implementation of most of the functions of our MOP is straightforward: they just retrieve and return particular meta objects. Implementation of the two functions for specifying how to read and store a particular type require a safety mechanism, however. We need to check whether it is a specified type and whether it includes the specified data members. To perform this check, we use the runtime type information our system provides. We then generate an iterator that allows clients to access all persistent data members in the specified order. An instance of this iterator is returned to clients if they call the `read_data` or `store_data` methods of the MOP. If no application-specific ways of storing and reading a particular type are specified, both functions return an iterator over all data members of the type.

EXAMPLE RESOLVED

In the previous sections we have explained the reflective architecture of our persistence-component example. How we will provide the runtime type information is still an open issue. One solution is to extend the compilation process with a special step. We collect type information from the source files of the application, generate code for instantiating the meta objects providing the type information, and link this code to the application.

VARIANTS

Reflective architecture with several meta levels.

Sometimes meta objects depend on one another. For example, consider the persistence component. Changes to the runtime type of information of a particular type also requires updating the meta objects. To coordinate such changes, you may introduce separate metaobjects, and, conceptually, a meta level for the meta level, (or, in other words, a meta meta level).

In theory this leads to an infinite tower of reflection. A software system has an infinite number of meta levels where each meta level is controlled by an even higher one and where each meta level has its own meta object protocol. However, in practice most existing reflective software comprises only one or two meta levels.

KNOWN USES

CLOS   The classic example of a reflective programming language is CLOS [Keene89]. In CLOS, operations defined for objects are called generic functions, and their processing is called generic function invocation. Generic function invocation is divided into three phases: first, the system determines what methods are applicable to a given invocation; second, it sorts the applicable methods in decreasing-precedence order; finally, the system sequences the execution of the list of applicable methods. Note that in CLOS more than one method can be executed in response to a given invocation.

The whole process of generic function invocation is defined in the CLOS MOP. Basically, it executes a certain sequence of meta-level generic functions. Through the CLOS MOP, users can vary the behavior of an application by modifying these generic functions or the generic functions of the meta objects they call.

MIP   MIP [Buschmann+92] is a runtime type information system for C++. It is mainly used for introspective access to an application's type system. Every type in a C++ software system is represented by a set of meta objects that provide general information about it, its relationships to other types, and its inner structure. All information is accessible at runtime through a MOP. MIP's functionality is separated into four layers:

- The first layer includes information and functionality that allows a program to identify and compare types. It corresponds to the standard runtime type identification facilities for C++ [Stroustrup+92].

- The second layer provides more detailed information about the application's type system. For example, clients can obtain information about classes' inheritance relationships or about their data and function members. This information can be used for implementing type-safe downcasts or for browsing type structures.

- The third layer provides information about the relative addresses of data members and offers functions for creating raw objects of user-defined types. In combination with Layer 2, this layer supports object I/O.

- Layer 4 provides full type information, such as information about friends of a class, protection of data members, or argument and return types of function members. This layer supports, for example, the development of flexible interprocess communications mechanisms or of tools, such as inspectors, that need very detailed information about the type structure of an application.

MIP is implemented as a set of library classes. Furthermore, MIP includes a toolkit to collect type information about an application and generate code for instantiating the corresponding meta objects. This code is linked to the application that uses MIP and is executed at the beginning of the main program. The toolkit can be integrated with the "standard" compilation process for C++ applications. A special interface allows users to scale the available type information for every individual class or type. PGen [Tichy+94] is a persistence component for C++ that is based on MIP. It allows an application to store and read arbitrary C++ object structures.

  The motivating example used to explain the Reflection architectural pattern is mainly based on MIP and PGen.

NEDIS   The car dealer system NEDIS [Eisenhauer+94] uses a reflective architecture to support its adaptation to customer- and country-specific requirements. NEDIS includes a meta level called runtime data dictionary. It provides the following services and system information:

- Default values for attributes of classes used to initialize new objects.

- Properties of certain attributes of classes (for example, their allowed value ranges).

- Functions for checking attribute values against their required properties. NEDIS uses these functions to evaluate user input (for example, to validate a date).

- Functions that specify the behavior of the system in case of user and system errors, such as wrong input or unexpected "null" values of attributes.

- Country-specific functions, such as those needed for tax calculations.

- Information about the specific look and feel of the software, such as the layout of input masks or the language to be used in the user interface.

The runtime data dictionary is implemented as a persistent database. Through a special interface, users can modify all the information and every service it provides. Whenever the runtime data dictionary changes, special tools check and eventually restore its consistency. The runtime data dictionary is loaded when starting the software. For reasons of safety and consistency, it cannot be modified while NEDIS is running.

Further examples of languages and systems that use a reflective architecture include Open C++ [Chiba+93], RbCl [Yonezawa+92], AL-1/D [Okamura+92], R2 [Honda+92], Apertos [Yokote92], and CodA [McAffer95]. Even more examples can be found in Yonezawa and Smith [Yonezawa+92], but note that although they all provide reflective facilities, not all of them really implement a reflective architecture as described by this pattern.

CONSEQUENCES

A reflective architecture supports designing for change. Thus, it helps with resolving many of the forces listed in the Problem section.

- *No explicit modification of source code.* You need not touch the existing code to modify a reflective system. Instead, you specify a change by calling a function of the MOP. When extending the software, you pass the new code to the meta level. The MOP itself is responsible for integrating the change requests: it performs any necessary modifications and extensions to meta-level code and, if necessary, dynamically recompiles the changed parts and links them into the running application.

- *Easy changes.* A reflective application is well prepared for modification. All aspects that can be changed are conceptually separate from those parts that will remain stable. Performing a change is easy—just call the appropriate MOP function.

- *Safe changes.* The reflective architecture opens an application's implementation without breaking its encapsulation. When calling MOP functions, clients need only specify a change. The MOP itself is responsible for its correct execution: it modifies certain meta objects (or their connection with the base level) and thereby modifies the subsequent behavior of the base level. In other words, users do not modify the software explicitly; they do it implicitly by using the MOP. In addition, a well-designed and robust MOP helps prevent undesired changes to the fundamental semantics of an application [Kiczales92].

- *Support for many kinds of changes.* Meta objects can objectify every aspect of a system—its behavior, state, and structure. Thus, a reflective software architecture potentially supports changes of almost any kind or scale (for example, the behavior of the software in case of exceptions [Honda+92], the current or initial state of system components [Eisenhauer+94], and the distribution of objects [McAffer95]).

- *Easy integration of unforeseen changes.* It is possible to address future changes that cannot be predicted today by objectifying general information about the software itself. For example, if a meta level provides information about the components of a system and also about their structural and communications relationships, it is easily possible to change a monolithic software system to a distributed software system.

- *Customization support.* With help of the MOP, it is possible to adapt software to meet specific needs of the environment, such as in RbCl [Ichisugi+92], or to integrate customer- or country-specific requirements, as in NEDIS [Eisenhauer+94].

A reflective architecture also has some significant drawbacks, however:

- *Complex inner structure.* Although a reflective software system eases the handling of complexity from the client's perspective, it is often very complex itself. Parts of the software are distributed over both the base level and the meta level; for example, a component's interface may be located at the base level, while various possible implementations may be located at the meta level. Reflective software also provides a dual interface: the user interface for the base level and the MOP for the meta level. When designing the MOP, you must clearly specify what aspects of the software can be changed and how clients can perform these changes. The correct implementation of the causal connection between the base level and the meta level is very important. Otherwise, you may run into problems keeping the levels coordinated.

- *Possible damage from modifications at the meta level.* You must design the MOP very carefully—its functions allow clients to step into the software and modify it. Even the safest MOP does not prevent users from specifying wrong modifications. These modifications may cause serious damage in the software or its environment. Therefore, a MOP's robustness is of great importance [Kiczales92]. Possible errors in change specifications should be detected before the change is performed. Every change should have only a limited effect on other parts of the software. Designing a robust MOP is difficult.

- *More components.* A reflective software system may include more meta objects than base-level components. The greater the number of aspects encapsulated at the meta level, the more meta objects there are. Group-wide reflection gives only some support to limiting the number of meta objects.

- *Lower efficiency.* Reflective software systems are usually slower than compiled, nonreflective programs. The reason for this is the complex relationship between the base level and the meta level. Whenever the base level cannot decide how to continue with a computation, it consults the meta level for assistance. This reflective capability requires extra computation: information retrieval, changing meta objects, consistency checking, and the communication between the two levels decrease the overall performance of the system. This performance penalty can be only partly reduced by optimization techniques, such as injecting meta-level code directly into the base level when compiling the system.

- *Greater storage overhead.* Reflective programs consume more storage space than nonreflective programs. The greater the number of meta objects, and the more complex the connection between the base level and the meta level, the more storage space the application consumes.

- *Incomplete support.* Although a reflective architecture helps developers design changeable software, it only supports changes that can be performed through the MOP. Thus, not every unforeseen change to an application can be easily implemented (changes and extensions to base-level code, for example, are not supported; see the following item).

- *No support for changes to the base level.* Reflective software supports changes to the meta level only. Modifications to the base level require explicit source code changes, which often cause additional changes to the meta level.

SEE ALSO

The Microkernel pattern supports the development of adaptable and extensible software. It separates the minimal functional core of an application—the microkernel—from its extended functionality and from customer-specific parts. The microkernel also serves as a socket for plugging in these extensions and coordinating their collaboration. Modifications can be made by exchanging these pluggable parts. In addition, the pattern helps in implementing a client-server architecture.

REFERENCES

[Buschmann+92] F. Buschmann, K. Kiefer, F. Paulisch, and M. Stal. "The Meta-Information-Protocol: Run-Time Type Information for C++." In *Proceedings of IMSA*, (1992): pp. 82–87.

[Chiba+93] S. Chiba and T. Masuda. "Designing an Extensible Distributed Language with a Meta-Level Architecture." In *Proceedings of ECOOP '93*, 1993, pp. 482–501.

[Coplien+95] J. O. Coplien and D. C. Schmidt (eds.). *Pattern Languages of Program Design*. Reading, MA: Addison-Wesley, 1995.

[Eisenhauer+94] R. Eisenhauer, S. Kumsta, F. Miralles, K. Mobius, U. Steinmuller, P. Stobbe, and C. Vester. *Architektur-Handbuch für Software-Architekten*. (Internal report, Siemens Nixdorf Informationssysteme AG), 1994.

[Gamma+95] E. Gamma, R. Helm, R. Johnson, and J. Vlissides. *Design Patterns: Elements of Reusable Object-Oriented Software*. Reading, MA: Addison-Wesley, 1995.

[Honda+92] Y. Honda and M. Tokoro. "Soft Real-Time Programming Through Reflection." *Proceedings of IMSA '92*, 1992, pp. 12–23.

[Ichisugi+92] Y. Ichisugi, S. Matsuoka, and A. Yonezawa. "RbCl: A Reflective Object-Oriented Concurrent Language Without a Run-Time Kernel." *Proceedings of IMSA '92*, 1992, pp. 24–35.

[Keene89] S. E. Keene. *Object-Oriented Programming in Common LISP: A Programmer's Guide to CLOS*. Reading, MA: Addison-Wesley, 1989.

[Kiczales92] G. Kiczales. "Towards a New Model of Abstraction in Software Engineering." *Proceedings of IMSA '92*, 1992, pp. 1–11.

[Knischewski94] K. Knischewski. *Funktionales Konzept für Lagerhaltungssysteme*. Siemens AG, Bereich Automatisierungstechnik, 1994.

[Konig/Ed.95] A. Konig (ed.), AT&T Bell Labs. *Programming Language C++*, (ANSI document X3J16/95 0088 WG21/N0688) (draft), 1995.

[McAffer95] J. McAffer. "Meta-Level Programming with CodA." *Proceedings of ECOOP '95*, Nuremberg, Germany, 1995, pp. 190–214.

[Nierstrasz93] O. Nierstrasz (ed.). "Object-Oriented Programming." In *ECOOP '93 Conference Proceedings*. Berlin: Springer-Verlag, 1993.

[Okamura+92] H. Okamura, Y. Ishikawa, and M. Tokoro. "AL-1/D: A Distributed Programming System with a Multi-Model Reflection Framework." *Proceedings of IMSA '92*, 1992, pp. 36–47.

[Olthoff95] W. Olthoff (ed.). "Object-Oriented Programming." In *ECOOP '95 Conference Proceedings*. Berlin: Springer-Verlag, 1995.

[Schmidt95] D. C. Schmidt. "A System of Reusable Design Patterns for Communication Software." In S. P. Berczuk (ed.), *The Theory and Practice of Object Systems*. New York: Wiley, 1995.

[Stroud+95] R. J. Stroud and Z. Wu. "Using Metaobject Protocols to Implement Atomic Data Types." *Proceedings of ECOOP '95*, 1995, pp. 168–189.

[Stroustrup+92] B. Stroustrup and D. Lenkov. *Run-Time Type Identification for C++. (*ANSI C++ standards document No. X3J16/92-0028), 1992.

[Tichy+94] W. F. Tichy, J. Heilig, and F. Newbery Paulisch. *A Generative and Generic Approach to Persistence: C++ Report.* New York: SIGS Publications, 1994.

[Yokote92] Y. Yokote. "The New Mechanism for Object-Oriented System Programming." *Proceedings of IMSA '92*, 1992, pp. 88–93.

[Yonezawa+92] A. Yonezawa and B. C. Smith (eds.). *Proceedings of the International Workshop on New Models for Software Architecture '92 — Reflection and Meta-Level Architecture.* Tokyo, Japan: ACM SIGPLAN, 1992.

[Zimmer94] W. Zimmer. "Relationships Between Design Patterns." in [Coplien+95] pp. 345–364.

Frank Buschmann can be reached at `frank.buschmann@zfe.siemens.de`.

18 Evolution, Architecture, and Metamorphosis

Brian Foote and Joseph Yoder

ABSTRACT

The dominant force driving software development in the 90's is the need to confront rapid change. Software that cannot adapt as requirements change will perish. This paper presents three patterns that address these forces. Software Tectonics shows how continuous evolution can prevent cataclysmic upheaval. Flexible Foundations catalogs the need to construct systems out of stuff that can evolve along with them. Metamorphosis shows how equipping systems with mechanisms that allow them to dynamically manipulate their environments can help them better integrate into these environments.

INTRODUCTION

This paper presents a trio of patterns that had their genesis in an unusual collaboration between the authors. Joseph Yoder is involved in a project investigating new approaches to software development for Caterpillar, one of the world's largest manufacturers of heavy construction equipment and, not incidentally, a major consumer and developer of software. Brian Foote is involved in research on object-oriented reflection and meta-level architectures, an area that has acquired a not altogether undeserved reputation for abstruseness. This collaboration was suggested by Ralph Johnson, who noticed an unusual and interesting connection between the Caterpillar group's goal of getting beyond traditional approaches to software design and some of the little-known findings coming out of the reflection community. This chapter represents an effort to cast these commonalties as patterns.

The primary focus of the chapter is on two patterns that attempt to show how the forces that drive contemporary software development lead to more reflective systems. It is difficult to properly comprehend the forces that give rise to these patterns, however, without setting them in the broader contexts of software reuse and evolution. As a result, this chapter begins, in the Alexandrian tradition, with a high-level pattern, Software Tectonics, pertaining to evolution and reuse. It describes the need to cope with unrelenting change as one of the principal forces driving the software development process, and it shows how this force can be dealt with. The second pattern, Flexible Foundations, attempts to resolve some of the forces unleashed by the first, by showing how to construct systems that can cope with change. The third pattern, Metamorphosis, shows how the need for flexibility is omnipresent and can often only be resolved dynamically. Our hope is that these patterns, taken together, will help the reader perceive how objects, with their continuous, highly iterative life cycles, encourage the emergence of the highly flexible, dynamic structural relationships that are characteristic of reflective architectures. We hope to show as well that these patterns are of genuine utility to real developers and not mere academic curiosities.

It is becoming increasingly clear that software architectures evolve in ways that are distinct from other, more traditional forms of architecture. The evolution of building styles is measured in centuries, or decades at best. The pace of software evolution is increasingly measured in months or even weeks. The ubiquitousness of change is one of the most striking factors that distinguishes software architectures. The possibility of change is one of the things that gives software its power. The need to confront and accommodate it is thus an issue that every software designer must address.

Change pervades the software life cycle. Systems stop evolving only when they are no longer used. Indeed, the most volatile and interesting part of a system's evolution frequently takes place during what was traditionally called the maintenance phase. Brad Cox [Cox86] observed the following about maintenance in 1986: "Software is not at all like wood or steel. Its paint does not chip and it does not rust or rot. Software does not need dusting, waxing, or cleaning. It often does have faults that do need attention, but this is not maintenance, but repair. Repair is fixing something that has been broken by tinkering with it or something that has been broken all along. Conversely, as the environment around software changes, energy must be expended to keep it current. This is not maintenance; holding steady to prevent decline. Evolution is changing to move ahead" (p. 6). Objects support fine-grained, graceful evolution in a way no other technology developed to date does.

This chapter presents examples drawn from the literature and from our experience with the development and evolution of a significant application in an academic/industrial setting. Caterpillar, Inc., joined the National Center for Supercomputing Applications at the University of Illinois as an industrial partner in December 1989. This partnership has spawned various projects, including an evaluation of supercomputers for analysis and the investigation of virtual reality as a design tool. This partnership with the NCSA has provided Caterpillar with a glimpse of an approach to software development that is radically different from traditional approaches. This approach involves rapid development of applications through incremental prototyping and continual evolution.

The most recent Caterpillar project, the Business Modeling project, is a pilot project to demonstrate how an appropriate tool might support financial analysis and business decision-making more effectively. This project aims to provide managers with a tool for making decisions about such aspects of their business as financial decision making, market speculation, exchange rates prediction, engineering process modeling, and manufacturing methodologies. It is very important that this tool be flexible, dynamic, and able to evolve to satisfy changing business needs. Therefore, it must be constructed in a way that facilitates change. It must also be able to coexist and dynamically cope with a variety of other applications, systems, and services.

The style in which these patterns are presented closely follows that used by Alexander in *A Pattern Language* [Alexander+77]. (In particular, this is where the diamond separators came from.)

SOFTWARE TECTONICS

Context   Aliases:

Evolve or Die

Evolution not Revolution

Grow Software, Don't Build It

Perpetual Incremental Development

A variety of forces drive software evolution. The fact that software evolves in response to changing technology and market forces is beyond dispute. However, the granularity at which particular programs evolve can differ tremendously. A large, mature application may change slowly, if at all, only to be replaced by a more nimble successor. In such cases, the extinct application influences the design of its successors only indirectly. At the other extreme, consider the notion that programs should be short, disposable artifacts that can be produced so cheaply they may be run once and thrown away. These too will evolve only to the extent that they influence subsequent programs.

This pattern considers the broad middle ground, wherein software artifacts are durable enough to be cultivated over a long period of time. We believe that this encompasses the quick, disposable type of program mentioned above, since these programs must rely on an infrastructure of relatively high-level, reusable elements.

Problem   Different people and organizations have different needs, and requirements change over time.

As software becomes increasingly complex, it can become more difficult to change. This ossification can become an obstacle to a system's evolving and impede its ability to cope with changing requirements. The inability of the system to adapt to the changing needs of its users can cause strain on the system to accumulate. Eventually, something must give.

It is becoming increasingly clear that the way software evolves today is at odds with the traditional, front-loaded, coarse-grained way of thinking about the process. Successful programs are no longer built from scratch, atop a simple programming language and a small runtime library. Instead they draw heavily from existing code, components, frameworks, and applications. It is no longer enough for programmers to merely learn the language and runtime vocabularies underlying their development tools. Today's programmers must comprehend and comply with a variety of interfaces in order to integrate their work with that of others. These interfaces are frequently *moving targets*.

Successful systems face unrelenting pressure to change. These pressures come from defect repairs, hardware evolution, operating system evolution, market competition, increasing user sophistication, and so on. It is impossible to predict and cope with these forces in a front-loaded fashion; the system must evolve to address these forces.

Traditional waterfall approaches to software development place analysis, design, and implementation early in the life cycle. This is followed by a lengthy maintenance phase. During this phase, a variety of activities occur. Bugs are repaired, and requests to accommodate new hardware or new features are addressed. After a while, a set of patches and enhancements may be bundled together as a new release. The maintenance phase is usually characterized by a gradual erosion of program structure, however. The following passage by Fred Brooks from *The Mythical Man-Month* [Brooks75, pp. 122–123] illustrates this inexorable decline: "All repairs tend to destroy the structure, to increase the entropy and disorder the system. Less and less effort is spent on fixing original design flaws; more and more is spent on fixing flaws introduced by earlier fixes. As time passes, the system becomes less and less well ordered" (pp. 122–123).

Software maintenance, it would seem, is like fixing holes in a failing dike. Eventually it fails and must be rebuilt. Only then can the lessons learned during its tenure be exploited.

For nearly a generation, researchers in a number of quarters have promoted an alternative view of the software life cycle. A number of these views came from researchers in the object-oriented vanguard of the 1970s. One such view is the notion of incremental perpetual development, proposed by Carl Hewitt. "The development of any large system (viewed as a society) having a long and useful life must be viewed as an incremental and evolutionary process. Development begins with specifications, plans, domain dependent knowledge, and scenarios for a large task. Attempts to use this information to create an implementation have the effect of causing revisions: additions, deletions, modifications, specializations, generalizations, etc." [Winston82, p. 462].

Different people and organizations have different needs. One of the most difficult design challenges facing software designers is how to balance the potential for generality with the need to confront a wide range of disparate individual concerns. An all-too-common approach to coping with individual needs is to simply force everyone to adapt to a single way of doing things. However, one size does not fit all. Therefore, it is better to take advantage of the malleability of software, to allow it to be individually tailored to better meet user needs.

Designing a system to meet the needs of a wide range of individuals or organizations can be an overwhelming task. It is better instead to provide a way for individuals to customize their system to meet their specific requirements. Such systems might be said to be "customizable" or "tailorable."

When faced with a system that almost, but not quite, meets one's needs, a customization mechanism can permit that system to be reused. The alternative is to construct an entirely new system. Making a system tailorable can greatly increase its reuse potential.

Tailorability can be useful at any level. Users can customize their desktop and provide shortcuts for common commands. Software architects can tailor existing abstract classes, frameworks, and components to precisely meet their needs. The mechanisms for achieving this can take several forms. A system that can be adapted to meet a designer's needs via simple parameter manipulations might be thought of as an "off-the-rack" solution. In traditional systems, when such a perfect fit is not achieved, the designer might resort to a cut-and-paste job on the original code. This practice, though initially effective (and, alas, still widespread), leads to a proliferation of sloppy, difficult-to-maintain copies of the original code. The proliferation of such expediently borrowed scraps of code has been dubbed *metastasization* [Foote88].

By using objects, designers can tailor existing code without disrupting its integrity. Customizations can be made using user-specific subclasses, via inheritance. This practice, though a great advance over slash-and-burn tactics, is not without its shortcomings. In particular, a good deal of knowledge is needed to use inheritance wisely to subclass existing objects. Johnson and Foote [Johnson+88] call this practice "white-box reuse."

An alternative is to specify the protocol for a component supplied to an existing framework as a *black-box*. The framework then calls the component back when its services are required. This approach has two benefits. First, the interface between the framework and the component is specified in terms of the component's public protocol. The designer need not know the internals of the existing code to design it. Second, any object that adheres to the framework/component protocol may be substituted for any other, even at runtime.

White-box, inheritance-based relationships can have a static, per-class quality, while black-box, component-based relationships can have a dynamic, per-instance character. We have observed that as a system matures, black-box, component-based reuse supplants white-box reuse. Because components are the end product of this evolution, some designers are tempted to design components directly, skipping the evolutionary process. Components designed in this fashion are seldom reusable. Attempting to short-circuit the evolutionary process by designing components most often yields components that resemble first-pass prototypes, *not* the mature, truly reusable components that emerge from an evolving system.

Therefore:

Solution   Give people the ability to tailor their systems to meet their individual needs. Build systems that can adapt to change as user requirements change. Allow systems to change in a series of small, controlled steps, in order to stay the potential upheaval that can result from massive changes that were too-long deferred.

One size does not fit all. Allowing a system to be customized or tailored can broaden its potential applicability and reuse potential. Building it to accommodate evolution can forestall premature obsolescence.

Seismologists have found that if tectonic plates release their energy in a series of small earthquakes, the strain that might have led to a major catastrophe is relieved. So it is with software as well. Systems that are permitted to evolve gracefully, in a series of small, controlled stages, can stay the seismic upheaval that often results from deferring change.

Not all software is built to last, and disposable programs have their place. Simple tutorial prototypes, quick-and-dirty macros, and small, one-shot applications often do not (or cannot) evolve beyond their initial incarnations. But even these require a substantial infrastructure of reusable elements to facilitate their production. This infrastructure is most often the result of the sort of evolutionary process described here.

One way to keep a system flexible is to build it out of flexible materials. This is the idea behind the Flexible Foundations pattern.

In turn, Flexible Foundations encourages *refactoring*, which allows systems to confront and reverse the entropic pressures Brooks warned against [Brooks75]. The fractal model of software design describes a set of evolutionary phases that embody this process. The heart of this process is a consolidation phase in which the system is refactored to better reflect structural insights that have accrued as it evolved. Foote and Opdyke [Foote+94] describe a nascent pattern language that encompasses this process, and the refactorings that drive it. The reader should refer to that paper for information on these and other evolutionary and refactoring patterns that help complete this pattern.

Metamorphosis encourages the construction of systems that retain enough runtime mechanics to allow themselves to be dynamic instruments of their own evolution.

The Business Model project is an excellent example of a system designed from the outset to cope with change. This project focuses on the use of object-oriented technology—specifically, the development of object-oriented frameworks—as a key strategy for reusing code and design.

Why is it inevitable that the requirements placed on this system will evolve, and why is it desirable that it be able to cope with change?

First, Caterpillar is a worldwide enterprise with many different business units and marketing companies. In the mid 1980s, Caterpillar made the bold decision to decentralize and let all its business units function with a certain degree of autonomy. Nonetheless, these units must still share the same tools and databases. Therefore, the business modeling tool must be able to adapt to each unit's needs while remaining compatible with shared, companywide resources. Also, as the business climate changes, the software must be able to keep pace.

To meet these requirements, our tool was developed around an object-oriented framework written in Smalltalk [Goldberg+83]. Smalltalk allowed us to quickly develop working prototypes and get immediate feedback from our users. Since VisualWorks (a Smalltalk environment by ParcPlace) is robust enough for production use, these prototypes were able to gracefully evolve into production applications.

Smalltalk is a pure object-oriented language, chosen for our project because of its extensibility, open architecture, tailorability, and ease of reuse. The use of Smalltalk has led to the development of a financial framework where key components have been reused and integrated into all the financial applications developed for Caterpillar's different business units. The specific needs of the individual business units have been realized by either making "small" changes to this framework or by adding new modules to it.

Systems that cannot cope with change will quickly be left behind by the marketplace. The same is true, of course, of corporations.

FLEXIBLE FOUNDATIONS

Context   Aliases:

Open Architectures

Open Implementations

Getting Under the Hood

Object-Oriented Object-Oriented Systems

Coevolution

Building software with Flexible Foundations helps resolve the need for continual, incremental evolution as described by the Software Tectonics pattern.

❖❖❖

Problem   As systems confront changing requirements, they must change as well. Tools, languages, and frameworks that cannot change along with systems will eventually become impediments to their evolution. Excessively rigid systems can be obstacles to their own evolution. It is not appropriate to expose the same face to every client.

Systems, tools, and languages that cannot evolve can eventually become obstacles to the evolution of the systems that use them.

A good way to open up a system is to selectively expose its internal architecture so that it can serve as a basis for changes and extensions. Note that the focus is on the system substructure, not the source code itself. The architecture is being opened up, not the entire implementation.

The views of a system exposed in this fashion are distinct from the primary public protocol through which the system is normally used. These views can be thought of as ways of "getting under the hood," whenever it's necessary to do so.

For instance, primary tasks (such as variable definition or assignment, for programming languages, and window definition, for window systems), are usually considered base-level rather than meta-level operations. However, facilities that allow either a language or window system to be queried to determine how much memory it is using are usually considered meta-level facilities.

Of course, those charged with shepherding the evolution of such systems should aim to accommodate as wide a range of requirements as possible using the system's public interface. If they are of general interest, modifications made via a system's reflective interfaces may be incorporated into the public interface. Some will be so exotic, mundane, or specific that they will not be appropriate for general exposure, however.

The reflection community's reputation for abstruseness is due in large part to its penchant for producing dense prose and coining exotic new terminology that exalts otherwise mundane, self-referential architectural insights. (*The preceding is a purposely self-referential sentence.*) What we hope to convey here is that a reflective, object-oriented system is simply one that

- Is constructed from parts and tools that are also built from objects
- Has access to the objects that make up these parts and tools

To further clarify this, it is useful to examine some of the criteria that traditionally define reflection. One premise of Smith's early reflection research [Smith83] was that a computational system is *about* something. For instance, an airline reservation system is about passengers, airplanes, arrivals, and departures, and an accounting system is about financial transactions of various sorts. A reflective system is one that has *itself* as its subject mater. The distinction between the model and the medium dissolves.

Maes [Maes87] identified three steps one must take to make a computational system reflective:

1. Build a *self-representation* of the system.
2. Provide a means by which this self-representation may be *manipulated.*
3. Make sure such manipulations really do *immediately affect* the underlying system.

The third requirement enforces the so-called causal connection requirement. A system's self-representation is said to be causally connected to the system itself when any operation performed on this representation is indistinguishable in its effect from one performed directly on the system. In other words, the self-representation should either be the system, or it should be implemented in such a way that it is impossible to tell that it isn't. Systems in which the self-representation actually implements the underlying system are said to be *procedurally reflective* systems. Systems in which this mechanism is less direct are called *declaratively reflective.*

Therefore:

Solution   Give tools, languages, or frameworks the ability to manipulate themselves. To do this, build these elements out of first-class objects.

Another way to think of this is to consider that self-manipulation might be a good test of whether a system's design has the power and flexibility to permit graceful evolution. If the underpinnings of a system are built from well-designed first-class objects, they get this power more or less for free.

When a system and the substrates from which it is built, including its languages and tools, are all built from objects, variants of these substrates can *coevolve* with the system. When the architecture of these elements is open, their potential for reuse is greatly increased. This can help the programmer avoid duplication in cases where the underlying system elements almost, but not quite, meet his or her requirements [Kiczales94].

Providing flexibility of this sort in systems built from traditional, compiled code can be difficult. Where only these sorts of tools are available, the cost of providing a flexible foundation may be prohibitive. Fortunately, modern object-oriented languages and environments provide viable alternatives to these antiquated approaches.

VisualWorks is a powerful object-oriented development environment for graphical, client-server applications. It includes an application framework and visual interface builders to help design graphical user interfaces (GUIs).

Visual interface builders (such as those provided by Smalltalk vendors today) let you quickly outline an interface, as long as it is composed of basic widgets such as buttons, text fields, menus, and scrolling fields. They generate empty methods, which you can fill in later to invoke the desired behaviors. One can also develop more complicated interfaces by grouping these widgets together and adding the appropriate behaviors, constraints, and tie-ins to your databases.

Visual languages like this are an important feature; they allow software developers to be more productive, not only in the early development/prototype stage of code writing but also in the production stage. Primary development of the financial aspects of the Business Model has been directed toward building or extending visual languages for the quick development of financial applications. Most of the code is automatically generated in drawing the interface and by the program's data flow.

The DuPont Model [Johnson+87] is a formulation which embodies the business rules for calculating a profit and loss statement. The results of this formulation are presented graphically as illustrated below. It provides a quick way for managers and accountants to view the return on their assets.

As can be seen from this example, a common interface widget is used many times. By adding a "DuPont widget" to the visual builder with methods for the automatic generation of related code, the developer can quickly tailor different DuPont models to meet the needs of different users.

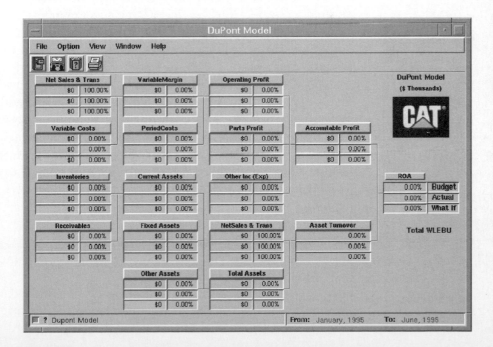

When building a DuPont model, as in the Caterpillar example, there are formulas and database queries associated with each graphical box on the screen. Normally this would require a lot of back-end coding. The developer would first use the VisualWorks Interface Builder to draw in all of the text fields and buttons, and then add in the associated behaviors such as defining all the queries and formulas along with all the associated constraints. If this only needed to be done once, it probably would be advantageous to develop the software this way. However, every business unit was looking at developing a DuPont Model with minor tweaks, including different boxes, constraints, formulas, and database queries. This, along with the fact that the data structure and layout needed to be somewhat different for each business unit, prompted us to extend the VisualWorks Interface Builder framework.

We were able to extend the framework to allow for the reuse of code and easy extension of the DuPont Model by creating another interface widget, like the DuPont box, which has all the fields and associated buttons. The developer could then draw the DuPont boxes quickly on the screen and use the property editor along with the builder's automatic Define method to automatically generate the formulas, the default query methods, and the needed constraints.

Many programming languages have been designed to provide developers with built-in functions, capabilities, and tools that allow quick and accurate development of software. Most often these languages are developed with specific needs in mind. If the software being developed maps easily into the domain of the language being used, then the developer can easily create the desired software. However, most large development projects do not easily map directly into the limited domain provided by the programming language. VisualWorks allows the developer to modify the language to map to different domains.

Since VisualWorks gives developers access to the insides of the visual builder, it opens up the system; thus they can easily add a new interface widget. We usually think of VisualWorks frameworks as the View and ApplicationModel subclasses. But the visual interface builder is itself composed of a set of frameworks that can be extended. These frameworks provide the reflective interfaces that make it possible for the developer to easily extend the visual interface builder. Extending the visual interface builder is often the quickest way to make flexible, powerful software that maps to the domain.

The Smalltalk-80 system is constructed from a set of objects that are themselves subject to modification. The language, framework, and tools with which the system is built all reside in the default system image, and hence they may be changed. These changes are usually done using abstract classes available within the Smalltalk image, thus allowing for a lot of reuse.

METAMORPHOSIS

Context   Aliases:

Changing the Rules

Changing the Performance

Dynamic Schema

Dynamic Object Incorporation

Dynamic Languages

Metainformation

Late Binding

Removing Your Own Appendix

Metamorphosis helps resolve the forces that arise in evolving systems by providing a means of augmenting a system's behavior without changing its primary interface. (These forces are described in the section on the Software Tectonics pattern.) Providing a system with the means to dynamically extend itself also resolves the gradual evolution criteria of that pattern.

Problem   It is difficult for statically compiled applications to manipulate objects that were unknown when the application was compiled. Sometimes it is necessary to augment or change a running system.

A *mutable* system is one in which the behavior of existing system parts can be changed. This is in contrast to an *extensible* system, which allows new elements to be added but does not allow modification of existing parts.

One example of a mutable system is one where extensions to existing tools can be incorporated in the menus for those tools. One does not create new tools; instead, one adds capabilities to existing tools. In order to do this, the tools' menus must be mutable.

A mutable language allows the behavior of existing constructs to be changed. Debugging tools can make use of such facilities. Because of the potential for circularity, programmers must exercise extreme care when they change the way existing language constructs behave. Typical programming environments implement debugging facilities in an ad hoc fashion beneath the language level. Hence, programmers cannot access and augment these facilities.

Consider an analogy drawn from the theater world. There are two ways to change what happens onstage during a play. The most direct way is to change the script. When that is not desirable, there is an alternative: you can change the performers or the nature of their performance. Most readers will, I trust, concede that a performance of *Macbeth* might take on a different character with someone like Jerry Lewis rather than Sir Laurence Olivier in the title role. Similarly, a production of *Macbeth* in a Kabuki style would have a decidedly different character than a traditional production.

What has this to do with software? If one wants to change the way a program works, one can change its code or data directly. Sometimes this is not desirable, however, or even possible. For instance, assumptions about a subsystem's primary interface may pervade the system. When this is the case, one can intervene indirectly, by changing the way some underlying element of the system works.

One layer that underlies every system is the machinery associated with the programming language in which it is written. Were one interested in changing all the formatted I/O in a C program, one could either change every call to `printf` in one's program or provide a new `printf`. Other linguistic facilities are more difficult to modify, however. Languages that do provide full runtime access to such mechanisms are said to be reflective.

This sort of relationship between an application and its substrates is not limited to the language layer. Facilities such as operating system calls, window systems, network services, mathematics libraries, and even other, user-written layers can all have the sort of relationship with an application that makes these kinds of interventions possible. When this is the case (and it is relatively easy to get at these facilities), changing the performance rather than changing the script can be an effective way of solving an otherwise intractable design problem.

Not only must systems provide a way for programmers to get under the hood, they must provide user-serviceable parts as well. What's more, they should ensure that these parts retain their serviceability in the field. For instance, languages without significant meta-level architectures, such as C++, trap objects in binary object files. Once C++ programs are compiled, information pertaining to layout, object and class identity, and the like is usually completely discarded. Some more modern systems have found it useful to retain some of this information in vendor-specific browsing and debugging structures. The growing movement to standardize runtime type information (RTTI) in the C++ community is evidence of a genuine need for meta information. Some of these proposals all but establish what are in effect first-class class objects in C++. This movement is driven not by linguistic purists but by the requirements of real programmers in the field. Programmers are frustrated because they must often build mechanisms to reconstruct information that the compiler knew in the first place but threw away. A good sign that a linguistic facility is necessary is that a number of people have gone to a great deal of trouble to independently invent it. This would seem to be the case with meta information. One can make the case that the extraordinary success of Visual Basic is due in part to the fact that the language is more reflective than C++.

Languages such as Smalltalk-80 and CLOS have what is in some ways the opposite problem. These languages provide fairly complete meta-level architectures, but they usually imprison objects in snapshots or images. For truly *autonomous* objects to break the umbilicals that tie them to single processes and images, the traditional division of responsibilities among system components must be refactored.

Autonomous objects must have access to global namespace services so they can find the objects to which they are tied. Autonomous objects that interact with object bases would benefit from the knowledge that truly first-class objects can glean about their own layouts.

For autonomous objects to function on platforms other than their home platform, code must be bound to them at runtime. Smalltalk, Self, and Java provide code portability by defining code in terms of byte codes for a virtual machine. Dynamic translation of the sort found in Smalltalk-80 [Deutsch+84] and Self [Chambers+89] might be factored into the operating system or provided as a runtime service, so that native code can be made available to any object on demand.

A vital factor in realizing autonomous objects is genuine "first-classness." They require a systemwide object model with a fully realized meta-level architecture, not one based exclusively on v-tables.

A good sign that a given programming language feature is needed is when a lot of people go to a great deal of effort to build it themselves, atop or beside existing languages. There is abundant evidence that first-class, dynamic, meta-level objects are such a feature.

Most programming systems that support GUIs now support mapped, dynamic data structures called *resources*. These are usually cast at about the level of C structs. However, since they are often created and manipulated using resource editing tools, they must usually employ their own conventions for manipulating what is, in effect, meta information. Some realizations add unique symbolic objects that resemble LISP atoms, and powerful, dynamic evaluators to allow runtime resource expressions to be processed. Often, elaborate schemes must be devised to set up runtime correspondences between names for routines in the resource namespace and the same routines as they were known to the compiler and linker. The irony here is that all the facilities that have to be created in an ad hoc, implementation-specific fashion by the architects of these systems are essentially duplicating things that the original programming system knew how to do just as well. In fact, the information the programmer must redundantly re-create for these systems is often information the compiler knew in the first place but compiled away.

For similar reasons, many developers are adding simple, interpreted macro languages to their applications even though these applications are implemented in a more powerful, object-oriented language. The system's architecture puts the object-oriented language out of reach. Building these applications in a more powerful, object-oriented language, one that by virtue of the system's architecture cannot be reused, is hence out of reach.

Consider the difficulty in trying to construct a query for an object in an object-oriented database, using C++, when one has never before encountered the object. The only way to address this issue is to once again construct a dynamic language, with its own meta-level data structures, on top of C++.

The potential for balkanization can be seen in current efforts to define object brokering services and object models. In many respects these seem to be architectural end-runs around the linguistic community. This evasiveness is justified, given the degree to which mainstream language designers have avoided the issues these efforts are trying to address. In the end it will be objects, not languages, that will be the central focus of system design efforts.

Therefore:

Solution   Provide mechanisms for augmenting the behavior of an object or system without changing its fundamental interface or behavior. Systems that allow dynamic access to compilation facilities or late binding of the namespaces in which objects reside can allow foreign objects to be incorporated into running applications at runtime.

When both applications and their substrates are built from objects, they can evolve together as requirements evolve or as specific users present specific needs. When the runtime mechanics of a system are thus accessible, the system can better integrate itself into a changing community of applications and services than can a system that is set in concrete.

Metamorphosis is a powerful technique. However, many conventional systems will place a premium on support for these facilities, if they provide them at all. When support is not provided, it will have to be provided by the user. Therefore, this technique should not be employed cavalierly. When objects can be redesigned in such a way that their layouts are knowable in advance, such a redesign should be considered and weighed against any loss of potential generality. In those cases in which applications simply cannot be given prior knowledge of certain kinds of objects, metamorphosis may be the only viable solution.

❖❖❖

In order to stay competitive, Caterpillar has noticed that it must be able to quickly evolve to new ways of doing business. It needs to be able to make new decisions quickly and change the way it does business according to those decisions. In order to do this, it needs to be able to dynamically choose its variables and business logic and then query from its data sources accordingly.

VisualWorks has provided a framework for creating static SQL database queries. The framework allows the developer to graphically create SQL queries that map to Oracle and Sysbase databases. These queries then get converted into a Smalltalk method that can be called upon when desired. Smalltalk objects can also be passed into the generated methods, and conversions and comparisons are supported by the framework. This framework can also query the database for the data model the developer is interested in and then create objects to map to the desired tables within the database. It is also easy to extend the framework to add undeveloped database functions or extend the mapping to other database vendors.

Basically what happens is that the generated methods are parsed, and SQL code is generated that includes the joins, projections, select-where, group-by, and order-by clauses. The generated SQL code is then packed up and shipped across the network via SQLNET. The returned database values are converted into objects that describe the attributes of each table within the database. These returned values can then be displayed, evaluated, or processed dynamically, just like any Smalltalk object.

A problem arises when one wants to dynamically change or create SQL queries during runtime. Since the SQL framework supplied by ParcPlace only provides pathways to predefined, static queries, we built a framework of SQL query objects that allowed for the creation of dynamic SQL queries through the use of Smalltalk expressions. For example, the experienced Smalltalk programmer might desire to be able to write code very similar to that of **example1**.

```
example1
    "Perform a natural join on Models and ProductFamily,
     projecting model number and family description.
     Then return the values."
    | models productFamily tmpQuery |
    models := TableQuery tableFor: #Models.
    productFamily := TableQuery tableFor: #ProductFamilies.
    tmpQuery := models naturalJoin: productFamily.
    tmpQuery := tmpQuery orderBy: (models fieldFor: 'modelNumber').
    tmpQuery := tmpQuery project:(models fieldFor: 'modelNumber'),
        (productFamily fieldFor: 'familyDescription').
    ^tmpQuery values
```

Also, it might be nice to take a query formed as illustrated above and then "wrap" some new constraints on it, such as "select only those in the above query for the current month." New constraints such as this might be realized only during runtime, however, thus making the static creation of queries insufficient.

Our solution to allowing for the dynamic creation of SQL objects was to define GroupQuery, OrderQuery, ProjectQuery, SelectionQuery, and TableQuery classes, which are all subclasses of the QueryObject abstract class. We also created QueryExpression objects that allow for the developer to build query expressions as in the previous example.

The Query objects know how to respond to the appropriate message to build the queries and wrap constraints to themselves during runtime. The design pattern that fits here is the Interpreter pattern [Gamma+95].

We were able to reuse all of the code from VisualWorks's original framework— parsing a method into SQL, submitting the SQL across the Net, and then creating objects that represent the desired values returned from the database.

Our dynamic SQL framework allows for late binding of constraints to SQL objects, by allowing the developer to build a parser for developing queries and wrap additional constraints to the SQL objects as the application runs.

This example demonstrates the principles of reuse, extension, and modifications. Reuse is accomplished by the simple approach of blindly reusing the framework for generating the SQL code and using SQLNET to get the desired results and populate objects with them. Extensions are based upon the addition of "Query Expression" objects, which allow the developer to write queries in Smalltalk-like expressions. Also, these objects can easily be dynamically extended by wrapping additional constraints before the SQL code is generated. Modifications can be made to the existing framework by adding in behaviors for additional desired SQL functionality, or the framework can be extended by adding database drivers not supported in the default image provided by ParcPlace.

Smalltalk allows dynamic translation of the sort performed in our SQL object example. Our example parses a field of possible queries and simply wraps additional constraints (which the end user can create) around SQL objects that are passed around. The dynamic translation is done through the simple parsing of strings that build SQL objects with the desired constraints and wrap them around the original SQL object.

CONCLUSION

It is no longer possible to avoid the fact that software must be able to rapidly adapt to changing conditions and requirements. Therefore, software developers must find new ways to confront this need for continual evolution. Software can no longer be designed up-front and left to drift as the marketplace passes it by. Nor can it be set in concrete, unable to adapt to the differing needs of different people or organizations. Instead, software must be designed so that it can change *along with* the requirements that drive evolution.

One way to do this is to build software out of objects. Objects can help an evolving system cope with change by confining variants to subclasses using inheritance and promoting the emergence of abstract classes and frameworks. Because objects can be *refactored*, the emergence of new components and better, more reusable frameworks is promoted too. System elements that are themselves objects, such as languages and tools, can evolve along with the applications that use them, rather than presenting obstacles to their evolution.

Today, no application is an island. Today's applications must integrate with a variety of objects, frameworks, services, and databases. Systems that can dynamically access the mechanisms they use to interact with the world can more effectively adapt to their environment.

We were gratified to discover that the cross-pollination of Caterpillar's effort with the heretofore Laputan world of reflection has led to what we think are genuinely useful, practical, and valuable ideas about how to build programs. In patterns we think we've found the ideal medium for capturing and disseminating these ideas.

ACKNOWLEDGMENTS

This collaboration was initiated by Ralph Johnson, who first noted the connection between what Joseph Yoder's group was doing and the often arcane claims of the reflection community. Professor Johnson also provided invaluable insights and observations as the chapter progressed.

We are grateful as well to the members of the University of Illinois Smalltalk Group: John Brant, Michael Chung, and Donald Roberts. We are also grateful to the participants in Professor Johnson's patterns seminar: Eric Scouten, Ron Absher, John McIntosh, Charles Herring, and Mark Kendrat, who soldiered through a particularly rough draft of this chapter and provided a variety of useful commentary and advice.

Desmond D'Souza shepherded our next, still unruly, draft through the PLoP '95 program committee.

Finally, we'd like to express our gratitude to the PLoP '95 Writers' Workshop participants, who with their candid but constructive criticism helped us shape and polish the current incarnations of these patterns.

REFERENCES

[Alexander+77] C. Alexander, S. Ishikawa, and M. Silverstein. *A Pattern Language.* New York: Oxford University Press, 1977.

[Brooks75] F. P. Brooks. *The Mythical Man-Month: Essays on Software Engineering.* Reading, MA: Addison-Wesley, 1975, pp. 122–123.

[Chambers+89] C. Chambers, D. Ungar, and E. Lee. "An Efficient Implementation of SELF, a Dynamically Typed Object-Oriented Language Based on Prototypes." *OOPSLA '89 Proceedings.* New Orleans, LA, October 1–6, 1989, pp. 49–70.

[Cox86] B. Cox. *Object-Oriented Programming: An Evolutionary Approach.* Reading, MA: Addison-Wesley, 1986, p. 6.

[Deutsch+84] L. P. Deutsch and A. M. Schiffman. "Efficient Implementation of the Smalltalk-80 System." *Proceedings of the Tenth Annual ACM Symposium on Principles of Programming Languages,* 1984, pp. 297–302.

[Foote88] B. Foote. *Designing to Facilitate Change with Object-Oriented Frameworks.* Unpublished master's thesis, University of Illinois at Urbana-Champaign, 1988.

[Foote+95] B. Foote and W. F. Opdyke. "Lifecycle and Refactoring Patterns That Support Evolution and Reuse." In J. O. Coplien and D. C. Schmidt (eds.), *Pattern Languages of Program Design.* Reading, MA: Addison-Wesley, 1995, pp. 239–258.

[Gamma+95] E. Gamma, R. Helm, R. Johnson, and J. Vlissides. *Design Patterns: Elements of Reusable Object-Oriented Software.* Reading, MA: Addison-Wesley, 1995.

[Goldberg+83] A. Goldberg and D. Robson. *Smalltalk-80: The Language and Its Implementation.* Reading, MA: Addison-Wesley, 1983.

[Johnson+87] H. T. Johnson and R. S. Kaplan. *Relevance Lost: The Rise and Fall of Management Accounting.* Boston: Harvard Business School Press, 1987.

[Johnson+88] R. E. Johnson and B. Foote. "Designing Reusable Classes." *Journal of Object-Oriented Programming,* 1(2) (1988): 22–35.

[Kiczales94] G. Kiczales. "Why Are Black Boxes So Hard to Reuse? (Towards a New Model of Abstraction in the Engineering of Software)." *ACM SIGPLAN Notices,* 29(10) (1994).

[Maes87] P. Maes. *Computational Reflection.* (Technical Report No. 87-2.) Brussels, Belgium: Vrije University, Artificial Intelligence Laboratory, 1987.

[Smith83] B. C. Smith. "Reflection and Semantics in LISP." *Proceedings of the 1984 ACM Principles of Programming Languages Conference,* 1983, pp. 23–35.

[Winston82] P. H. Winston and R. H. Brown. Artificial Intelligence: An MIT Perspective, 2nd ed. Cambridge, MA: MIT Press, 1982, pp. 433–465.

Brian Foote can be reached at `foote@cs.uiuc.edu`. Joseph Yoder can be reached at `yoder@cs.uiuc.edu`.

PROCESS AND ORGANIZATION

PART 5

Patterns first made inroads in the software community as a tool of program structure. Process and organization patterns made a strong showing as misfit patterns at PLoP '94 [Coplien+95]. This volume breaks new ground as well, particularly with the Exposition patterns of Part 6, but the process and organization patterns are back in force. Part 5 collects the patterns that focus explicitly on process and organization, but it permeates other sections as well (see, for example, Steven Berczuk's Organizational Multiplexing in Chapter 12). This genre appears to have staying power.

This is a result both of an increased awareness of the importance of organizational issues in software development, and of the surprising acceptance of such patterns in the pattern community. Perhaps we should not be so surprised, given the pattern community's Alexandrian legacy of balancing human forces.

Even though organizational and process patterns are enjoying exposition in the pattern form only in recent years, such patterns have ageless roots. Cultural anthropologists have consciously studied such patterns, and called them such, for at least half a century. As the pattern form maps out timeless patterns, it also explores the fine points to apply these patterns to the native environment of the contemporary pattern community, *viz.*, the culture of software development. Software development has its own social mores, structures, ceremonies, practices, and language that reach beyond the studies of classic cultural anthropology. And it has its own subcultures: small teams, legacy organizations, entrepreneurial organizations—each emerges from its own pattern languages.

One might think there is an infinite variety of such organizational patterns to mine and catalog, given all this diversity. Yet even the modest profusion of organization patterns of the past two years has pushed them onto common ground. Neil Harrison's Diversity of Membership (Chapter 21) and Allen Hopley's Executable Models (Chapter 20) tweak Prototype patterns that were mapped out at PLoP '94 (see also Todd Coram's Demo Prep pattern language in Chapter 25). This suggests either that there may be a relatively small number of interesting patterns in this area—a phenomenon we're starting to notice in object-oriented design patterns as well—or just that everyone likes to write patterns about the same problems, because the problems themselves are interesting. But the overall shape of the organizational pattern language fabric is starting to appear, both in the recurring themes among these patterns and through the citations to the existing body of pattern literature by the majority of these chapters.

Alistair Cockburn's chapter "Prioritizing Forces in Software Design" (Chapter 19), explores a new pattern form called *principle patterns*. Principle patterns present common software problems and their forces, accompanied by an almost stereotypical, pat solution. But the pat solution is just another force, and a principle pattern shows the forces that are too often left unbalanced by pat solutions. The form serves well to gore sacred cows, to help designers *think* about the principles they hold dear. Having set the stage, a principle pattern segues into a conventional pattern form whose solutions are controversial, but which can be justified by the forces exposed in the preceding principle pattern. Alistair uses the form to present patterns that weave staff considerations with the structure of the architecture. This concern for the people issues, and the deep, indirect nature of the solutions, recalls quintessential Alexandrian principles of human comfort and generativity.

Allen Hopley's pattern language on Decision Deferral and Capture (Chapter 20) looks at fundamental patterns of software modeling, drawing from experience with what the author believes to be the largest object-oriented project in the world, at this writing. Rather than falling into the trap of answering the question "What is a model?", Allen's patterns lay down principles applicable to a wide variety of modeling techniques. The patterns solve problems of traceability, granularity, consistency and correctness (which is where prototyping comes in), and change propagation. The pattern language originally bore methodological ornamentation, but Allen found the methodological principles similar enough to a published work that he could factor them out.

Martin Fowler's chapter, "Accountability and Organization Structures" (Chapter 22), guides how we capture the structure of a human organization: the construction of organization architecture models, if you will. Martin maps OO modeling constructs to institutional organization structure, drawing on experience with the United Kingdom's National Health System as an example. Each pattern captures increasingly complex structure, starting with an abstraction that unifies individuals and groups, going through multiple interleaved hierarchies, into reification of relationships ("Accountability Abstraction") and state-dependent type information reminiscent of the GOF State pattern [Gamma+95] in the programming domain. While we traditionally ascribe deep hierarchies to legacy organizations (as we might expect applies in Martin's example), we find that even legacy structures contain amazingly complex structures—patterns—such as multiple interlaced hierarchies and layers.

These patterns address the general context of software development organizations. Two of the chapters solve problems in more specific contexts: software development teams, and entrepreneurial development organizations. Neil Harrison looks at self-selecting teams, the small communities of interest that arise as instrumental organizations in software development projects of all sizes. Not every company, department, or group is a true *team* in spite of the apparent universal appeal of the term. Teams are bound by "Unity of Purpose," and work best when Neil's pattern's are present. This is a wonderful pattern language, small enough to get your mind around, yet rich in links to the existing body of organizational and process patterns.

Ward Cunningham's EPISODES pattern language (Chapter 23) relates his experience as a member and observer of entrepreneurial organizations. He presents 16 patterns of a pattern language that will eventually comprise about 40 patterns. Perhaps most interesting about this pattern language is its organization and "taxonomy." Ward splits the patterns into three subsections: product, development, and programming. (A fourth task, operations, foresees problems not yet captured here in pattern form.) He also maps the patterns—all 40 of them—in a two-dimensinsal space delineated by "Tasks" and "Agents." This classic taxonomy is appealing and powerful; it makes it clear how the patterns relate, and it makes it clear that these patterns form a language.

Like Alistair's patterns, Neil's patterns and Ward's patterns elevate our awareness of the emotive and sociological human forces that overshadow most activities of software development. Allen's patterns add a more traditional process perspective of what-gets-considered-when, and Martin's patterns bring new dimensions to traditional flat-earth model organization charts. Even this small sample of patterns serves to illustrate the richness of perspectives and complexity of managing human endeavors. Perhaps we'll see these patterns converge over the years, or perhaps we'll learn which patterns solve the most important problems. In the meantime, all these patterns serve to put our technical patterns in the larger perspective of the human context they were meant to serve. Remember these patterns as you work through the other chapters.

REFERENCES

[Coplien+95] J. Coplien and D. Schmidt, (eds.). *Pattern Languages of Program Design*. Reading, MA: Addison-Wesley, 1995.

[Gamma+95] E. Gamma, R. Helm, R. Johnson, and J. Vlissides. *Design Patterns: Elements of Reusable Object-Oriented Software*. Reading, MA: Addison-Wesley, 1995.

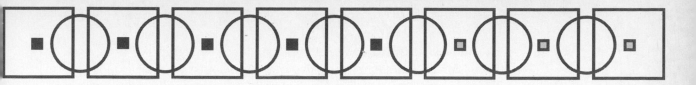

19

Prioritizing Forces
in Software Design

Alistair Cockburn

INTRODUCTION

The purpose of this chapter is to describe a new pattern form that highlights
the competition between different principles of software design. It presents
13 patterns: 5 are prioritized design principles, and 8 are design decisions
derived from them. Some of the patterns are new, some are old; the old ones
are included to demonstrate how they fit into the larger context.

A design principle captures past experience. It quickly reduces the design
space and eliminates unsuitable ideas. It acts as a force on a design, and it
has a counterforce that limits its value. Despite the existence of these forces,
the consequences of a design principle are rarely obvious. Nor are design
principles remembered and followed as time and design projects move on.
The result of such forgetfulness is a system that becomes slowly more
complicated over time. An example is the idea of separating the application
model from the user interface, a well-known design principle that is seldom

fully followed. It is treated in Pattern 3 (Application Boundary), along with a discussion of some nonobvious design decisions that it drives.

Principles compete, and thus they must be prioritized. This prioritization is as subjective as the initial selection of principles. Since you will undoubtedly disagree with some of the priorities, principles, or decisions of your colleagues, you should be able to tell how far back to go in making a change. You should see your point of divergence and its implications. The pattern form tries to make this more explicit.

A "pattern" is a shape of forces with a resolution, a shape found in many projects. A "principle," which is itself a kind of pattern, reacts to forces by adding two other forces (itself and its counter). A "design decision" is also a pattern, but one that simply reacts to forces without creating new forces. Given the differences between them, I label and present patterns, principles, and design decisions slightly differently.

Principles are described as follows:

Intent: The intended benefit from the pattern
Force: An external force acting on the project or design
Principle: A new driving force, from a freely chosen principle
Counterforce: A counter and limiting force against the principle's force

The design decisions are given in the "standard" form:

Intent: The pattern's intended benefit
Context: The situation in which the decision takes place
Forces: What is pulling the designer in various directions
Resolution: A suitable means of dealing with these forces in this context

Figure 1 shows the principles in priority order. Figure 2 shows the design decisions that come from them. Note that decision 2.1 was based on principles 2 and 4, so clearly not every decision is tied to just one principle.

The design task used for the example is an object-oriented (OO) client workstation connected to a relational database server. I started by applying New Clients with Old Servers, a pattern language for client-server frameworks

FIGURE 1 The five principles and their relationships

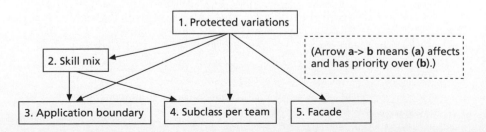

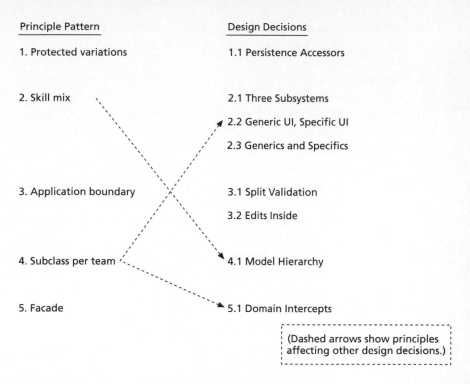

Principle Pattern

1. Protected variations

2. Skill mix

3. Application boundary

4. Subclass per team

5. Facade

Design Decisions

1.1 Persistence Accessors

2.1 Three Subsystems

2.2 Generic UI, Specific UI

2.3 Generics and Specifics

3.1 Split Validation

3.2 Edits Inside

4.1 Model Hierarchy

5.1 Domain Intercepts

(Dashed arrows show principles affecting other design decisions.)

FIGURE 2   The five principles and eight design decisions

[Wolf+95]. I found that it presupposed the use of a software architecture that one might not have. I also found myself more concerned with managing competing principles to settle design questions than with determining the (also important) usage dependencies of the design patterns. Thus I present here my experience as it showed itself—as principles competing for attention. The principles are those of technical OO design plus those of team organization, all competing for effect on the software architecture.

PATTERN 1: PROTECTED VARIATIONS

Intent   This pattern protects system integrity across changes.

Force   Requirements change.

Principle   Identify points of predicted variation; create a stable interface around them.

Counterforce   Too many points of variation create excessive complexity and performance loss due to intermediary handoffs.

Precursor Patterns   None.

Discussion   When a design provides a natural place to make a change, the change requires less learning and does less damage to the system. This principle is so well ingrained in good designers' minds that they scarcely recognize its existence. It is behind the notions of encapsulation (Parnas's papers in the mid 1970s) and object-oriented design. The reason for mentioning it is that it drives the rest of the patterns here and is responsible for a controversial decision (1.1, Persistence Accessors). To disagree with this decision, the designer must rework this pattern of forces.

Designers sometimes try to anticipate all variations, thereby producing excess code that slows down the software but never really gets used. Often, needed protection is not included or is considered too expensive and is thus not implemented (a common example is a project that is given domain components that use a different persistence layer interface and hence cannot be used).

Most patterns are based on protected variations, so this is a root pattern. Two examples are Application Boundary (Pattern 3) and Bridge [Cunningham95].

Pattern 1.1: Persistence Accessors

Intent   This pattern lets designers defer (or change) decisions about how instance data are stored and accessed, without overregulating the developers.

Context   You are designing OO software-accessing server data. The persistence infrastructure is considered likely to change its interface. Some processing is required on each data read/write (for persistence, is the data in memory yet? for transactions, is the instance variable getting a new value? for identity management, do two instance variables point to same object?). There is controversy, however, over whether instance variable accessor methods are good or bad.

Forces   Accessor methods are good, because they provide a constant interface should the data access technique change. Accessor methods are also bad, however, because they slow the software and add complexity to the object's interface. Using accessor methods for every instance variable is good, because it makes the code uniform and hence easier to read and modify (an example of the consistency principle). Using accessor methods for every instance variable is also bad, however, because it exposes more of an object's inside than may be desirable (an example of the abstraction principle). In other words, accessor methods are controversial: some people swear by them, and others swear at them.

Resolution   Require "persistence accessor methods," getters and setters for the persistent instance variables of persistent objects. These are the property of the infrastructure, not the domain designers, and may thus be regenerated at any time. Access to other instance variables is considered a "local matter" by each design group.

Discussion   The infrastructure team decides whether a domain object's persistent data is held by the domain object or by another object on its behalf (using one of the two designs discussed below). The choice is likely to change during the project. Without accessors, all client access to persistent data will have to be modified when the choice changes.

Under these circumstances, the "Protected Variations" principle outweighs any personal preferences regarding accessors *for persistent instance variables of persistent classes*. By this rule, they may be regenerated, in any form, anytime the persistence design changes—without impact to client calls. For other instance variables, no hard-and-fast rule applies: a UI and domain team may decide consistency is important and thus always use accessors; an infrastructure team may feel that abstraction is important and thus decide against accessors.

The example used to generate the tight wording on the resolution was that of an OO client—getting data from an intermediate, relational data server—that talked to a back-end database. The workstation infrastructure software was considered likely to change. The role of the intermediate system was also in question: either it would not change (variation 1), object creation and transactions would be put onto the server (variation 2), it would be replaced with an OO database (variation 3), or it would be removed entirely (variation 4).

The infrastructure was considered likely to change, as noted above. One nominated design, called Records, removes instance data from the domain class and puts it under the control of a Record object (see Objects from Records [Wolf+95]). The Record object holds both the raw (relational) database record and the object data values. It optimizes materialization, conversion, and update, always knowing what has been touched or changed. The Records pattern requires the Persistence Accessors design decision. It handles variations 1 and 4 well, but not 2 and 3.

An alternative design, which works for all variations, leaves the instance data in the domain object. It puts the accessors within the persistence layer, where it notices every time an instance variable is read or set and controls materialization and transaction rollback. This also relies on Persistence Accessors (as well as Three Subsystems [Pattern 2.1] and Model Hierarchy [Pattern 4.1]).

The point to be made is that Patterns 1 and 1.1 do not force one of these designs but permit either, according to the perceived likelihood of change and the designer's preference. The purpose of Pattern 1 is to protect our ability to defcr or alter design decisions; the decision to use it is paying off.

PATTERN 2: SKILL MIX

Intent   This pattern protects system development against the effects of shifting staff.

Force   People have differing skills and specialties.

Principle   Separate subsystems by staff skill requirements.

Counterforce   Having too many subsystems increases the number of interfaces and handoffs, thereby making the system slower and harder to understand.

Precursor Pattern   Pattern 1 (Protected Variations).

Discussion   On a small enough project, the few people involved may have multiple skills that enable them to mix UI design with infrastructure design and domain design. Unhappily, their successors may not; this makes system evolution more difficult and costly. On larger projects, the many people are more likely to have specialized skills. If their code is intermingled, two expensive difficulties appear: getting the different people to understand one another and come to common decisions, and dealing with the same system evolution difficulty as appears in the smaller system. Separating their specialties into different subsystems

- Lets them work with their special issues in their special vocabulary
- Lets their successors see those issues in isolation
- Makes the project easier to staff, since the staff need not be so multi-disciplinary.

Skill Mix depends upon Pattern 1, Protected Variations. The variation protected is that in staff skills over time. This may be the basis for Conway's Law [Conway95], which states that a system's design consists of copies of its communication structures. (This is also recorded in Organization Follows Architecture [Coplien95], albeit within a larger context of forces.)

Pattern 2.1: Three Subsystems

Intent This pattern allows specialization of skills and skill levels in three areas: application domain, UI, and computer science.

Context You are developing workstation application software for which all parts of the system above the operating system will have to operate for the next 6 to 12 years.

Forces Infrastructure frameworks are difficult to create but not so hard to use. Domain classes are easier, but they require knowledge of the company's operation. UI design wants human factors and good programming skills. It is hard to get people with this combination of attributes.

Resolution Create three subsystems: the infrastructure, the UI, and the application domain. This way, the UI people can concentrate on human factors and UI programming; the application domain people can concentrate on application requirements, data needs, and model object behavior; and the infrastructure people can concentrate on system structure.

Discussion This is a straightforward application of Pattern 2 (Skill Mix) to the situation at hand. The infrastructure team will consist of the computer scientists; relative novices and domain experts can be put on the domain subsystem; and the UI people will have to know either human factors, programming, or both. The fortunate part is that the skills fall into groups that make suitable technical boundaries.

Pattern 2.2: Generic UI, Specific UI

Intent This pattern allows the designer to make use of different skill levels in UI programming.

Context It allows context design of OO code for the user interface (UI), using a mix of novices and experts.

Forces A large percentage of novices must be used; using novices everywhere is bad (results in weak designs, cut-and-pasted code).

Resolution Create two class layers and teams in the UI subsystem: the generic and the specific. Let the generic UI people *create* frameworks, and let the specific UI people *use* them. Use only highly skilled programmers or designers for the generic classes, and allow novice programmers or designers to work on only the specific classes.

Discussion Within UI programming work, there are expert programmers who can construct new UI widgets and UI frameworks and novice programmers who put them together with the domain classes. The issues they face are quite different. Using the pattern Skill Mix, the UI widget/framework group is separated from the UI specifics group. Pattern 2.2 also uses Pattern 4, Subclass Per Team, to keep the work and issues separate. The UI frameworks group makes generic superclasses, and the UI specifics group subclasses those generic superclasses.

Pattern 2.3: Generics and Specifics

Intent This pattern allows the designer to make use of different skill levels in OO programming.

Context You are working on the design of an OO system, using a mix of novices and experts.

Forces A large percentage of novices must be used; using novices everywhere is bad (results in weak designs, cut-and-pasted code).

Resolution In general, separate the generic from the specific parts of problems. Use an expert framework designer to design the generic parts, and let the novice programmers design the specific parts.

Discussion This is applicable to any technology that lends itself to plug-in frameworks. OO programming is one such technology, as it uses inheritance and polymorphism.

Such separation of subsystems can go on indefinitely, down to the work of one person or even the parts of a single person's work. In fact, this is what led to encapsulation (and, by extension, OO programming) in the first place! When, then, does the counterforce enter into the picture? In the sense of objects, it may never. In the sense of groups of people communicating to other groups of people, the number of interfaces between the groups forces more talking, writing, and meetings, eventually driving the cost of development up. In the sense of program communication, calls across interfaces consume time, eventually slowing system performance. This is perhaps the only thing that prevents each person from being assigned his or her own level in the inheritance hierarchy.

PATTERN 3: APPLICATION BOUNDARY

Intent   This pattern protects system integrity against changing external components.

Force   User interface requirements are notorious for changing.

Principle   Define the user interface to be outside the application proper. Make all functions of the application accessible through a program-driven interface.

Counter   It is easier on the user if input errors are brought up directly upon entry. The principle separates the input from error detection.

Precursor Principles   Patterns 1 (Protected Variations) and 2 (Skill Mix).

Discussion   First the UI will change. Then electronic interchange or another application should drive the application, not using the human interface. What is really "the application"? Where is the scratch copy of a domain object kept: in the domain or the UI? Is that inside or outside "the application"? Is input validation done within or without?

To address these questions, determine the services of the application. Create a program-driven (not human-driven) interface, on the assumption that one day the application will be driven by a computer system. The UI is one of several drivers. All functions of the application must be accessible to the driving system (that is the sticky part).

This pattern is a double application of Protected Variations. The volatile UI was isolated as a subsystem in Three Subsystems (Pattern 2.1); it is now put outside the application boundary, since the very notion of a human driver means the driver is likely to change. Sufficiently experienced designers know this; less-experienced designers keep trying to avoid it. This is essentially the Model-View-Controller pattern, cast so that its less-than-obvious ramifications become clearer. It has significant consequences, particularly for input validation and searching.

Two examples of this pattern in use are the AppleScript interface and the Model-View-Controller framework. Many other examples are around.

Pattern 3.1: Split Validation

Intent   This pattern allows the designer to take advantage of GUI generators without violating the Application Boundary pattern.

Context   This is not "heads-down" data entry, so time can be taken for data validation. Is input validation performed before the application is called, or is it performed by the application itself?

Forces   Validation should not be performed at the UI (according to the Application Boundary pattern, values may come from any source). Keystroke validation should be performed in the UI, as it is efficiently generated by the GUI generator (and costly if hand-coded).

Resolution   Entry validation is performed in two stages. Keystroke validation is performed in the UI, and value validation is performed within the application. The application boundary provides a way to pass information about the error out to the driver program.

Discussion   The user types an incorrect value into an entry field. One design possibility (to be rejected) is to place the validation rules at the point of input, in the user interface. That violates Application Boundary, though it satisfies the counterforce (getting feedback to the user directly). So value validation must be performed within the "application proper." So far, so good.

A driving program sends complete parameters, not individual keystrokes. GUI generators generate good keystroke validation code, enforcing input field length and character type. So Keystroke validation can be done in the UI, outside the application.

Split Validation is more completely described by Ward Cunningham in the CHECKS pattern language [Cunningham95].

Pattern 3.2: Edits Inside

Intent   This patterns makes driving the application from other platforms easier.

Context   The user can cancel a transaction after making changes but before committing. The efficacy of this action depends upon where the editing copy of the domain object is kept.

Forces   If the editing copy of a domain object is kept in the UI, then it is local, disposable, and will not disrupt other objects. If it is kept in the application proper, it is usable by other application drivers. If it is kept in the persistence layer, it is right at the database cache. None of these options are viable, however; it should be just a shallow copy of the domain object, so it cannot tamper with persistence issues.

Resolution   The editing copy of a persistent domain object resides inside the application, not in the user interface.

Discussion   The user starts working with an object from the database, alters it, then decides against the change and cancels it. To allow this change of heart, there must be two copies of the object: the safe and the editing copy.

There are several ways to arrange these two copies: put the editing copy in the UI and the safe copy inside the application somewhere; put the editing copy in the domain layer and the safe copy in the domain or persistence layer; put both in the persistence layer.

The Application Boundary pattern requires us to consider the application as being driven by a batch job, electronic data interchange, or other external subsystem. These cannot be expected to cache an editing copy of a domain object. The first choice above is therefore ruled out, and the editing copy must be kept inside the application. Canceling a partial change to that object is done by a request to the application. The remaining choices are available for later design decisions, as permitted by the Protected Variations pattern.

PATTERN 4: SUBCLASS PER TEAM

Intent   Give teams a private design space to work on their issues; protect system integrity against having unrelated issues colocated.

Force   Your development teams have differing interests and need to optimize differently.

Principle   When design needs coincide for the same class, assign people working on different subsystems to work on different layers of the class hierarchy.

Counterforce   Excessive levels of inheritance makes the system slower and harder to understand.

Precursor Principles   Patterns 1 (Protected Variations) and 2 (Skill Mix).

Discussion   This principle is selected when Skill Mix runs into changing requirements. The input-validation, persistence, and domain subsystems all intersect at the domain class. Mixing all three in the same class runs counter to Protected Variations, since a change in one causes potential damage to all three.

Ideally, the description of the application's business behavior should be independent of the particular persistence mechanism used so that the persistence mechanism can be changed without damaging the business behavior. The person who best knows the behavior of the business objects (as a result of his or her job description and expertise) is not likely the person who knows about persistence mechanisms, and vice versa.

The three teams will be making changes to their interfaces and implementations concurrently. Since they have different interests, they are likely to have different ideas about what is "best." If the subsystems are put into one level, fights between the groups are likely. Introducing two or even three layers of subclassing allows the three groups to hone their designs with minimal impact upon one another (see Pattern 4.1, Model Hierarchy).

This principle would make a wonderful, universal argument-mediation technique, except that addition of a new level of subclassing for every disagreement might produce a system that is difficult to understand (i.e., the counterforce).

Pattern 4.1: Model Hierarchy

Intent   This pattern provides the primary subsystem teams with separate design spaces.

Context   You are working on OO client design and developing domain objects that need persistence services.

Forces   Validation, domain, and persistence are three parts of any persistent domain object. They are being designed by different teams, per Skill Mix.

Resolution   The class hierarchy for persistent domain classes consists of Model, to contain the common domain issues; ValidatedModel, to contain the validation issues; and PersistentModel, to contain the persistence issues. Model and ValidatedModel may be merged or broken apart, depending on the design. Different people may be responsible for each.

Discussion   As in the Subclass Per Team discussion, ValidatedModel may be a separate layer, using Pattern 2.3, Generics and Specifics; and 3.1, Edits Inside. On some projects there may not be enough left in Model to warrant one extra layer. An example of keeping Model separate is ParcPlace's ObjectWorks class hierarchy.

PATTERN 5: FACADE

Intent   This pattern protects developers against massive rework due to an interface change. It also provides a unified interface to a set of interfaces.

Force   Tracking down every call to an interface that is being changed is a time-consuming and error-prone process.

Principle   Provide a single point of call to volatile interfaces.

Counterforce   Excessive call levels make the system slower and harder to understand.

Precursor Pattern   Pattern 1 (Protected Variations).

Discussion   This pattern is exactly the same as the Facade pattern presented by Gamma and his colleagues [Gamma+95]. It is included here to show how it fits into the larger context of forces and because it drives Pattern 5.1, Domain Intercepts. It is a direct consequence of Pattern 1, Protected Variations.

   If the thing that will vary is an interface, then there must be an interface to that interface. However, the counterforces of Patterns 1 and 5 demand minimizing the number of times an interface to an interface is created.

Pattern 5.1: Domain Intercepts

Intent   This pattern protects developers against massive rework due to persistence-layer interface changes.

Context   You are working on an OO client-server design with persistent domain objects. The UI needs to communicate with the persistence mechanism. The persistence mechanism is considered likely to change its interface.

Forces   The UI objects should talk with the persistence mechanism directly so the software runs faster and it is easier to read the program. Only domain objects should talk with the persistence mechanism, because the interface to the persistence mechanism might change.

Resolution The UI never calls the persistence subsystem directly. Instead, it makes its call to a domain object, whose superclass provides a single point of implementation for the service.

Discussion The user indicates when a domain object has been updated and is ready to be stored. The user interface may either store the object away directly, tell the persistence layer to store the object, or tell the domain layer, which will tell the persistence layer to store the object.

Protected Variations eliminates the first choice, since the persistence layer is likely to change. Pattern 4.1, Model Hierarchy, establishes that there need only be one place, PersistentModel, that is sensitive to the persistence interface. The primary forces acting on the design are performance degradation due to forwarding (versus difficulty of change if forwarding is not done). The context defines risk of change as high, so Facade is used to select the third choice.

This design decision is valid in a fairly narrow context. If the persistence mechanism were considered highly stable, the decision would be reexamined.

EVALUATION OF THE FORM

The "standard" form of this pattern language—building a pattern by identifying an external force, selecting a principle to respond to it, finding the principle's counterforce, and prioritizing the set—seems to work for the high-level patterns in which new forces are created. Prioritizing the patterns helps designers who wish to vary either the principles or priorities, and it certainly helps with the design decisions. The form was also useful in putting existing material (Conway's Law, MVC, Facade, Split Validation) into a larger context. This is needed as the number of patterns grows.

The new form did not appear to be better in describing design decisions (which is why it was not used). A design decision is made by examining a given set of forces and making a personal choice, rather than by introducing a new principle. The experiment with the new form gave me added confidence in the usefulness of the standard form (Intent, Context, Forces, Resolution) for expressing design decisions. The prioritization of the principles did help sequence the design decisions so that it was clear which ones were locked at any moment and which could be varied.

REFERENCES

[Conway95] M. E. Conway. "How Do Committees Invent?" *Datamation, 14*(4) (1995):28–31.

[Coplien95] J. O. Coplien. "A Generative Development-Process Pattern Language." In J. O. Coplien and D. C. Schmidt (eds.), *Pattern Languages of Program Design.* Reading, MA: Addison-Wesley, 1995, pp. 183–239.

[Cunningham95] W. Cunningham. "The CHECKS Pattern Language of Information Integrity." In J. O. Coplien and D. C. Schmidt (eds.), *Pattern Languages of Program Design.* Reading, MA: Addison-Wesley, 1995, pp. 145–155.

[Gamma+95] E. Gamma, R. Helm, R. Johnson, and J. Vlissides. *Design Patterns: Elements of Reusable Object-Oriented Software.* Reading, MA: Addison-Wesley, 1995.

[Wolf+95] K. Wolf and C. Liu. "New Clients with Old Servers: A Pattern Language for Client/Server Frameworks." In J. O. Coplien and D. C. Schmidt (eds.), *Pattern Languages of Program Design.* Reading, MA: Addison-Wesley, 1995, pp. 51–64.

Alistair Cockburn can be reached at `acockburn@aol.com`.

Decision Deferral and Capture Pattern Language

20

Allen Hopley

INTRODUCTION

This pattern language captures the structure and relationships of the various models used in designing the Generic Services Framework (GSF), an object-oriented call processing system developed by Bell-Northern Research for Northern Telecom's DMS family of digital switches. (The development of GSF is currently the world's largest object-oriented project.) An earlier version of this chapter discussed some of the methodologies used in working with these models. However, because an excellent reference on Desmond D'Souza's Catalysis methodology has recently been made available on the World Wide Web [D'Souza+95], much of my discussion on methodology is now omitted; the reader is instead referred to this other source. Although Catalysis is not the methodology used in the development of GSF, the similarities are striking (as noted by both D'Souza and myself). Thus, I have increased confidence that this pattern language captures more than a single (albeit large) project's experience.

OVERVIEW

This pattern language is applicable for systems developed using a model-refinement methodology.[1] Figure 1 illustrates the relationship between *refined* (higher-level) models and *refining* (lower-level) models.

The patterns discussed here focus on how to deal with those models. Specifically, Decision-Based Models (Pattern 1) defines the criteria for deciding the models' content. Appropriate Living Models (Pattern 2) helps the designer decide which models are valuable enough to maintain over the long term. Executable Models (Pattern 3) helps ensure consistency in the design. Upward Traceability (Pattern 4) keeps consistency between the models. And Downward Changes (Pattern 5) keeps the higher-level models from becoming irrelevant.

FIGURE 1 Refinement of models

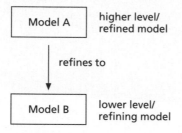

PATTERN 1: DECISION-BASED MODELS

Problem   When defining a system by means of successive refinement of models from a problem domain level down to an implementation level, how do you decide what "refinement" is? How is the refining model different from the refined model?

Context   You are developing a system, using successive refinement of models.

Forces   There are many choices regarding what to make different in a refined model. You could add more entities to the model, break existing entities into smaller-grained entities, make finer-grained operations, or localize opera-

---

[1] Refinement is one of the key ideas behind the Catalysis methodology [D'Souza+95]; refinement of models is one aspect of this.

tions to specific entities in the model, to name just a few. But what type of refinement will lead to the model's being of enough value to justify the effort in developing it?

Solution Define the model content on the basis of the decisions that are *captured* in that model and *deferred* to refining models. Any particular decision is either captured in a model or deferred to some later, refining model, as illustrated in Figure 2.

   Two distinct attributes determine whether a particular model is valuable. The first is defined by the decisions that have been captured, because those decisions have to be made and cannot be put off forever. The second is defined by the decisions that have been deferred, because the model does not have to change if the deferred decisions change (i.e., the model is independent of those decisions). In either instance, these decisions are often based on *what* is being done, *who* (which entities in the model) is doing it, and *how* it is being done [D'Souza+95]. The Appropriate Living Models pattern (Pattern 2) helps the designer decide which of these decision-based models should be maintained.

FIGURE 2 Deferral and capture of a decision

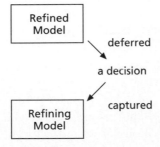

Resulting Context You now have a set of models that are defined in terms of the decisions captured in each model.

PATTERN 2: APPROPRIATE LIVING MODELS

Problem A large number of decisions must be made during the course of defining a system. How can you choose an appropriate number of models to capture those decisions so that you don't spend all your time developing those models instead of developing the system?

Context   You are developing a system, using successive refinement of models. Each model's content is based on the decisions made in that model and those decisions deferred to other models.

Forces   You could try to make a model valuable by including all the decisions necessary to create the system, but that would be difficult to accomplish in a single step. You could try to make a model valuable by making no decisions, but that would not get you to a solution. No one model can both capture and be independent of a particular decision, so adding multiple models is necessary. If there are too many models, the cost of creating and maintaining them may exceed their value.

Solution   Maintain models (that is, make them continue living) that are independent of decisions that are likely to change. For example, if you suspect that the system's hardware platform is likely to change, you should create and maintain a model that is independent of that platform. The number of "living" models is greater for a product family than for a product or a project,[2] because the number of decisions that are likely to change (or be different in different circumstances) will be greater.

A particular model can capture, or be independent of, multiple decisions. This can reduce the total number of models.

Resulting Context   You have chosen the appropriate models to fit the system (the bigger the system, the higher the number of appropriate models). If the choices have been made appropriately, these models will reduce the costs of the product (or product family) over its lifetime.

Example Models   Table 1 shows some examples of models used in the GSF project. The table describes the reasons why each model is considered valuable, both in terms of the decisions it captures and those it defers. Note how the deferred decisions of one model become the captured decisions of the next model.

PATTERN 3: EXECUTABLE MODELS

Problem   How can you ensure that a model is a correct, or even consistent, representation of a solution to a problem?

---

[2]   A project is a single application; a product is an application over its lifetime [D'Souza+95].

Model Name	Captured Decisions	Deferred Decisions
Requirements Model	Representation of the requirements in the customer's terminology	Abstraction of multiple requirements into more general concepts
Domain Model	Abstraction of multiple requirements into more general concepts	The overall structure of the system that can meet the requirements
Architecture Model	The overall structure of the system that can meet the requirements	The mapping of the solution onto a hardware architecture
Mapped Architecture Model	The mapping of the solution onto the hardware architecture	How to implement the solutions within each part of the hardware architecture
Implementation Model	How to implement the solutions within each part of the hardware architecture	The code

TABLE 1 The captured and deferred decisions of some example models

Context   You are designing a system, using iterative refinement of models.

Forces   The human power of self-delusion is immense. System designers may lie to themselves about the correctness of a model without knowing they are doing so.

Solution   Build an executable version of a model. Designers cannot hide from the fact that a model doesn't work. This model doesn't have to be written in the same language and environment as the final system. (And ensuring that it isn't will ward off any customer or management notions that the system is almost done.)

   This is a form of prototyping (there are patterns referencing prototyping in [Whitenack95] and [Coplien95]). However, the main customers of the executable model are the model builders themselves (to see if it works), not necessarily the customers or end-users of the system.

   Note that Catalysis [D'Souza+95] uses formalisms in its model definitions to check consistency.

Resulting Context   If the executable model does not work, any inconsistencies in the model will be apparent. The findings can then be used to fix up the model. As a bonus, there is now something tangible to show management.

Examples   The GSF project has an executable version of its architecture model in Smalltalk.

PATTERN 4: UPWARD TRACEABILITY

Problem   How can you ensure that information is not lost in moving from one model to another?

Context   You are working on a system represented by two or more levels of models, with different individuals or groups maintaining the different models.

Forces   If the development of different models takes place in isolation, the different models will be discontinuous and thus of little (or even negative) value. People do not like being dictated to; therefore, to have a true sense of ownership, the owners of a model refined from another model must have an opportunity to provide real input. Therefore, the owners of a higher-level model cannot directly specify what the lower-level model should look like. But if designers have free reign in refining higher-level models, how can the owners of those models feel that they have had real input?

Solution   Maintain upward traceability between models and downward approval of that traceability (as illustrated in Figure 3). The designers of the refining model are responsible for owning and maintaining the traceability to the refined model. The designers of the refined model give approval of, or take exception to, that traceability.

FIGURE 3 Upward traceability and downward approval of traceability

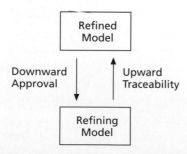

Resulting Context   You now have a system described by several layers of models, with the relationship between models clearly established. With good *conceptual continuity* [D'Souza93], many of the concepts will be recognizable all the way from the highest-level model down to the lowest-level model (for example, from the domain model down to the implementation model). The designers of both refined and refining models will have both an opportunity to provide input and a strong incentive to maintain good traceability between models.

This approach also yields a side benefit: the designers of the refining model must know and understand the refined model in order to maintain the traceability. The designers of the refined model must understand the refining model in order to give their approval. This means that model owners can understand at least one level above and one level below where they normally do their work. This aids in making changes, as described in Downward Changes (Pattern 5).

PATTERN 5: DOWNWARD CHANGES

Problem   Given multiple models at various levels of abstraction, how do you go about developing and making changes to those models?

Context   You are designing a system in which problems are often encountered at more detailed levels of abstraction. These problems require changes.

Forces   It is a given that the model in which the problem was encountered must change (otherwise, there wouldn't have been a problem). Why not just fix it there? Is it OK to just fix the problem and let the more abstract models be changed later to reflect the new system? What happens if the more abstract models don't keep up?

Solution   Official changes to the models are made starting from the highest level of abstraction down to the lowest level, maintaining traceability all the way. This is shown in Figure 4. The necessary changes can be incorporated into each living model by starting with the highest-level model that needs to be changed. The change is not complete until all models have been changed and are again consistent and traceable.

Resulting Context   The "living" models will continue to live because they are always kept up-to-date.

In some cases, it may be impossible to avoid changing a lower-level model without at least identifying and validating the changes to the higher-level models (and, preferably, incorporating them as well). This should be captured

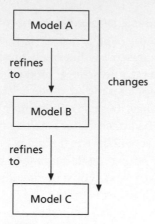

FIGURE 4 Changes start at the highest level model and propagate downward.

and tracked as a serious issue; you must fully accept that resolving the issue may entail "undoing" your changes to the lower-level model.

ACKNOWLEDGMENTS

The concepts discussed here are the result of much hard work by teams and individuals within Bell Northern Research during a series of meetings and workshops about what it means to have an architecture and to develop framework. In particular, Gerard Meszaros and the other members of the Framework Evolution Team deserve special mention. Also, thanks to Gerard for acting as the shepherd for this contribution.

Thank you as well to the members of the writer's workshop. Your input on making this a better contribution is much appreciated. Also, I am indebted to Desmond D'Souza, who was a member of my review group, and Alan Wills for creating Catalysis and thus enabling me to defer discussing methodology and focus on the core of the pattern language.

REFERENCES

[Coplien95] J. Coplien. "A Generative Development-Process Pattern Language." In J. O. Coplien and D. C. Schmidt (eds.), *Pattern Languages of Program Design*. Reading, MA: Addison-Wesley, 1995, pp. 183–238.

[D'Souza+95] D. D'Souza and A. Wills. "CATALYSIS—Practical Rigor and Refinement," 1995. URL: http://www.iconcomp.com

[D'Souza93] D. D'Souza. "A Comparison of OO Methods." *OOPSLA '93* tutorial notes, 1993.

[Whitenack95] B. Whitenack. "RAPPeL: A Requirements-Analysis-Process Pattern Language for Object-Oriented Development." In J. O. Coplien and D. C. Schmidt (eds.), *Pattern Languages of Program Design*. Reading, MA: Addison-Wesley, 1995, pp. 259–292.

Allen Hopley can be reached at alhop@bnr.ca.

Organizational Patterns for Teams

21

Neil B. Harrison

THE PATTERN LANGUAGE: DESIGN BY TEAM

Problem   How can people work together to design and develop software?

Context   The system you need to develop is too large for one person to design alone. In very small teams of two or three people, individual personalities strongly influence group dynamics, so the context begins with teams of four or more people. There is no upper bound on the size of the project, although larger projects will generally divide into smaller subteams.

Depending on the particular organization and circumstances involved, the problems of team design may be best handled by either managers and project leaders or the team members themselves.

Forces   The following general forces affect the dynamics of teams:

- People have all different ideas and concepts.
- Multiperson development requires people to share information.

- Programmers tend to be introverted, and thus they often prefer to work alone.

There are other, more specific, forces at play as well; these will be discussed later in the chapter.

Solution The real key is to recognize that you can't throw a bunch of programmers together and expect an effective team to form automatically; you need to take overt action to make it happen. The following patterns will help you:

1. Unity of Purpose lays the groundwork for an effective team and helps reconcile differing opinions.

2. Diversity of Membership deals with the composition of teams. It suggests getting representation from different communities to take advantage of different ideas.

3. Lock 'em Up Together helps deal with the natural tendency of programmers to work independently.

4. Validation by Teams helps bring people and their different ideas together, and it facilitates the sharing of information.

These patterns are described below. They all work within the context described above. Each resolves a different set of forces in addition to the above-named common forces.

PATTERN 1: UNITY OF PURPOSE

Problem How do you get a bunch of different people all pointed in the same direction?

Forces
- Every person is different and has different views and opinions.
- A single product needs consistency across its functions and interfaces.
- If people have differing concepts of the product, there is little hope of it coming together in a timely and consistent manner.

Solution The leader[1] of the project must instill a common vision and purpose in all the members of the team. The following actions can help form a common vision and create the necessary unity in the team. All team members

---

[1] The leader is not to be confused with the project manager. The leader is the person in the team who naturally rises above his or her peers and is supported by them. Nearly every successful team has a leader.

participate in these actions, but it is the ultimate responsibility of the leader to ensure that the team has a common vision.

1. Create a common vision of the product by discussing the following aspects: What is the product supposed to do? Who are the target customers? How will the product help them? All team members should have a chance to express their views, but the most important thing is that all members fully understand the nature of the product.

2. Agree on a target schedule. It is important that team members feel personally committed to the date, so concerns about the feasibility of target dates and the proposed product content must be aired and differences resolved. The idea is that the schedule must be something that everyone feels good about; if they do, it stands a much better chance of being met.

3. Outline the competition. A sense of working against a common enemy has a strong unifying effect.

4. "Team-building" exercises should be aligned with the goals of the team. Because such exercises are often geared toward managing interpersonal relationships, they are generally most successful with teams of managers.[2] For technical staff, it is usually more meaningful to rally around the project itself than to foster teamwork through contrived team-building exercises.

Developing unity of purpose sounds like no more than good sense, and indeed it is just that. Too many people believe unity will just happen, however. Sometimes you are lucky, and it does; but in most cases, you need to make an overt effort to ensure that such unity is achieved.

Rationale   Personal experience has shown that unity generally does not happen automatically.

Studies of numerous successful projects have shown that in every highly successful project there was a strong sense of identity and unity. DeMarco and Lister [DeMarco+87] treat this subject extensively.

Related Patterns   Self-Selecting Team [Coplien95] describes how a team should come together. As a leader with a vision emerges, people with similar visions will gravitate to that leader, thus helping satisfy the Unity of Purpose pattern.

---

[2]   K. Switzer, personal conversation, May 16, 1995.

PATTERN 2: DIVERSITY OF MEMBERSHIP

Problem   How do you get the information you need about your product's required capabilities, the resources needed for its completion, and other relevant issues?

Forces
- Information and expertise is distributed among different individuals, roles, or organizations.
- All too often, software designers are removed from users.
- Users often don't know exactly what they want, anyway.
- System testers want closure on system specifications as soon as possible so they can begin planning for testing.

Solution   Put together a team to specify user requirements. The team should include a developer, a user or user's representative, and a system tester (at least one of each). These individuals will work through the issues surrounding product requirements, often using small prototypes to identify the requirements and determine testing criteria. The use of prototypes can be closely tied to using use cases or similar usage scenarios as analysis and validation tools.

   One area in which this approach is especially useful is in the specification and design of the user interface. The developer creates mock-ups of the user interface, and the user and system tester examine them. In this way, this small subteam can go through many different designs of the user interface and select the best one.

   This approach of making fast iterative prototypes should help reduce overall development time. In addition, reviewing various interfaces will help users better understand their own needs.

Rationale   Highly effective developments are tightly coupled to users as well as validation teams. Such teams have a strong awareness of their customers' needs. A particularly striking example of this was a project where a team consisting of a system engineer, system tester, and user interface designer worked together closely for several weeks. They produced numerous iterations of the user interface, sometimes as many as three per week. This close interaction was a key to the success of the project.

Variation   An interesting variation on this pattern is to have team members come from different backgrounds. They may have not only different professional experience but also different cultural, ethnic, racial, gender, or even religious backgrounds. Jim Coplien[3] related a software architecture exercise in which teams of all-men, all-women, and mixed-gender teams worked to create software architectures for various problems. The mixed groups consistently outperformed the others.

Related Patterns This pattern is similar to Whitenack's Prototype pattern [Whitenack95].

Coplien's Engage Customers pattern describes the necessity of having a close association with customers; Diversity of Membership provides a pattern for achieving and using that association. It acts as a bridge between Engage Customers and Whitenack's Requirements Specification pattern [Whitenack95], which describes ways to capture requirements.

PATTERN 3: LOCK 'EM UP TOGETHER

Problem How can a team of different people come up with a single, coherent architecture?

Context A team has been formed, preferably by following the Self-Selecting Team pattern, and has achieved unity of purpose.

Forces
- A product needs a single architecture that is self-contained and consistent.
- Programmers have a tendency to work separately.
- One person's design bears that person's unique signature; many people working on separate parts of an architecture will produce parts that do not necessarily work well together.
- "Designs by committee" usually look that way.
- If one person has all the key architectural knowledge, the project is very vulnerable if that person gets hit by a truck (or leaves the project by any other means).

Solution Gather everyone together to work out the architecture. Put them all in the same room (literally). Every person should commit to total participation until the architecture is complete (or complete enough that a clear picture

---

[3] J. O. Coplien, personal communication, May 5, 1994.

has emerged). The following techniques can help make the process more effective and prevent the "designed by committee" syndrome:

- Use a small team of architects, usually not more than five or six. These people must be able to not only design the system but also carry the architectural vision back to the rest of the project.

- Have an acknowledged "chief architect." The chief architect is responsible for the overall vision and for imparting that vision to everyone on the team. A strong chief architect can be very effective in making the Unity of Purpose pattern happen, and he or she can resolve opposing viewpoints. See Coplien's pattern Patron [Coplien95].

- Use CRC cards and/or other user action-oriented methods to perform analysis.

- Constrain the problem. There is a tendency to want to add additional features during design. This tendency can be kept in check during group designing by a strong chief architect.

- Recognize the iterative nature of software design and implementation; do not try to get the details right yet.

Rationale   See Coplien's architect patterns, including Architect Also Implements [Coplien95]. See also various case studies describing the use of CRC cards [Beck89].

Allen [Allen76] suggests that the work areas of members of engineering teams should be as physically close to each other as possible to enhance the information flow within the team.

Project studies within AT&T have yielded the following anecdotes and scenarios:

- A project used small design teams within the context of a larger project. The teams were formed and convened by the (technical) person responsible for the feature, who assumed the leader role. The team worked closely together to design the feature.

- All members of a small project worked together constantly for a period of weeks to complete the architecture. Although the project was geographically split, the team members came together in one location until the architecture was complete. The architecture remained strong throughout the project.

- A related experience that supports this pattern is a project the author studied that conducted group debugging sessions. Besides providing assistance in debugging, it helped everyone learn everyone else's code. See also Validation by Teams.

PATTERN 4: VALIDATION BY TEAMS

Problem   How do you make sure that designs are valid?

Forces
- The interfaces among people's work need to be clear. Many of the problems in software development are internal interface issues.
- Designers work separately on their own parts of the project.
- You are too close to your own stuff to see all of its bugs.
- Other people do not know your area and your design very well, so it is difficult for them to assess your design.
- Traditional reviews of design documents have generally not worked well [Parnas95]. Often, people get hung up on the grammar, wording, and form of the document.
- It is necessary for a designer to somehow impart knowledge of the design to other team members, to reduce the "truck number."[4]
- Certain elements of a design are often not clear until one writes the code. In fact, for most programmers, writing code and designing it go hand-in-hand, and they are sometimes hard to differentiate.
- There is usually schedule pressure by this time.

This is a formidable list of forces, and it may not even be complete. This is a tough but important problem.

Solution   Leverage team members to validate one another's designs. The Unity of Purpose pattern is an important prerequisite, and the Diversity of Membership pattern can provide a solid foundation. Do the following to resolve the many forces:

1. At the review, have the designer explain the design to the other team members. This should be an oral presentation; blackboards, overhead projectors, visual aids, and even code fragments may be used, but the focus should remain on the oral presentation. The stated purpose of this activity is to impart an understanding of the design to the team. (Note that understanding a design is different than validating it.)

2. Do not use formal design documents at the review. The Mercenary Analyst pattern [Coplien95] may be useful.

3. Each team member should check the internal interfaces to make sure that the others' views of the interfaces are consistent with his or her

---

[4] The "truck number" is the number of critical people on a project; if any one of them were to get hit by a truck, the project would lose essential knowledge and not be able to continue.

own views. Team members may wish to pull out the CRC cards they used to see if the design is consistent with the architecture. This is the beginning of the process of validating the design.

4. The team should execute the design orally. This is essential. They may wish to each assume the identity of one or more components in the design, and thus animate it. They should execute several scenarios so as to cover both normal and exceptional execution. They may wish to use some of the scenarios/use cases that they (hopefully) used during the CRC card analysis. The goal of this exercise is to validate the internal design.

Rationale Numerous successful projects have used similar techniques for reviewing designs (not design documents). One project at AT&T performed design reviews with a team and then wrote the design document later.

My personal experience attests to the necessity of oral design execution. In one case, a design review without a design execution left me with a vague, uneasy feeling but no concrete objections to the design. Some time later, the design was found to be fatally flawed; this would have been discovered during a design execution.

REFERENCES

[Allen76] T. J. Allen. *Managing the Flow of Technology*. Cambridge, MA: MIT Press, 1976.

[Beck91] K. Beck. "Think Like an Object." *UNIX Review*, September 1991.

[Beck89] K. Beck and W. Cunningham. "A Laboratory for Teaching Object-Oriented Thinking." *Proceedings of the Object-Oriented Programming Systems, Language, and Applications (OOPSLA) Conference.* New Orleans, LA, October 1–6, 1989, pp. 1–6.

[Coplien95] J. Coplien. "A Generative Development-Process Pattern Language." In J. O. Coplien and D. C. Schmidt (eds.), *Pattern Languages of Program Design*. Reading, MA: Addison-Wesley, 1995, pp. 183–237.

[DeMarco+87] T. DeMarco and T. Lister. *Peopleware.* New York: Dorset House, 1987.

[Parnas95] D. Parnas and D. M. Weiss. "Active Design Reviews." Paper presented at the Eighth International Conference on Software Engineering, London, August 28–30, 1995.

[Whitenack95] B. Whitenack. "RAPPeL: A Requirements-Analysis-Process Pattern Language for Object-Oriented Development." In J. O. Coplien and D. C. Schmidt (eds.), *Pattern Languages of Program Design*. Reading, MA: Addison-Wesley, pp. 259–292.

Neil B. Harrison can be reached at AT&T Bell Laboratories, 11900 N. Pecos St., Denver, CO; nbh@dr.att.com.

22 ACCOUNTABILITY AND ORGANIZATIONAL STRUCTURES

Martin Fowler

INTRODUCTION

This chapter is something of a PLoP black sheep. So far, PLoP has not had much to do with analysis and design methods, and methodologists have been conspicuously absent from PLoP conferences. This chapter is about using patterns with analysis and design methods. It also uses a conceptual analysis method, that of Odell [Martin+95].

This chapter covers two broad themes. First, it is about choosing a conceptual model to describe organizational structures. Second, it is about using patterns to explicate the logic that moves a modeler from one conceptual model to another. Thus, two types of patterns are described here: some are specific to the process of modeling organizational structures (e.g., Pattern 5, Organizational Structure–Typed Relationship); other patterns describe more general patterns in conceptual modeling (e.g., Pattern 7, Typed Relationship). Whenever a general pattern is discussed, it is placed after the specific pattern that uses it. This presentation format was chosen because it is often easier to understand a specific statement first and then extrapolate to a general statement.

It should be stressed that this chapter is about *choosing* a model to represent an organizational structure, not about how to use a model that has already been chosen for this purpose.

The patterns presented here are based on various consulting work I have done over the last few years. A principal inspiration for these patterns is the work of the Cosmos Project [Cairns+92]. [Fowler96] discusses these and other analysis problems in more detail. Many of these concepts have also been described elsewhere [Fowler95], although not in terms of patterns. This chapter applies the pattern-language concept to these ideas. I discuss the implications of these and other conceptual modeling issues in a nonpatterned environment in a separate book [Fowler96].

THE PROBLEM OF ORGANIZATIONAL STRUCTURES

The United Kingdom's National Health Service (NHS) is a complex organization. A regional structure divides the country hierarchically for management purposes. The various types of clinical professionals are organized differently, but all have important obligations to their employers (e.g., hospitals), professional societies (the Royal Colleges), and the Department of Health. Patients' links to this structure are similarly varied. They must register with general practitioners (GPs) and for regular treatments with numerous secondary caregivers. They may give explicit consent for a clinical procedure, or they may give only implicit consent (such as when a patient turns up unconscious in an emergency room). Although payment for medical services is usually assumed (as it is a state-run system), private care does exist, often alongside NHS care. Foreign nationals are not necessarily given free NHS care.

The NHS is also experiencing a period of unprecedented change. A new organizational system has been introduced by the government. Instead of hospitals and GPs being organized through regional hierarchies, they are encouraged to act as independent trusts or fund holders. Regions negotiate contracts with hospitals and GPs to manage the costs of health care. As patients are treated, it is important to track whether regional contracts or individual GP fund holders are responsible for paying for treatment.

These lines of responsibility play an essential part in the clinical process. As mentioned earlier, they may indicate the payment mechanism. More importantly to clinicians, they show who bears clinical responsibility for the patient. Patients are often assigned to an individual caregiver rather than a clinical department. This caregiver is responsible for coordinating care within a particular area of expertise. These responsibilities indicate who is allowed to see a given patient's record. If a patient is referred by another clinician, responsibilities exist to that referring clinician. The way these lines of responsibility are determined change from hospital to hospital, depending on the working practices of individual doctors. Yet they must be understood so that care can be properly coordinated.

Many large organizations have similarly complex organizational structures. Others have simpler structures, for which a simpler model can be used.

OVERVIEW OF PATTERNS

Pattern 1, Party, introduces the concept of party, a valuable tool for many aspects of conceptual modeling. Pattern 2, Recursive Structures for Organizations, is the first potential model for organizational structures. It is based on the modeling principle used in Pattern 3, Abstract Models with Constraints in Subtypes. Pattern 4, Multiple Hierarchic Associations, builds on Pattern 2 to handle slightly more complex examples. As the structures become significantly more complex, the modeler is led to Pattern 5, Organizational Structure–Typed Relationship. Pattern 5 uses the principles of Pattern 6, Objectify Associations, and Pattern 7, Typed Relationship. Pattern 5 is very capable, but it can be further abstracted by using the party concept from Pattern 1, yielding Pattern 8, Accountability Abstraction. As the structures get even more complicated, modelers should consider Pattern 9, Accountability Knowledge Level. This applies the abstract Pattern 11, Knowledge Level, which is based on the modeling principle behind Pattern 10, Put Frequently Varying Structures in Instances.

The pattern map (Figure 1) gives an overview of the pattern language. The patterns that model organizational structure (2, 4, 5, 8, and 9) compose a sequence of increasing complexity. The general modeling patterns, together with Pattern 1, influence these patterns as shown by the arrows. You should choose one of the organizational structure models for your work, depending on the forces at play in your problem. The general modeling patterns should help you understand the trade-offs involved, and they will perhaps lead you to other patterns, should those presented here be inappropriate.

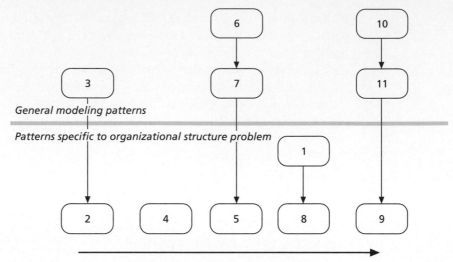

FIGURE 1 Pattern map

MODEL NOTATION

To define the models used by the patterns in this chapter, I need to use a system of notation. Arguments about which notation to use are perhaps the most tedious in software engineering. I use Martin and Odell's system [Martin+95], because it is the most conceptual of the major notations. This section outlines the principal points.

Types are represented as rectangles. I use type to denote the conceptual notion of concept and the programming notion of interface. I do make a distinction between type (for interface) and class (for implementation). These patterns are about types.

Associations are represented by lines between types. Associations model connections between instances of types. Each association is viewed as a pair of directed *mappings*. The two mappings in the association are inverses. The term *inverse*, in this context, indicates that when both mappings in an association are traversed from some object, the starting object is a member of the resulting set. Each mapping has a *cardinality*, usually expressed as a lower and upper bound (see Figure 2). Mappings with an upper bound of one are termed *single-valued*; those with an upper bound of more than one are called *multivalued*. Multivalued mappings are assumed to return a set, unless otherwise indicated. Mappings indicate

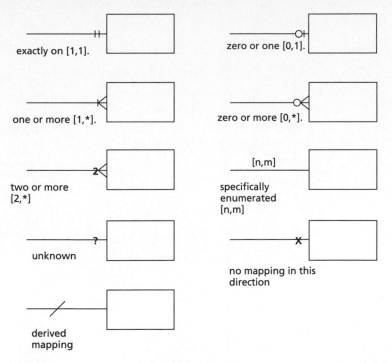

FIGURE 2 Symbols for mappings

responsibilities rather than implementation data structures [Odell+95a]. Mappings may be marked as derived; this indicates that their value is determined from other mappings.

Generalization is expressed through the partition notation. A *partition* box includes several disjointed subtypes of the type connected to the box (see Figure 3). A type may have several partitions, indicating multiple classifications. Subtyping is assumed to be dynamic, unless otherwise indicated by a constraint. An *incomplete partition* indicates that an instance of the supertype need not be an instance of a subtype within that partition. *Complete partitions* indicate that every instance of the supertype must also be an instance of a subtype within the partition. Subtyping does not necessary imply inheritance of classes in an implementation [Odell+95b].

Additional *semantic statements* (see Figure 4) are added to the model in two forms. A short semantic statement is added in square brackets. The only such statement used in this chapter is "[hierarchy]" on a recursive association, which indicates that objects connected by this association

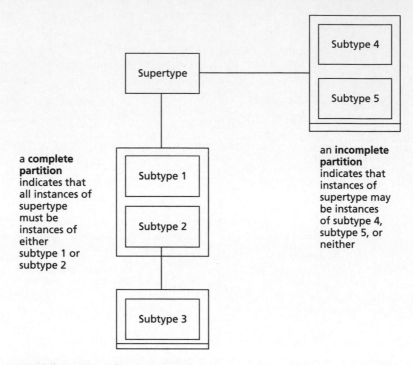

FIGURE 3 Generalization notation

form a hierarchy. Longer statements are placed in a note box attached to the relevant part of the diagram. Longer statements are given an italicized heading to indicate what they are. Constraints are usually stated in informal English.

FIGURE 4 Notation for semantic statements

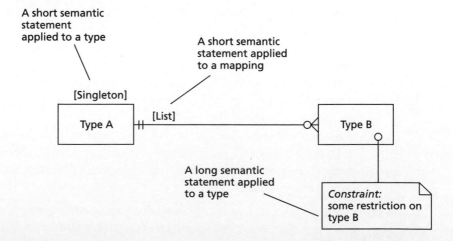

PATTERN 1: PARTY

Problem   Behaviors are frequently shared by people and organizational units.

Forces   The same thing should not be defined in different places. People and organizations are both recognized concepts. Similar features suggest generalization.

Solution   Create a party type that is a supertype of person and organization. Assign all common behavior to the party (see Figure 5).

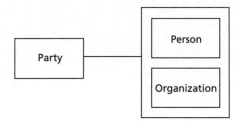

FIGURE 5 Party

Rationale   Supertyping is a common device used to factor common behavior between types. The concept of a party is frequently present, although it is often not explicated.

Examples   In contracts, legal entities may be either people or companies (company is a subtype of organizations). Medical procedures can be carried out by individuals or by teams. Bank accounts can be held by people or by organizations. Addresses can be given to both people and organizations.

PATTERN 2: RECURSIVE STRUCTURES FOR ORGANIZATIONS

Problem   You need to describe an organization with a strict hierarchy and defined levels within that hierarchy.

Context   The levels change but not frequently. A history of past hierarchies is not required.

Forces   You need to be able to navigate the hierarchy easily. Thus you want to add new levels without affecting the ease of navigation. You must ensure that organizations are inserted correctly without breaking the strict levels that are defined.

Solution   Use a recursive relationship on organization. Subtype the organization for the levels. Add constraint rules (invariants) to enforce the position of the levels (see Figure 6).

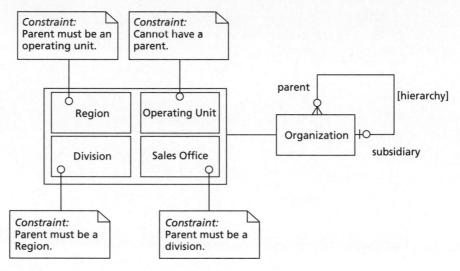

FIGURE 6 Organization with a single recursive hierarchy and defined levels

Rejected Solution   The associations could also be placed between the specific levels (see Figure 7).

Rationale   The use of a supertype to hold the interlevel relationships allows any navigation to be done without the client knowing what the levels are. This simplifies the use of this structure. If a change in the levels occurs, then this change can be done by introducing a new subtype that only affects clients if they need to know the subtypes. The rejected solution forces clients to be aware of the associations between each level. This makes navigation of the structure more awkward. A recursive approach can be used with the solution illustrated in Figure 6 but not the one in Figure 7. Furthermore, using the rejected solution would force all clients to change should the levels change.

FIGURE 7 Rejected solution

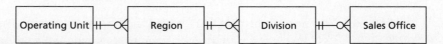

By using a more abstract and flexible model, you achieve something that is easier to change and manipulate at an abstract level. However, the rejected solution does support the need for new organizations to be inserted in a fixed manner. To do this with an abstract organization requires placing structural constraint rules on the subtypes. Changing the levels means that we must add subtypes and change the rules for all subtypes affected by the change.

Example The traditional structure of the UK's NHS divides the country into regions, which are divided into districts, which are divided into units. Many large enterprises have a hierarchical control structure similar to this.

Related Patterns This is a use of Pattern 3: Abstract Models with Constraints in Subtypes.

PATTERN 3: ABSTRACT MODELS WITH CONSTRAINTS IN SUBTYPES

Problem In modeling a situation, should you choose a more abstract model or a more specific one?

Forces An abstract model is more flexible; changes in the enterprise can be dealt with more easily. But an abstract model is also more difficult to create and explain. Rules inherent in the specialized domain must not be lost.

Solution Create an abstract model for flexibility, and use subtypes to enforce the rules.

Rationale A small abstract model has many advantages in enterprise modeling.

- It provides for greater consistency. Users of the model need to learn only one mechanism, which they can then use in several places. Although the mechanism is harder to learn since it is so abstract, once learned it has greater applicability.

- Enterprises change a great deal. These changes cause problems if business concepts and the software based on them are not sufficiently flexible.

- Different parts of the enterprise need information to be stored in a consistent manner to allow enterprisewide integration of information.

- A small model yields less code. The less code there is, the less there is to go wrong and the less there is to alter during maintenance.

Using subtypes to enforce the specialized rules means that only those users of the structure that care about the rules need know about them. More rules can be added without affecting the structure or other applications of the abstract model.

Example   See Pattern 2: Recursive Structures for Organizations.

PATTERN 4: MULTIPLE HIERARCHIC ASSOCIATIONS

Problem   The enterprise is a matrix organization with more than one hierarchy.

Context   Pattern 2 would be usable for each separate hierarchy. There are only a small number of hierarchies. The hierarchies change but not frequently. A history of past hierarchies is not required.

Forces   You need to easily navigate the hierarchies. You want to add new levels without affecting this navigation. You must ensure that organizations are inserted correctly, without breaking the strict levels that are defined.

Solution   Apply Pattern 2 for each hierarchy. Each hierarchy gets an association on organization and a partition of subtypes for the levels.

Example   An organization could have two hierarchies, one for sales and one for product groups (see Figure 8).

Rationale   The associations must be independent for each hierarchy, so clients can navigate each hierarchy separately. Separate partitions of subtypes are required to enforce the rules of each hierarchy.

FIGURE 8   An example of Pattern 4, Multiple Hierarchic Associations

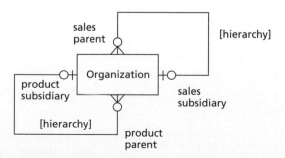

Limitations   This pattern does not scale to more than a few hierarchies.

PATTERN 5: ORGANIZATIONAL STRUCTURE–TYPED RELATIONSHIP

Problem   There are many organizational links in the enterprise.

Context   There are a large number of hierarchic and other links. The kinds of organization links may change frequently. We may need to keep a history of past structures.

Forces   Pattern 4 becomes unwieldy with too many relationships. You need to easily navigate the hierarchies. Too many associations on organization are difficult to remember and lead to a large interface on the software classes. You may need to be able to add new structures easily. You must ensure that organizations are inserted correctly without breaking the strict levels that are defined.

Solution   Turn the association into a specific type (organizational structure, Figure 9). Add an organizational structure type. Each instance of an organizational structure type represents a kind of organizational relationship. A time period may be added to an organizational structure to record a history of organizational

FIGURE 9   Organizational structure

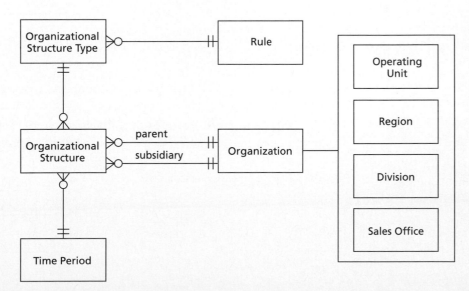

links. A rule can be added to instances of organizational structure type to enforce configuration constraints for that organizational relationship.

Rationale   As the number of organizational relationships grows, Pattern 4 becomes increasingly unwieldy. Each additional association is something else to remember and increases the interface of the resulting software. If the structure changes frequently, this leads to a model change for each new change.

   This pattern deals with this problem by moving the knowledge of different organizational relationships from associations on organization to instances of organizational structure type. It is easier to add instances than to add associations. Similarly, we can dynamically query to find what instances exist and then manage them with other classes as we need them.

PATTERN 6: OBJECTIFY ASSOCIATIONS

Problem   A feature needs to be added to an association.

FIGURE 10 Context for Pattern 6

Context   See Figure 10.

Forces   It is inappropriate to add the feature to either participating type.

Solution   Turn the association into a type with associations to the participating types. The feature can then be added to the association (see Figure 11).

FIGURE 11 An objectified association

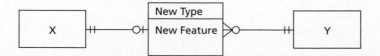

Rationale   Features can only be given to types, so to add a feature to an association it is necessary to turn it into a type. This is quite a straightforward process. Note the way the cardinalities are formed. The cardinalities from the new type to the existing types are both single-valued. If the method supports it, they are usually immutable. The existing cardinalities are transferred to the mappings to the new type. Hence the cardinality of the mapping X->Y is transferred to X->New Type.

Variants   Many modeling methods allow features to be added to associations directly. A special notation is provided for this. This may or may not be semantically equivalent to this pattern. The trade-off is between the convenience provided by the new notation versus the extra effort involved in learning it.

PATTERN 7: TYPED RELATIONSHIP

Problem   There are many similar associations that are bloating a type.

Forces   Having too many associations on a type makes it too complex. A large number of associations makes types difficult to remember and understand. A large number of associations also leads to a large interface on a software component.

Solution   Objectify the association (Pattern 6), and add an association type attribute. One instance of the association type attribute is created for each association subsumed into this structure.

Rationale   A single structure can support what would require several structures otherwise. New association types can be added dynamically by creating new instances of the association type.

Limitations   This pattern should only be used for large numbers of similar associations. It is best used when similar processing is done on the associations, with any variations depending on the association type handled by polymorphism within the association. Used indiscriminately, it can effectively hide the interface of the participating types. This pattern cannot take advantage of static type checking.

Examples   See Pattern 5, Organizational Structure–Typed Relationship.

PATTERN 8: ACCOUNTABILITY ABSTRACTION

Problem Similar structural relationships exist between organizations, between people, and between people and organizations.

Context The logic for describing and interrogating these relationships is similar. Some processing requires switching between relationships in the three categories.

Forces Similar features suggest generalization.

Solution Abstract these relationships into a single typed relationship (Pattern 7) between parties (Pattern 1). Call this type "accountability" (see Figure 12).

Rationale Supertyping is a common device used to factor common behavior between types. Accountabilities provide a single structure to handle these kinds of relationships. This provides a greater consistency for users of the types, as they all handle the same thing in the same way (see Pattern 3).

Examples A region is part of a district (accountability type = hierarchical reporting). A doctor works for a unit (employment). A patient consents to a doctor's treating him (consent). A consultant leads her team (leader). A payer contracts with a

FIGURE 12 Accountability

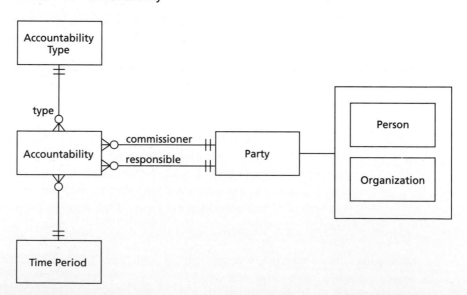

hospital to provide health care services (service contract). A patient contracts with an insurance company to provide coverage (insurance contract).

PATTERN 9: ACCOUNTABILITY KNOWLEDGE LEVEL

Problem Certain accountabilities can only be formed between certain kinds of parties.

Context Pattern 8, Accountability Abstraction, is being used. There are many accountability types. Different environments have different accountability types. New accountability types are frequently defined.

Forces It is easier to change instances of objects than to change the model. We want people to be able to configure the model for use in their environment without changing the model. We want people to be able to add new accountability types without changing the model.

Solution Define a knowledge level for accountability that contains rules about how accountabilities can be configured.

Rationale The links at the knowledge level define which party types may be used for a particular accountability type (see Figure 13). The constraint rule on accountability type enforces the rule on the accountabilities.

The constraint is placed on accountability type rather than accountability so that it can be overridden for accountability types with different constraint behavior, such as those that require a strict hierarchy.

Examples The commissioner for patient consent must be a patient, and the responsible party must be a doctor. The commissioner for medical registration must be a royal college, and the responsible party must be a doctor.

PATTERN 10: PUT FREQUENTLY VARYING STRUCTURES IN INSTANCES

Problem Models cannot be changed easily.

Context Models are used for the description of business practices. Similar models are used to specify software interfaces (or implementations).

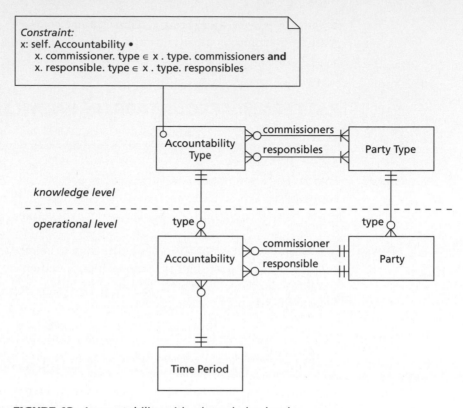

FIGURE 13 Accountability with a knowledge level

Forces Changing a model causes domain experts to rethink their view of the world. Frequent changes make it difficult for domain users to understand a model. Frequent changes reduce the value of a model to the domain experts. Changing a model leads to interface changes in software. Interface changes require a lot of maintenance.

Solution Design the model so that any frequent changes affect instances of types within the same type structure.

Rationale Models are designed to allow frequent changes in instances (i.e., to record new objects coming into the world). Changes in a model are expensive, however. It is thus valuable to come up with a model that can represent changes as changes in instances of objects rather than changes in types. This is often not easy, but it leads to a more flexible model. Taken to extremes, however, it results in a model that is too abstract to be of much use.

PATTERN 11: KNOWLEDGE LEVEL

Problem   Frequent changes in the structure of types may occur due to changes in business practice.

Context   A model for the day-to-day operational aspects of the problem has been developed. There are many variations on this model, and new ones are regularly developed. Different environments require different variations.

Forces   Model changes are expensive (see Pattern 10).

Solution   Create a knowledge level for the model. Each type on the operational level is given a corresponding type on the knowledge level. An association links the operational type to its corresponding knowledge type. Relationships between the knowledge types define the possible links between the operational types. A rule on a knowledge type can be used to enforce this.

     Thus, from Figure 14, a mapping from an instance of type X (x1) to an instance of type Y (y1) is only permissible if x1's X type has y1's Y type as a member of the x1's X type's α mapping (see Figure 14).

Rationale   The knowledge level defines the possible configurations for the operational level in a similar way that the model defines the possible configurations for the objects. The knowledge can be thought of as a (partial) metamodel for the operational level. Associations at the knowledge level are rulcs that govern operational objects.

     The model can be configured for different environments by creating new instances at the knowledge level for each environment. New configurations can be added by adding or altering knowledge objects.

FIGURE 14 Knowledge Level

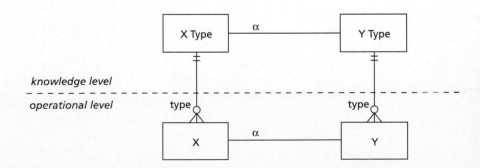

Limitations   Use of this pattern implies that integrating two systems requires that both the model and the instances of the knowledge level be mapped to each other.

Examples   Pattern 9, Accountability Knowledge Level.

ACKNOWLEDGMENTS

Many of the ideas discussed in this chapter, including the key concept of accountability, were developed with Tom Cairns and Hazim Timimi while eating the best pizza in Paddington.

From PLoP I thank my shepherd, Jim Coplien, for getting the chapter into an appropriate form, the working group at PLoP for their valuable comments, and Kent Beck and Ralph Johnson for their support.

REFERENCES

[Cairns+92] T. Cairns, A. Casey, M. Fowler, M. Thursz, and H. Timimi. *The Cosmos Clinical Process Model.* (NHS Reports ECBS20A & ECBS20B.) Birmingham, England: National Health Service, Information Management Centre, 1992. (http://www.ihi.aber.ac.uk/pubs.html).

[Fowler95] M. Fowler. "Modelling Organisation Structures." *Report on Object Analysis and Design,* 2(2), (1995):20–23.

[Fowler96] M. Fowler. *Object Blueprints: Patterns for Business Analysis.* Reading, MA: Addison-Wesley, 1996.

[Martin+95] J. Martin and J. Odell. *Object-Oriented Methods: A Foundation.* Englewood Cliffs, NJ: Prentice-Hall, 1995.

[Odell+95a] J. Odell and M. Fowler. "From Analysis to Design Using Templates. Part I." *Report on Object Analysis and Design,* 1(6) (1995):19–23.

[Odell+95b] J. Odell and M. Fowler. "From Analysis to Design Using Templates. Part II." *Report on Object Analysis and Design,* 2(1) (1995):10–14.

Martin Fowler can be reached at 88 Worcester St., #3, Boston, MA 02118; 100031.3311@compuserve.com.

EPISODES: A Pattern Language of Competitive Development

23

Ward Cunningham

This pattern language describes a form of software development appropriate for an entrepreneurial organization. We can assume that the organization's developers work in small teams of bright and highly motivated people. We can also assume that time to market is highly valued by the organization, as it often is where market windows close quickly and development dollars are in short supply. But, unlike some entrepreneurs, this organization also places high value on being able to get a second version out the door in a timely way (and a third version, and an *n*th version, many years down the road). That is, it expects to be successful, and it has every intention of exploiting that success by continuing development for as long as its customers desire it.

These patterns describe how to develop software. They could be fairly described as *process* patterns, though they don't actually describe a process the way a methodology document might. Nor do they describe *designs* or *organizations*, as other patterns do. Being patterns, they describe *things*— things that solve problems that occur in the software development process. These things can be physical, like a document or a group of developers, or they can be mental, like a commitment or a state of mind.

We are particularly interested here in the sequence of mental states that leads to important decisions. I call this sequence an *episode*. An episode builds toward a climax, where a decision is made. Before making this decision, however, developers must find facts, share their opinions, build their concentration, and generally prepare for an event that cannot be known in advance. After the climax, the decision is known, but the episode continues. In the tail of an episode, developers act on their decision, promulgate it, and follow it through to its consequences. They also leave a trace of the episode behind in their products. It is from this trace that they must often pick up the pieces of thought in some future episode.

I won't be so naive as to suggest that the thoughts leading to a decision must be written down. These thoughts are too complex, and decisions are too numerous, for this to be practical. What I do suggest is that hints and pointers be placed in strategic locations so that preparing for subsequent episodes might go more smoothly. Of course they won't go *much* more smoothly. That's because each new episode begins with greater expectations. Software developers can only hope to rise to the occasion. They will know that they have done so if their episodes remain well shaped: not too heavy in the front or back, and not always getting longer.

There is an old saying that laments, "There is never time to do it right but always time to do it over." I take this to be a fact of competitive life. Developers find themselves unable, under competitive pressure, to make the kind of careful decisions they would like. These patterns tell what decisions can be made—in fact should be made—to maintain continuous forward motion through iterative development.

One does not have to compete to find these patterns useful. The developments they create are equally applicable for entrepreneurial groups within large organizations, or any other group that wants to develop code quickly and indefinitely.

The idea of an episode is related to, but not the same as, DeMarco and Lister's notion of "flow" [DeMarco87]. An individual achieves flow much like they begin an episode. Flow, however, is conceived of as continuing indefinitely, at least until the next interruption. Work groups in this paper are assumed to operate as high-performance teams, as described by Katzenbach and Smith [Katzenbach93]. They emphasize concrete deliverables and a culture of responsibility as key factors leading to performance. So do I. Finally, I would not have thought this material amenable to the pattern form were it not for the example set by Coplien's organizational patterns [Coplien95]. In fact, this work found its start in a workshop exercise performed by Jim Coplien, Kent Beck, and myself in the spring of 1995.

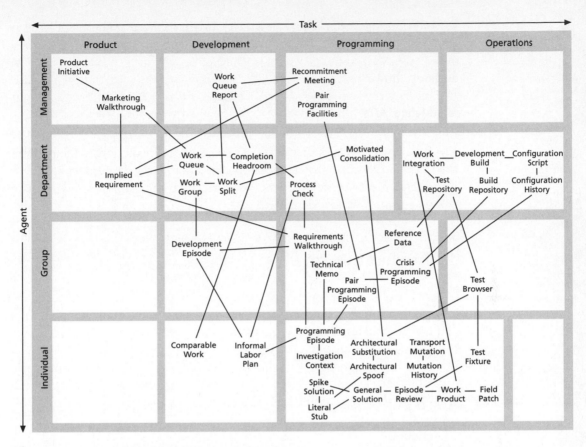

Figure 1 Map of EPISODE patterns and their relations

This pattern language addresses a wide variety of development issues. These have been organized into topic areas that could be described as top-down or chronological. Don't think that any real development effort is so structured or sequenced. In practice, these patterns will be applied over and over, in and out of order, sometimes by people whose job description says they should do so, and sometimes not. Figure 1 presents a map of the language, with the patterns positioned by task and agent. Here *task* implies the kind of work being done while *agent* implies the kind of person doing it. These aren't to be taken too seriously. Far more important are the relationships between patterns. Patterns are related when one leads to another. This happens when the strong forces bearing on a pattern are brought into balance: it's a balance as its solution. Such resolutions of strong forces inevitably expose weaker forces to which attention should then be applied. It is this shift of attention that we capture in the relationships between the patterns. These relationships turn a bunch of patterns into a pattern language; a system that (like a spoken language) is employed without a great deal of conscious thought.

1 PRODUCT

We pick up the development process somewhere in the long middle, after the first few versions have shipped and well before the customers have lost interest in future enhancements. We start with the longest and largest of nested episodes, the Product Initiative.

1.1 Product Initiative

Problem   Market conditions or operating conditions may indicate the need for increased or modified product functionality. Or, an in-place product plan may call for specific functionality on a given date. Anyway, it is time to direct the attention of multiple groups of developers toward specific product goals.

Everyone involved with a product accumulates a wish list of features and functions they would add if given half a chance. A product designed to absorb an ever-increasing complement of features is at particular risk of losing any sense of coherence or direction.

Therefore:

Solution   Articulate clearly the most important direction for improving a product. Expect all members of all involved groups to be able to at least summarize the initiative and defend its business rationale. A new initiative need not align with previous initiatives. There is no need to retreat on past accomplishments by withdrawing them from the product or withholding proper support. There is, however, a need to reduce or displace less-than-relevant thoughts in every mind within the initiative.

Expect an initiative to come from upper management, where the responsibility for major resource allocations rests. It is possible for a product initiative to boil up from the development ranks. What is important is that everyone accept the initiative as the direction of the moment, no matter how such agreement may be reached.

A clear initiative will imply requirements that should be talked through carefully in a market walk-through. Definite schedule and resource goals further enhance the focus of an initiative. Throughout the initiative, management should track work groups' completion windows on each requirement.

Initiative slips result in over allocation of attention to one subject, at the expense of good will and future initiatives. In the worst case, implied requirements may need to be reviewed and possibly deferred or discarded in an organization-wide recommitment meeting.

1.2 Market Walk-through

Problem   A product initiative will be expressed in marketing or business terms. A product is more than a program or any other piece of technology. Davidow makes this clear in his book *Marketing High Technology* [Davidow86]. It is the marketing function that makes one from the other. And Marketing must have good communication with both sides of its operations—the product's customers and its developers. Likewise, Development must understand the customer needs served by an initiative and have the confidence and resources to peruse market questions as they arise.

Therefore:

Solution   Begin every initiative with a walk-through of program and product concepts. Involve most of the Development and Marketing staffs. Understand an initiative from the buyer's and user's perspective and from Development's point of view too. Should an initiative come from or involve contract terms, now is a good time to review them. Finally, all should agree on basic terminology, such as that used in implied requirements.

> *Example:* A trading software company responds to its growing fear of derivative contracts by adding improved pricing models and related analytic tools. The Marketing department has selected key customers with derivative portfolios and a willingness to work with software developers. In a market walk-through, the company president outlines changes in the derivatives market, the New York region customer representative summarizes the newest pricing models popular "on the street," and the staff domain specialist outlines a vision for incorporating similar function in the company's products. The walk-through ends with a long question-and-answer period in which Marketing and Development begin to match customer needs with implementation possibilities.

1.3 Implied Requirements

Problem   A product initiative has identified the direction for further development, and a marketing walk-through has explored customer motivation and the developmental possibilities behind it. The organization expects positions and attitudes to be understood, but it has yet to make any commitments beyond everyone's general commitment to do a good job for the company.

A commitment implies an agreement between people. Development commitments generally obligate developers to meet some customer need in a timely and satisfactory way. The tension here is to define a need in sufficient detail that commitments have meaning without exhausting up-front analysis or overconstraining a solution.

Therefore:

Solution   Select and name chunks of functionality. Use names that will have meaning to customers and be consistent with the product initiative. Allow these names to imply customer requirements without actually enumerating requirements in the traditional sense.

Examples:

- *Year-end tax reports,*
- *Dollar-denominated Japanese bonds,*
- *High-quality printing,*
- *Disconnected operation on lap-tops.*

These items will fill in the blank in this recurring question: Who's handling the programming (or specification, or customer contact, or manual update, or release notes) for _____.

2 DEVELOPMENT

The following patterns generate development team activity leading to frequent and regular releases of increasingly functional programs. An important idea is the simultaneous development of requirements, specifications, design, and implementation. When these responsibilities fall to single individuals, those individuals are assumed to be able to wear the appropriate hat at the appropriate time. Similarly, should a different person fill each role, each individual is assumed to be able to coordinate his or her activities such that he or she is both productive and benefits from the others' work.

The patterns also generate a schedule of sorts, while preserving considerable latitude to do what makes the most sense at the moment. Our general strategy is to develop a few fixed target dates. When a delivery date arrives, we would like to look back over the development period and say with confidence that we used every available minute wisely.

2.1 Work Queue

Problem Implied requirements suggest deliverable program enhancements that will have various necessities, dependencies, risks, and rewards associated with them. Deliverables may be ill-defined, being represented more by a vision or desire than anything concrete or measurable.

If the development team were to work up a conventional schedule, it would probably begin with a block of requirements analysis for each item. From these would be hung blocks of specification, design, implementation, and, eventually, integration and testing. Add to this some wild guesses and a few ordering constraints, and, presto, you have thirty feet of diagram saying what will be finished when and by whom. Such a document takes on a life of its own, striking fear in developers' hearts and generally distracting everyone else from the real scheduling task, which is to get better input, not larger output.

Therefore:

Solution Produce a schedule with less output than you have input. Use the list of implied requirements (really just names) as a starting point, and order them into a likely implementation sequence, favoring the more urgent or higher-priority items. When work can be factored from two or more entries, go ahead and do so, giving the common element a name that establishes its worth and implies its implementation precedence.

Examples:

1. *Settlement date positions*
2. *Settlement date–based tax reports*
3. *Trade vs. settlement accounting preference by portfolio*

Be prepared to reorder this list as unforeseen interactions surface or business realities demand new priorities. Remove work from the list as it is completed. Observed defects are not enough to return completed work to the list; however, independently scheduled repair activity may uncover omissions that are more appropriately removed from defect tracking and scheduled in competition with all the other work on the work queue.

2.2 Work Group

Problem You have a work queue that describes product initiative–relevant work, is ordered by urgency, and shifts up as completed work is removed from the top. You must now allocate staff without overwhelming or under-utilizing any individual.

Therefore:

Solution   Allocate to staff roughly two month's worth of work at the head of the work queue. Seek their commitment to work together as needed to understand the real and implied requirements, develop suitable specifications, complete or extend a design, assemble tests, and implement all aspects of the deliverable. Expect individuals to apply themselves to their most-urgent assigned tasks. Allow some latitude to compensate for impossible-to-forecast dependencies between projects and individuals. Expect the work of any given item to be performed with the usual rise and fall of concentration, revolving around a burst of decision making that marks the center of a development episode.

2.3 Work Queue Report

Problem   With a fairly consistent mix of analysts, designers, and implementers, one can assume that a consistent amount of analysis, design, and implementation gets done every week. This can be confirmed in a weekly status meeting in which every attendee is given five minutes to describe his or her progress. However, it can be amazingly difficult to detect a slipping schedule in the status meeting venue.

Therefore:

Solution   Collect status reports in regular personal interviews conducted weekly. Solicit estimates of days of remaining effort, using contrasts with comparable work.

> **Example:** *"I put two full days into the new tax calculations, and one day with Joe on his U/I."*
> *"How many uninterrupted days do you think you need to finish the calculations?"*
> *"Oh, say two. It's no different from the accruals."*
> *"And, working with Joe?"*
> *"Well, we didn't get to the real work. I had three down last week? Must still be three days."*

Use these estimates along with individual dilution factors (how many uninterrupted days of development does the individual have access to a week?) to predict elapsed days to completion for each assigned deliverable. Compute and publish completion headroom from this data. Include a cover page with a few sentences explaining numbers that might have shifted in an interesting way.

2.4 Comparable Work

Problem Developers are surprisingly bad estimators when it comes to dates. On the other hand, they have a good memory of which circumstances lead to what problems in past projects, and they have a sixth sense for uncovering the same circumstances in a new project.

Therefore:

Solution Let developers estimate effort by selecting comparable work. A job that is two-thirds as complex as some previous job will probably take about two-thirds as long. Comparable estimates are usually accurate even for ill-defined projects, unless there is hidden complexity that is not taken into account when selecting a comparable effort. Hidden complexity usually shows within a few days of actually starting work. It's OK to challenge an estimate that is not taken seriously, but don't try to hold developers to last week's estimate when they've uncovered hidden complexity. Take heart—there is such a thing as hidden simplicity, and it does surface on occasion.

As an aid to memory, record the number of uninterrupted days applied to current efforts, as illustrated in the table below. This data will be a handy reference when today's projects become tomorrow's source of comparison. Do not expect a week on the job to yield more than two or three full days of development. Also, don't try to use the data for performance evaluations. To

Example Work Queue Report

Work in Progress (ordered by priority)	Uninterrupted Days to Completion						Earliest Possible Finish	Head room
	Sue	Bill	Joe	Kay	Ed	Ray		
Availability	60%	70%	25%	70%	10%	75%		
Settlement-Date Positions		3	2				June 5	12
Settlement-Date Tax Reports		2				2	June 8	9
Trade vs. Settle Preferences			1	4			June 7	10
etc.	5				5		June 21	8
etc.				9		3	June 25	4

do so would betray the frankness required for good estimating. Besides, it's not clear whether bigger or smaller numbers indicate improved performance. It will be necessary to prorate accumulated effort data should a project undergo a work split. Some ratio will suggest itself; just don't count days twice.

2.5 Completion Headroom

Problem   Every project must commit to delivering product on a few hard-and-fast dates. This is actually fortunate, because it is about the only way to get out of work that is going poorly. A work split provides a graceful exit by allowing one to defer portions of the work that are not understood or going poorly while saving the parts that do work or will save face. A work split does require some advance notice, however, since some portion of the work must still be completed before the deadline.
   Therefore:

Solution   Project work group completion dates from the remaining effort estimates in the work queue report. For each project, calculate each contributor's earliest possible completion date, find the latest of these, and compare that to the hard delivery date for the project. The difference between these figures is your completion headroom. This headroom will often fluctuate, plus or minus a day or two, from week to week. But steady evaporation of headroom for any work group is a sure indicator of the need for management attention. Techniques at your disposal for dealing with such a situation include reordering the work queue, possibly deferring whole items to a later release date, the work split already mentioned, or the public embarrassment of a recommitment meeting.

2.6 Development Episode

Problem   The members of a work group are selected based on the needs inferred from the implied requirement. Each member brings specific skills that will be important at some point in the development effort. For this you can be thankful. However, if you overemphasize a member's specific strengths, you diminish everyone's general abilities. Unnecessarily narrowing members' focus to particular specialties risks creating ambiguity concerning who is responsible for non-specialized tasks, and it discourages members from learning new skills.
   Therefore:

Solution   Approach all development as a group activity, as if no one had anything else to do. Expect the activity to follow the usual course of an episode, in which energy builds to a decision-making climax and then dissipates. At the height of the episode, the purpose should be clear, the terminology well understood, the "knowns" well explored, and the "unknowns" identified. It is at exactly this point that individual strengths merge into a sort of common consciousness. Landmark decisions come easy. Breakthroughs are common. A creative act will have been shared.

Besides yielding better decisions, the collective episode has very positive effects on its participants. Looking back, people often have trouble identifying the actual source of key ideas. Non-specialists gain invaluable insight into the thought processes of specialists. Specialties are demystified, shared, spread throughout the group. Specialists come to realize that this sharing will not diminish their status within the group. As insight wells up in the master, he will delay slightly, expecting others to be close to the same insight. He will know that their recognition experience will be of tremendous value to them and only a small loss to himself. Seymour Papert calls this an "Ah Ha!" and admonished instructors not to "steal their students' Ah Ha!"[Papert80].

2.7 Informal Labor Plan

Problem   The development episode presents an ideal that must be worked into the lives of people trying to get a big job done quickly. Developers will often find themselves obligated to more than one in-progress development episode at a time. The work queue offers one prioritization, though one that ignores the many small trade-offs possible when the work is at hand.

Therefore:

Solution   Let individuals devise their own short-term plans. Accept that much of the group activity implied in a development episode will take place in pairs of group members that find the time to tackle some issue together. Avoid the temptation to call a meeting where a developmental climax is intended to happen. It won't. Instead, let individuals express their interests and make commitments to each other spontaneously. And let them revise these intentions on a moment's notice when the energy of some episode reaches an irresistible level.

A development episode is actually composed of a series of programming episodes, some of which must take place in (at least) pairs if any approximation of group consciousness is to form. An individual's labor plan is his tool to make these connections happen. Paired programming facilities are configurations of the physical environment which can reduce this planning to an occasional promise in the hallway.

2.8 Work Split

Problem   A work group commits to resolve and deliver implied requirements in the most timely and satisfactory way it can find. The group is not committed to specific dates, but it does have an obligation to make its efforts visible through what becomes the ultimate trouble signal, low completion headroom. Headroom disappears when developmental activities fail to match those of comparable work. A common problem is the (well-meaning) escalation of requirements by people too close to a problem.

Therefore:

Solution   Divide a task into urgent and deferred components. No more than half of the developmental work should be in the urgent half. Defer even more work if necessary to acquire sufficient completion headroom. Defer analysis and design for parts that won't be implemented. This advice runs counter to conventional wisdom. Often a split is just a way to get back to the basic work that had been originally planned. Trust architectural substitution to cover for omissions and inconveniences caused by incomplete "up-front" work. Both halves of the split will appear in the work queue with distinctly different urgencies.

2.9 Recommitment Meeting

Problem   Work splits offer a scheduling mechanism that can be initiated from within a development group. If a product initiative is in jeopardy because implied requirements cannot be met through schedule and work queue adjustments, then it is unlikely that any other development-initiated activity will help. Management up to at least the level that began the initiative will suddenly take an interest in all the circumstances that lead up to the current situation. Some of this is natural and appropriate. But it won't be a time of high productivity, and it shouldn't be allowed to continue for too long.

Therefore:

Solution   Assemble a meeting of interested management and key development people. Allow them to review the development history until all present agree that simple adjustments (like working weekends or adding staff) won't help. Eventually a solution will appear, usually expressed as a question in this form: "What is the least amount of work required to do X?" X is one person's idea of the most important part of the initiative. The question should be answered quickly and confidently by consulting a recent work queue report. The process may be repeated for plans Y and Z. Ultimately a plan will be selected. Then the remainder of the meeting can be devoted to talking through the implications of the decision and getting all the parties committed to the new plan and/or schedule.

This, of course, is another form of episode. Because the decisions pertain to allocating business resources, they belong in upper management. All present can contribute, however, and should do so in a frank, honest, nondefensive, and constructive way.

3 Programming

Programming is the act of making and encoding decisions about future behavior. Encoding requires careful consideration of the basis and consequence of every decision. Often, decisions are found incomplete, and new questions are raised. In this section I discuss decision making in the presence of incomplete, obscure, or questionable facts. I include patterns for the assembling of knowledge in artifacts and individuals and for limiting decision making when knowledge requirements exceed what is immediately available.

3.1 Requirement Walk-through

Problem   Not all members of a work group will start to consider the implied requirements of a piece of work at the same time. Unpredictable circumstances lead individuals to work through their portions of the work queue at different rates. Although all members' efforts should be considered a contribution, the first to address the problem may seem to others to have inappropriate influence over decisions affecting others.

Therefore:

Solution   Assemble the whole work group as soon as one member begins to consider any part of the implied requirement. Consider the expressed needs and desires of the group, the individuals who hold them, and likely strategies to satisfy them. This is the beginning of the development episode, and it is a good time to sketch the first informal work plan. This can lead to adjustments in group membership. It is also a good place for CRC-level design.

3.2 Technical Memo

Problem   A development episode may intertwine with other activities demanding the attention of the work group. Further, some concepts may require quiet contemplation for group members to absorb them, or they may involve sufficient detail that they cannot be recalled without aid.
  Therefore:

Solution   Maintain a series of well formatted technical memoranda addressing subjects not easily expressed in the program under development. Focus each memo on a single subject, and keep the text short and to the point. Carefully selected and well-written memos can easily substitute for traditional, comprehensive design documentation. The latter rarely shines except in isolated spots. Elevate those spots in technical memos and forget about the rest.

3.3 Reference Data

Problem   The requirement walk-through will identify relevant information sources, which will be retrieved, reviewed, and absorbed as the development episode begins. The various data may require transformations before they are easily interpretable. Such activities build the awareness that makes for the intensity characteristic of a decision-making climax. However, after a climax the focus is on the decisions and its implications; the data and processing that contributed to it are easily forgotten.
  Therefore:

Solution   Collect examples, test cases, and customer data as machine-readable examples. Use a spreadsheet program to organize and transform the data as appropriate. Leave notes and observations as text annotations to the sheets so key observations won't be forgotten. Keep this handy throughout the development process, and make sure it is easily imported into the development environment when useful. Check the program against this data throughout the development process, possibly by incorporating it in test suites developed for the application.

3.4 Programming Episode

Problem Programming is the act of deciding now what will happen in the future. A programming language offers an operationally precise way to encode decisions—through a process called simply *coding*. Programmers reason about future behavior by interpreting previously coded decisions and integrating these with their own decisions and with their interpretations of other sources (like technical memos and domain experts). The depth, quality, and value of programming decisions are determined by the programmers ability to concentrate.

Therefore:

Solution Develop a program in discrete episodes. Select appropriate deliverables for an episode, and commit sufficient mind share to deliver them. Be aware of the rise in concentration as the episode progresses. Consider each source (as noted above) and consciously include or exclude its recommendations.

Use the fear that often accompanies a not-yet-made decision as a motivation. Try to compare your position within an episode to similar points in previously successful episodes.

> **Example:** *"I feel like we've been around twice now on the possible ways we can bind the six terms of this bond analytic to the four calculation classes we have in our library."*
>
> *"Yeah, right now I'd be happy if we could place the four primary terms, look at the error cases, and see if that gives us a hint how to proceed after lunch."*

Push for the decisions that can be made. Don't abandon an episode; that will leave you feeling defeated and unable to achieve even the same level of concentration at a future time. Make the decisions that seem possible. Code the decisions. Then review the code to be sure that the extent of your decisions and your confidence in them is apparent in the code. Coding occurs on the downhill side of a programming episode. Coding is the most direct way to promulgate programming decisions.

SUPPLEMENTAL PATTERNS

Space does not allow for the inclusion of all EPISODE patterns.

Patterns to Be Included in Part 2 of EPISODES Pattern Language

Pattern	Solution
Pair Programming Episode	Add reflective articulation, subliminal process check, pattern propagation, search space pruning, and general goodwill to the programming episode.
Pair Programming Facilities	Arrange the furniture. Adjust the fonts. Stretch the cables. Use a private office with an open door and two chairs. Abandon authorship/ownership.
Crisis Programming Episode	Assemble a possibly larger-than-necessary work group. Let members drop off as a solution becomes clear.
Investigation Context	Use inspection and cross-referencing tools to assemble a mental model of the as-is program.
Spike Solution	Patch, debug, and/or code a minimal solution of representative functions in the task. Code protocol before variables, using literal stubs to make progress.
Literal Stub	Return the value that you know you will eventually compute in the current investigation context.
Generalized Solution	Code for skipped/missing parts of the solution. Stub still-remaining functions or allow them to fault when encountered.
Process Check	What are you working on? Why are you working on it? Don't work on that anymore.
Architectural Substitution	Create a new architecture for functions that does not fit well in the existing architecture. Develop that architecture in isolation if necessary to understand mechanisms required by the new functions.
Architectural Spoof	Add sufficient compatibility protocols to an obsolete architecture and/or its substitution so that both can coexist. Reuse names so that modification lists will include both architectures.
Motivated Consolidation	Clean only that part of the architecture that is necessary to support a motivated (funded) set of functions.
Episode Review	Examine the episode product from a solution-sharing rather than a problem-solving perspective.

Pattern	Solution
Work Product	Create a transmittable, integrateable summary of changes necessary to duplicate the solution.
Field Patch	Bundle the work product in a form that can be efficiently distributed to field locations in an emergency. Integrate these patches as you would any other work product. Patches can induce sweep mutations, but these must be considered part of one continuous development. Where truly one-time modifications are required, use a subclass and script it out of standard configurations.
Sweep Mutation	Sweeping is the process of traversing clusters of application data as it is exported from or imported to the runtime memory environment. Expect to find any possible version of any object in the external world. Mutate these to the most current form as they are read. Write the most current form as new or modified objects are written.
Mutation History	Sweep mutation requires that we remain familiar with all previous versions of any given object. Keep this history in an "evaluatable comment" in the mutating sweep method of the affected classes.
Work Integration	Assemble recent work products. Check for completeness and conflicts. Edit as appropriate.
Developmental Build	Reassemble an image from complete sources. Run regression tests and save the results in a distributible image. Post this image to the build repository with the work products uniquely included.
	Mechanically assemble episode products. Supervise conflict resolution.
Build Repository	Collect developmental builds with the auxiliary information used to construct and test them. Cull non-released builds when they are covered by a release and all open forks have been closed.
Test Suite Repository	Collect tests from reference data, programming episodes, and normal test development. Distribute tests to programming episodes and developmental builds. Preserve and protect them as if they were code.

Pattern	Solution
Test Suite Browser	Drill down from build statistics to suites, cases, variables, inspectors, and, finally, debuggers. Import, enter, and compute expected values. Visualize failure distributions (systematic vs. sporadic).
Test Fixture	Construct or retrieve objects suitable for performing a test. If a tcst case is an interrogation, then the fixture is the interrogator, who calls up the interrogated and starts asking questions. Long-term fixture maintenance is a Development responsibility. Make sure the fixtures appear in a development episode's investigation context.
Configuration Script	Develop in a full configuration. Deploy by applying scripts that remove or disable unwanted functions.
Configuration History	Accumulate a history of configuration scripts and field patches applied to a particular product. Make sure the history is available in crisis programming episodes so that debuggable versions of faulty configurations can be reconstructed.

REFERENCES

[Coplien95] J. Coplien. "A Generative Development-Process Pattern Language." In J. Coplien and D. Schmidt (eds.), *Pattern Languages of Program Design*. Reading, MA: Addison-Wesley,1995, pp. 183–238.

[Davidow86] W. H. Davidow. *Marketing High Technology*. New York: Macmillan, 1986.

[DeMarco87] T. DeMarco and T. Lister. *Peopleware: Productive Projects and Teams*. New York: Dorset House, 1987.

[Katzenbach93] J. R. Katzenbach and D. K. Smith. *The Wisdom of Teams: Creating the High-Performance Organization*. Cambridge, MA: Harvard Business School Press, 1993.

[Papert80] S. Papert. *Mindstorms: Children, Computers, and Powerful Ideas*. New York: Basic Books, 1980.

Ward Cunningham can be reached at ward@c2.com.

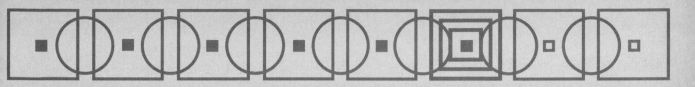

EXPOSITION

PART **6**
The following three chapters attest to the versatility of the pattern form. Unlike other pattern languages in the book, these are not concerned with software modeling or design or implementation, and yet they are no less relevant to computer professionals. They impart skills almost everyone needs: expository skills.

In Chapter 24, titled "Patterns for Classroom Education," author Dana Anthony captures essentials of effective teaching in just a handful of patterns. The language reflects her experience teaching Smalltalk, though she believes the principles carry over to a wider instructional context.

Some of the patterns may seem obvious at first, but knowing how and when to apply them profitably takes experience. Consider the first pattern, Iterative Course Development. It explains why it's nearly impossible to develop course materials in one pass, which makes iteration inevitable. The pattern delegates the criteria for iteration to other patterns in the language. For example, one criterion is how well students assimilate the material. Frequent misunderstanding indicates a problem to be fixed in the next iteration of the course. On this point, Pattern 1 leads to Pattern 4, Pitfall Diagnosis and Prevention. That transition is but one thread in Dana's tapestry of teaching expertise.

Chapter 25 takes us to another form of exposition: the "demo." What software professional hasn't been called upon to demonstrate his or her handiwork? A demonstration can make or break a project, yet the secrets of effective demonstration are rarely articulated. Todd Coram's "Demo Prep" is a glimpse at those very secrets.

No discussion of exposition would be complete without considering what may be the ultimate expositional medium: the World Wide Web. The Web's rapid rise to ubiquity is cliché by now. Everyone—from schoolchildren to multinational corporations—has a home page. It's remarkably easy to establish a presence on the Web, but as any surfer can tell you, the quality of Web pages varies drastically. It's obvious which Web pages work well and which don't; what *makes* them work well or not is much less obvious. The last pattern language in this part, by Robert Orenstein (Chapter 26), shows how to structure and connect Web pages to best effect.

It's tempting to draw a parallel between these pattern languages and the reflection-oriented patterns of Part 4. Patterns and pattern languages are, after all, an expository medium. So, what could be more reflective than using them as a conduit of expository expertise? Thinking reflectively about patterns could unleash some bold new insights. Then again, it may be reflective only of the tendency, best characterized by Kent Beck, of computer scientists "to go meta at the drop of a bit." Still, don't be surprised to find patterns that are themselves reflective at a future PLoP conference.

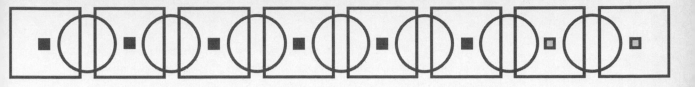

Patterns for Classroom Education

24

Dana L. G. Anthony

ABSTRACT

This chapter describes patterns used to teach difficult technical topics (such as object-oriented programming). There are patterns for games, examples, flow of the course, and dealing with different learning styles. Each pattern is divided into four sections. The first two sections, "Problem" and "Constraints and Forces," lay out the pattern's context for the third section, "Solution." The fourth section points out connections between Related Patterns. The last part of this chapter discusses how the patterns may be used together to develop a course.

INTRODUCTION

Although there are a few unusual aspects to teaching object-oriented programming, a lot of the techniques apply to a variety of other contexts. That's why I titled this chapter "Patterns for Classroom Education" instead of "Patterns for Smalltalk Education," even though I found the patterns while teaching Smalltalk.

THE PATTERNS

These are patterns I have discovered both by teaching and by talking to other instructors. They apply primarily in the context of a class where a heterogeneous group of students works with one or two instructors, but some could be useful in nearly any educational setting.

In the "Problem" section of each pattern you will find the problem or group of problems that the pattern solves. The "Constraints and Forces" section describes any additional context necessary to determine when to apply the pattern; often this includes a more detailed restatement of the problem. The "Solution" section resolves the constraints and forces and solves the problem. The "Related Patterns" section refers both to other patterns in this chapter and to patterns that haven't been written (or I haven't read them).

The patterns that follow are arranged from most abstract to most concrete. Several of the patterns, especially the more abstract ones, are strategies that *lead* to a solution. Others, especially the more concrete ones, are ready to implement. Pattern 1 has the highest level of abstraction, Patterns 2 through 6 have the next-highest, and Patterns 7 through 14 are at the most concrete level. Within this arrangement, closely related patterns are placed together. For instance, Patterns 8 through 10 all relate to examples. There's no need to read the patterns in the order presented.

At the end of the chapter is a part called "The Pattern Language" that attempts to tie together the patterns into a system of course development. That section also discusses additional forces that may affect the patterns as a group; for example, the three "learning styles"—learning by doing, learning by seeing, and learning by hearing—which form part of the context of many of the patterns presented here.

PATTERN 1: ITERATIVE COURSE DEVELOPMENT

Problem   How can you develop a course that takes the needs of all kinds of students into account?

Constraints and Forces   A single course developer is only one person, and no matter how experienced, he or she may have trouble accommodating widely differing learning styles. The developer's own learning style will naturally tend to attract the most attention. Even a team of course developers may still leave gaps. Some presentation concepts may seem like great ideas on paper but aren't successful in practice. Others fail only due to some mistake or oversight in preparation.

For example, Pattern 4, Pitfall Diagnosis and Prevention, requires you to figure out where students will have the most trouble. The easiest and most accurate way to do this is by teaching the course and seeing where students have great difficulty.

If a course is taught by different people, each using different techniques, it becomes difficult to tell which techniques work best. It may even be tricky to tell which techniques have been tried at all.

Solution   Develop courses iteratively. The developer or team can make their best isolated development effort and then take the course out and actually present it. As audiences change over the long run, the course will continue to grow and improve.

Related Patterns   To document the iterative changes in a course, use patterns as much as possible. This will help those working on the next iteration know what to try next and what has worked in the past.

PATTERN 2: CHICKEN AND EGG

Other possible names for this pattern include Need to Know, Simplified Mutual Prerequisites, Illusion of Understanding. This pattern is named after its problem, while most of the other patterns are named after their solution.

Problem   Two concepts are each a prerequisite of the other. It's a "chicken and egg" situation: a student who doesn't know A, won't understand B; but a student who doesn't know B, won't understand A.

Constraints and Forces   You could just explain one concept and then the other, but at the halfway point, everyone would be confused. Many people, if confused, stop trying; this invalidates a "just go ahead" approach. You could simplify each concept to the point of incorrectness, just for the sake of explaining the other one. But many people object to being lied to, even for their own good. This invalidates the "Santa Claus and Easter Bunny" approach.

Solution
: Give students the illusion of understanding, by explaining each of A and B very superficially, but essentially correctly. Iterate your explanations over and over, each time going into more detail. Be sure to maintain the illusion of understanding at each step.

Related Patterns
: Pattern 3, Mix New and Old, is related. As you iterate through a chicken-and-egg pair of topics, mix new material on each topic with a review of material already covered. Also, vary the "learning style" each time through.

PATTERN 3: MIX NEW AND OLD

Problem
: Basic concepts must be reviewed over and over, but this gets boring for many students. New concepts must be introduced, but few can handle more than 10 to 15 percent new material at a time [Howe77].

Constraints and Forces
: In addition, students vary in their learning style; some learn better by doing something, others by seeing diagrams or demonstrations, and others by hearing explanations [Gagne70] [Goldstein74].

Solution
: Iterate over a concept several times. Each time, present the material in a different way to accommodate a different learning style. Each time, mix in some new material with the old. This both maintains students' interest through the review period and helps them absorb the new material.

Related Patterns
: Pattern 12, Simulation Games, provides an alternative to exercises for students with the learn-by-doing learning style. Pattern 7, Visible Checklist, provides extra stimulus for students that learn by seeing. Pattern 11, Colorful Analogy, provides a boost for the learn-by-hearing students.

PATTERN 4: PITFALL DIAGNOSIS AND PREVENTION

Problem
: Certain concepts are vital yet easily missed. I call these concepts "pitfalls," because students have a disproportionate amount of trouble with them.

  When the same course is repeatedly taught the same way, you may notice students making the same kinds of mistakes every time. Although the pitfalls are given the same emphasis as other, equally important concepts, students understand the others but miss the pitfall concepts.

Constraints and Forces   Usually it's difficult or impossible to predict, without actually teaching the course, what concepts will be pitfalls. When you change the structure or style of a course, you may change the pattern of pitfalls. You have to see the trouble to figure out what causes it.

Solution   The solution is to use an ounce of prevention: if something was a problem in one session of a course, place extra emphasis on that material when it first comes up in later sessions. Make sure to highlight that it is a vital part of the subject matter, not to be forgotten.

For example, I found that students who don't know much about sorting algorithms often find it hard to believe that you can specify a sorting order by providing a function that sorts only two values. Students' confusion on this point leads to their being unwilling to use this kind of sort routine. Having diagnosed this pitfall, I had to find a way to prevent it.

To avoid having to either explain sorting algorithms or leave my students doubtful about their utility, I constructed a simulation game. I provided them with several typical objects: a pair of scissors, an apple, a candle, and so on. I gave them a balance, with which they could see which of any two items was the heavier, and asked them to arrange the items in order, from lightest to heaviest. After doing this, the pitfall never reappeared.

Another pitfall I diagnosed in Smalltalk was that many students could not remember the message printString and always tried to use asString instead. This I prevented by writing "printString" on the whiteboard in fancy letters and leaving it up. Every time a student got an error from sending asString, I just pointed at the board.

For a third example of pitfall prevention, see the Solution section for Pattern 11, Colorful Analogy.

Related Patterns   Pattern 1, Iterative Development, tells you to record your pitfalls so you can later apply this pattern. Pattern 7, Visible Checklist; Pattern 11, Colorful Analogy; and Pattern 12, Simulation Games, all provide possible ways to highlight difficult concepts and thus prevent pitfalls.

PATTERN 5: MODULE'S STORY

Problem   How do you make a module feel like a coherent whole, not just one thing after another? (A module is one segment of a course, a unit of the presentation.)

Constraints and Forces You may have a module that really is just a bunch of bits and pieces, or you may have one that consists of things that only seem disconnected when a student first learns them, or a sequence of things that are each a prerequisite for the next but are otherwise unconnected.

One idea would be to break such a module into separate modules. But the resulting modules might be too short, or have no use on their own, or otherwise be too small.

Solution Come up with an example, exercise, or goal that makes use of all the topics in the module. Make the flow of the module into a story. The preview becomes a foreshadowing of where the story will lead and a motivation for its end goal; the review takes care of itself, as you can just recite how the series of steps led to a resolution of the story's conflict.

Often, keeping the "story" foremost in your mind will make the module flow this way. You may not even have to explicitly tell the story to the students. If that is not enough, think of writing the module as creating a story, and think of delivering the module as telling that story. Or explain the exercise or goal as the preview of the module, letting students tell the story to themselves as the module progresses. Then review how each topic covered in the module fits that introductory exercise or goal.

Related Patterns Pattern 8, Acquaintance Examples, will help you choose an example or exercise topic. Pattern 7, Visible Checklist, can support the story flow of a module. For a module that has sufficient natural cohesion, a checklist alone can even provide the story.

PATTERN 6: SEVEN PARTS

Problem How do you choose an appropriate size for a module?

Constraints and Forces You want students to be able to keep the entire set of topics for a module in mind and be able to relate them to one another. Modules should be short enough to finish without taking a break but long enough to keep the course from seeming choppy.

A person's short-term memory can hold about seven things, give or take two. This is often called the Miller Limit, after psychologist George Miller [Miller56].

Solution If you can divide the module into about seven steps or subtopics, it will seem about right to most people.

PATTERN 7: VISIBLE CHECKLIST

Problem Previewing a module or course at the beginning and reviewing it at the end are standard teaching style. How can you relate the preview and review to each other and to the material presented in between?

  Often the instructor or the students (or both) forget exactly how a piece of detail in the middle of a section relates to the overall purpose of the section, as defined in the preview or review. People have only so much memory, and when it's being taken up with details, they may forget the high-level concepts.

Constraints and Forces You want to make sure that students not only understand their ultimate goal but also learn how each detailed step brings them closer to that goal. When all the technical detail is presented, however, students can get bogged down in trivia, and lose track of the big picture. Therefore, you want to keep connecting the specifics back to the general concepts.

Solution When previewing a module or course, use a visual aid that serves as a checklist. The checklist must remain on display throughout the module, while you go through the main body of the material. Each time you go on to the next step, refer back to the checklist. At the end, use the checklist for the review.

  Although it is of greatest use to students who primarily learn by seeing, the checklist pattern supports all three learning styles:

- The visible checklist acts as an aid or cue to the visual learner. This effect can be heightened by using a pointer to indicate visually where the current topic falls on the checklist.

- Each word or phrase on the checklist will be repeated many times by the instructor, who otherwise might use a synonymous word or phrase. This will act as a cue to the verbal/learn-by-hearing learner.

- The checklist can also be used as an aid in actually carrying out the task or analyzing the problem covered by the module. Thus the checklist can help the kinesthetic/learn-by-doing group as well.

Related Patterns   Review and Preview (covered in the Pattern Language part), in which a preview of the material is performed at the beginning of a module or course and a review at the end, is related to this pattern. Pattern 6, Seven Parts, recommends the number of things to include on the checklist. Pattern 5, Module's Story, suggests an alternate way to organize a module and solve a similar problem, if this pattern is a poor fit.

PATTERN 8: ACQUAINTANCE EXAMPLES

Problem   How do you choose specific examples to use for a class?

Constraints and Forces   There is a range of example domains, from those totally unfamiliar to those in which the student has professional expertise.

If a student is completely unfamiliar with an example's basis, the instructor can end up spending more time explaining the example than using it. If the instructor is trying to demonstrate the creation of abstract classes, and uses as the example "Control Chart," which has "Non P Control Chart" and "X Bar Chart" as concrete subclasses (among others), he doesn't want to spend more time explaining what X Bar means than what the difference between abstract and concrete is.

On the other hand, if a student is an expert in the example domain, the student can become bogged down in the example's domain details and fail to see the point the example was intended to illustrate. If the instructor is trying to explain when to use a Phone Number object instead of an array of strings representing a phone number's area code, exchange, and station, she doesn't want the telephone expert student arguing whether exchanges are a valid description of how phone numbers work these days.

Solution   Choose examples that are the most likely to be familiar to students but not be within their area of expertise. One way to do this is to choose businesses that students patronize but don't run, such as a hotel or a video rental store. You may wish to have two alternatives ready and use the one that is most appropriate for each group of students. Choosing appropriate acquaintance examples can be a very difficult task.

If a class is homogeneous, with all students having expertise in the same domain, an acquaintance example can serve as an icebreaker to get students to see how to apply their new knowledge. The instructor can then supplement the acquaintance example with an example closer to the students' domain, to demonstrate that their new knowledge applies to their domain of expertise as well.

Related Patterns   Pattern 10, Reference Examples, provides one way to give students a greater variety of example domains than there is time to cover in the course.

PATTERN 9: EXAMPLE LASTS ONE WEEK

Problem   Should you continue to use an already established example, or should you introduce a fresh, new example?

Constraints and Forces   There are pros and cons to each alternative:

- *Established example:* Students are already familiar with it, and therefore time does not need to be taken out of the course to explain it. Since the example is familiar, students can concentrate on learning the concept it illustrates rather than on trying to understand the example. Of course, this only works if students remember the details of the example.

- *A fresh example:* You don't have to depend on students' possibly faulty memories of the details of an example. Instead, you present all the relevant details, so they will be completely fresh in students' minds (and your own as well) when you use the example to illustrate the current topic. Of course, presenting all those details takes time, especially if the example is complex.

Another constraint is that courses are usually divided into week-long units. A semester-style course usually has two or three meetings a week (usually with no more than one day between meetings). Some semester-style courses, often called seminars, have only one meeting a week. In a training session, an entire course may be completed in a single week. During the week, examples tend to remain fresh in everyone's mind. Over the weekend, everyone turns to other tasks, and the details of examples are largely forgotten.

Solution   If an example is used, it may and should be continued throughout a week-long unit. This means that a seminar needs new examples each meeting, while a training session should make use of examples that continue to be elaborated throughout the session.

Related Patterns   Pattern 8, Acquaintance Examples, explains how to choose the domain of examples used in a class.

PATTERN 10: REFERENCE EXAMPLES

Problem   A course must fit into tight time constraints but still cover all the required material. How can you provide examples when you can't afford to spend any time on them?

Constraints and Forces   Often, if the course developer doesn't provide adequate examples in the course materials, students insist that the instructor provide them. This can be impossible in the time available, yet some students really require examples for any complex topic.

Solution   Provide references to examples students can refer to after a session ends. For example, in a Smalltalk course, all students should have access to a base Smalltalk image. A reference example in such a course could be simply a reference to an example in the base image. For almost any course, instructors can provide references to papers and journal articles that include detailed examples illustrating the topics covered.

PATTERN 11: COLORFUL ANALOGY

Problem   A very important concept has a lot of boring, detailed ramifications. It is not suitable for a simulation game, and it is easily forgotten until it becomes a problem and causes trouble.

Constraints and Forces   The concept's name may be memorable, but its explanation is not. People may tend to remember that there's something called that, but they forget what it means. Simply emphasizing the importance of this concept tends to just confuse students or bore them so that they tune out.

Solution   A dry concept can be highlighted with a colorful analogy that provides a place to go back to recall the details.

   The example I see most frequently is used in explaining the difference between identity and equality in objects. The analogy is a story of a restaurant patron who sees another diner eating a delicious-looking plate of lasagna. He tells the waiter, "I want what she's having." Equality would mean the waiter goes into the kitchen and gets another plate of lasagna for him. Identity would mean that the waiter takes the lasagna the other customer is eating and gives it to him. With the right analogy, a single word (in this case, "lasagna") can become a touchstone that helps students recall enough of the details of the explanation to make sense of the concept.

PATTERN 12: SIMULATION GAMES

Problem You need to both explain tricky concepts and provide interaction.

- *Explain tricky concepts*: Many problems are hard to learn from the explanation provided. If you've ever tried to learn to play a complex game just by reading the rules, you know what I mean. It's much easier to just play the game, and watch what happens, than to try to figure out the game from the written rules.

- *Provide interaction*: Interactive games provide a way to get students involved in the material. They engage all types of learners, but especially those who learn best by doing. Having some interaction in the course will help increase the amount of interaction going on in exercises and lectures, too, by setting a tone that encourages this.

Constraints and Forces Some individuals may not get involved in the class because they think they will do best by just sitting still and listening, even when they don't understand the material. They plan to sit down alone later and try to *do* the things they learned. (Most of these students come from the group that learns primarily by doing.) Therefore, it is most vital to get these particular students to interact with the group. Otherwise, they may get completely lost and never let on.

Interaction at the very beginning of a class lets the students loosen up and feel free to ask questions, answer them, and generally relax. But you also need to provide periodic "boosters" to keep up the interactive atmosphere.

Solution Playing a simulation of a complex activity often provides students with a much better understanding of what is going on than a straight explanation would. Plus, such activities serve as an occasion for interaction.

Related Patterns Pattern 13, Quiz Games, also provides interaction when no suitable topic for simulation is on the agenda. There are also various general-purpose, icebreaker games that are often suitable at the very beginning of a class.

These are not covered in this chapter, but there are books available that describe them [Greene-Forbess83] [Pike94].

PATTERN 13: QUIZ GAMES

Problem   Several problems are resolved by this pattern:

- Review is necessary, but it can be boring.

- Testing students' comprehension and absorption of the material is useful for both the instructor and the course designer. But tests make students nervous, and students don't like being graded or evaluated.

- No section of the day's material is suitable for a simulation game, but you still want to provide interaction to keep students interested and motivated.

Constraints and Forces   There are several different problems involved, and therefore there are several categories of constraints and forces:

- In addition to a review specific to each section or module, there's a need for a review that ties together all the topics covered in the class.

- Activities that simulate or elucidate the concept being learned are the best, but they are difficult to design and to get right, and there are a lot of subjects that don't lend themselves to appropriate activities.

- Most students will not answer questions if the answers are embarrassingly simple and obvious. This can mislead the instructor into believing that the class has failed to absorb the information.

- Even if you are teaching in an environment that requires testing, tests may not always be the best way to determine students' absorption of the material. Tests are often not exactly reflective of learning, because "test anxiety" can cause students to do less well than they should. Classroom environments that don't include testing make it even harder to measure what students have learned.

Solution   Quiz games, modeled on sports, board games, or TV game shows, are entertaining to students as well as a familiar, safe format. They provide a review by raising questions on the topics covered in the class (answers should be provided for questions that students miss). Students will be eager to answer the simplest questions, since they give easy points in the game. The quiz game also gives the instructor a rough gauge of student absorption of the information. Questions that give students trouble can provide material for further review.

Related Patterns   Pattern 4, Pitfall Diagnosis and Prevention, is related, because quiz games can help the instructor discover pitfalls. Pattern 7, Visible Checklist, can provide material for quiz game questions.

PATTERN 14: DEBRIEF AFTER ACTIVITIES

Problem   Sometimes after an exercise or simulation game, some students haven't grasped the concepts the exercise or game was intended to convey, or else they don't see the point of those concepts or how they relate to the course content. How can you ensure that these students still get the maximum value out of the exercise or game?

Constraints and Forces   Students often achieve better retention and buy-in if they discover something themselves. Not all students discover the same things, however. How can they share their discoveries with one another to leverage this "aha!" factor?

Solution   After an activity, exercise, or simulation game designed to stimulate students to discover something, lead a discussion of what the students learned. Ask open-ended questions (ones without a yes or no answer) to draw out comments and insights from each student. Students will value one another's discoveries almost as much as their own, and they will value them more than what is simply told to them by the instructor.

Related Patterns   A debriefing is often useful after a simulation game (Pattern 12, Simulation Games).

THE PATTERN LANGUAGE

In the beginning, there was the course concept. For example, a course developer might have intended to create a course that would serve as an introduction to object-oriented programming. My assumptions (as an instructor) about the course developer are as follows: he or she knows the central ideas and skills the course should communicate, has those skills, and has some expertise with the material the course will contain.

Developing a course, like developing a program, involves specifying requirements, performing analysis and design, and implementing and refining the content based on experience.

During the design phase, the course developer lays out the sequence in which the material will be presented and decides upon the means of presentation. Usually the material will not organize itself neatly—often it takes a great deal of effort (and a number of iterations; see Pattern 1, Iterative Course Development) to effectively organize it for presentation. For any given body of material, three natural groupings of topics often occur:

A *dependent group* is a group of topics that belong together and must be explained together. An understanding of each topic is necessary to facilitate understanding of the rest. This causes an obvious problem: in order to explain each topic, you must have already explained the others. Placing these topics together in a module is an obvious step: they belong together. Organizing their order within the module is more problematic. (See Pattern 2, Chicken and Egg.)

A *series* is a group of topics that follow logically, one after another, each building on the previous one. The most natural way to proceed is to address each topic in sequence. One benefit of this approach is that it is very motivational, as each new topic provides a use and purpose for the preceding topic. However, there is a great risk to using this approach. If a student fails to understand a topic, he or she will (in domino fashion) fail to understand all the subsequent topics in the group. (For some ways to help prevent this, see Patterns 3, Mix New and Old, and 4, Pitfall Diagnosis and Prevention.) And even students who understand each section can lose sight of the overall picture of how each topic leads to the next. (See Pattern 7, Visible Checklist.)

An *independent group* is a group of topics that are independent of one another; each could be presented without reference to the others. They form a group because of some external reason, such as the following:

- Another topic, covered before the group, is a prerequisite of all of them.
- All the topics in the group are a prerequisite of some single task, topic, or topic group.
- They are all steps in performing some larger task.
- They all share a common use or goal (for example, each is a way to do I/O).
- They all share a common tool or facility (for example, things to build with a component kit).

Or there could be another common thread.

The problem the course developer faces with this third kind of grouping is to create unity for the group. A student's interest must transfer to the next topic as the course moves along; it must not remain behind with the previous topic. (One approach to solving this problem is to use Pattern 5, Module's Story.) In addition, sometimes this lack of cohesion means the group should be subdivided into smaller groups. (To determine when to break a group down further, see Pattern 6, Seven Parts.)

Course design also involves creating examples that demonstrate the course's concepts. (See Pattern 8, Acquaintance Examples; Pattern 9, Example Lasts One Week; and Pattern 10, Reference Examples.)

Once a course is designed and the developer has determined the sequence of topics and their division into modules, the next step is to create presentation materials that will support the actual delivery of the course. The presentation materials should target all three kinds of sensory learning styles: learning by seeing, learning by hearing, and learning by doing. I'm not sure if Three Learning Styles is a pattern or just a major part of the context of the patterns described in this chapter. The patterns refer to these three learning styles often.

Courses must begin with preview material so that students know what to expect. Include an overall outline of what they will learn, and follow a predetermined sequence so students won't ask questions on topics that will be covered in a later section. Delivery must contain explanations students can understand, so they will learn the new material. And courses must include review, both because the instructor must verify that prerequisites have been learned and because most people can't continuously absorb new material and have any hope of remembering it and applying it later.

There's a commonly known pattern that I call Preview and Review because of this necessity to preview and review at all levels of presentation. It's also referred to colloquially as "Tell them what you're going to tell them, then tell them, then tell them what you've told them." The patterns in this paper refer to previews and reviews often.

Presentation materials can include checklists (Pattern 7, Visible Checklist) and games (Pattern 12, Simulation Games, and Pattern 13, Quiz Games). Modules can be organized around topic groups that naturally occur, around exercises, and/or around the checklists and games. Each module should contain some new material and some review material.

When a course is first presented, usually the instructor will discover weak areas where the course needs more material, more review, and/or more emphasis. (See Pattern 4, Pitfall Diagnosis and Prevention.) Extra emphasis can be achieved using any or all of the following techniques: highlighting or using larger text in the presentation materials, conducting a special exercise or review exercise on the topic, placing special emphasis on a particular question during a quiz game (see Pattern 13, Quiz Games), or using a colorful analogy (see Pattern 11, Colorful Analogy).

REFERENCES

[Howe77] M. J. A. Howe (ed.). *Adult-Learning-Psychological Reseach and Applications.* New York: Wiley, 1977.

[Gagne70] R. M. Gagne. *The Conditions of Learning* (2nd ed.). Troy, MO: Holt, Rinehart & Winston, 1970.

[Goldstein74] I. L. Goldstein. *Training: Program Development and Evaluation.* Pacific Grove, CA: Brooks/Cole, 1974.

[Greene-Forbess83] S. Greene-Forbess. *The Encyclopedia of Icebreakers: Structured Activities That Warm-up, Motivate, Challenge, Acquaint, and Energize.* CA: University Associates, 1983.

[Miller56] G. A. Miller. "The Magical Number Seven, Plus or Minus Two: Some Limits on Our Capacity for Processing Information." *Psychological Review, 63,* 1956:81–97.

[Pike94] B. Pike. *Dynamic Openers & Energizers.* Minneapolis, MN: Lakewood Publications, 1994.

Dana L. G. Anthony can be reached at danthony@ksccary.com.

Demo Prep: A Pattern Language for the Preparation of Software Demonstrations

25

Todd A. Coram

INTRODUCTION

If you develop customer-driven software, you will find yourself subject to providing on-demand demonstrations of what you are building. These demos show the customer what to expect of the delivered software. Preparing for software demos can be as easy as mocking up a GUI prototype of the deliverable system or as complex as developing working models of the final system. The following pattern language attempts to address preparing for demos that approach the latter level of complexity.

Successful demos are integral to the development effort, as customers must be kept enthusiastic at all times. If your demo is not effective, then you may have to deal with a customer that does not want your final product.

Given the reality of having to provide on-demand demos, you can either choose to approach each occurrence as a panic situation or develop techniques to make demos that are less disruptive of the development effort and that even help speed the effort along.

A balance must be maintained between providing effective demos and remaining on course toward developing the final product. Presented here is the beginning of a pattern language that can aid in maintaining that balance. The Demo Prep language is primarily concerned with demos that show capability and progress.[1] Even with this in mind, the language is by no means complete. It is certainly not morphologically complete [Alexander79]; there are definite gaps. However, this language can be taken as a subset of a more complete pattern language that covers the full spectrum of software demonstrability. Each pattern described here also fits into the "bigger picture" of a full software development pattern language.

The Demo Prep language consists of the following patterns:

1. Element Identification

2. Catalytic Scenarios

3. Mutable Code

4. Prototyping Languages

5. Lightweight User Interfaces

6. Judicious Fireworks

7. Archive Scenarios

The patterns can be used in a context in which you have already derived initial requirements specifications from your customer and are preparing to commit to a schedule for developing the end product.

PATTERN 1: ELEMENT IDENTIFICATION

Problem   Correctly identifying what should be demonstrated is a critical part of keeping the customer's confidence.

Context   Requirements have been documented, and you have begun to consider what you can demo to ease any doubts the customer may have about committing to the development effort.

Forces   Customers will want to see the product's *face*. The user interface shows the customer what she is getting.

---

[1]   Software demonstrations are multifaceted. They are used to communicate many things to your customers, such as your company's skills, your product's capabilities, work in progress, and the finished product's usability.

Customers demand to see some level of functionality, to demonstrate your capability in delivering "things that work." You may see a certain function of the product as trivial, but if the customer is concerned with it, you need to put her at ease.

If a customer is not satisfied by a demo, then she probably won't be satisfied by the end product. A demo builds confidence and creates anticipation.

Solution   Identify the key areas that concern the customer. Demos exist to alleviate a customer's concerns about whether what is being developed is correct and will work the way she expects it to work.

Talk to the customer and try and draw her out. Key elements will often appear as repeated phrases or stressed points. If the customer keeps going on about speed or ease of use, then you better show it. Once you have identified the major concerns, you are ready to develop Catalytic Scenarios (Pattern 2).

Stay away from excessive animation or other visual embellishments—the customer wants a demonstration of something that will help her accomplish a task. The customer isn't interested in using your product for its own sake. She is interested in using the product to help her accomplish her work [Heckel92].

The product's face can be shown through developing Lightweight User Interfaces (see Pattern 5); its functionality can be addressed by Prototyping Languages (see Pattern 4).

PATTERN 2: CATALYTIC SCENARIOS

Problem   Even though the customer has specified what he thinks he wants, you don't want to go off and build the wrong thing.

Context   You are about to start a project to deliver a system or application based on requirements and specifications that have already been agreed on.

Forces   Customers expect to be given some idea of how a finished product will look and operate. Often, a customer has a specific vision that may not have been accurately communicated by his initial list of requirements.

Sometimes a customer doesn't know what he really wants. Many requirements specifications are ambiguous, especially when a user interface is involved.

Any capability shown during the demo that is not reflected in the requirements specifications may be expected to become part of the end product.

Demos impact development schedules in unpredictable ways. They can eat up tremendous amounts of resources and time. They can take on a life of their own, draining momentum from the development effort.

Problems with any customer-generated requirements need to be brought out into the open.

Solution Use demonstrable scenarios as a catalyst to open a dialogue between you and your customer. You want to make sure that you and the customer agree on what is being built. Develop clarifying scenarios. If you have identified usage scenarios [Love93] as part of your design, some of these may be candidates for good demo scenarios.

If the requirements specifications are ambiguous, then you may want to develop scenarios that offer alternatives to the customer. For example: your customer, a network administrator, wants the product to have the ability to highlight an icon representing a faulty workstation in order to keep an eye on it. He does not know exactly how this should be done. He suggests drawing a yellow border around the workstation. Perhaps a better idea would be to place the icon in a special window reserved for workstations that need closer watching. A good demo will include a scenario showing what the customer requested, and other scenarios that offer your ideas as alternatives.

You should be careful not to demonstrate such scenarios if the demonstrated capabilities are not easily incorporated back into your design plan. The customer may want these features but not allow for the additional resources required for them to be delivered on schedule and within budget. Because of this, you want to demo any proposed features or suggestions as early as possible so the requirements specifications can be reworked before they become an immutable part of the development effort.

If you do not want to modify the requirements specifications, then keep your demo scenarios true to the specifications and only hint at future possibilities. Refer to Judicious Fireworks (Pattern 6) for a discussion of the dangers involved in doing this.

Above all, keep your demo scenarios uncomplicated and succinct. Develop only as many scenarios as needed to show off the requested capability. If you can identify and develop alternative scenarios that suggest other approaches to implementing a capability, then do so, but don't lose sight of the real goal: to deliver an end product that is complete and that performs up to the customer's expectations. You must now consider how much effort to put into your scenarios and how much Mutable Code (Pattern 3) is allowable.

PATTERN 3: MUTABLE CODE

Problem   The level of coding that you should put into developing demos is unclear. It is even more unclear if the resulting code will be usable in the actual development effort.

Context   You have identified your Catalytic Scenarios (Pattern 2) and are evaluating the amount of effort required to develop them.

Forces   Some identified scenarios seem to require too much development time, and you cannot afford the impact this will have on the development schedule. This becomes an even greater problem if you find that you cannot use the artifacts of the developed scenarios in the actual development effort.

Demo code is usually very specific to the particular scenario it demonstrates, and it thus may contain facades in place of functionality.

There is sometimes pressure to treat the prototype as the end product [Love93]. No customer wants to think she is paying for two development efforts, so she may be led into believing that the demo code is actually production code.

Solution   Build modifiable code. Look for tools that support a high level of abstraction. GUI builders and scripting languages allow you to address the problem at hand—the demo.

You want to write only as much code as is necessary to pull off a successful dcmo. Try to incorporate as much real development code as is feasible (i.e., don't create copious amounts of demo code where real code will do).

If the code can be reused for the end product, then do so. However, do not try to forcibly rework the code into the end product. "Plan to throw one away" [Brooks75, p. 116]—just don't tell the customer.

If you find yourself building mostly screens, then you will be concerned with Lightweight User Interfaces (Pattern 5). If you need to work on the stuff behind the screens, then you will probably be writing a bit of code. Prototyping Languages (Pattern 4) discusses how you may be able to integrate the code developed for the demos into the end product, as well as reduce the amount of code written.

PATTERN 4: PROTOTYPING LANGUAGES

Problem   If you are developing software using a language that is difficult to prototype (or make rapid changes) with, then developing demos can be as involved as developing the end product, especially if you need to demonstrate some of the proposed functionality.

Context   You are considering how to demonstrate various functional aspects of the product in the defined Demo Scenarios. You are also looking for efficient ways to code the scenarios.

Forces   Although the customer typically sees only the product's interface (or face), you are often required to show that something is going on "behind the scenes."

Functional demonstrations usually involve writing a substantial amount of code. This code may not be usable for the end product. Often, requested functionality is not ready for demonstrations, and the customer wants to see more than just pretty screens.

Solution   If you cannot implement the end product in a language that provides for rapid prototyping, then consider adopting a Prototyping/Scripting language (such as TCL, Perl, or XLisp) that works with your implementation language.

Often such prototyping languages can be embedded in the implementation language and carried over into the final product. Perhaps the Prototyping language can even become an extension language for the product. For example, TCL is commonly used as both a prototyping language and a scripting language.

If your product includes a database functionality, consider all the ways a customer may want to manipulate data. Extensibility can often save you from explaining to an angry customer why you didn't implement the obviously needed reverse-sort-on-maiden-name function.

A flexible Prototyping Language can be used to demonstrate a design's actual functional capabilities. However, if you cannot demonstrate its functionality, then you can fake it by using Judicious Fireworks (Pattern 6) in your Lightweight User Interfaces (see Pattern 5).

PATTERN 5: LIGHTWEIGHT USER INTERFACES

Problem   The customer wants some indication that you are building what he wants the end product to look and feel like, and you can end up spending a great amount of time getting the interface "just right."

Context   You are preparing for a demo that must show some level of interactivity. It is difficult to document interactivity requirements in specifications, so building a demo is inevitable.

Forces   The customer sees the interface as the application. Although a considerable amount of work may go on behind that interface, this may not be evident to the customer.

If the interface is too complete too early, the customer may falsely believe that the product is nearing completion.

The customer may demand a change to the interface that goes against all logic and makes fulfilling the requirements specifications impossible.

Solution   A minimal amount of development effort should be spent on developing a demonstration of the user interface. If at all possible, you should acquire tools that will allow you to rapidly change the interface without writing a lot of code. GUI builders are good for this.

Be prepared to discuss the rationale behind some of your interface decisions. Often the easiest way to do this is to provide alternate scenarios that demonstrate why your choice is better. You also want to make sure that you can change interface resources on the spot. That way, if a customer suggests something questionable such as "red text on a blue background," you can demonstrate why it may be a bad idea. Refer to Catalytic Scenarios (Pattern 2) for other reasons why you want to suggest alternate scenarios.

It is important to make the customer realize that the prototype interface is part of a demonstration, not part of the end product. Intentionally leave parts of the display incomplete, and don't spend too much time getting the layout "just right." You still want to impress the customer (Pattern 6, Judicious Fireworks), but you don't want to lead the customer into thinking that you are closer to finishing the product than you really are.

PATTERN 6: JUDICIOUS FIREWORKS

Problem   A demo needs to engage the customer but not give her unrealistic expectations.

Context   You want the demo to excite the customer. You also want to provide some substitute for parts of the product that are not yet functional.

Forces   An enthusiastic customer is a good thing. A satisfying demonstration can pacify a potentially angry customer if a schedule slippage occurs.

The customer wants to be pleasantly surprised and to feel that she is getting "more bang for the buck."

You or other developers feel a need to impress the customer with ad hoc features added outside the scope of the requirements specifications.

There is an overwhelming urge to dazzle the customer with senseless—but impressive—embellishments.

Solution   Dazzle the customer with just enough fireworks to leave her wanting for more. As discussed in the section on Lightweight User Interface (Pattern 5), the interface should not be too complete. However, certain parts of the interface can be given more attention than others. Pick a part of the interface that can put on the best show at the demonstration, and concentrate on it.

Be careful not to demo "extras" that will not appear in the final product. Clicking on icons of workstations and popping up graphic images of the people populating those stations may provide a good demo effect, but remember, the things a customer remembers most vividly about the demonstration should appear in the final product.

Sometimes, functional capabilities aren't ready yet and must be faked. This is one area where you can use "slick animation" and other fireworks to show what a certain function will look like when it is implemented. For example, if your product will highlight the best road to travel between two points on a map, then drawing a precomputed highlight instead of actually doing the calculation may be acceptable. But you must be certain that the customer realizes what she sees in the demo is a fake.

Another way you can provide fireworks is to demonstrate the product's extensibility (if extensibility is a required feature). Demonstrable examples of extensibility can often be provided by Prototyping Languages (Pattern 4).

Resist the urge to add dazzling new features to a design that has already been agreed upon. All too often, a customer is enticed by such features and will expect them to be delivered for free. Remember, by seeing the feature demonstrated, the customer may think that the work is already done, even if you have stressed that it is something you are only developing for possible future implementation. For example, resizing video displayed in a window looks great during a demo, even if you haven't properly dealt with pixelation, aspect ratios, and frame rates. However, your customer will expect resizing to work flawlessly in the delivered product, even if you explain that the demo was intended "just to show potential capabilities."

Once you've got your best fireworks coded, you want to make sure they are repeatable and saved for future demos; therefore, make sure that you Archive Scenarios (Pattern 7).

PATTERN 7: ARCHIVE SCENARIOS

Problem   Many developers are lulled into believing that they have given the customer all the demos he wants; thus they end up scrambling when another demo is requested.

Context   You have finished defining (and perhaps executing) your Demo Scenarios and are ready to continue with product development.

Forces   Surprise demos are exactly what they sound like. You will often have to give the same demo more than once, without having adequate time to prepare for it each time.

Each defined demo scenario needs to be consistent. Anyone who attends a demo of a particular scenario should leave with the same impression of product capabilities as someone who attended a previous demonstration.

Solution   Demo Scenarios should be archived. The code, scripts, results, and even bugs should be saved. While new scenarios will be developed or enhanced in the development effort, any old demos should be easily repeated. Any new features added to an archived demo should cause that demo to be rearchived as a new demo scenario. You can improve the presentation and flow of an archived demo, but resist the urge to make modifications, no matter how slight, without retaining the older version. Remember, a customer that is unsatisfied by new directions in development (even if he instigated them) may ask to see how something *used to* work.

You will find that customers will want you to show a successful demo to other important people. If you are developing business software, you may end up doing demos for the customer's accountants, investors, and employees. If you are developing government software, you may need to give demos for your customer's bosses, auditors, and consultants. Try to impress everyone equally.

CONCLUSION

Building high-quality software requires paying attention to details. Often, demo preparation details are not given much thought. We expect the customer to be patient. We say, "Trust us, it will be great." But that is not enough. We are selling a vision, and we must sell it every step of the way. Customer confidence is a primary concern; any doubts must be quelled. Demonstrations are mechanisms for engaging the customer in a dialogue in which his concerns can be addressed.

The Demo Prep language should be applied early in the software development process. Once it has been applied, demonstrations become easier, and you can focus on developing the actual product. In fact, you may find yourself offering more demos to your customer—to draw her comments out or to generate more enthusiasm. And, as we all know, an enthusiastic customer is indeed a good thing.

REFERENCES

[Alexander79] C. Alexander. *The Timeless Way of Building.* New York: Oxford University Press, 1979.

[Brooks75] F. P. Brooks. *The Mythical Man-Month.* Reading, MA: Addison-Wesley, 1975.

[Heckel92] P. Heckel. *The Elements of Friendly Software Design.* Alameda, CA: SYBEX, 1992.

[Love93] T. Love. *Object Lessons.* New York: SIGS Books, 1993.

Todd A. Coram can be reached at todd@btg.com.

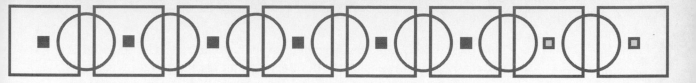

26 A Pattern Language for an Essay-Based Web Site

Robert Orenstein

The patterns described in this chapter express a method of writing and organizing essays on a World Wide Web site. The language was developed in the process of creating Anamorph, a server located at `http://www.anamorph.com/`.

Most of the essays at Anamorph contain interactive material; for example, a document about the growth of the Internet allows the user to enter a date and see how many people are expected to be on the Internet on that date. Many of the patterns discussed here are specific to an essay-based Web server, but others are more general and can be applied to almost any kind of Wcb sitc.

The patterns presented here are of two types:

- Fully developed patterns.
- Patterns that I believe exist, but haven't yet been fully expressed. These should probably be called pattern ideas rather than patterns.

These pattern ideas are presented here so that the fully developed patterns can refer to them. In general, the developed patterns can be used at any Web site, while the pattern ideas are specific to creating Web essays. A few of the pattern ideas (such as Interlaced Images) are descriptions of common solutions to problems that have been discussed elsewhere.

The fully formed patterns are presented in this format:

- The name of the pattern is given, along with a number for the pattern.
- This is followed by either two, one, or zero asterisks, which rank the pattern (see below).
- A description of the larger patterns that this pattern is a part of is presented [in brackets].
- A description of the **problem** is given, in boldface.
- The discussion of the problem and a justification for the solution are presented, in plain text.
- A **solution** to the problem is presented, in boldface.
- Subsidiary patterns that help form this pattern appear next [in brackets].
- A few of the patterns are followed by notes, which express thoughts and questions about the pattern.

For the pattern ideas, the name is presented in parentheses, followed by a general description of the problem and solution.

I've followed Alexander's ranking system for his patterns:

- Two asterisks (★★) means the pattern is probably invariant; the solution as stated is thought to summarize a property common to all possible ways of solving the problem.
- A single asterisk (★) indicates that the solution is either incomplete or can be improved upon.
- Patterns without asterisks represent just one way of solving the problem; other solutions are possible.

Some of these patterns contain examples of phrases with textual hyperlinks; in these, the links are underlined. For example, in the phrase "**See if you're on the list of <u>people I thank</u>**," the link would be found in the phrase "**<u>people I thank</u>**."

A version of this material in HTML is available at `http://www.anamorph.com/docs/patterns/default.html`. It is probably best read there, since the Web version was written using the patterns it describes.

A: TEXT STYLE PATTERNS

How should the text in a Web essay be written? Is there any need to differentiate Web text from printed text? These patterns provide guidelines for writing Web essays.

A.1: Natural Text Flow**

Many Web documents contain words and phrases that call attention to the fact that they are located on the Web. This is unnecessary.

In general, a book doesn't call attention to the fact that it is a book. *The Grapes of Wrath* isn't called *The Grapes of Wrath Book*, and its pages don't contain instructions saying "Please turn the page to continue reading."

Yet many Web documents call attention to their format. Titles on opening pages of Web sites say "My Home Page"; hyperlinks are often worded "Click here to see . . ." This is unnecessary, and it distracts readers from the natural flow of the text.

Therefore:

When creating Web documents, write text that reflects the content of the document. Write the text in your native tongue; avoid phrases that call attention to the "Webness" of the document.

[Natural Text Hyperlinks (A.2) describes a method for writing hyperlink text that meets this criteria, and Natural Text Directories (A.3) is a pattern for creating navigational tools for your document tree. Also, links to other documents can be created with a Natural Text Flow in your site's reference section (B.11).]

A.2: Natural Text Hyperlinks*

[You are writing your documents using a Natural Text Flow (A.1).]

One of the outstanding features of the Web is the ability to create hyperlinks to other documents. Yet the wording of these links can distract readers from the natural flow of the text.

One common method of dealing with this is to use pictorial links. But these are not always desirable; a document that is too heavy with images can slow down document retrieval (D.2). Textual links must often be used; how best to write these?

Natural Text Flow (A.1) states that link phrases like "Click here . . ." are distracting and bring the user out of the information flow and back into a realization of the information's format. But there is another reason not to write links in this fashion: a casual reader, speed-reading through your document, might only be scanning for links. If your links are written as above, a reader scanning for links may see nothing more than "here . . . here . . . here . . . ," which contains no useful information. In creating Anamorph, I discovered that if I wrote my pages as straight text, with no thought to the wording of the links, there were almost always natural links in the text. Instead of "Click here to see a card trick," I would write "About a year ago, I saw an interesting card trick," using the natural link suggested by the text.

Other examples of natural text hyperlinks at Anamorph are:

- I've written a number of fun little programs.
- See if you're on the list of people I thank.

(Clicking on the first of these takes you to an archive of programs, and the second link leads to a thank-you page.)

The benefits of this approach are that the text flows naturally, as if you are reading a book, newspaper, or magazine; also, speed-reading these pages for hyperlinks becomes easy.

Therefore:

Write your text document as if you were creating printed text in your native tongue, and look for the natural hyperlink phrase in the text you've written. It will almost always be there; if it isn't, tweak the text.

[Include links to other sites using Natural Text Hyperlinks in your Reference Section (B.11); use Natural Text Directories (A.3) to navigate through your document tree.]

A.3: Natural Text Directories

[Your site contains a Natural Text Flow (A.1), and your links to other documents are all Natural Text Hyperlinks (A.2). Now, your documents must be organized in a Low-Depth Document Trees (B.2).]

It can be difficult to find your way around the pages of a Web site. Some mechanism must be provided to allow your users to maneuver through your site's document set.

Graphic toolbars can provide such a navigational device, but they don't usually contain information telling the user where he or she is in relation to other documents. Another common method is to use links such as these in the headers and footers:

[Up] [Next] [Previous]

But these types of links aren't part of a Natural Text Flow, and they don't give the user a sense of where he or she is in the document set.

At Anamorph, the directory links at the tops and bottoms of the documents look something like this:

A Pattern from the <u>Pattern Language</u> at <u>Anamorph</u>

Reading from left to right, this indicates that

- The current document is a pattern.
- It is located in the document tree directly underneath the main pattern-language document.
- That document is located directly underneath the Anamorph site's opening page.

There are two advantages to this technique:

- It allows the user to get to any page on your Web site with a few clicks.
- The hyperlink text flows naturally.

Therefore:

Provide a series of natural text hyperlinks in your headers and footers. Write these hyperlinks as parts of a single sentence fragment. Reading from left to right, the user should know exactly where he or she is located in your document tree, with the leftmost position representing the current document and the rightmost position representing the site's home page. Pages between the current page and the top page should also be linked to this sentence fragment. Clicking on the proper links will take the user back up the document tree.

[Place the Natural Text Directories in Consistent Headers and Footers (B.6). Provide Next and Previous Reference Links (B.12) in the Reference Section (B.11).]

Note: This is one of my favorite patterns, but it is one of the hardest to understand without actually seeing it in use. In general, first-time users haven't appreciated this pattern; it is only after repeated visits that readers tell me they like this device. It should be pointed out that this technique won't work well with a document tree depth of four or more pages; I haven't yet had to face this problem at Anamorph.

B: ESSAY FORMATTING PATTERNS

All the essays at Anamorph are formatted in the same fashion. This section describes the patterns that make up this format.

Most of the patterns in this section are incomplete pattern ideas; thus they are not expressed as fully as I would prefer.

B.1: (Active Essays*)

Reading a pure-text essay can be uninvolving. Your essays can be made more interesting via interactive demonstrations of the principles described. This concept is often used in science museums, where texts about scientific mechanisms are balanced with active exhibits that demonstrate the ideas in a more intuitive, fun manner.

Clearly this does not always apply. For example, it is hard to imagine how a history of the 19th-century American communitarian movement could have a CGI program added to it. But scientific essays can usually be made more involving with interactivity.

B.2: (Low-Depth Document Trees*)

Keep your Web site's document depth low. This has been much discussed elsewhere.

B.3: (Document Format Consistency**)

Format all the documents on your server consistently. This provides a sense of continuity between the documents at your site, makes them easily identifiable by their appearance, and makes it easier to write programs to serve HTML documents in different formats. Present all documents in this format, even error pages.

This principle has been much discussed elsewhere.

B.4: (Section-Based Essays*)

Divide your essays into sections, each no longer than a single screen of text. Give each section its own title, and make them easily accessible from the Introductory Section (B.7) via a Document Content Listing (B.10). You can use Short, Single-Page Essays (B.5) to present these sections in a single document, or you can present each section on a separate page. Ideally, your users will have a choice in how they wish to view the essay—as a complete document or one section at a time.

B.5: (Short, Single-Page Essays)

Much has been written in Web style guides about dividing site material into pages; some sites prefer to divide documents into many pages, and other sites use one page per document. At Anamorph, most of the essays are presented as single pages. They are all relatively short, and presenting them as single pages keeps their loading time to a minimum.

B.6: (Consistent Headers and Footers**)

The headers and footers on each document on a Web site should be formatted the same way as the site's other headers and footers. At Anamorph, the headers contain only a Natural Text Directory (A.3), and the footers contain a Natural Text Directory, the Relevant Dates (C.3), a link to the Author Biography (C.2), and the Reachable Author's E-mail address (C.6).

B.7: (Introductory Section)

For each essay, provide an introduction that contains both text and an Introductory Picture (B.8). Summarize the contents of the essay in the introductory text, and, ideally, add an interactive CGI to this section to heighten the user's interest (B.9, Activity Toward the Top).

B.8: (Introductory Picture)

Provide a picture at the top of each essay. Make each document's picture unique, and have the image summarize the main point of the document visually. Ideally, the image will make the user want to look at your other documents just because the pictures are so intriguing.

B.9: (Activity Toward the Top*)

Present interactivity close to the top of the essay. This allows users to try your page as if it's a hands-on exhibit in a museum; if they like what they see, they can read more about the topic later in the essay.

Most successful science museums use this pattern. Exhibits involve user participation in some form, with detailed scientific information available on the side. Watching museumgoers is instructive; they will almost always try an exhibit first, and only read the supporting material if what they've seen interests them.

B.10: (Document Content Listing)

At the end of an essay's Introductory Section (B.7), provide a table of contents that describes what the rest of the essay contains. This Document Content Listing should contain hyperlinks to the proper sections of the essay. At Anamorph, the titles of the different sections are identical to the text of the corresponding hyperlink in the Document Content Listing.

B.11: Reference Section

[You are writing your documents using a Natural Text Flow (A.1).]

There may be many documents on the Web that discuss material related to your essays. How do you best point interested readers to these other pages?

One way of providing links to related pages at other sites is to intersperse them as needed within your text. This can distract the user from the flow of your text, however, and it may be incomplete or inaccurate (there might be *similar* documents on the Web that don't relate *directly* to what you're writing).

For example, the HTML version of this essay at Anamorph should contain links to other pattern language sites, but such links don't always fit in with the natural flow of the text. How can these links be provided without compromising the flow of the document?

Once again, it is worthwhile to look at books, and see how references are handled there. Rather than providing all the information about related material within the text, many books present a bibliography at the end. The same technique can be implemented in a Web essay.

Therefore:

Provide a Reference Section as the last section in your essay, formatted as an HTML unordered list. In this section, supply links to related Web pages, along with a description of these pages. If there are related newsgroups, provide links to these as well.

[Write the links as Natural Text Hyperlinks (A.2). Provide links to your Home Version Essays (E.2) here; if your essay is divided into multiple parts, place your Next and Previous Reference Links (B.12) here.]

B.12: (Next and Previous Reference Links)

When a particular essay is large, it might be broken into a series of smaller documents. "Next" and "previous" links are necessary; place these in your Reference Section (B.11) and write them as Natural Text Hyperlinks (A.2).

C: META-INFORMATIONAL PATTERNS

So far this discussion has centered on creating essays and documents that carry the information you want to communicate. But there is another type of information that needs to be expressed: information about the creation of the material at your site. These patterns express ways of communicating this meta information.

C.1: Exposable Guts**

When information is found to be valuable, users will want to know more about the creation of the information itself.

The desire for meta information takes many forms. When readers like a book, they want to know more about the author. If a Web page contains constructs that a Web author has not seen before, he will want to know how the corresponding HTML code was written.

One of the features of almost every Web browser is the ability to view HTML source code. This is invaluable for learning HTML; when a user asks, "How did they do that?" the answer is immediately available. Many HTML guides recommend providing an Author Biography (C.2) so the author's credentials can be seen and users can make their own decision as to the reliability of the presented information.

But these measures don't go far enough. When a large image loads particularly quickly, a user might want to know how the image file is formatted. If a particular essay seems incomplete, a user may want to know what changes are planned for that essay in the future. If a user is learning how to do CGI programming, he or she may want to view your CGI source code.

In short, almost every piece of information on a Web site has some meta information that goes with it. Most readers won't care about the meta information, but some of them will. It is useful to provide interested users access to your meta information without overwhelming the casual reader.

Therefore:

At your Web site, provide meta information that explains the techniques you used to gather and present your main body of work. The meta information should never be the first thing the user sees, but it should be easily accessible from the primary information.

[Relevant Dates (C.3) and Author Biography (C.2) are simple, often-used examples of this. Worksheet Documents (C.4) can provide information on what changes are intended for a particular document in the future, and Downloadable CGIs (C.5) provides a natural extension of the browser's "View Source" menu.]

C.2: (Author Biography**)

Provide short biographies of your essays' authors. This allows the user to judge the credentials of the author, provides information about related work that the author has done, and satisfies the reader's curiosity.

C.3: (Relevant Dates**)

For each essay, provide its creation date and the date it was last modified. This allows users to judge the timeliness of the information, and it lets them quickly see if a document has been changed since the last time they read it. Place these dates in your Consistent Headers and Footers (B.6).

C.4: Worksheet Documents*

[You are using Exposable Guts (C.1) to present the meta information at your site, and you have a Reference Section (B.11) at the bottom of each page.]

You want to publish a document on the Web, but it isn't finished yet.

Anamorph, like most Web sites, is in a permanent state of construction. An essay can be incomplete for many reasons:

- Its completion is dependent on input from users after they've seen a preliminary version.

- Images are to be added to the essay, but there hasn't been time to draw them yet.
- A CGI is working, and you want to show it, but the explanatory text isn't finished.

One common way of dealing with such problems is to add an "Under Construction" sign to the document. But this method has two problems: it mixes the meta information with the primary information, and it doesn't provide any picture of how the document will look once it's complete. Another solution is necessary.

Therefore:

For any unfinished page, create a separate Worksheet Document. In this document, provide information describing why the page is unfinished and what you expect to add.

[Provide a link to the Worksheet Document from the incomplete document's Reference Section (B.11). Format the Worksheet Document according to the patterns you've chosen from Document Format Consistency (B.3).]

C.5: (Downloadable CGIs)

CGI source code can be provided. This pattern is particularly useful for teachers.

C.6: (Reachable Author*)

The author of a document should be easily reachable by E-mail from the documents the author has written, via the HTML "mailto" tag. This allows the user to get more information, ask relevant questions, and give corrections immediately.

C.7: (Immediate Document Discussion)

A mechanism for group discussion of essays can be provided. This might consist of a link from the document's Reference Section (B.11) to a page where readers can write their comments about the documents or make comments about the comments.

C.8: New Document Notification**

[You are using Exposable Guts (C.1) to provide meta information to your readers.]

As you add new essays to your site, users who have visited previously will be unaware of the new material unless they decide to connect to your site again to see what's changed.

Of course, there's no guarantee that they'll do so. Bookmark lists grow; revisiting becomes infrequent; favorite sites are forgotten. And when a user does revisit, there may not be any new documents available, or perhaps the new documents at the site aren't relevant to that reader's needs. Much of the user's time is spent panning the Web for new nuggets of information that may or may not exist.

Some of the regularly changing Web sites, like *HotWired*, now send their users E-mail listing the new material for a given week. So far this has been done mostly at sites that call themselves Web magazines, but there's no reason not to do this for *every* Web site. If your users are notified whenever a new document is added to the site, they can decide for themselves whether or not to revisit, depending on whether or not the new essay is relevant to them. The end result is less work for your users.

Therefore:

On the opening page of your Web site (close to the bottom), include a form with a single field for collecting users' E-mail addresses. Use these addresses to send out notices whenever new documents are added to the site. If the site contains documents on many different topics or subtopics, include checkboxes so users can choose what kind of new information they want to be notified about.

[Changed Document Notification (C.9) can be used to inform a user when the contents of a particular document have changed.]

Note: On the Web, quality is often confused with quantity: overwhelmingly, the most oft-cited statistic about Web sites is the number of hits they receive. New Document Notification may in fact reduce the number of hits your site takes, but it certainly won't reduce its quality.

C.9: (Changed Document Notification*)

Provide a mechanism for collecting the E-mail addresses of users who want to know when an oft-changed document has been modified. This is similar to a New Document Notification (C.8).

C.10: (Temporal Document Versioning)

As documents are changed, keep the old versions around, and make them available from a hyperlink in the Reference Section (B.11).

D: SLOW MODEM SPEED PATTERNS

Different users will receive information from your server at different speeds. When developing Web pages, it is easy to forget to plan for the user connecting at 14.4 kbps. These patterns express ways of developing documents that can be more painlessly retrieved at slower speeds.

D.1: 14.4 Kbps Testing*

The documents at some Web sites can take a minute or longer to load at 14.4 kbps.

It has been reported that 48 percent of all Web users connect at 14.4 kbps (see `http://www.cc.gatech.edu/gvu/user_surveys/survey-04-1995/bulleted/use_bullets.html`). Yet many sites seem oblivious to this, presenting large pictures with high bit depths and QuickTime movies that take a long time to load. Some users will wait around for a large image to finish loading, but others will leave once they realize how long it will take. It is not unreasonable to assume that the longer an image takes to load, the greater the number of viewers that will be lost.

One client's opening page presented a single ISMAP image, well laid out and easy to navigate. The image was beautiful, but there was one problem: it took one and a half minutes for it to load at 14.4 kbps! This isn't a long time for someone who has the intention to visit the site, but for the casual viewer, this is too long. It turned out that the client had been testing their pages over an Ethernet network; every time they looked at their images, loading was almost instantaneous. They didn't understand the problem until days after the site opened, when one of their employees began to demo the site at a party. He was shocked at how long it took.

This problem could have been easily prevented:

Therefore:

When creating a Web site, test pages with large images on slower-speed systems. Near the development machines, set up a computer that is connected

to the Net via a 14.4 kbps modem, and test all pages from this machine before signing off on them.

[Loading time can be shrunk substantially by using Low-Bit-Depth Images (D.4) to shrink the size of the image and Sparse Images (D.2) if it fits in with the goals of the site.]

D.2: (Sparse Images)

If the content of your site does not depend on images to communicate the information there, and if it is not an overtly "commercial" Web site, use images sparingly.

D.3: (Interlaced Images*)

Interlace your images, particularly large images. A detailed discussion on this topic is available at `http://info.med.yale.edu/caim/M_III_3.HTML`.

D.4: (Low-Bit-Depth Images*)

Use images with lower bit depths whenever possible. At Anamorph, all images are three-bit GIFS or smaller.

E: OTHER PATTERNS

This section presents a small collection of pattern ideas that don't fit naturally into any of the other categories.

E.1: (Link-Type Distinction*)

Provide a mechanism by which links to on-site documents can be distinguished visually from links to off-site documents. At Anamorph, links to off-site documents are italicized. It would also be useful to have a visual mechanism to distinguish links to other site documents from links to other sections in the same document, but HTML does not make this easy.

E.2: (Home Versions*)

There are two problems with active essays: too many simultaneous hits to your CGIs can slow down your server, and the user may want to experiment with your programs at different times, sometimes while not connected to the Web. One solution is to provide home versions of your Web programs that can be downloaded and run on the user's machine.

For example, a downloadable card trick is available on the Anamorph site. If a user chooses five cards from a deck, and one of them is hidden, the server can be told the other four cards and respond by correctly guessing the hidden fifth card. How is this done? The server takes many hits as users try to figure out the trick's mechanism; the load has been alleviated somewhat by providing a downloadable version of the card trick.

ACKNOWLEDGMENTS

This document is based on lessons learned while building Anamorph (`http://www.anamorph.com/`), and it couldn't have been completed here without Kent Beck's encouragement, Ward Cunningham's extensive help, and the insightful comments I received from the PLoP '95 reading group.

WEB SITE REFERENCES

An excellent manual on Web design has been published by the Center for Advanced Instructional Media. It can be read at

`http://info.med.yale.edu/caim/StyleManual_Top.HTML`

The Graphics, Visualization and Usability Center has been conducting a series of surveys on Web usage. Their results can be viewed at

`http://www.cc.gatech.edu/gvu/user_surveys/`

Alan Kay coined the term *active essay*. **His Web document on the subject is available at**

`http://www.atg.apple.com/areas/Learning_Concepts/`

`Evolution_Active_Essay/active_essay.html`

Robert Orenstein can be reached at `rlo@netcom.com`.

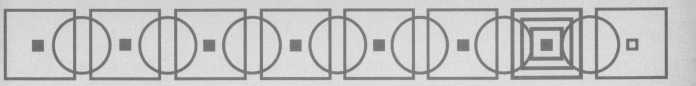

CONCURRENT PROGRAMMING/
DISTRIBUTED SYSTEMS

PART 7

Programming concurrent and distributed systems has always been challenging. Initially, the challenge was to make the most of a valuable resource—the computer. Today, concurrent and distributed systems have grown in importance, and we still want to make the most of valuable resources, but the resources have changed! *Information* is now key—as the explosive growth of the Internet and World Wide Web so clearly illustrates—and computing systems must be tailored to it, not the other way around. With information the hot commodity, the world is hungry for distributed, concurrent systems that can handle vast information flows flexibly and efficiently.

Although network and computer power have increased dramatically over the years, developing software for concurrent and distributed systems is as difficult as ever. One cause is inherent complexity. Race conditions, deadlock, and synchronization overhead are just a few of the peculiar hazards these systems pose. Meanwhile, the diversity of hardware and software platforms makes it hard to reuse algorithms, detailed designs, interfaces, implementations, and tools. But a deeper problem is that the patterns of concurrent and distributed systems aren't widely taught or even documented. Too many developers learn only how to program sequentially, and most popular applications target stand-alone personal computers exclusively. The dearth of training and experience, coupled with inherent complexity, severely limits the number of concurrent and distributed systems that succeed.

A successful developer of these systems needs much more than a knowledge of object-oriented design methods and language mechanisms. Distributed and concurrent systems teem with recurring design problems; expert developers learn their solutions through years of hands-on experience. Often they solve new problems by appealing to existing systems: "We'll be more robust in the face of crashes if we use a stateless server like the one in NFS. . . ." The experts succeed largely because they've learned the patterns of concurrency control, distribution, resource sharing, and a host of others.

Studying the chapters in this part of the book will help you learn several of these patterns. Each of the first four chapters presents a single pattern aimed at a pervasive problem in the concurrent/distributed field. The fifth and last chapter presents a pattern language for concurrent applications that run on parallel platforms.

In Chapter 27, titled Half-Sync/Half-Async, Doug Schmidt and Charles Cranor show how to simplify complex concurrent software architectures without sacrificing performance. They focus on how to decouple asynchronous programming tasks (such as handling hardware interrupts) from synchronous ones (such as rendering an image). Asynchronous tasks are efficient but can be hard to program, while synchronous tasks are easier to program but can be inefficient if they aren't integrated carefully using this pattern.

A second pervasive problem is addressed in Resource Exchanger (Chapter 28), another contribution from Aamod Sane and Roy Campbell (their first was Detachable Inspector in Part 3). Here they explain how to resolve common resource starvation problems in systems with concurrent producers and consumers. Their pattern discusses ways to manage resources (such as memory buffers or disk blocks) that will not penalize producers or consumers unfairly when resource contention is high. The Resource Exchanger pattern has been used in stand-alone systems as well as in client-server distributed systems.

Client-server systems are the topic of Chapter 29, "The Client-Dispatcher-Server Design Pattern," by Peter Sommerlad and Michael Stal. Their pattern introduces the notion of a "dispatcher," which decouples the location of a particular distributed service from its use. The dispatcher determines the location of a suitable server in a distributed system when a client program requests a service.

Greg Lavender joins Doug Schmidt (coauthor of "Half-Sync/Half-Async") to address yet another pervasive problem. Theirs is a widely used pattern that hides the complexity of concurrent and distributed programming within "Active Objects." This pattern lets different tasks in an application execute independently while localizing the complexity of synchronization. Many RPC and distributed object computing systems (DCE and CORBA, for example) implement network servers as Active Objects. This pattern is commonly used to implement the synchronous tasks in the Half-Sync/Half-Async pattern.

The last chapter in this part (Chapter 30), "Selecting Locking Designs for Parallel Programs," differs from the others in that it does not try to solve just one design problem. Rather, author Paul McKenney examines a variety of problems that synchronization primitives were invented to address. His pattern language guides you to the right primitive for a particular context based on forces such as speedup, contention, overhead, granularity, cost, and complexity. Paul's analysis makes it obvious that no synchronization mechanism is clearly best in every circumstance. What's compelling about his pattern language is that it lays bare the strengths and weaknesses of each mechanism. Far better to design the right primitive into your system at the outset than to have to root out the wrong one later.

Excellence in concurrent programming and distributed systems requires more than just experience. Samuel Taylor Coleridge suggests that "experience is like the stern lights of a ship, which illumine only the track it has passed."[1] The goal of patterns is to avoid repeating the mistakes of the ship ahead; to avoid the rough seas and the rocky reefs it encountered. Instead, we write notes and leave them in bottles for the benefit of those who follow. A pattern or pattern language that addresses problems in concurrent programming and distributed systems is a welcome gift.

---

[1] Samuel Taylor Coleridge (1772–1834), English poet, critic. Interview reported by Thomas Allsop in *Table Talk*, 1820 (published in *Letters and Conversations of S. T. Coleridge*, Vol. 1, 1836; reprinted in *Collected Works*, Vol. 14, ed. by Kathleen Coburn, 1990). From *The Columbia Dictionary of Quotations*, licensed from Columbia University Press. Copyright © 1993 by Columbia University Press.

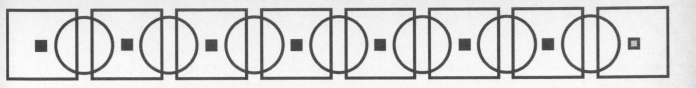

Half-Sync/Half-Async:
An Architectural Pattern
for Efficient and Well-Structured
Concurrent I/O

27

Douglas C. Schmidt and Charles D. Cranor

Abstract This chapter describes the Half-Sync/Half-Async pattern, which integrates synchronous and asynchronous I/O models to support both programming simplicity and execution efficiency in complex concurrent software systems. In this pattern, higher-level tasks use a synchronous I/O model, which simplifies concurrent programming. In contrast, lower-level tasks use an asynchronous I/O model, which enhances execution efficiency. This pattern is widely used in operating systems such as UNIX, Mach, Windows NT, VMS, and other complex concurrent systems.

Intent The Half-Sync/Half-Async pattern decouples synchronous I/O from asynchronous I/O to simplify concurrent programming efforts without degrading execution efficiency.

Motivation To illustrate the Half-Sync/Half-Async pattern, consider the software architecture of the BSD UNIX networking subsystem [Leffler+89], shown in Figure 1. The BSD UNIX kernel coordinates I/O between asynchronous communication devices (such as network adapters and terminals) and applications running on the operating system (OS). Packets arriving on communication devices are

delivered to the OS kernel via interrupt handlers. These handlers are initiated asynchronously by hardware interrupts. Interrupt handlers receive
packets from devices and trigger processing of higher-layer protocols such as
IP, TCP, and UDP. Valid packets containing application data are queued at
the Socket layer. The OS then dispatches any user processes waiting to
consume the data. These processes synchronously receive data from the
Socket layer using the read system call. A user process can make read calls
at any point; if the data is not available, the process will sleep until the data
arrives from the network.

In the BSD architecture, the kernel performs I/O asynchronously in response to device interrupts. In contrast, user-level applications perform I/O
synchronously. This separation of concerns into a half-synchronous, half-
asynchronous concurrent I/O structure resolves the following two forces:

1. **Need for programming simplicity.** Programming an asynchronous I/O
   model can be complex, because input and output operations are triggered
   by interrupts. Asynchrony can cause subtle timing problems and race
   conditions when the current thread of control is preempted by an interrupt

FIGURE 1 BSD UNIX software architecture

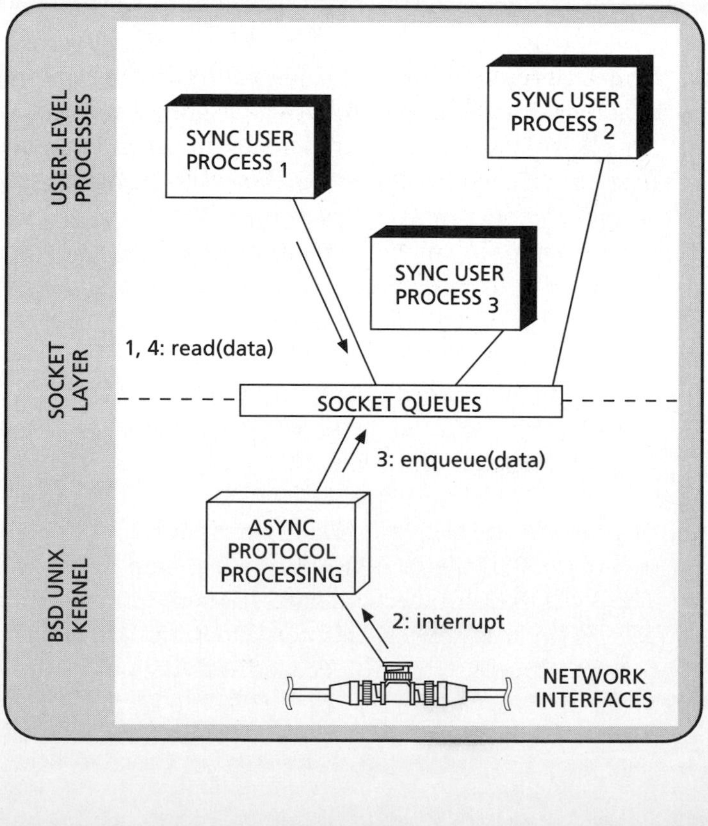

handler. Moreover, interrupt-driven programs require extra data structures in addition to the runtime stack. These data structures are used to save and restore states explicitly when events occur asynchronously. In addition, debugging asynchronous programs is hard, since external events occur at different points of time during program execution. In contrast, programming an application with a synchronous I/O model is easier, because I/O operations occur at well-defined points in the processing sequence. Moreover, programs that use synchronous I/O can block while awaiting the completion of I/O operations. The use of blocking I/O allows programs to maintain state information and execution history in a runtime stack of activation records rather than in separate data structures. Thus there is a strong incentive to use a synchronous I/O model to simplify programming.

2. **Need for execution efficiency.** The asynchronous I/O model maps efficiently onto hardware devices driven by interrupts. Asynchronous I/O enables communication and computation to proceed simultaneously. In addition, context switching overhead is minimized, because the amount of information necessary to maintain the program state is relatively small [Schmidt+95a]. Thus there is a strong incentive to use an asynchronous I/O model to improve runtime performance. In contrast, a completely synchronous I/O model may be inefficient if each source of events (such as a network adapter, a terminal, or a timer) is associated with a separate active object (such as a process or thread). Each of these active objects contains a number of resources (such as a stack and a set of registers) that allow it to block while waiting on its source of events. Thus, this synchronous I/O model increases the time and space required to create, schedule, dispatch, and terminate separate active objects.

Solution To resolve the tension between the need for concurrent programming simplicity and execution efficiency, use the Half-Sync/Half-Async pattern. This pattern integrates synchronous and asynchronous I/O models in an efficient, well-structured manner. In this pattern, higher-level tasks (such as database queries or file transfers) use a synchronous I/O model, which simplifies concurrent programming. In contrast, lower-level tasks (such as servicing interrupts from network controllers) use an asynchronous I/O model, which enhances execution efficiency. Because there are usually more high-level tasks than low-level tasks in a system, this pattern localizes the complexity of asynchronous processing within a single layer of the software architecture. Communication between tasks in the synchronous and asynchronous layers is mediated by a queueing layer (the Socket layer).

Applicability Use the Half-Sync/Half-Async pattern when

3. A system possesses all of the following characteristics:

   ■ It must perform tasks in response to external events that occur asynchronously.

   ■ It is inefficient to dedicate a separate thread of control to perform synchronous I/O for each source of external events.

   ■ The higher-level tasks in the system can be simplified significantly if I/O is performed synchronously.

4. One or more tasks in the system *must* run in a single thread of control, while other tasks may benefit from multithreading. For example, legacy libraries like X Windows and Sun RPC are often nonreentrant. Therefore, multiple threads of control cannot safely invoke these library functions concurrently. However, to ensure quality of service or to take advantages of multiple CPUs, it may be necessary to perform bulk data transfers or database queries in separate threads. The Half-Sync/Half-Async pattern can be used to decouple the single-threaded portions of an application from the multithreaded portions. This decoupling enables nonreentrant functions to be used correctly, without requiring changes to existing code.

Structure and Participants Figure 2 illustrates the structure of participants in the Half-Sync/Half-Async pattern. The participants in the Half-Sync/Half-Async pattern are described below.

1. **The Synchronous task layer (e.g., user processes).** The tasks in this layer perform high-level I/O operations that transfer data synchronously to message queues in the queueing layer. Unlike the asynchronous layer, tasks in the synchronous layer are *active objects* (see Chapter 30) that have their own runtime stack and registers. Therefore, they can block while performing synchronous I/O.

2. **Queueing layer (the Socket layer).** This layer provides a synchronization and buffering point between the synchronous task layer and the asynchronous task layer. I/O events processed by asynchronous tasks are buffered in message queues at the queueing layer for subsequent retrieval by synchronous tasks (and vice versa).

3. **Asynchronous task layer (BSD UNIX kernel).** The tasks in this layer handle lower-level events from multiple external event sources (such as network interfaces or terminals). Unlike the synchronous layer, tasks in the asynchronous layer are *passive objects* that do not have their own runtime stack or registers. Thus, they cannot block indefinitely on any single source of events.

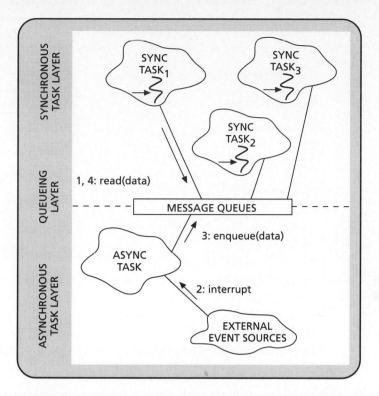

FIGURE 2   The structure of participants in the Half-Sync/Half-Async pattern

4. **External event sources (network interfaces).** External devices (such as network interfaces and disk controllers) generate events that are received and processed by the asynchronous task layer.

Collaborations   Figure 3 illustrates the dynamic collaboration among participants in the Half-Sync/Half-Async pattern when input events arrive at an external event source (output event processing is similar).

These collaborations are divided into the following three phases:

1. **Async phase.** In this phase, external sources of events interact with the asynchronous task layer via interrupts or asynchronous event notifications.

2. **Queueing phase.** In this phase, the queueing layer provides a well-defined synchronization point that buffers messages passed between the synchronous and asynchronous task layers in response to input events.

3. **Sync phase.** In this phase, tasks in the synchronous layer retrieve messages placed into the queueing layer by tasks in the asynchronous layer. Note

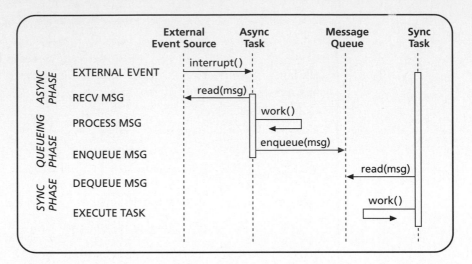

FIGURE 3 Collaboration between participants in the Half-Sync/Half-Async pattern

that the protocol used to determine how data is passed between the synchronous and asynchronous task layers is orthogonal to how the queueing layer mediates communication between the two layers.

The asynchronous and synchronous layers in Figure 3 communicate in a "producer/consumer" manner by passing messages. The key to understanding the pattern is to recognize that synchronous tasks are active objects. Thus, they can make blocking read or write calls at any point in accordance with their protocol. If the data is not yet available, tasks implemented as active objects can sleep until the data arrives. In contrast, tasks in the asynchronous layer are passive objects. Thus, they cannot block on read calls. Instead, tasks implemented as passive objects are triggered by notifications or interrupts from external sources of events.

Consequences   The Half-Sync/Half-Async pattern yields the following benefits:

- **Higher-level tasks are simplified.** Because higher-level tasks are shielded from lower-level asynchronous I/O, they are simplified. Complex concurrency control, interrupt handling, and timing issues are delegated to the synchronous task layer. This layer handles the low-level details (such as interrupt handling) of programming an asynchronous I/O system. The asynchronous layer also manages the interaction between the OS and hardware-specific components (such as DMA, memory management, and device registers).

- **Synchronization policies in each layer are decoupled.** Therefore, each layer need not use the same concurrency control strategies. For example, in the single-threaded BSD UNIX kernel, the asynchronous task layer implements concurrency control via low-level mechanisms (such as raising and lowering CPU interrupt levels). In contrast, user processes in the synchronous task layer implement concurrency control via higher-level synchronization constructs (such as semaphores, message queues, condition variables, and record locks).

- **Inter-layer communication is localized at a single point.** This happens because all interaction is mediated by the queueing layer. The queueing layer buffers messages passed between the other two layers. This eliminates the complexity of locking and serialization that would occur if the synchronous and asynchronous task layers directly accessed each other's memory.

- **Performance is improved on multiprocessors.** The use of synchronous I/O can simplify programming *and* improve performance on multiprocessor platforms. For example, long-duration data transfers (such as downloading a large medical image from a database) can be simplified and performed efficiently using synchronous I/O. One processor can be dedicated to the thread transferring the data, which enables the instruction and data cache of that CPU to be associated with the entire transfer operation.

The Half-Sync/Half-Async pattern has the following drawbacks:

- **A boundary-crossing penalty may be incurred.** This may result from synchronization, data copying, and context switching overhead. This overhead typically occurs when data is transferred between the synchronous and asynchronous task layer via the queueing layer. In particular, most operating systems that use the Half-Sync/Half-Async pattern place the queueing layer at the boundary between the user and kernel protection domains. A significant performance penalty may be incurred when crossing this boundary. For example, the socket layer in BSD UNIX accounts for a large percentage of the overall TCP/IP networking overhead [Hutchinson+91].

- **Asynchronous I/O for higher-level tasks is lacking.** Depending on the design of the system interface, it may not be possible for higher-level tasks to utilize low-level asynchronous I/O devices. Thus, the system I/O structure may prevent applications from utilizing the hardware efficiently, even if external devices support asynchronous overlap of computation and communication.

Implementation This section describes how to implement the Half-Sync/Half-Async pattern by factoring tasks in the system into synchronous and asynchronous layers that communicate through a queueing layer.

Long-Duration Tasks

Many tasks in a system can be simplified by allowing them to perform synchronous I/O. Often these are long-duration tasks that transfer large streams of data [Schmidt+95b] or perform database queries that may block for prolonged periods while waiting for responses from servers.

Implement these long-duration tasks using an active-object model as in Chapter 30 [Lavender+95]. Since active objects have their own runtime stack and registers, they can block while performing synchronous I/O. Implementing an active-object mechanism requires a means of switching between different threads of control. At the lowest level, this means having a place to *store* the current thread's hardware state (e.g., the values in all its registers, including its stack pointer) and *load* the new thread's state. This functionality is sufficient to implement a nonpreemptive threading mechanism with no memory protection. Packages of user-level threads typically provide this type of functionality.

However, more functionality is required in order to implement active objects as threads and processes in a robust, multitasking operating system. In this case, each thread of control has its own address space, which is managed by the processor's memory management unit (MMU). When switching between threads, the new process's address space information must be loaded into the MMU. Cache flushing may also be required, especially with certain types of virtually addressed caches. In addition to an address space, an OS process often has a "user identification." This tells the operating system what access rights the process has and how much system resources it can consume.

To prevent a single process from taking over the system indefinitely, there must be a way to preempt it. Preemption is generally done with a timer. Periodically (e.g., 1/100 of a second), the timer generates a clock interrupt. During this interrupt the operating system checks to see if the currently running process needs to be preempted. If so, it saves the process's state and loads the state of the next process to run. When the interrupt returns, the new process will be running.

Short-Duration Tasks

Certain tasks in a system cannot block for prolonged periods of time. Often these tasks run for a short time and interact with external sources of events (such as GUIs or interrupt-driven hardware network interfaces). To increase efficiency and ensure adequate response time, these sources of events must be serviced rapidly, without blocking.

Implement these short-duration tasks using a reactive, passive-object model [Schmidt95a]. Passive objects borrow their thread of control from elsewhere (such as the caller or a separate interrupt stack). Therefore, these tasks must use asynchronous I/O, since they cannot block for long periods of time. The primary motivation for not blocking is to ensure adequate response time for other system tasks (such as high-priority hardware interrupts, like clock timers).

There are several ways to develop a well-structured framework for asynchronous I/O, as discussed below.

Demultiplexing Events

The Reactor pattern [Schmidt95a] manages a single-threaded event loop that supports the demultiplexing and dispatching of multiple *event handlers*, which are triggered concurrently by multiple events. This pattern combines the simplicity of single-threaded event loops with the extensibility offered by object-oriented programming. The Reactor pattern serializes event handling within a process or thread and often eliminates the need for more complicated threading, synchronization, or locking.

A reactor may be implemented to run atop synchronous and/or asynchronous sources of events. The behavior it provides to its event handlers is distinctly asynchronous, however. Thus, a handler cannot block without disrupting the response time for other sources of events.

A Multilevel Interrupt Scheme

These implementations allow non-time-critical processing to be interrupted by higher-priority tasks (such as hardware interrupts) if higher-priority events must be handled before the current processing is done. Data structures used by the asynchronous layer must be protected (e.g., by raising the processor priority or using semaphores) to prevent interrupt handlers from corrupting shared states while they are being accessed.

For example, in an operating system kernel, the need for a multilevel interrupt scheme is strongly influenced by the hardware interrupt service time. If this time can be reduced significantly, it may be more efficient to perform all processing at the hardware interrupt level to avoid the overhead of an extra software interrupt. Implementations of TCP/IP have reduced in-bound packet protocol processing overhead to the point where the cost of the two-level interrupt scheme dominates the overall packet processing time.

The Queueing Layer

The queueing layer provides a synchronization point for buffering messages exchanged by tasks in the asynchronous and synchronous layers. The following are several topics that must be addressed when designing the queueing layer:

- **Concurrency control.** If tasks in the asynchronous and synchronous layers execute concurrently (due to either multiple CPUs or hardware interrupts), it is necessary to ensure that concurrent access to a shared queue state is serialized (to avoid race conditions). Thus, the queueing layer is typically implemented using concurrency control mechanisms such as semaphores, mutexes, and condition variables. These mechanisms ensure that messages can be inserted and removed to and from the queueing layer without corrupting internal queue data structures.

- **Layer-to-layer flow control.** Systems cannot devote an unlimited amount of resources to buffer messages in the queueing layer. Therefore, it is necessary to regulate the amount of data passed between the synchronous and asynchronous layers. For example, layer-to-layer flow control prevents synchronous tasks from flooding the asynchronous layer with more messages than can be transmitted on network interfaces. Tasks in the synchronous layer can block. Therefore, a common flow control policy is to put a task to sleep if it produces and queues more than a certain amount of data. When the asynchronous task layer drains the queue below a certain level, the synchronous task can be awakened to continue. In contrast, tasks in the asynchronous layer cannot block. Therefore, if they produce an excessive amount of data, a common flow control policy is to have the queueing layer discard messages. If the messages are associated with a reliable connection-oriented network protocol, the sender will eventually time out and retransmit.

- **Data copying overhead.** Some systems (such as BSD UNIX) place the queueing layer at the boundary between the user and kernel protection domains. A common way to decouple these protection domains is to copy messages from users to kernels and vice versa. However, this increases system bus and memory load, which may degrade performance significantly when large messages are moved across domains. One way to reduce data copying is to allocate a region of memory shared between the synchronous task layer and the asynchronous task layer [Druschel+93]. This allows the two layers to exchange data directly, without copying data into the queueing layer. For example, Cranor and Parulkar [Cranor+95] present an I/O subsystem that minimizes boundary-crossing penalties by using polled interrupts to improve the handling of continuous media I/O streams. This approach also provides a buffer management system that allows efficient page remapping and shared memory mechanisms for use between user processes, the kernel, and kernel devices.

Sample Code   This section provides examples of code using the Half-Sync/Half-Async pattern in two different parts of the BSD UNIX operating system [Leffler+89]. These examples illustrate how the Half-Sync/Half-Async pattern is used by the BSD kernel to enable user processes to operate synchronously while ensuring that the kernel operates asynchronously. The first example illustrates how this pattern is used in the networking subsystem to input data through the TCP/IP protocol stack over Ethernet. The second example illustrates how this pattern is used in the file subsystem to implement interrupt-driven output for disk controllers.

BSD Networking Subsystem

This example illustrates how the Half-Sync/Half-Async pattern is used to structure the synchronous invocation of a `read` system call, asynchronous reception and protocol processing of data arriving on a network interface, and synchronous completion of the `read` call. Figure 1 illustrates the participants in and structure of this pattern in BSD UNIX. For a comprehensive explanation of the BSD UNIX networking subsystem, see *TCP/IP Illustrated*, by W. R. Stevens [Stevens93].

Synchronous Invocation   Consider a user process that creates a passive-mode TCP stream socket, accepts a connection, and receives TCP data from the connected socket descriptor. To the user process, the `read` system call on the connection appears to be a synchronous operation (i.e., the process makes the call, and the data is returned). However, many steps occur to implement this system call. When the `read` call is issued, it gets trapped in the kernel and vectored into the network socket code synchronously. The thread of control ends up in the kernel's `soreceive` function, which performs the half-synchronous part of the processing. The `soreceive` function is responsible for transferring the data from the socket queue to the user. It must handle many types of sockets (such as datagram sockets and stream sockets). A simplified view of what `soreceive` does is shown below, with emphasis on the boundary between the synchronous and asynchronous layers:

```
/* Receive data from a socket. */

int soreceive ( ... )
{
```

```
for (;;) {
  sblock (...);   /* lock socket recv queue */

  /* mask off network interrupts to protect queue */
  s = splnet ();

  if (not enough data to satisfy read request) {
    sbunlock (...); /* unlock socket queue */

    /***** Note! *****
        The following call forms the boundary
        between the Sync and Async layers. */

    sbwait (...); /* wait for data */
    splx (s); /* drop splnet */
  }
  else
    break;
}

splx (s); /* drop splnet */

/* copy data to user's buffer at normal priority */
uiomove (...);

s = splnet (); /* mask off network interrupts */

sbunlock (...);    /* unlock socket queue */
splx (s);          /* restore spl */

return (error code);  /* returns 0 if no error */
}
```

The preceding code illustrates the boundary between the synchronous user layer process and the asynchronous kernel layer. Although the user process can sleep while waiting for data, the kernel cannot be suspended, because other user processes and devices in the system may require its services.

There are several ways in which the user's read request is handled by soreceive, depending on the characteristics of the socket and the amount of data in the socket queue:

- **Completely synchronous.** If the data requested by the user is in the socket queue, it is copied out immediately and the operation completes synchronously.

- **Half-synchronous and half-asynchronous.** If the data requested by the user has not yet arrived, the kernel will call the sbwait function to put the user process to sleep until the requested data arrives.

Once `sbwait` puts the process to sleep, the OS scheduler will context-switch to another process that is ready to run. To the original user process, however, the `read` system call appears to execute synchronously. When one or more packets containing the requested data arrive, the kernel will process them asynchronously. When enough data has been placed in the socket queue to satisfy the user's request, the kernel will wake up the original process, which completes the `read` system call.

Asynchronous Reception and Protocol Processing The half-asynchronous part of the user's read request starts with a packet arriving on a network interface, which causes a hardware interrupt. All inbound packet processing is done in the context of an interrupt handler. It is not possible to sleep during an interrupt, because there is no UNIX process context and no separate thread of control. Therefore, an interrupt handler must borrow the caller's thread of control (i.e., its stack and registers). The BSD UNIX kernel uses this strategy to borrow the thread of control from interrupt handlers and from user processes that perform system calls.

Most interrupt-driven computers assign priority levels to the interrupts. For example, on a SPARC there are fifteen interrupt levels, with Level 1 the lowest level and Level 15 the highest level. Other processors have different levels (e.g., the Motorola 68030 has seven interrupt levels). Under BSD UNIX, processor-specific interrupt levels are assigned machine-independent symbolic names known as SPL levels (the term SPL originated in the PDP-11 days of UNIX). For example, the highest network hardware interrupt level is called SPLIMP, the clock interrupt is called SPLCLOCK, and the highest possible interrupt level is called SPLHIGH. For each of these levels there is a corresponding function of the same name that sets the processor interrupt level to that value. Thus, the `splimp` function is called to block out all network hardware–level interrupts. All the `spl` functions return the previous processor priority level, which represents what the priority should be restored to when the operation completes.

Conventional versions of BSD UNIX use a two-level interrupt scheme to handle packet processing. Hardware-critical processing is done at a high priority (SPLIMP), and less time-critical software processing is done at a lower priority level (SPLNET). This two-level interrupt scheme prevents the overhead of software protocol processing from delaying the servicing of other hardware interrupts. The two-level BSD UNIX packet processing scheme is divided into hardware-specific processing and protocol processing. When a packet arrives on a network interface, it causes an interrupt at that interface's interrupt priority. All networking interfaces have priority of <= SPLIMP.

The operating system services the hardware interrupt and then inserts the packet on the input queue in the protocol layer (such as the IP protocol). A network software interrupt is then scheduled to service that queue at a lower priority (e.g., SPLNET). Once the network hardware interrupt is serviced, the rest of the protocol processing is done at the lower priority level, as long as there are no other, higher-level interrupts pending. The BSD kernel is carefully designed to allow hardware interrupts to occur during a software interrupt without losing data or corrupting buffers.

As an example, consider a host with an AMD LANCE Ethernet NIC chip. The device driver for this chip is called `le` (for "LANCE Ethernet"). Upon the packet's arrival, the `lerint` function is called from the interrupt handler. Its job is to acknowledge and clear the interrupt. It then extracts the packet from the network interface and copies it into memory buffers called "mbufs," as follows:

```
int lerint (...)
{
   /* perform hardware sanity checks */
  while (inbound buffers to process) {

    /* get length and clear interrupt ... */
    /* read the packet into mbufs */

    ether_input (interface, ether_type, packet);
    /* free buffer */
  }
}
```

The mbufs are then handed off from `lerint` to the following Ethernet function, called `ether_input`. Each network protocol has a packet queue associated with it (e.g., the IP packet queue). The `ether_input` function first determines which network protocol is being used and puts the packet on the correct queue. It then arranges for a network software level interrupt to occur. This interrupt will occur at the lower-priority SPLNET level. At this point, the hardware interrupt has been handled and the interrupt service routine exits. The relevant code for the `ether_input` function is shown below:

```
int ether_input (char *intf, int etype,
                 struct mbuf *packet)
{
  switch (etype) {
  case ETHERTYPE_IP:
    /* schedule network interrupt */
    schednetisr (NETISR_IP);
    inq = &ipintrq;
    break;
```

```
    /* etc... */
    }

    s = splimp ();

    /* Try to insert the packet onto the IP queue. */

    if (IF_QFULL (inq)) {
      /* queue full, drop packet */
      IF_DROP (inq);
      m_freem (packet);
    } else
      /* queue packet for net interrupt */
      IF_ENQUEUE (inq, m);
    splx (s);
}
```

Once the hardware interrupt is done, a network software interrupt occurs at the SPLNET level (provided there are no higher-level interrupts pending). If the inbound packet is an IP packet, the kernel calls the IP interrupt routine (ipintr). IP protocol processing (such as header parsing, packet forwarding, fragmentation, and reassembly) is performed in this routine. If the packet is destined for a local process, then it is handed off to the transport protocol layer. The transport layer performs additional protocol processing (such as TCP segment reassembly and acknowledgments). Eventually, the transport layer appends the data to the receive socket queue and calls sbwakeup. This call wakes up the original process that was sleeping in soreceive while waiting for data on that socket queue. Once this is done, the software interrupt is finished processing the packet.

The following code illustrates the general logic of the thread of control running from ipintr up through tcp_input to sowakeup, which forms the boundary between the asynchronous and synchronous layers. The first function is ipintr, which handles inbound IP packets:

```
int ipintr (...)
{
  int s;
  struct mbuf *m;

  /* loop, until there are no more packets */
  for (;;) {
    s = splimp ();
    IF_DEQUEUE (&ipintrq, m); /* dequeue next packet */
    splx(s);
    if (m == 0) return;  /* return if no more packets */
```

```
    if (packet not for us) {
      /* route and forward packet */
    } else {
      /* packet for us... reassemble */

      /* call protocol input, which is tcp_input() */
      (*inetsw[ip_ protox[ip->ip_ p]].pr_input)(m,
       hlen);
    }
  }
}
```

Since our current example involves a TCP/IP packet, the "protocol switch" `inetsw` invokes the `tcp_input` function, which handles an inbound TCP packet:

```
int tcp_input (m, iphlen)
{
  /* lots of complicated protocol processing... */

  /* We come here to pass data up to the user */
  sbappend (&so->so_rcv, m);
  sowakeup((so), &(so)->so_rcv);
  /* ... */
}
```

The `sowakeup` function wakes up the user process that was asleep in `read` while waiting for the packet to arrive. As discussed in the following section, this function forms the boundary between the asynchronous and synchronous layers.

Synchronous Completion When the data is appended to the socket queue, the `sowakeup` is invoked if a user process is asleep waiting for data to be placed into its buffer.

```
void sowakeup (so, sb)
{
  /* ... */
  if (a user process is asleep on this queue) {

    /***** Note! *****
       The following call forms the boundary
       between the Async and Sync layers. */

    wakeup ((caddr_t) &sb->sb_cc);
  }
}
```

When a process goes to sleep, there is a "handle" associated with that process. To wake up a sleeping process, the `wakeup` call is invoked on that handle. A process waiting for an event will typically use the address of the data structure related to that event as its handle. In the current example, the address of the socket-receive queue (`sb->sc_cc`) is used as a handle.

If there are no processes waiting for data on a socket queue, nothing interesting will happen. However, in the example shown earlier, the original process was sleeping in `soreceive`, waiting for data. The kernel will wake up this process in the `soreceive` function, which loops back to check if enough data has arrived to satisfy the `read` request. If all the data requested by the user has arrived, `soreceive` will copy the data to the user's buffer, and the system call will return.

To the user process, the `read` call appears to be synchronous. However, this is an illusion supported by the Half-Sync/Half-Async pattern. In particular, asynchronous processing and context switching are performed while the process is sleeping. Note that the kernel never blocks and is always doing something, even if that something is to run an "idle" process.

Disk Controller

This example illustrates another use of the Half-Sync/Half-Async pattern in the context of the BSD UNIX file subsystem. The previous example illustrated how the pattern is used to *input* data from the Ethernet interface through the TCP/IP protocol stack and up to a user process. This example illustrates how the pattern is used to *output* data from a user process through the BSD UNIX raw I/O subsystem and to a disk.

There are two ways to access UNIX storage devices such as disks. One is through their block-special devices in `/dev`; the other is through their character-special devices. Accesses through the block-special devices go through a layer of software that buffers disk blocks. This buffering takes advantage of the locality of data references. In contrast, access through the character-special device (called "raw" I/O) bypasses the buffering system and directly accesses the disk for each I/O operation. Raw I/O is useful for checking the integrity of a file system before mounting it, or of user-level databases that have their own buffering schemes.

Synchronous Invocation If a process does an `open` on a character-special file (e.g., `/dev/rdk0a`) and then does a `write`, the thread of control will end up in the device driver's write entry point. This performs the half-synchronous part of the processing. Most raw disk devices have a `write` entry point that references a global raw I/O routine stored in the `cdevsw` vector. The following illustrates this entry:

```
/* Do a write on a device for a user process. */
int raw_write (dev_t dev, struct uio *uio)
{
  return physio (cdevsw[major(dev)].d_strategy,
                 (struct buf *) NULL,
                 dev, B_WRITE, minphys, uio);
}
```

This entry point causes a synchronous redirect into `physio`, which is a routine that does physical I/O on behalf of a user process. Physical I/O writes directly from the raw device to user buffers, bypassing the buffer cache. The `physio` routine is implemented as follows:

```
int
physio (int (*strategy)(),
        struct buf *bp,
        dev_t dev,
        int flags,
        u_int (*minphys)(),
        struct uio *uio);
{
  struct iovec *iovp;
  struct proc *p = curproc;
  int error, done, i, nobuf, s, todo;

  /* ... */

  /* read and write, from above */
  flags &= B_READ | B_WRITE;

  bp->b_flags = B_BUSY | B_PHYS | B_RAW | flags;

  /* call driver's strategy to start the transfer */
  (*strategy) (bp);

  /***** Note! *****
     The following call forms the boundary
     between the Sync and Async layers. */

  while ((bp->b_flags & B_DONE) == 0)
    /* Wait for the transfer to complete */
    tsleep ((caddr_t) bp, PRIBIO + 1, "physio", 0);

  /* ... */
}
```

The `physio` routine is given a user buffer, a device, and that device's `strategy` routine. The strategy routine's job is to initiate a read or write operation on a buffer and return immediately. Because the pointer to the user's buffer is provided by the user process, `physio` must first validate the buffer's address. Once the buffer has been validated, it is encapsulated in a `buf` structure. The flags in the `buf` structure are set to indicate if this is a read or a write operation. The flags are also set to indicate that this is a raw I/O operation. Once the `buf` structure is set up, it is passed to the device-specific `strategy` routine. The `strategy` routine schedules the I/O operation and returns. Next, `physio` sleeps until the I/O operation is done.

Asynchronous Processing Both buffered and raw I/O requests enter the device driver synchronously, via the device's `strategy` routine:

```
void strategy (struct buf *bp)
{
  /* ... */

  s = splbio (); /* protect the queues */

  /* sort the buffer structure into the
     driver's queue (e.g., using disksort()) */

  if (drive is busy) { splx (s); return; }

  /* flow control is here.... if the
     drive is busy the request stays in the queue */

  /* start first request on the queue */

  /* done! */

  splx (s);
  return;
}
```

The `strategy` routine is designed to be general so that most device I/O can be routed through this interface (the exception being some `ioctl` calls that perform control operations on a device, such as formatting a cylinder on a disk). The bookkeeping information required to store state information during the asynchronous I/O is stored in a data structure accessible to the driver. The example above assumes that the driver handles only one request at a time. It is possible to have a device that handles multiple requests at a time. In that case, multiple lists keep track of which buffers are active and which are waiting for I/O.

Synchronous Completion A hardware interrupt is generated by the disk controller when the write request completes. This triggers an interrupt routine that ties the asynchronous task layer back into the synchronous task layer, as follows:

```
int intr (void *v)
{
    struct buf *bp;
    /* get current request into "bp" */

    /***** Note! *****
      The following ties the Async layer back into
      the Sync layer. */

    biodone (bp); /* Wakeup the sleep in physio(). */
    /* start next request on queue */
    return (1); /* done */
}
```

The interrupt function services and clears the hardware interrupt. This involves looking in the driver's state table to determine which I/O request has completed. The I/O request is represented by a `buf` structure. Once the `buf` structure has been identified, the `biodone` function is called to signal the higher-level kernel software that the write request is complete. This causes the sleeping process to return from `tsleep`. The interrupt function must also start any queued write requests if necessary.

Variations For input, the conventional form of the Half-Sync/Half-Async pattern uses "push-driven" I/O from the asynchronous task layer to the queueing layer and "pull-driven" I/O from the synchronous task layer to the queueing layer. These roles are reversed for output. The following variations appear in some systems:

- **Combining asynchronous notification with synchronous I/O.** It is possible for the synchronous task layer to be notified asynchronously when data is buffered at the queueing layer. This is how signal-driven I/O is implemented by the UNIX SIGIO mechanism. In this case, a signal is used to "push" a notification to higher-level user processes. These processes then use `read` to "pull" the data synchronously from the queueing layer.

- **Spawning synchronous threads on demand from asynchronous handlers.** Another way to combine asynchronous notification with synchronous I/O is to spawn a thread on demand when an asynchronous event occurs. I/O is then performed synchronously in the new thread. This approach ensures that the resources devoted to I/O tasks are a function of the number of work requests being processed in the system.

- **Providing asynchronous I/O to higher-level tasks.** Some systems extend the preceding model still further by allowing notifications to push data along to the higher-level tasks. This approach is used in the extended signal interface for UNIX System V, Release 4. In this case, a buffer pointer is passed along with the signal-handler function. Windows NT supports a similar scheme using overlapped I/O and I/O completion ports [Custer93]. In this case, when an asynchronous event completes, an overlapped I/O structure contains an indication of the event that completed, along with the associated data.

- **Providing synchronous I/O to lower-level tasks.** Single-threaded operating systems (such as BSD UNIX) usually support a hybrid synchronous/asynchronous I/O model only for higher-level application tasks. In these systems, lower-level kernel tasks are restricted to asynchronous I/O. Multithreaded systems permit synchronous I/O operations in the kernel if multiple wait contexts are supported via threads. This is useful for implementing polled interrupts, which reduce the amount of context switching for high-performance continuous media systems by dedicating a kernel thread to poll a field in shared memory at regular intervals [Cranor+95]. If the asynchronous task layer possesses its own thread of control, it can run autonomously and use the queueing layer to pass messages to the synchronous task layer. Microkernel operating systems typically use this design. The microkernel runs as a separate process that exchanges messages with user processes [Black90].

Known Uses The BSD UNIX networking subsystem [Leffler+89] and the original System V UNIX STREAMS communication framework [Ritchie84] use the Half-Sync/Half-Async pattern to structure the concurrent I/O architecture of user processes and the OS kernel. All I/O in these kernels is asynchronous and triggered by interrupts. The queueing layer is implemented by the Socket layer in BSD and by STREAM heads in System V STREAMS. I/O for user processes is synchronous. Most UNIX applications are developed as user processes that call the synchronous, higher-level read/write interfaces. This design shields developers from the complexity of asynchronous OSs handled by the kernel. There are provisions for notifications (via the SIGIO signal) that asynchronously trigger synchronous I/O.

 The multithreaded version of Orbix 1.3 (MT-Orbix) [Horn93] uses several variations of the Half-Sync/Half-Async pattern to dispatch CORBA remote operations in a concurrent server. In the asynchronous layer of MT-Orbix, a separate thread is associated with each HANDLE that is connected to a client. Each thread blocks synchronously reading CORBA requests from the client. When a request is received, it is formatted and then enqueued at the queueing layer. An active object thread in the synchronous layer then wakes up, dequeues the request, and processes it to completion by performing an upcall on the CORBA object implementation.

A large-scale telecommunications system uses the Half-Sync/Half-Async pattern in an application-level gateway that routes messages between satellites and ground-control stations [Schmidt95b]. The Gateway implements the Half-Sync/Half-Async pattern with the ADAPTIVE Service eXecutive (ASX) framework [Schmidt94]. The Reactor class category from the ASX framework [Schmidt95a] implements an object-oriented demultiplexing and dispatching mechanism that handles events asynchronously. The ASX `MessageQueue` class implements the queueing layer, and the ASX `Task` class implements active objects in the synchronous task layer.

The Conduit communication framework [Zweig90] from the Choices OS project [Campbell+93] implements an object-oriented version of the Half-Sync/Half-Async pattern. User processes are synchronous active objects, an adapter conduit serves as the queueing layer, and the conduit microkernel operates asynchronously.

Related Patterns
- The synchronous task layer uses the Active Object pattern (see Chapter 30).

- The asynchronous task layer may use the Reactor pattern [Schmidt95a] to demultiplex asynchronous events from multiple sources of events.

- The queueing layer provides a facade [Gamma+95] that simplifies the interface to the system's asynchronous task layer.

- The queueing layer is also a mediator [Gamma+95] that coordinates the exchange of data between the asynchronous and synchronous task layers.

ACKNOWLEDGMENTS

We would like to thank Lorrie Cranor and Paul McKenney for their comments and suggestions on improving this chapter.

REFERENCES

[Black90] D. L. Black. "Scheduling Support for Concurrency and Parallelism in the Mach Operating System." *IEEE Computer, 23* (1990): 23–33.

[Campbell+93] R. Campbell, N. Islam, D. Raila, and P. Madany. "Designing and Implementing Choices: An Object-Oriented System in C++." *Communications of the ACM, 36,* (1993): 117–126.

[Cranor+95] C. Cranor and G. Parulkar. "Design of Universal Continuous Media I/O." In *Proceedings of the 5th International Workshop on Network and Operating Systems Support for Digital Audio and Video (NOSSDAV '95)*, pp. 83–86.

[Custer93] H. Custer. *Inside Windows NT*. Redmond, WA: Microsoft Press, 1993.

[Druschel+93] P. Druschel and L. L. Peterson. "Fbufs: A High-Bandwidth Cross-Domain Transfer Facility." In *Proceedings of the 14th Symposium on Operating System Principles (SOSP)*, 1993.

[Gamma+95] E. Gamma, R. Helm, R. Johnson, and J. Vlissides. *Design Patterns: Elements of Reusable Object-Oriented Software*. Reading, MA: Addison-Wesley, 1995.

[Horn93] C. Horn. *The Orbix Architecture.* Technical Report, IONA Technologies, 1993.

[Hutchinson+91] N. C. Hutchinson and L. L. Peterson. "The x-kernel: An Architecture for Implementing Network Protocols." *IEEE Transactions on Software Engineering, 17* (1991): 64–76.

[Lavender+95] R. Greg Lavender and Douglas C. Schmidt. "Active Object: An Object Behavioral Pattern for Concurrent Programming." Chapter 30, this volume.

[Leffler+89] S. J. Leffler, M. McKusick, M. Karels, and J. Quarterman. *The Design and Implementation of the 4.3BSD UNIX Operating System*. Reading, MA: Addison-Wesley, 1989.

[Ritchie84] D. Ritchie. "A Stream Input-Output System." *AT&T Bell Labs Technical Journal, 63* (1984): 311–324.

[Schmidt94] D. C. Schmidt. "ASX: An Object-Oriented Framework for Developing Distributed Applications." In *Proceedings of the 6th USENIX C++ Technical Conference*. USENIX Association, 1994.

[Schmidt95a] D. C. Schmidt. "Reactor: An Object Behavioral Pattern for Concurrent Event Demultiplexing and Event Handler Dispatching." In J. O. Coplien and D. C. Schmidt (eds.), *Pattern Languages of Program Design*. Reading, MA: Addison-Wesley, 1995, pp. 529–546.

[Schmidt95b] D. C. Schmidt. "A System of Reusable Design Patterns for Application-Level Gateways." In S. P. Berczuk (ed.), *The Theory and Practice of Object Systems (Special Issue on Patterns and Pattern Languages)*. New York: Wiley, 1995.

[Schmidt+95a] D. C. Schmidt and T. Suda. "Measuring the Performance of Parallel Message-Based Process Architectures." In *Proceedings of the Conference on Computer Communications (INFOCOM)*. IEEE, April 1995.

[Schmidt+95b] D. C. Schmidt, T. H. Harrison, and E. Al-Shaer. "Object-Oriented Components for High-Speed Network Programming." In *Proceedings of the Conference on Object-Oriented Technologies*. USENIX, 1995.

[Stevens93] W. R. Stevens. *TCP/IP Illustrated*, Vol. 2. Reading, MA: Addison-Wesley, 1993.

[Zweig90] J. M. Zweig. "The Conduit: A Communication Abstraction in C++." In *Proceedings of the 2nd USENIX C++ Conference*. USENIX Association, 1990, pp. 191–203.

Douglas C. Schmidt and Charles Cranor can be reached at the Department of Computer Science, Washington University, St. Louis, MO 63130. Douglas Schmidt can also be reached at schmidt@cs.wustl.edu.

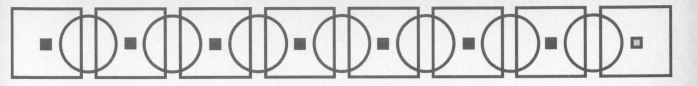

Resource Exchanger: A Behavioral Pattern for Low-Overhead Concurrent Resource Management

28

Aamod Sane and Roy Campbell

ABSTRACT

Consider a machine that runs multiple servers, such as an ftp server and an http server. Clients of such servers may request resources like ftp connections and http connections at varying rates and hold them for varying durations. The servers must compete for resources like connection records and I/O memory on the same machine. As a result, one server may starve another. Similarly, one fast but loaded server might keep critical resources (such as network drivers) busy and thereby starve other servers. This chapter presents a pattern that can be used to avoid such imbalances and at the same time allow efficient communication.

Intent Use Resource Exchanger to reduce overall server load, allocate resources fairly, get fast responses, and achieve a simple, flexible program structure.

Aliases Resource Exchanger is also known as Neither Client Nor Server Be.

Motivation In a concurrent system, servers have to do more work than clients, such as allocating and initializing resources. Thus servers can become computation and communication bottlenecks. Further, multiple servers on one machine must compete with one another for shared facilities such as network drivers. Thus one fast but busy server with many clients can starve another server, depriving its clients of services even when noncritical resources are available. Ideally, we want both fast servers *and* balanced server loads.

Consider servers' interaction with the network driver.[1] If a server is slow copying data from the driver to its local memory, it depletes the memory available to the driver. This may result in lost packets for a different server. While a driver might attempt to allocate new buffers, such allocation wastes communication time. On the other hand, if a server is normally fast but experiences bursty traffic (i.e., rapidly receives many client requests), it will end up holding more driver memory for its data and starving other servers. To prevent such imbalances, we wish to minimize the time and memory a network driver allocates to each server.

In the usual scheme,[2] the network driver hands a buffer to a server, which then copies it and eventually returns it to the driver. The copying can take a considerable amount of time. Further, if a server later discovers that the communicated data was in fact unnecessary (e.g., it was a duplicate fragment), the processing time is wasted. Also, if there are multiple servers, then each may use different amounts of network buffer space, so one server may starve other servers. So we have two problems: unnecessary data processing and server load imbalances. Therefore, the network driver must decide as early as possible (possibly before or as part of demultiplexing), to deliver packets or drop them, and it must make this decision quickly. Thus we need a solution that can resolve the following forces:

- The network driver (or any other critical shared facility) cannot wait too long for servers to return buffers.

- The network driver should not spend time on extraneous activities like copying or allocating memory.

- We cannot allocate too much memory to one server, and servers should be able to optimize packet processing without affecting the network driver.

- Clients must get reasonable service, which means every server must be able to communicate sufficiently often.

- The software structure must be simple, fast, and easy to understand.

---

[1] For explanatory purposes, let us pretend that http/ftp servers interact directly with the network driver; in reality, real-time protocols, distributed shared memory [Sane+90, Sane+95] and other special servers may need direct interaction for proper performance.

[2] That is, the one used in the absence of special hardware such as scatter-gather direct memory access.

The solution presented here is not restricted to networking in particular; similar problems arise in allocating resources like CPUs and disk drivers. The Known Uses section on page 471 considers other applications, and solutions for different constraints are mentioned in the section Variations.

SOLUTION

Our solution resolves the forces described above by combining a variant of double buffering with a credit scheme.

In the scheme described above, the network driver hands a buffer to a server; the driver cannot use that buffer while the data is being copied. The data is of no consequence to the driver, however; it merely wants a buffer to replace the one it gave up. Therefore, instead of giving away a buffer to a server, the network driver *exchanges* a buffer with the server. Then, while the server is busy copying and processing the data, the network driver's buffer pool is left intact; the driver need never allocate new buffers or copy them itself. In turn, the server is free to optimize packet processing (such as in-place demarshaling) in any way, without penalizing the network driver.

Thus, every server must have a buffer it can exchange with the driver. To deal with varying server loads, a server negotiates with the memory system and keeps a pool of buffers according to the traffic it expects. The number of buffers allowed depends on the *credit* a server has with the memory system. By "charging" a server for the amount and duration of memory it holds, the memory system can balance memory allocation and deallocation to the servers if the server load fluctuates. The memory allocation algorithm can execute independently of the network driver, and each server is responsible for maintaining its own pools. If a server keeps driver buffers for too long, it eventually runs out of buffers to exchange with the driver. At such time, the driver will drop any messages sent to that server, thus throttling the data flow and penalizing each server according to its buffer usage. Furthermore, the exchange routine is simple and can be executed very quickly.

The classes for the resulting driver-server architecture are shown in Figure 1. The demultiplexer is the exchanger, from the viewpoint of the network driver. Servers must register themselves with the demultiplexer and identify a packet id used by `lookup()` for demultiplexing. When the network driver gives a packet (`newBuffer()`) to the demultiplexer, the demultiplexer determines the destination server and exchanges buffers with the server.

The solution resolves the forces as follows:

■ Buffer exchange minimizes the time a network driver must wait for the servers.

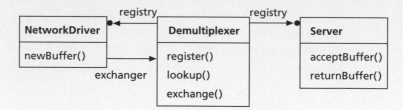

FIGURE 1 A network driver that exchanges buffers

- The credit scheme allocates memory fairly, and the exchange decouples server processing from network driver execution.
- The network driver has a constant supply of buffers and does not need to allocate or copy them.
- Servers with high loads will eventually expend their credit and run out of exchangeable buffers. At this time, servers with low loads will get service.

The resource exchanger is a simple, symmetric architecture. The credit scheme can be developed independently of the exchange scheme; indeed, static memory allocation may suffice in many cases. The pattern also guarantees that resources like buffers are not aliased, so resource allocation and deallocation can be decentralized. Further, as we will see in the Implementation section below, the primary exchange scheme easily admits variations.

APPLICABILITY

Use this pattern to manage resources shared among multiple processes. The pattern is applicable when the following requirements are met:

- The processes act as resource generators and acceptors.
- Once a generator generates a resource, it does not use the resource again before it is returned by the acceptor.
- It is possible to preallocate at least one resource per process that can be exchanged.
- Resource allocation and usage is expensive, but exchange is cheap.

Due to its simplicity and flexibility, Resource Exchanger may also be applicable to nonconcurrent resource manangement. However, Resource Exchanger is less suitable if you need preemptive allocation or occasionally need to collect all resources in one place.

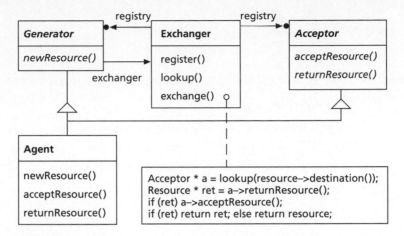

FIGURE 2   A static structure for a resource exchanger

STRUCTURE

The diagram in Figure 2 generalizes the structure in Figure 1. Note that Acceptor and Generator are roles, and the same agent may be an acceptor or a generator at different times. In our example from the Motivation section, the NetworkDriver is a generator and a Server is an acceptor. Agents need not implement both interfaces, but they can do so if required. Note that the credit scheme is implemented by acceptors as part of the `returnResource()` method.

Classes, Responsibilities, and Collaborators

Generator
(`NetworkDriver`)

Generators generate resources to be consumed by acceptors.

Responsibilities:

Generate resources, set resource destinations, and exchange resources.

Collaborators:

Exchanger.

Exchanger
(`Demultiplexer`)

Exchangers implement resource exchange.

Responsibilities:

Register generators and acceptors.

Route exchange requests from a generator to an acceptor.

Collaborators:

Acceptor, Generator.

Acceptor Acceptors consume generated resources and return used resources in exchange.
(Server)

Responsibilities:

Consume resources using `acceptResource()`.

Maintain exchangeable resources by interacting with some resource manager (e.g., a memory manager for network buffers).

Return resources using `returnResource()`.

Collaborators:

Exchanger.

Agent`(NetworkDriver, Server)`

Agents implement the acceptor, the generator, or both interfaces. An agent may be an acceptor or a generator at different times.

Dynamic Collaborations

The interaction diagram in Figure 3 shows the dynamic collaborations. We have shown generators as generating resources using `newResource()` and exchanging them using `exchange()`. However, for our networking example, the resource is "generated" as the data received from the network. Also, we have shown different acceptors and generators, but the same agent may act like one or the other at different times.

CONSEQUENCES

The resource exchanger is a mediator [Gamma+95]. Like any mediator, it decouples various agents, abstracts the collaborations, and simplifies object interfaces. Resource Exchanger is particularly good at improving resource management in the presence of concurrency.

The benefits of the Resource Exchanger are:

1. *Concurrency control.* Although the exchanger centralizes generator/ acceptor interaction, concurrency control remains simple, since agents access Resource Exchanger code for a limited duration.

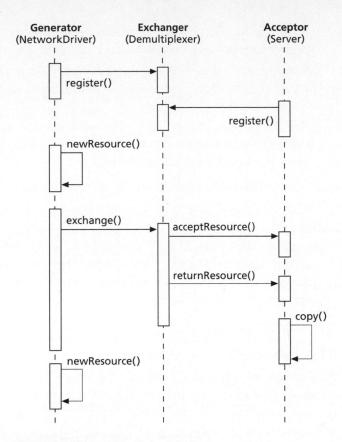

FIGURE 3 Dynamic collaborations

2. *Deadlock.* As long as resources are always exchanged, resource users cannot deadlock waiting for resources.

3. *Fairness.* Servers are penalized fairly. For instance, if a server holds a resource for too long, it will not have one available for exchange and will lose data.

4. *Decoupling.* Concurrent activities become nearly independent of each other. In our example, after a server receives a packet, it may do whatever it likes with the packet and keep it as long as it wishes.

5. *Passive exchange.* The Exchanger need not be a process—it is usually a passive interface. Thus there is no context-switching overhead due to the exchanger.

Another set of advantages accrues from the simple software architecture:

1. *A simple interface.* Processes have a symmetric structure and behavior, so all agents—generators or acceptors—can be instances of a single class.

2. *Flexibility.* Any number of acceptors and generators can be accommodated. An agent can act as a generator or a receiver at different times.

3. *Decentralized allocation and deallocation.* Allocation and deallocation can be decentralized, since the pattern guarantees that there are no aliases.

4. *Degradation to nonexchange.* If necessary, the resource exchanger gracefully degrades into a traditional resource manager and admits other variations (see the Variations section).

Some limitations of Resource Exchanger are as follows:

1. *Need for cooperation.* One noncooperating client can cause problems for other agents. Also, agents may succeed or fail in exchanging resources, but they should not suspend their operation under any circumstances. However, since agent behavior is straightforward, implementors can ensure that agents use system library code to interact with the exchanger.

2. *Exchanger becomes critical.* System designers must be careful not to overload the Exchanger subsystem. If it becomes a bottleneck, system performance can seriously degrade.

3. *Overuse of resources.* Resource Exchanger involves a resource-time trade-off, trading resources for time, since every acceptor must have at least one resource to exchange.

4. *No preemption.* Resource Exchanger is nonpreemptive in that agents do not force other agents to relinquish resources.

IMPLEMENTATION

Implementing Resource Exchanger involves many variations in policies and requirements. Many of the variations are unavoidable (often they are dictated by the hardware configuration), while others are motivated by agent requirements. The other primary issue in using Resource Exchanger is concurrency control. We will first consider examples where hardware configuration leads to difficulties:

1. Occasionally, hardware restrictions may conspire to prevent direct use of the resource exchanger. For example, network buffers may have to be allocated from a fixed area of memory where DMA is possible. In such

cases, use an allocation agent that allocates and deallocates resources. The exchanger knows that agent and interacts with it for buffer allocation.

2. In the case of networking, protocol stacks may require the driver to fill particular buffers. In that case, the driver must first obtain an appropriate buffer and then return it, rather than swapping arbitrary buffers.

Other variations are due to different policies of mediation and differences in the roles of agents. Some possibilities are as follows:

1. Network protocols often have to examine packet headers. Such "peeking" is usually very fast, since only a small region is examined. This is an excellent example of when resource usage is best implemented within the exchanger, where it can be shared among agents and highly optimized.

2. Sometimes one process is more central than others. For instance, one agent may be the primary generator while other agents play more passive roles. In this case, the process can double as the exchanger and dictate system policies. For instance, the actual exchange of packets in a networking system might be implemented by the driver, and the registry would be implemented separately. This simplifies interfaces to multiple servers whose requirements differ due to diverse hardware constraints. Following the pattern strictly may clutter the demultiplexer with hardware details.

The next implementation issue is concurrency. Agents may exhibit concurrent access

- When two generators attempt to exchange resources with each other
- When two generators attempt to exchange resources with one receiver
- When registering new agents
- When looking up old agents

For a successful implementation, none of these cases can lead to bottlenecks.
   However, two prerequisites for using Resource Exchanger are that agent interaction (e.g., invocation of `returnResource()` or `newResource()`) must be very fast and agents must not suspend. Therefore, all four cases of contention among agents can be handled using spin locks.
   Thus, it remains for the implementor to build a fast and safe agent registry. A hash table with a lock-per-bucket often suffices when a good hash function is available.

SAMPLE CODE AND USAGE

We will now consider the structure of our networking system example (see Figure 1) in greater detail. The class `Demultiplexer` is the exchanger. It also doubles as a memory manager, but only because network buffer management is often system- and hardware-dependent, and the demultiplexer can ask the driver for hardware-specific allocation. The class `NetworkBuffer` is the resource, class `Server` is the acceptor, and class `NetworkDriver` is the generator.

The `Demultiplexer` maintains the registry of servers and methods for acceptors and generators to request buffers and return them upon termination (either via a `returnBuf()` method or by overriding `operator delete` to get "buffers that know how to deallocate themselves"). The heart of the pattern is implemented in the `exchange()` method:

```
class Demultiplexer {
public:
    Demultiplexer() { // alloc buffers... };

    void register(Server *);
    Server * lookup(NetworkAddress *);
    NetworkBuffer * exchange(NetworkBuffer * in);

private:
    HashTable * _registryOfServers;
    NetworkBuffer * _bufferList;
};
```

In the `exchange()` method, `Demultiplexer` combines demultiplexing and exchange. It examines `NetworkBuffer` to determine the server to which the packet in the `NetworkBuffer` was sent, so no server address is necessary in the `exchange()` method:

```
NetworkBuffer   *
Demultiplexer::exchange(NetworkBuffer * in)
{
    Server * server = lookup(in->address());
    if (0 == server) return in;
    NetworkBuffer * out = server->returnBuffer();
    if (0 != out) {
        server->acceptBuffer(in);
        return out;
    } else {
        return in;
    }
}
```

`Demultiplexer` may also implement server interactions other than exchange, copying, peeking (copying a small portion of the buffer), etc. The client must then register the policy to be used.

`Server` is the acceptor that must implement `returnBuffer()` and `acceptBuffer()`. It must also register itself with the demultiplexer. The `Server` instance gets control during `returnBuffer()` and `acceptBuffer()`, and it must respond quickly to these calls. Usually the calls will simply remove and insert (respectively) buffers into a list, so this part can be standardized:

```
class Server {
public:
    void acceptBuffer(NetworkBuffer *);
    Server * returnBuffer();
};
```

`NetworkDriver` is the generator. Upon receiving a packet, it executes `generateBuffer()`, which invokes `exchange()`:

```
class NetworkDriver {
public:
    void generateBuffer();
private:
    // Called by a friend InterruptHandler
    void packetArrived();
};
```

KNOWN USES

This pattern was discovered while developing a fast distributed virtual memory (DVM) system [Sane+90, Sane+95]. The DVM system uses the raw network with a specialized protocol stack, so time spent in copying data has a large impact. In trying to eliminate copying, I discovered Resource Exchanger.

Resource Exchanger is also useful in maintaining the pages in an operating system. For instance, the Sprite operating system [Ousterhout+88] multiplexes pages between the virtual memory and the file system. This makes the system simpler and allows flexible page allocation policies.

A variant of resource exchangers are ticketing schedulers [Waldspurger+94], which issue tickets to processes to determine priorities or time. Processes get resources in proportion to their tickets. Ticketing schedulers are typically more versatile and responsive than standard schedulers.

RELATED PATTERNS

The pattern Mediator [Gamma+95] is related. A resource exchanger is a mediator with a special structure.

VARIATIONS

Resource Exchanger is very versatile and allows many variations:

- *No exchange.* Resource Exchanger can gracefully degrade into a traditional resource manager that gives resources without asking for any back. Such "degradation" is implemented as a policy of the mediation protocol (i.e., method exchange is changed to allow acceptors to accept resources without first requiring return of resources).

- *Mixed exchange.* It may not be possible to have all agents exchange resources. Some agents may exchange data; others may force allocation of new resources. Such combinations are typically programmed by introducing a set of policies that agents can register with the exchanger (see the example in the Implementation section).

- *Data processing while multiplexing.* In some cases it may not be desirable to have all agents exchange data. For example, a network packet demultiplexer has to examine data headers, so it could be altered to do a little more processing.

- *Delayed exchange.* The resource exchange can be *delayed*. For instance, the network driver may keep buffers when asked to transmit data. Thus its buffer pool will increase. Later, it can return them to the proper server when that server receives data.

- *Preemption.* The demultiplexer can keep track of resource allocation. Thus it is possible to use that information to institute resource preemption, if necessary. However, this reduces the speed of resource exchange.

ACKNOWLEDGMENTS

Willy Liao [Liao+95] used this pattern in the Network Interface Framework and suggested incorporating "peeking." Russ Williams's comments led me to clarify allocation-deallocation issues. Ellard Roush, John Coomes, and Amitabh Dave helped with the presentation. We would also like to thank our shepherd, Desmond D'Souza, and the writers' workshop Group One for their many improvements.

REFERENCES

[Gamma+95] E. Gamma, R. Helm, R. Johnson, and J. Vlissides. *Design Patterns: Elements of Reusable Object-Oriented Software.* Reading, MA: Addison-Wesley, 1995.

[Liao+95] W. Liao and R. Campbell. *A Fast, Flexible Network Interface Framework.* (Technical report.) University of Illinois at Urbana-Champaign, Dept. of Computer Science, 1995.

[Ousterhout+88] J. K. Ousterhout, A. R. Cherenson, F. Douglis, M. N. Nelson, and B. B. Welch. "The Sprite Network Operating System." *IEEE Computer*, 23–36, 1988.

[Sane+90] A. Sane, K. MacGregor, and R. Campbell. "Distributed Virtual Memory Consistency Protocols: Design and Performance." *Second IEEE Workshop on Experimental Distributed Systems*, pp. 91–96, Huntsville, AL, 1990.

[Sane+95] A. Sane and R. Campbell. *Coordinated Memory: A Distributed Memory Model and Its Implementation on Gigabit Networks.* (Technical report.) University of Illinois at Urbana-Champaign, Dept. of Computer Science, 1995.

[Waldspurger+94] C. A. Waldspurger and W. E. Weihl. "Lottery Scheduling: Flexible Proportional-Share Resource Management." *First Symposium on Operating Systems Design and Implementation, Monterey Association for Computing Machinery, Monterey, CA, pp. 1–11, 1994.*

Aamod Sane can be reached at sane@cs.uiuc.edu; Roy Campbell can be reached at rhc@uiuc.edu.

The Client-Dispatcher-Server Design Pattern

29

Peter Sommerlad and Michael Stal

When we need to distribute software components over a network of computers, the location-transparent communication between them becomes an important aspect of their design. In the Client-Dispatcher-Server design pattern, an intermediate layer between clients and servers is introduced: the dispatcher component. It provides location transparency by means of a name service and hides the details of establishing the communication connection between client components and their servers.

Example   Suppose you are developing a software system that will allow people to retrieve brand new scientific information. The information services are on your own local network and are distributed over the world. To use one of these services, it is necessary to specify the location of the service provider as well as the service to be executed. When a service provider (e.g., a NASA workstation offering data from the Hubble space telescope) receives a request, it will execute the appropriate service and return the requested information to your local workstation.

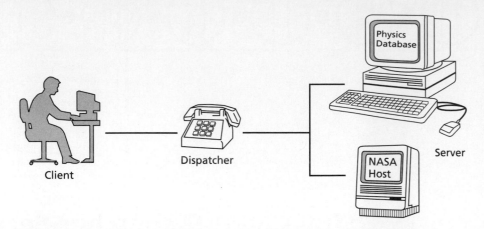

FIGURE 1 Example of an application of the Client-Dispatcher-Server pattern

Context   A software system should utilize or consist of a set of separate services. The service components may run locally, or they may be distributed over a network.

Problem   When a software system utilizes components that may be distributed over a network, it has to provide a means for communication between them. In many cases, depending on the underlying platform, a communication connection between components must be established before communication can take place. However, the core functionality of the components should be separated from the details of communication. In particular, we have to balance the following forces:

- A component should be able to use a service independent of the location of the service component.
- The code implementing the functional core of a component should be separated from the code to establish a connection with other components.
- The communications channels (e.g., port numbers) may be a limited resource, depending on the underlying platform.

Solution   The Client-Dispatcher-Server design pattern separates the communication establishment from the services and data processing performed by clients and servers. Furthermore, it allows location transparency by providing name service for servers. For this it introduces three kinds of participants—a dispatcher, clients, and servers (Figure 2):

- The dispatcher offers the functionality needed by clients to establish a communications channel to a server. The interface takes the name of a

Class Client	*Collaborators* Dispatcher Server(s)
Responsibility • implements a system task • uses servers via communication channels • requests server connections from dispatcher	

Class Server	*Collaborators* Dispatcher Client(s)
Responsibility • provides services that are used by clients • registers itself at the dispatcher (or is registered)	

Class Dispatcher	*Collaborators* Server(s)
Responsibility • establishes communication connections between clients and servers • manages communication channel resources • locates servers • registers servers • maintains a map of server locations	

FIGURE 2 Participants in the Client-Dispatcher-Server design pattern

server component and maps this name to the location of the server component. The dispatcher manages the available communications channels if they are a limited resource. For example, if the dispatcher cannot initiate a communication link with the requested server, it informs the client about the error it encountered. To provide its name service, the dispatcher implements functions to register and locate servers.

■ A server provides a set of operations it can execute on behalf of a client. It either registers itself or is registered with the dispatcher by its name and address. A server component may be located on the same computer as a client or reachable via a network.

■ The task of a client is to perform the domain-specific computations for which it was designed. In order to get its work done, the client accesses service operations offered by servers. Before a client can send any request to a server, it asks the dispatcher for a communications channel to the server. It then uses this channel to communicate with the server.

Structure The following OMT diagram (Figure 3) shows the components of the Client-Dispatcher-Server design pattern and their relationships.

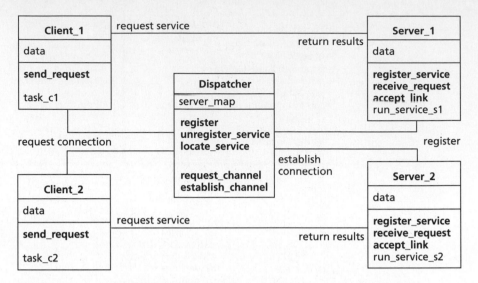

FIGURE 3 The components of the Client-Dispatcher-Server design pattern

Dynamics   A typical scenario (see Figure 4) for the Client-Dispatcher-Server design pattern includes the following events:

- A server registers itself with the dispatcher component.
- A client asks the dispatcher for a communications channel with a specified service provider.
- Depending on the service specified in the client's request, the dispatcher looks up in its registry which server is responsible for executing the request. Then it establishes a communications link to the server. If the dispatcher can successfully initiate the communications connection, it returns the communications channel to the client.
- The client uses the communications channel to send a request directly to the server. After receiving notification of the incoming request, the server executes the appropriate service. When the service execution is completed, the server sends the results to the client.

Implementation   1. Organize the software system into a set of decoupled components. (This separation may have already been created by the demand to use existing servers.) Decide which components will act as servers, which are clients, and which may be both. Define the logical interfaces of the participating components.

In our motivating example, the client component handles the display and the user interface of the local workstation. The servers are the information sources, distributed over the network.

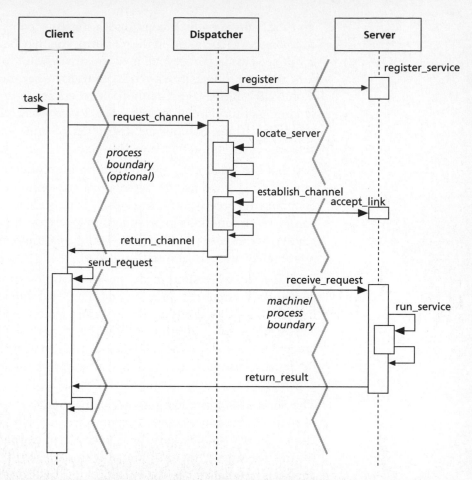

FIGURE 4 Collaborations within the Client-Dispatcher-Server design pattern

2. Decide how you will name and address the servers. You will typically use or modify an established naming and addressing schema. For example, on the Internet you have domain names (DNS), like `zfe.siemens.de`, and 4-byte Internet Protocol (IP) addresses, like `127.0.0.0`. The naming schema determines the implementation of the dispatcher component's naming service, and it provides the basic mechanism for achieving location transparency.

The IP adressing schema fits nicely in our example. We need to extend it by specifying the concrete service as well as the information source on the computer we want to address. For our example, we might use a universal resource locator (URL) address, the format used on the World Wide Web: `service://server.name/information_path`.

3. You must decide which communications mechanism to use for your components. Depending on the platform, you may have several choices. If you need to support several mechanisms or want to defer the decision of which one to use, it is a good idea to use a separate layer of proxies [Rohnert95, BMRSS96, Gamma+95] to encapsulate further details of sending and receiving requests. Such a proxy will take the role of the communications channel the dispatcher returns after the connection between client and server is established.

Say that our local network is based on a proprietary protocol but for remote servers we use IP connections. Assume we have proxy components supporting both protocols, with an identical client interface consisting of functions for sending and receiving requests and available results. In this case the dispatcher would create and initialize the appropriate proxy and return it to the clients.

4. With the above decisions made, you can now design and implement the dispatcher component. In designing the dispatcher it must be decided how the clients and servers will communicate with it. For example, if the dispatcher is located within the client's address space, local procedure calls will be used by the client; servers can then be registered by putting the current system configuration in a file read by the dispatcher.

The selected communications mechanisms define the detailed structure of requests, responses, and error messages used by the system. If the choice of communications mechanism implies that the channels are limited resources, you must also provide a means of managing how the channels are allocated to clients. Since these platform-dependent details go beyond the scope of this pattern, we will not discuss them further here.

The dispatcher in our example is a component similar to an httpd-daemon that provides access to information located locally or on the World Wide Web. The example dispatcher takes the URL, establishes a connection to the appropriate server, and hands the connection proxy over to the display client.

5. Implement the client and server components according to your desired solution and the decisions made concerning the dispatcher interface. Configure the system and register the servers with the dispatcher.

For our example, we have to implement the display client that will allow the user to enter the information designators (URLs) and will show the user the requested information. For simplicity, let us assume that only the local information servers have to be developed and that the remote servers are implemented with the already established http protocol.

Known Uses Sun Microsystems' implementation of remote procedure calls (RPCs) [SUN90] is based on the principles of the Client-Dispatcher-Server design pattern. The portmapper process takes the role of the dispatcher. A process initiating an RPC is then the client, and the receiving process is the server. The registry of services is contained in the file /etc/services.

The OMG CORBA "Common Object Request Broker" specification [OMG92] follows the principles of the Client-Dispatcher-Server design pattern, extending it with further functionality.

Consequences The Client-Dispatcher-Server design pattern gives you several benefits:

- **Dynamic enrichment and replacement of behavior.** In the Client-Dispatcher-Server design pattern, a software developer can change or add new services without impacting the dispatcher component or the clients.

- **Location transparency and reconfiguration.** Since clients do not need to know where servers are located, the developer can defer deciding which network nodes servers should run until system startup or even runtime. Therefore, the Client-Dispatcher-Server design pattern allows developers to prepare a software system to become a distributed system.

There are some drawbacks to the Client-Dispatcher-Server design pattern as well:

- **Less efficiency due to indirection and explicit connection establishment.** The performance of a system developed using the Client-Dispatcher-Server pattern depends on the overhead introduced by the dispatcher due to locating and registering servers and the cost of explicitly establishing the connection.

- **Changing the interfaces of the dispatcher component.** Because the dispatcher plays the central role, the software system is sensitive to changes in the dispatcher interface.

REFERENCES

[BMRSS96] F. Buschmann, R. Meunier, H. Rohnert, P. Sommerlad, and M. Stal. *Pattern-Oriented Software Architecture: A System of Patterns.* New York: Wiley, 1996.

[Gamma+95] E. Gamma, R. Helm, R. Johnson, and J. Vlissides. *Design Patterns: Elements of Reusable Object-Oriented Software.* Reading, MA: Addison-Wesley, 1995.

[OMG92] OMG, Inc. *The Common Object Request Broker: Architecture and Specification.* (OMG Document No. 91.12.1.) 1992.

[Rohnert95] H. Rohnert. "The Proxy Design Pattern Revisited." Chapter 7, this volume.

[SUN90] Sun Microsystems, Inc. *Sun OS Documentation Tools.* 1990.

Peter Sommerlad and Michael Stal can be reached at Siemens AG, Corporate Research and Development, Dept. ZFEBT SE2, Otto-Hahn-Ring, D-81730 Munich, Germany; `{peter.sommerlad,michael.stal}@zfe.siemens.de`.

Active Object:

An Object Behavioral Pattern

30

for Concurrent Programming

R. Greg Lavender and Douglas C. Schmidt

ABSTRACT

This chapter describes the Active Object pattern, which decouples method execution from method invocation in order to simplify synchronized access to a shared resource by methods invoked in different threads of control. The Active Object pattern allows one or more independent threads of execution to interleave their access to data modeled as a single object. A broad class of producer/consumer and reader/writer problems are well suited to this model of concurrency. This pattern is commonly used in distributed systems requiring multithreaded servers. In addition, client applications (such as windowing systems and network browsers) are increasingly employing active objects to simplify concurrent, asynchronous network operations.

Intent The Active Object pattern decouples method execution from method invocation in order to simplify synchronized access to a shared resource by methods invoked in different threads of control.

Aliases Concurrent Object, Actor, Serializer

Motivation   To illustrate the Active Object pattern, consider the design of a connection-oriented gateway. A gateway decouples cooperating components in a distributed system and allows them to interact without having direct dependencies upon each other [Buschmann+96].

For example, the gateway shown in Figure 1 routes messages from one or more source processes to one or more destination processes in a distributed system [Schmidt95a]. Sources and destinations communicate with the gateway using TCP connections. Internally, the gateway contains a set of `Input Handler` and `Output Handler` objects. Input handlers receive messages from sources and use address fields in a message to determine the appropriate output handlers associated with the destination. The `Output Handler` object then delivers the message to the destination.

Since communications between the sources, destinations, and gateway use TCP, output handlers may encounter flow control from the transport layer. Connection-oriented protocols like TCP use flow control to ensure that a fast source does not produce data faster than a slow destination (or slow network) can buffer and consume it.

FIGURE 1 A connection-oriented gateway

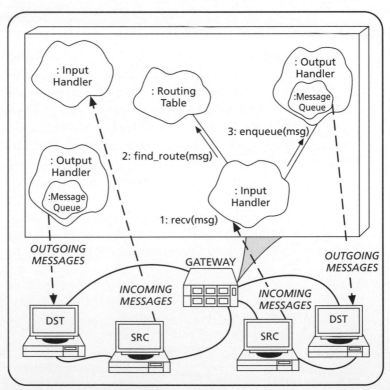

To reduce end-to-end delay, an `Output Handler` object must not block the entire gateway waiting for flow control to abate on any single connection to a destination. One way to ensure this is to design the gateway as a single-threaded reactive state machine that uses asynchronous network I/O. This design typically combines the Reactor pattern [Schmidt+95a], nonblocking sockets, and a set of message queues (one per output handler). The Reactor pattern and the nonblocking sockets provide a single-threaded cooperative event loop model of programming. The Reactor demultiplexes "OK to send" and "OK to receive" events to multiple `Input Handler` and `Output Handler` objects. These handlers use nonblocking send and receive messages to prevent the gateway from blocking. The message queues are used by the output handlers to store messages in FIFO order until they can be delivered when flow control abates.

It is possible to build robust single-threaded connection-oriented gateways using the approach outlined above. There are several drawbacks to this approach, however:

- **Complicated concurrent programming.** Subtle programming is required to ensure that the output handlers in the gateway never block while routing messages to their destinations. Otherwise, one misbehaving output connection can cause the entire gateway to block indefinitely.

- **Performance bottlenecks.** The use of single threading does not take advantage of the parallelism available from the underlying hardware and software platform. Since the entire gateway runs in a single thread of control, it is not possible to transparently alleviate performance bottlenecks by running the system on a multiprocessor.

A more convenient and potentially more efficient way to develop a connection-oriented gateway is to use the Active Object pattern. This pattern enables a method to execute in a thread of control separate from the one that originally invoked it. In contrast, passive objects execute in the same thread as the object that called a method on them.

Implementing `Output Handler` objects as active objects in the gateway enables them to block independently, without adversely affecting each other or the `Input Handler` objects. The active-object gateway design resolves the following forces:

- **Simplify flow control.** Since an `Output Handler` active object has its own thread of control, it can block waiting for flow control to abate. If an `Output Handler` active object is blocked due to flow control, `Input Handler` objects can still insert messages onto the message queue associated with the `Output Handler` object. After completing its current send, an `Output Handler` active object dequeues the next message from its queue. It then sends the message across the TCP connection to its destination.

- **Simplify concurrent programming.** The message queue used by the `Output Handler` active objects allows `enqueue` and `dequeue` operations to proceed concurrently. These operations are subject to synchronization constraints that guarantee serialized access to a shared resource and depend on the state of the resource (e.g., full vs. empty vs. neither). The Active Object pattern makes it simple to program this class "producer/consumer" application.

- **Take advantage of parallelism.** The gateway can transparently take advantage of the inherent concurrency between `Input` and `Output Handler` objects to improve performance on multiprocessor platforms. For example, the processing at output handlers can execute concurrently with input handlers that pass them messages to be delivered.

The structure of the gateway application implemented using the Active Object pattern is illustrated in the Booch class diagram in Figure 2.

Applicability   Use the Active Object pattern when

- **The design and implementation of a concurrent program can be simplified.** Concurrent programs can often be simplified if the thread of control of an object that executes a method can be decoupled from the thread of control of objects that invoke methods on that object.

FIGURE 2 Booch diagram of active object components in a connection-oriented gateway

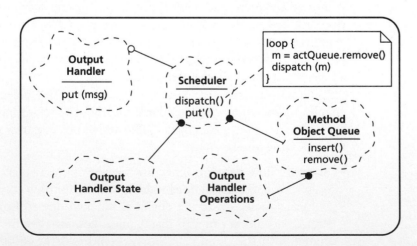

- **Multiple threads of control require synchronized access to shared data.** The Active Object pattern shields applications from low-level synchronization mechanisms rather than having them acquire and release locks explicitly.

- **The order of method execution can differ from the order of method invocation.** Methods invoked asynchronously are executed based on a synchronization policy, not on the order of invocation.

- **The operations on a shared object are relatively coarse-grained.** In contrast, if operations are very fine-grained, the synchronization, data movement, and context switching overhead of active objects may be too high [Schmidt+95b].

Structure and Participants

The structure of the components that make up the Active Object pattern is illustrated in Figure 3.

The key participants in the Active Object pattern include the following classes:

- **Client interface (output handler interface).** The client interface is a proxy that presents a method interface to client applications. The invocation of a method defined by the client interface triggers the construction and queueing of a Method object (see next item).

- **Method objects (output handler operations).** A Method object is constructed for any method call that requires synchronized access to a shared

FIGURE 3   Booch diagram of the components of a generic active object

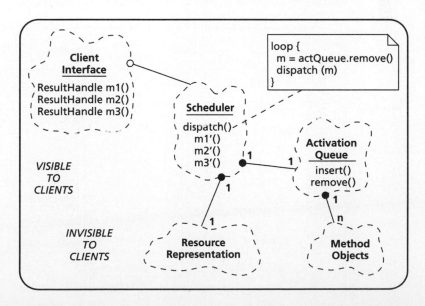

resource managed by the scheduler. Each Method object maintains context information necessary to execute an operation following a method invocation and return any results of that invocation through the client interface.

- **Activation queue (Method object queue).** The activation queue maintains a priority queue of pending method invocations, which are represented as Method objects created by the client interface. The activation queue is managed exclusively by the scheduler (see next item).

- **Scheduler (Method object scheduler).** A scheduler is a "meta object" that manages an activation queue containing Method objects requiring execution. The decision to execute an operation is based on mutual exclusion and condition synchronization constraints.

- **Resource representation (output handler implementation).** This represents the shared resource that is being modeled as an active object. The resource object typically defines methods that are defined in the client interface. It may also contain other methods that the scheduler uses to compute runtime synchronization conditions that determine the scheduling order.

- **Result handle.** When a method is invoked on the client interface, a result handle is returned to the caller. The result handle allows the method result value to be obtained after the scheduler finishes executing the method.

Collaborations   Figure 4 illustrates the three phases of collaborations in the Active Object pattern.

FIGURE 4 Interactions among the internal components of an active object

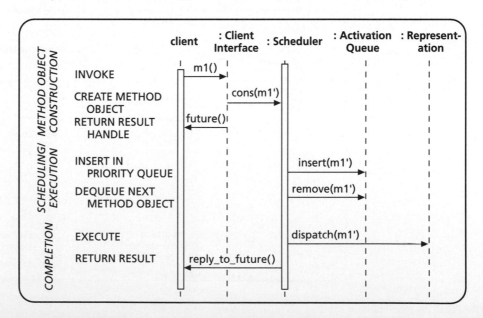

1. **Method object construction.** In this phase, the client application invokes a method defined by the client interface. This triggers the creation of a Method object, which maintains the argument bindings to the method as well as any other bindings required to execute the method and return a result (for example, a binding to a Result Handle object returned to the caller of the method). A result handle is returned to the client unless the method is "one way," in which case no result handle is returned.

2. **Scheduling/execution.** In this phase the scheduler acquires a mutual exclusion lock and consults the activation queue to determine which Method object(s) meet the synchronization constraints. The Method object is then bound to the current representation, and the method is allowed to access/update this representation and create a result.

3. **Return result.** The final phase binds the result value, if any, to a *Future* [Halstead85, Liskov+88] object that passes return values back to the caller when the method finishes executing. Future is a synchronization object that enforces "write-once, read-many" synchronization. Subsequently, any readers that rendezvous with the Future object will evaluate it and obtain the result value. The Future and Method objects will be garbage-collected when they are no longer needed.

Consequences   The Active Object pattern offers the following benefits:

1. **It enhances application concurrency while reducing synchronization complexity.** This is especially true if objects only communicate via messages.

2. **It leverages the parallelism available from the hardware and software platform.** If the hardware/software platform supports multiple CPUs, this pattern can allow multiple active objects to execute in parallel (subject to their synchronization constraints).

The Active Object pattern has the following drawbacks:

1. **It potentially increases context switching, data movement, and synchronization overhead.** Depending on how the scheduler is implemented (e.g., in user space vs. kernel space), overhead may occur in scheduling and executing multiple active objects.

2. **It may be difficult to debug programs that contain active objects, due to the concurrency and nondeterminism of the scheduler.** Moreover, many debuggers do not adequately support the debugging of concurrent programs.

Implementation   The Active Object pattern can be implemented in a variety of ways. This section discusses several issues that arise when implementing it.

Interface, Implementation, and Synchronization Policies

A common way to implement a shared resource (such as a message queue) is to use a single class whose methods first acquire a mutual exclusion ("mutex") lock. The code then proceeds to access the resource, subject to conditional synchronization constraints (e.g., the dequeue operation in the Sample Code section example cannot execute when message queue is empty and the enqueue operation cannot execute when the message queue is full).

```
class MessageQueue
{
public:
  // Enqueue message.
  int enqueue (Message *new_msg)
  {
    mutex.acquire ();

    while (is_full ()) {
      // Release the lock and wait for
      // space to become available.
      notFullCond.wait ();

    // Enqueue the message here...

    mutex.release ();
  }

private:
  Mutex mutex;
  Condition<Mutex> notFullCond;
};
```

A drawback to using this technique is that it embeds code representing the synchronization policy into methods that access the message queue representation. This tight coupling often inhibits reuse of the resource implementation by derived classes that require specialized or different synchronization policies. This problem is commonly referred to as the *inheritance anomaly* [America87, Kafura+89, Matsuoka+91, Papathomas89].

A more flexible means of implementation is to decouple the explicit synchronization policy code from the methods that access and update the shared resource. This decoupling requires that the client interface be defined separately. It is used solely to cause the construction of a Method object for each method invocation.

A Method object is an abstraction of the context (or *closure*) of an operation. This context includes argument values, a binding to the resource representation that the operation will be applied to, a Result object, and the code for the operation. Method objects are constructed when a client application invokes a method on a client interface proxy.

Each Method object is queued on a method-activation queue. A scheduler that enforces a particular synchronization policy on behalf of a shared resource will compute whether or not a Method object operation can execute. Predicates can be defined as those parts of the resource implementation that represent the different states of the resource.

Rendezvous and Return Value Policies

A rendezvous policy is required since active objects do not execute in the same thread as callers that invoke their methods. Different implementations of the Active Object pattern choose different rendezvous and return value policies. Typical choices include the following:

- **Synchronous waiting.** Block the caller synchronously at the client interface until the active object accepts the method call.

- **Synchronous timed wait.** Block the caller only for a bounded amount of time, and fail if the active object does not accept the method call within that period. If the timeout is zero, this scheme is often referred to as "polling."

- **Asynchronous.** Queue the method call and return control to the caller immediately. If the method produces a result value, then some form of future mechanism must be used to provide synchronized access to the value (or the error status, if the method fails).

In the context of the Active Object pattern, a *parametric future* pattern may be required for asynchronous invocations that return a value to the caller [Lavender+95]. A polymorphic future allows parameterization of the eventual result type represented by the future and enforces the necessary synchronization. When a Method object computes a result, it acquires a write lock on the future; it then updates the future with a result value of the same type as that used to parameterize the future. Any readers of the result value that are currently blocked waiting for the result value are awakened and may concurrently access the result value. A future object is eventually garbage-collected after the writer and all readers no longer reference the future.

Leveraging Off Related Patterns

The Active Object pattern requires a set of related patterns for different forms of synchronization (such as mutual exclusion, producer-consumer, and readers-writers), and it requires reusable mechanisms for implementing them (such as mutexes, semaphores, and condition variables). A current area of research is working on defining a collection of reusable building block synchronization patterns to complement the use of the Active Object pattern in a wide set of circumstances.

Sample Code   This section presents sample code that illustrates an implementation of the Active Object pattern. The following steps define an active object for use as a message queue by `Output Handler` objects (see the gateway example described in the Motivation section).

Defining a Nonconcurrent Queue Abstraction That Implements a Bounded Buffer

The resource implementation should not be concerned with implementing explicit mutual exclusion or condition synchronization, since the synchronization policy is enforced by the scheduler. The following `MessageQueueRep` class presents the interface for this queue:

```
// The template parameter T corresponds to
// the type of messages stored in the queue:

template<class T>
class MessageQueueRep
{
public:
  void enqueue (T x);
  T dequeue (void);

  bool empty (void) const;
  bool full (void) const;

private:
  // Internal resource representation.
};
```

The methods in the `MessageQueueRep` representation should not include any code that implements synchronization or mutual exclusion. A key goal of the Active Object pattern is to ensure that the synchronization mechanisms remain external to the representation. This approach facilitates specialization of the class representing the resource while avoiding the inheritance anomaly. The two predicates `empty` and `full` are used to distinguish three internal states: empty, full, and neither empty nor full. They are used by the scheduler to evaluate synchronization conditions prior to executing a method of a resource instance.

Defining a Scheduler That Enforces the Particular Mutual Exclusion and Condition Synchronization Constraints

The scheduler determines the order to process methods, based on synchronization constraints. These constraints depend on the state of the resource being represented. For example, if the `MessageQueueRep` abstraction is used to implement an `Output Handler` object, these constraints would indicate whether the queue was empty, full, or neither. The use of constraints ensures fairly shared access to the `MessageQueueRep` representation. Each method of a `MessageQueueRep` representation is represented by a class derived from a `MethodObject` base class. This base class defines pure virtual `guard` and `call` methods that must be redefined by a derived class. The type parameter `T` defined in the `MessageQueueScheduler` template is the same type of message that is inserted and removed from the `MessageQueue` object:

```
template<class T>
class MessageQueueScheduler
{
protected:
  class Enqueue : public MethodObject
  {
  public:
    Enqueue (MessageQueueRep<T> *r, T a)
      : rep (r), arg (a) {}

    virtual bool guard (void) const {
      // Synchronization constraint
      return !rep->full ();
    }

    virtual void call (void) {
      // Insert message into message queue
      rep->enqueue (arg);
    }

  private:
    MessageQueueRep<T> *rep;
    T arg;
  };

  class Dequeue : public MethodObject
  {
  public:
    Dequeue (MessageQueueRep<T> *r, Future<T> &f)
      : rep (r), result (f) {}

    bool guard (void) const {
```

```
            // Synchronization constraint.
            return !rep->empty ();
        }

        virtual void call (void) {
            // Bind the removed message to the
            // future result object.
            result = rep->dequeue ();
        }

    private:
        MessageQueueRep<T> *rep;
        Future<T> result;    // Future result value
};
```

Instances of the Method object–derived classes `Enqueue` and `Dequeue` are inserted into an activation queue according to the synchronization constraints, as follows:

```
... // as above
public:

    ... // constructors/destructors, etc.

    void enqueue (T x) {
        MethodObject *method = new Enqueue (rep, x);
        queue->insert (method);
    }

    Future<T> dequeue (void) {
        Future<T> result;

        MethodObject *method = new Dequeue (rep, result);
        queue->insert (method);
        return result;
    }

    // These predicates can execute directly since
    // they are "const."

    bool empty (void) const {
        return rep->empty ();
    }
    bool full (void) const {
        return rep->full ();
    }

protected:
    MessageQueueRep<T> *rep;
```

```
    ActivationQueue *queue;
    ...
};
```

The `MessageQueueScheduler` object executes its `dispatch` method in a thread of control that is separate from client applications. Within this thread, the activation queue is searched. The scheduler selects a Method object whose `guard` method (which corresponds to a condition synchronization constraint) evaluates to "true." This Method object is then executed. As part of the method execution, a Method object receives a runtime binding to the current representation of the `MessageQueueRep` object (this is similar to providing a "this" pointer to a sequential C++ method). The method is then executed in the context of that representation. The following code illustrates how the `MessageQueueScheduler` object dispatches Method objects:

```
virtual void dispatch (void) {
    for (;;) {
      ActivationQueue::iterator i;

      for (i = queue->begin();
           i != queue->end();
           i++) {
      // ...
      // Select a Method Object 'm'
      // whose guard evaluates to true.
      m = queue->remove ();
      m->call();
      delete m;
      }
    }
}
```

In general, a scheduler may contain variables that represent the synchronization state of the shared resource. The variables defined depend on the type of synchronization mechanism required. For example, with reader-writer synchronization, counter variables may be used to keep track of the number of read and write requests. In this case, the values of the counters are independent of the state of the shared resource, since they are only used by the scheduler to enforce the correct synchronization policy on behalf of the shared resource.

Defining a Client Interface

A message queue is a Method object factory. It constructs instances of methods that are sent to the scheduler for subsequent execution.

If the active object's condition synchronization constraints, enforced by the scheduler, prohibit the execution of a Method object when a method is invoked, the object is queued for later activation. In some cases, an operation may not create a Method object if it is not subject to the same synchronization constraints as other operations (e.g., the "const" methods `empty` and `full` shown on pages 494–495). Such operations can be executed directly, without incurring synchronization or scheduling overhead.

If a method in the client interface returns a result `T`, a `Future<T>` is returned to the application that calls it. The caller may block immediately, waiting for the future to complete. Conversely, the caller may evaluate the future's value at a later point by using either an implicit or explicit type conversion of a `Future<T>` object to a value of type `T`:

```
template <class T>
class MessageQueue
{
public:
  enum { MAX_SIZE = 100 };
  MessageQueue (int size = MAX_SIZE) {
    sched_ = new MessageQueueScheduler<T> (size);
  }

  // Schedule enqueue to run as an active object.
  void enqueue (T x) { sched->enqueue (x); }

  // Return a Future<T> as the "future" result
  // of an asynchronous dequeue operation.

  Future<T> dequeue (void)  {
    return sched->dequeue ();
  }

  bool empty (void) const { sched->empty (); }
  bool full (void) const { sched->full (); }

private:
  MessageQueueScheduler<T> *sched;
};
```

A `Future<T>` result can be evaluated immediately by a client, possibly causing the caller to block. For example, a gateway output handler running in a separate thread may choose to block until new messages arrive from an input handler:

```
// Make an MessageQueue specialized for the Gateway.
typedef MessageQueue<RoutingMessage> MESSAGE_QUEUE;

MESSAGE_QUEUE messageQueue;
// ...
```

```
// Type conversion of Future<Message> result causes
// the thread to block pending result of the dequeue

Message msg = messageQueue.dequeue ();

// Transmit message to the destination.
sendMessage (msg);
```

Alternatively, the evaluation of a return result from an Active Object method invocation can be delayed. For example, if no messages are available immediately, an output handler can store the `Future<T>` return value from `messageQueue` and perform other "bookkeeping" tasks (such as exchanging "keep-alive messages" to make sure its destination is still active). When it's done with these various tasks, it may choose to block until a message arrives from an input handler, as follows:

```
// Invocation does not block
  Future<Message> future = messageQueue.dequeue ();

... // Do something else here

// Evaluate future by implicit type conversion --
// may block if the result is not yet available.

Message msg = future;
```

Known Uses The Active Object pattern is commonly used in distributed systems requiring multithreaded servers. In addition, the Active Object pattern is used in client applications, such as windowing systems and network browsers, that employ multiple active objects to simplify concurrent programs that perform nonblocking network operations.

The gateway example from the Motivation section is based on the communication services portion of a communication services gateway. `Output Handler` objects in gateways are implemented as active objects to simplify concurrent programming and improve performance on multiprocessors. The active-object version of the gateway uses the preemptive multitasking capabilities provided by Solaris threads [Eykholt+92]. An earlier version of the gateway [Schmidt95a] used a reactive implementation. The reactive design relied on a cooperative event loop–driven dispatcher within a single thread. This design was more difficult to implement, and it did not perform as well as the active object version on multiprocessor platforms.

The Active Object pattern has also been used to implement actors [Agha86]. An actor contains a set of instance variables and behaviors; these react to messages received from other actors. Messages sent to an actor are queued in the actor's message queue. In the Actor model, messages are executed in order of arrival by the "current" behavior. Each behavior nominates a replacement behavior to execute the next message, possibly before the nominating behavior has completed its execution. Variations on the basic Actor model allow messages in the message queue to be executed based on criteria other than arrival order [Tomlinson+89]. When the Active Object pattern is used to implement actors, the scheduler corresponds to the actor scheduling mechanism, Method objects correspond to the behaviors defined for an actor, and the resource representation is the set of instance variables that collectively represent the state of an actor [Kafura+92]. The client interface is simply a strongly typed mechanism used to pass a message to an actor.

Related Patterns   The Mutual Exclusion (Mutex) pattern is a simple locking pattern that can occur in slightly different forms (such as a spin lock or a semaphore) and can have subtle semantics (such as recursive mutexes and priority mutexes).

The Consumer-Producer Condition Synchronization pattern is a common pattern that occurs when the synchronization policy and the resource are related by the fact that synchronization is dependent on the state of the resource.

The Reader-Writer Condition Synchronization pattern is a common synchronization pattern that occurs when the synchronization mechanism is not dependent on the state of the resource. A readers-writers synchronization mechanism can be implemented independent of the type of resource requiring reader-writer synchronization.

The Future pattern describes a typed future result value that requires write-once, read-many synchronization. In this pattern, whether a caller blocks on a future depends on whether or not a result value has been computed. Hence, the future pattern is a hybrid pattern that is partly a reader-writer condition synchronization pattern and partly a producer-consumer synchronization pattern.

The Half-Sync/Half-Async pattern [Schmidt95b] is an architectural pattern that decouples synchronous I/O from asynchronous I/O in a system to simplify concurrent programming efforts without degrading execution efficiency. This pattern typically uses the Active Object pattern to implement the synchronous task layer, the Reactor pattern [Schmidt95b] to implement the asynchronous task layer, and a Producer/Consumer pattern to implement the queueing layer.

REFERENCES

[Agha86] G. Agha. *A Model of Concurrent Computation in Distributed Systems.* Cambridge, MA: MIT Press, 1986.

[America87] P. America. "Inheritance and Subtyping in a Parallel Object-Oriented Language." In *ECOOP '87 Conference Proceedings.* New York: Springer-Verlag, 1987, pp. 234–242.

[Buschmann+96] F. Buschmann, R. Meunier, H. Rohnert, P. Sommerlad, and M. Stal. *Pattern-Oriented Software Architecture: A System of Patterns.* New York: Wiley, 1996.

[Eykholt+92] J. Eykholt, S. Kleiman, S. Barton, R. Faulkner, A. Shivalingiah, M. Smit, D. Stein, J. Voll, M. Weeks, and D. Williams. "Beyond Multiprocessing: Multithreading the SunOS Kernel." In *Proceedings of the Summer USENIX Conference.* San Antonio, TX, 1992.

[Halstead85] R. H. Halstead, Jr. "Multilisp: A Language for Concurrent Symbolic Computation." *ACM Transactions on Programming Languages and Systems, 7* (1985):501–538.

[Kafura+89] D. G. Kafura and K. H. Lee. "Inheritance in Actor-Based Concurrent Object-Oriented Languages." In *ECOOP '89 Conference Proceedings.* New York: Cambridge University Press, 1989, pp. 131–145.

[Kafura+92] D. Kafura, M. Mukherji, and R. G. Lavender. "ACT++: A Class Library for Concurrent Programming in C++ Using Actors." *Journal of Object-Oriented Programming* (October 1992): 47–56.

[Lavender+95] R. G. Lavender and D. G. Kafura. "A Polymorphic Future and First-Class Function Type for Concurrent Object-Oriented Programming in C++." Forthcoming; available on the World Wide Web from http://www.cs.utexas.edu/users/lavender/papers.html.

[Liskov+88] B. Liskov and L. Shrira. "Promises: Linguistic Support for Efficient Asynchronous Procedure Calls in Distributed Systems." In *Proceedings of the SIGPLAN '88 Conference on Programming Language Design and Implementation.* ACM Press, 1988, pp. 260–267.

[Matsuoka+91] S. Matsuoka, K. Wakita, and A. Yonezawa. "Analysis of Inheritance Anomaly in Concurrent Object-Oriented Languages." *SIGPLAN OOPS Messenger, 2*(2) (April 1991).

[Papathomas89] M. Papathomas. "Concurrency Issues in Object-Oriented Languages." In D. Tsichritzis (ed.), *Object Oriented Development.* Geneva, Switzerland: Centre Universitaire D'Informatique, University of Geneva, 1989, pp. 207–245.

[Schmidt95a] D. C. Schmidt. "A System of Reusable Design Patterns for Application-Level Gateways." In S. P. Berczuk (ed.), *The Theory and Practice of Object Systems (Special Issue on Patterns and Pattern Languages).* New York: Wiley, 1995.

[Schmidt+95a] D. C. Schmidt and C. D. Cranor. "Half-Sync/Half-Async: An Architectural Pattern for Efficient and Well-Structured Concurrent I/O." Chapter 27, this volume.

[Schmidt95b] D. C. Schmidt. "Reactor: An Object Behavioral Pattern for Concurrent Event Demultiplexing and Event Handler Dispatching." In J. O. Coplien and D. C. Schmidt (eds.), *Pattern Languages of Program Design.* Reading, MA: Addison-Wesley, 1995, pp. 529–546.

[Schmidt+95b] D. C. Schmidt and T. Suda. "Measuring the Performance of Parallel Message-Based Process Architectures." In *Proceedings of the Conference on Computer Communications (INFOCOM). IEEE,* 1995, pp. 624–633.

[Tomlinson+89] C. Tomlinson and V. Singh. "Inheritance and Synchronization with Enabled-Sets." In *OOPSLA '89 Conference Proceedings. ACM Press, 1989, pp. 103–112.*

R. Greg Lavender can be reached at ISODE Consortium, Inc., 3925 West Braker Lane, Suite 333, Austin, TX 78759; g.lavender@isode.com. Douglas C. Schmidt can be reached at the Department of Computer Science, Washington University, St. Louis, MO 63130; schmidt@cs.wustl.edu.

31 Selecting Locking Designs for Parallel Programs

Paul E. McKenney

1. ABSTRACT

The only reason to parallelize a program is to gain performance. The synchronization primitives needed in parallel programs can cause contention, overhead, and added complexity. These problems can overwhelm the performance benefits of parallel execution. Therefore, it is necessary to understand the performance and complexity implications of synchronization primitives, in addition to their correctness, liveliness, and safety properties. This chapter presents a pattern language to assist you in selecting locking designs for parallel programs.

Section 2 presents an example used throughout the chapter to demonstrate the use of these patterns. Section 3 describes contexts in which the patterns are useful. Section 4 describes the forces common to all of the patterns. Section 5 presents several indexes to the patterns. Section 6 presents the patterns themselves.

2. EXAMPLE ALGORITHM

A simple hashed lookup table illustrates the patterns in this chapter. This example searches for a specified key in a list of elements and performs operations on those elements. Both the individual elements and the list itself may require mutual exclusion.

Figure 1 shows the data structure for a monoprocessor implementation. The lt_next field links the individual elements together, the lt_key field contains the search key, and the lt_data field contains the data corresponding to that key. Each pattern will embellish this data structure as needed. You might implement a search for a member of a list of looktab_t's, as shown in Figure 2.

FIGURE 1 Lookup-table element

```
typedef struct looktab {
    struct looktab_t *lt_next;
    int      lt_key;
    int      lt_data;
} looktab_t;
```

3. OVERVIEW OF CONTEXTS

Use the patterns in this chapter for development or maintenance efforts in which parallelization is a central issue. An example of such an effort is when you "Share the Load" among several processors in order to improve the capacity of reactive systems (see Chapter 35).

For new development, use the following steps:

1. Analyze the architecture and design:
   - Identify activities that are good candidates for parallelization.
   - Identify shared resources.
   - Identify communications and synchronization requirements.

   These items, combined, will define the critical sections. You must guard all critical sections with synchronization primitives in order for the program to run correctly on a parallel processor.

```
/* Header for list of looktab_t's. */

looktab_t *looktab_head[LOOKTAB_NHASH] =
        { NULL };
#define LOOKTAB_HASH(key) ((key) % LOOKTAB_NHASH)

/*
 * Return a pointer to the element of the
 * table with the specified key, or return
 * NULL if no such element exists.
 */

looktab_t *
looktab_search(int key)
{
        looktab_t *p;

        p = looktab_head[LOOKTAB_HASH(key)];
        while (p != NULL) {
                if (p->lt_key == key) {
                        return (p);
                }
                p = p->lt_next;
        }
        return (NULL);
}
```

FIGURE 2 Lookup-table search

2. Use the patterns in this chapter to select a locking design.[1]

3. Measure the results. If they are satisfactory, you are done! Otherwise, proceed with the maintenance process described below.

Use prototypes as needed to help identify candidate activities. Relying on the intuition of architects and designers is risky, particularly when they are solving unfamiliar problems. If you cannot scale the prototype up to production levels, use differential profiling [McKenney95] to help predict which activities are most prone to scaling problems.

For maintenance, use the following steps:

1. Measure current system.

2. Analyze measurements to identify bottleneck activities and resources.

---

[1] It may also be necessary to select designs for notification (and versioning). Pattern languages covering these aspects of design are beyond the scope of this chapter.

3. Use the patterns in this chapter to select a locking design.
4. Measure the results. If they are satisfactory, you are done! Otherwise, repeat this process.

Use the pattern language presented in this chapter for Step 2 of the development procedure and Step 3 of the maintenance procedure. The other steps of both procedures are the subject of other pattern languages.

4. FORCES

The following forces affect the performance of parallel programs:

- **Speedup.** Getting a program to run faster is the only reason to go to all of the time and trouble required to parallelize it. Speedup is the ratio of the time required to run a sequential version of the program to the time required to run a parallel version.
- **Contention.** If you run a parallel program on more CPUs than the program's speedup can support, then contention will consume the excess CPUs.
- **Overhead.** A monoprocessor version of a given parallel program does not need synchronization primitives. Therefore, any time consumed by these primitives is overhead that does not contribute directly to that program's job. Note that the important measure is the relationship between the synchronization overhead and the serial overhead—critical sections with greater overhead may tolerate synchronization primitives with greater overhead.
- **Read-to-write ratio.** You can often protect an infrequently changed data structure with lower-overhead synchronization primitives than you can use for a data structure with a high update rate.
- **Economics.** Budgetary constraints can limit the number of CPUs available, regardless of the potential speedup.
- **Complexity.** A parallel program is more complex than an equivalent sequential program, because the parallel program has a much larger state space than the sequential program. A parallel programmer must consider synchronization primitives, locking design, critical-section identification, and deadlock in the context of this larger state space. This greater complexity often translates to higher development and maintenance costs. Therefore, budgetary constraints can limit the number and types of

modifications made to an existing program—a given degree of speedup is worth only so much time and trouble.

These forces will act together to enforce a maximum speedup. The first three forces are deeply interrelated. The remainder of this section analyzes these interrelationships.[2]

Note that these forces may also appear as part of the context. For example, economics may act as a force ("cheaper is better") or as part of the context ("the cost must not exceed $100").

An understanding of the relationships between these forces can be very helpful in resolving the forces acting on an existing parallel program:

1. The less time a program spends in critical sections, the greater the potential speedup.

2. The fraction of time a program spends in a given critical section must be much less than the reciprocal of the number of CPUs for the actual speedup to approach the number of CPUs. For example, a program running on 10 CPUs must spend much less than one-tenth of its time in the critical section if it is to scale well.

3. Should the actual speedup be less than the number of available CPUs, contention effects will consume the excess CPU and/or wallclock time. The larger the gap between the number of CPUs and the actual speedup, the less efficiently the CPUs will be used. Similarly, the greater the desired efficiency, the smaller the achievable speedup.

4. If the available synchronization primitives have high overhead compared to the critical sections they guard, reduce the number of times your program invokes the primitives, in order to improve speedup. You can do this by fusing critical sections, using Data Ownership, or moving toward a more coarse-grained parallelism such as Code Locking.

5. If the critical sections have high overhead compared to the primitives guarding them, the best way to improve speedup is to increase parallelism by moving to Reader/Writer Locking, Data Locking, or Data Ownership.

6. If the critical sections have high overhead compared to the primitives guarding them and your program rarely modifies the data structure, you can increase parallelism by moving to Reader/Writer Locking.

---

[2] A real-world parallel system will have many additional forces acting on it, such as data-structure layout, memory size, memory-hierarchy latencies, and bandwidth limitations.

5. INDEX TO LOCK-DESIGN PATTERNS

This section contains indexes based on relationships between the patterns (Section 5.1), forces resolved by the patterns (Section 5.2), and problems commonly encountered in parallel programs (Section 5.3).

5.1 Pattern Relationships

Section 6 presents the following patterns:

1. Sequential Program (6.1)
2. Code Locking (6.2)
3. Data Locking (6.3)
4. Data Ownership (6.4)
5. Parallel Fastpath (6.5)
6. Reader/Writer Locking (6.6)
7. Hierarchical Locking (6.7)
8. Allocator Caches (6.8)
9. Critical-Section Fusing (6.9)
10. Critical-Section Partitioning (6.10)

See Figure 3 and the following paragraphs for relationships between these patterns.

Parallel Fastpath, Critical-Section Fusing, and Critical-Section Partitioning are meta patterns.

Reader/Writer Locking, Hierarchical Locking, and Allocator Caches are instances of the Parallel Fastpath meta pattern. Reader/Writer Locking and Hierarchical Locking are themselves meta patterns; think of them as modifiers to the Code Locking and Data Locking patterns. Parallel Fastpath, Hierarchical Locking, and Allocator Caches are ways of combining other patterns; thus they are template patterns.

Critical-Section Partitioning transforms Sequential Program into Code Locking and Code Locking into Data Locking. It also transforms conservative Code Locking and Data Locking into more aggressively parallel forms.

Critical-Section Partitioning transforms Data Locking into Code Locking and Code Locking into Sequential Program. It also transforms aggressive Code Locking and Data Locking into more conservative forms.

Assigning a particular CPU or process to each partition of a data-locked data structure results in Data Ownership. A similar assignment of a particular CPU,

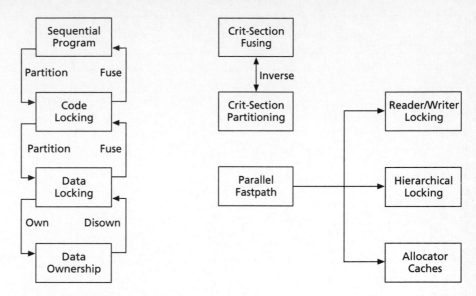

FIGURE 3 Relationships between the patterns

process, or computer system to each critical section of a code-locked program produces Client/Server (used heavily in distributed systems but not described in this paper).

5.2 Force Resolution

Table 1 compares how each of the patterns resolves each of the forces.

Plus signs indicate that a pattern resolves a force well. For example, Sequential Program resolves contention and overhead perfectly due to a lack of synchronization primitives; it resolves budgetary forces perfectly since Sequential Programs run on cheap, single-CPU machines; and it resolves complexity perfectly because sequential implementations of programs are better understood and more readily available than parallel versions.

Minus signs indicate that a pattern resolves a force poorly. Again, Sequential Program provides extreme examples, for example, with speedup since a sequential program allows no speedup[3] and with read-to-write ratio because multiple readers cannot proceed in parallel in a sequential program.

Question marks indicate that the quality of resolution is quite variable. Programs based on Data Ownership can be extremely complex if CPUs

---

[3] If you run multiple instances of a sequential program in parallel, you have used Data Locking or Data Ownership instead of Sequential Program.

Speedup	Contention	Overhead	R/W	$	Complexity	Pattern
----	+++	+++	--	+++	+++	Sequential Program
0	--	0	----	0	+	Code Locking
+	+	0	+	-	--	Data Locking
+++	+++	+?	+	----	?	Data Ownership
+	+	+	+	--	--	Parallel Fastpath
+	+	+	+++	--	-	Reader/Writer Locking
+	+	-	0	-	----	Hierarchical Locking
+	+	+	N/A	--	-	Allocator Caches
0	-	+	0	0	--	Critical-Section Fusing
0	+	-	0	0	+	Critical-Section Partitioning

TABLE 1 Force resolution

must access each other's data. If no such access if needed, you can use a simple script that runs multiple instances of a sequential program in parallel.

See the individual patterns for more information on how they resolve the forces.

5.3 Fault Table

Use Table 2 to locate a replacement pattern for a pattern that is causing more problems than it is solving. This table provides a summary of the contexts where the patterns are most useful.

6. LOCK-DESIGN PATTERNS

This section contains patterns for selecting locking designs. See Section 5 for a full index to these patterns.

Old Pattern	Problem	Pattern to Use or Apply

Sequential Program	Need faster execution.	Code Locking
		  Data Locking
		  Data Ownership
		  Parallel Fastpath
		  Reader/Writer Locking
		  Hierarchical Locking
		  Allocator Caches

Code Locking	Speedup limited by contention.	Data Locking
		  Data Ownership
		  Parallel Fastpath
		  Reader/Writer Locking
		  Hierarchical Locking
		  Allocator Caches

Code Locking
  Data Locking
  Hierarchical Locking
	Speedup is limited by both contention and synchronization overhead.	Data Ownership
		  Parallel Fastpath
		  Reader/Writer Locking
		  Allocator Caches

Sequential Program
  Code Locking
  Data Locking
  Reader/Writer Locking
	Speedup limited by contention and synchronization is cheap compared to noncritical-section code in critical sections.	Critical-Section Partitioning

Code Locking
  Data Locking
  Reader/Writer Locking
	Speedup limited by synchronization overhead and contention is low.	Critical-Section Fusing

Code Locking Data Locking	Speedup limited by contention and readers could be in parallel.	Reader/Writer Locking

Data Locking
  Data Ownership
  Parallel Fastpath
  Reader/Writer Locking
  Hierarchical Locking
  Allocator Caches
	Speedup is greater than necessary and complexity is too high (e.g., it takes too long to merge changes for new versions of the program).	Sequential Program
		  Code Locking

(continued)

TABLE 2   Locking-design fault table

Old Pattern	Problem	Pattern to Use or Apply
Code Locking	Speedup is greater than necessary and complexity is too high (e.g., it takes too long to merge changes for new versions of the program).	Sequential Program
Data Ownership	Complexity of passing operations to the data is too high (e.g., it takes too long to merge changes for new versions of the program).	Data Locking

TABLE 2 *(continued)* Locking-design fault table

6.1 Sequential Program

Problem   How do you eliminate the complexity of parallelization?

Context   You are working on an excessively complex parallel program that runs fast enough on a single processor.

Forces   **Contention (+++):** There is no parallel execution, so there is absolutely no contention.

Overhead (+++): There are no synchronization primitives, so there is no synchronization overhead.

Economics (+++): The program runs on a single CPU. Single-CPU systems are usually cheaper than parallel systems.

Complexity (+++): Pure sequential execution eliminates all parallel complexity. In fact, any sequential programs are available as freeware. You need only understand how to install such programs to run them sequentially. In contrast, you would need to intimately understand the program, your machine, and parallelism in order to produce a parallel version.

Speedup (– – –): There is no parallel execution, so there is absolutely no speedup.

Read-to-Write Ratio (– – –): There is no parallel execution, so there is absolutely no opportunity to allow readers to proceed in parallel.

Solution   Construct an entirely sequential program. Eliminate all use of synchronization primitives, thereby eliminating the overhead and complexity associated with them.

Resulting Context   The resulting context is a completely sequential program with no complexity, overhead, contention, or speedup from parallelization.

Design Rationale   If the program runs fast enough on a single processor, remove the synchronization primitives and spare yourself their overhead and complexity.

6.2 Code Locking

Problem   How can you parallelize and maintain existing third-party code in an inexpensive and efficient way?

Context   You are working with an existing sequential program that has only one resource. Its critical sections are very small compared to the parallel portion of the code, which requires only a modest speedup. (Or, development or maintenance cost constraints rule out more complex and effective parallelization techniques.)

   Alternatively, suppose you are working on an excessively complex, aggressively parallel program that runs fast enough on a small number of CPUs.

Forces   **Complexity (++):** The monitorlike structure of code-locked programs is more easily understood.

   Speedup (0): Code Locking usually permits only modest speedups.

   Overhead (0): Code Locking uses a modest number of synchronization primitives and so suffers only modest overhead.

   Economics (0): Code Locking scales modestly, so it requires a system with few CPUs.

   Contention (– –): Code Locking often results in high contention.

   Read-to-Write Ratio (– – –): There is no parallel execution of critical sections sharing a specific resource, so there is absolutely no opportunity to allow readers to proceed in parallel.

Solution   Parallelize and maintain existing third-party code inexpensively and efficiently using Code Locking when the code spends a very small fraction of its execution in critical sections or when you require only modest scaling.

See Figure 4 for an example. Note that you must surround calls to the `looktab_search()` function and later uses of the return value by a synchronization primitive, as shown in the figure. Do not try to bury the locks in the `looktab_search()`, since this would allow multiple CPUs to update the element simultaneously, which would corrupt the data. Instead, hide the locking within higher-level functions (member functions in an object-oriented implementation) that call `looktab_search()` as part of specific, complete operations on the table.

It is relatively easy to create and maintain a code-locking version of a program. You need not restructure the program; you need only do the (admittedly nontrivial) task of inserting the locking operations.

This program might scale well if table search and update are a very small part of the program's execution time.

Resulting Context   The result is a moderately parallel program that is very similar to its sequential counterpart, resulting in relatively little added complexity.

Design Rationale   Code Locking is the simplest locking design. It is particularly easy to retrofit an existing program to use Code Locking in order to run it on a multiprocessor. If

FIGURE 4 Code-locking lookup table

```
/*
 * Global lock for looktab_t
 * manipulations.
 */

slock_t looktab_mutex;

. . .

/*
 * Look up a looktab element and
 * examine it.
 */

S_LOCK(&looktab_mutex);
p = looktab_search(mykey);

/*
 * insert code here to examine or
 * update the element.
 */

S_UNLOCK(&looktab_mutex);
```

the program has only a single shared resource, Code Locking will even give optimal performance. However, most programs of any size and complexity require much of the execution to occur in critical sections, which in turn sharply limits the scaling, as specified by Amdahl's Law.

Therefore, use Code Locking on programs that spend only a small fraction of their runtime in critical sections or from which you require only modest scaling. In these cases, Code Locking will provide a relatively simple program that is very similar to its sequential counterpart.

6.3 Data Locking

Problem How can you obtain better speedups than can be provided by straightforward parallelizations such as Code Locking?

Context You are working on an existing sequential or parallel program requiring greater speedup than can be obtained via Code Locking. The program's data structures may be split up into independent partitions so the different partitions may be operated on in parallel.

Alternatively, you are working on a Data Ownership program that uses excessively complex operation-passing techniques.

Forces **Speedup (+):** Data Locking associates different locks with different data structures or with different parts of data structures. Contention and overhead still restrict speedups.

Contention (+): Accesses to different data structures proceed in parallel. However, accesses to data guarded by the same lock still result in contention.

Read-to-Write Ratio (+): Readers accessing different data structures proceed in parallel. However, readers attempting to access structures guarded by the same lock are still serialized.

Overhead (0): A data-locked program usually uses about the same number of synchronization primitives to perform a given task as a code-locked program.

Economics (–): Greater speedups require bigger machines.

Complexity (– –): Data-locked programs can be extremely complex and subtle—particularly when critical sections must be nested—leading to deadlock problems.

Solution   Partition the data structures to process each of the resulting portions in parallel. Data Locking often results in better speedups than straightforward parallelizations such as Code Locking can provide. The following paragraphs present two examples of Data Locking.

The first example is trivial but important: lock on instances of data structures rather than on the code operating on those data structures.[4] For example, if there were several independent lookup tables in a program, each could have its own critical section, as shown in Figure 5. This figure assumes that you modified `looktab_search()` to take an additional pointer to the table being searched. Structuring the code in this manner allows searches of different tables to proceed in parallel, although searches of a particular table will still be serialized.

Alternatively, allocate a lock for each hash line in the hash line header data structure,[5] as shown in Figures 6 and 7. These locks allow noncolliding searches to proceed in parallel. You can use per-hash-line locks only if the elements in the table are independent of one another.

A major difference between these two examples is the degree to which locking considerations have constrained the design. For example, you can change the first example's design to use a linked binary search tree without changing the locking design. A single lock still guards a single table, regardless of that table's implementation.

FIGURE 5 Conservatively data-locked table lookup

```
/* Global lock for looktab_t manipulations. */

slock_t my_looktab_mutex;
looktab_t *my_looktab[LOOKTAB_NHASH];

. . .

/* Look up a looktab element and examine it. */

S_LOCK(&my_looktab_mutex);
p = looktab_search(my_looktab, mykey);

/* insert code to examine or update the element. */

S_UNLOCK(&my_looktab_mutex);
```

[4] Or, in object-oriented terminology, lock on instances of a class rather than the class itself.

[5] In object-oriented programs, this level of data locking results in many independent critical sections per instance.

```
/*
 * Type definition for looktab header.
 * All fields are protected by lth_mutex.
 */

typedef struct looktab_head {
        looktab_t *lth_head;
        slock_t *lth_mutex;
} looktab_head_t;

/* Header for list of looktab_t's. */

looktab_head_t *looktab_head[LOOKTAB_NHASH];
#define LOOKTAB_HASH(key) ((key) % LOOKTAB_NHASH)
```

FIGURE 6 Aggressively data-locked table lookup data structures

However, the second example's locking design forces you to use a hashing scheme. The only degree of freedom is your choice of design for the overflow chains. The benefit that accompanies this constraint is unlimited speedup—you can increase speedup simply by increasing the size of the hash table.

In addition, you can combine these two techniques to allow fully parallel searching within and between lookup tables.

Resulting Context The result is a more heavily parallel program that is less similar to its sequential counterpart but exhibits much lower contention and overhead and thus higher speedups.

Design Rationale You can partition many algorithms and data structures into independent parts, with each part having its own independent critical section. Then the critical sections for each part can execute in parallel (although only one instance of the critical section for a given part can execute at a given time). Use Data Locking when you need to reduce critical-section overhead and when synchronization overhead does not limit potential speedup. Data Locking reduces this overhead by distributing the instances of the overly large critical section into multiple critical sections.

6.4 Data Ownership

Problem How can you make programs with frequent, small critical sections achieve high speedups on machines with high synchronization overhead?

```
/*
 * Return a pointer to the element of the table
 * with the specified key, or return NULL if no
 * such element exists.
 */

looktab_t *
looktab_search(int key)
{
        looktab_t *p;

        p = looktab_head[LOOKTAB_HASH(key)].lth_head;
        while (p != NULL) {
                if (p->lt_key > key) {
                        return (NULL);
                }
                if (p->lt_key == key) {
                        return (p);
                }
                p = p->lt_next;
        }
        return (NULL);
}

/* . . . */

        /* Look up a looktab element and examine it.
*/
        looktab_head_t *p

        p = &looktab_head[LOOKTAB_HASH(mykey)];
        S_LOCK(&(p->lth_mutex));
        p = looktab_search(mykey);

        /* code to examine or update element. */

        S_UNLOCK(&(p->lth_mutex));
```

FIGURE 7 Aggressively data-locked table lookup code

Context You are working on an existing sequential or parallel program. You can partition the program so that only one process accesses a given data item at a time, thereby greatly reducing or eliminating the need for synchronization but likely increasing complexity.

Forces **Speedup (+++):** Since each CPU operates on its data independently of the other CPUs, Data Ownership provides excellent speedups.

Contention (+++): No CPU accesses another CPU's data, so there is absolutely no contention.

Read-to-Write Ratio (+): Each CPU can read its own data independently of the other CPUs, but since only one CPU owns a given piece of data, only one CPU may read a given piece of data at a time.

Overhead (+?): In the best case, the CPUs operate independently, free of overhead. However, if the CPUs must share information, this sharing will exact some sort of communications or synchronization overhead.

Complexity (???): In the best case, a program constructed using Resource Ownership is simply a set of sequential programs that run independently in parallel. The main issue here is how to balance the load among these independent programs. For example, if one CPU does 90 percent of the work, then there will be at most a 10 percent speedup.

In more complex cases, the CPUs must access one another's data. In these cases, you must design and implement arbitrarily complex sharing mechanisms. For Data Ownership to be useful, the CPUs must access their own data almost all of the time. Otherwise, the overhead from sharing can overwhelm the benefit of ownership.

Economics (– – –): Excellent speedups require lots of equipment. This means lots of money, even if the equipment is a bunch of cheap PCs connected to a cheap LAN.

Solution Use Data Ownership to partition data used by programs with frequent, small critical sections running on machines with high synchronization overheads. This partitioning can eliminate mutual-exclusion overhead, thereby greatly increasing speedups.

The last example in the previous section split a lookup table into multiple independent classes of keys, where the key classes were defined by a hash function.

If you can assign each key class to a separate process, you will have a special case of partitioning known as Data Ownership. Data Ownership is a very powerful pattern, as it can entirely eliminate synchronization overhead. This is particularly useful in programs that have small critical sections whose overhead is dominated by synchronization overhead. If the key classes are well balanced, Data Ownership can allow virtually unlimited speedups.

Partitioning the lookup-table example over separate processes requires a convention or mechanism to cause the proper process to do lookups for keys of a given class. For example, Figure 8 shows a simple modular mapping from key to CPU. The on_cpu() function is similar to an RPC call; the function is invoked with the specified arguments on the specified CPU.

Note that the algorithm's form has changed considerably. The original, serial form passed back a pointer that the caller could use as it saw fit. However, Data Ownership requires that a specific CPU perform all the operations on a

FIGURE 8 Partitioning key ranges

```
/* Header for list of looktab_t's. */

looktab_t *looktab_head[LOOKTAB_NHASH] = { NULL };
#define LOOKTAB_HASH(key)   ((key) % LOOKTAB_NHASH)

/*
 * Look up the specified entry and invoke the
 * specified function on it.  The key must be one
 * of this CPU's keys.
 */
looktab_t *
looktab_srch_me(int key, int (*func)(looktab_t *ent))
{
        looktab_t *p;

        p = looktab_head[LOOKTAB_HASH(key)];
        while (p != NULL) {
                if (p->lt_key == key) {
                        return (*func)(p);
                }
                p = p->lt_next;
        }
        return (func(NULL));
}

/*
 * Look up the specified entry and invoke the
 * specified function on it.  Force this to happen
 * on the CPU that corresponds to the specified key.
 */

int
looktab_search(int key, int (*func)(looktab_t *ent))
{
        int which_cpu = key % N_CPUS;

        if (which_cpu == my_cpu) {
                return (looktab_srch_me(key, func));
        }
        return (on_cpu(which_cpu,
looktab_srch_me(key, func)));
}
```

particular data structure. We must therefore pass an operation to the CPU that owns the data structure.[6] This operation passing usually requires synchronization, so we have simply traded one form of overhead for another. This trade-off may nevertheless be worthwhile if each CPU processes its own data most of the time, particularly if each data structure is large. For example, a version of OSF/1 for massively parallel processors used a `vproc` layer to direct operations (such as UNIX signals) to processes running on other nodes [Zajcew+93].

Data Ownership might seem arcane, but it is used very frequently:

1. Any variables accessible by only one CPU or process (such as `auto` variables in C and C++) are owned by that CPU or process.

2. An instance of a user interface owns the corresponding user's context. It is very common for applications that interact with parallel database engines to be written as if they were entirely sequential. Such applications own the user interface and its current action. Explicit parallelism is thus confined to the database engine itself.

3. Parametric simulations are often trivially parallelized by granting each CPU ownership of its own region of the parameter space.

This is the paradox of Data Ownership. The more thoroughly you apply it to a program, the more complex the program will be. However, if you structure a program to use *only* Data Ownership, as in these three examples, the resulting program can be *identical* to its sequential counterpart.

Resulting Context   The result is a more heavily parallel program that is often even less similar to its sequential counterpart but exhibits much lower contention and overhead and thus higher speedups.

Design Rationale   Data Ownership allows each CPU to access its data without incurring synchronization overhead. This can result in perfectly linear speedups. Some programs will still require one CPU to operate on another CPU's data; these programs must pass the operation to the owning CPU. The overhead associated with this operation's passing will limit the speedup, but this may be better than directly sharing the data.

---

[6] The Active Object pattern [Lavender+95] describes an object-oriented approach to this sort of operation passing. More complex operations that atomically update data owned by many CPUs must use a more complex operation-passing approach, such as two-phase commit [Tay87].

6.5 Parallel Fastpath

Problem How can you achieve high speedups in programs that cannot use aggressive locking patterns throughout?

Context You are working on an existing sequential or parallel program that can use aggressive locking patterns for the majority of its work load (the fastpath) but must use more conservative patterns for a small part of its work load.

You must need high speedup badly enough to invest the resources needed to develop, maintain, and run a highly parallel version of the program.

The program must be highly partitionable, and its speedup must be limited by synchronization overhead and contention. The fraction of the execution time that cannot be partitioned limits the speedup. For example, if the off-fastpath code uses Code Locking and 10 percent of the execution time occurs off the fastpath, then the maximum achievable speedup will be 10. Either the off-fastpath code must not execute very frequently, or it must itself use a more aggressive locking pattern.

Forces **Speedup (++):** Parallel fastpaths have very good speedups.

Contention (++): Since the common-case fastpath code uses an aggressive locking design, contention is very low.

Overhead (++): Since the common-case fastpath uses either lightweight synchronization primitives or omits synchronization primitives altogether, overhead is very low.

Read-to-Write Ratio (+): The Parallel Fastpath may allow readers to proceed in parallel.

Economics (– –): Higher speedups require larger, more expensive systems with more CPUs.

Complexity (– –): Although the fastpath itself is often very straightforward, the off-fastpath code must handle complex recovery for cases the fastpath cannot handle.

Solution Use Parallel Fastpath to aggressively parallelize the common case without incurring the complexity required to aggressively parallclize the entire algorithm.

You must understand not only the specific algorithm you wish to parallelize but also the workload that the algorithm will run. Great creativity and design effort are often required to construct a parallel fastpath.

Resulting Context The result is a more heavily parallel program that is even less similar to its sequential counterpart but exhibits much lower contention and overhead and thus higher speedups.

Design Rationale Parallel Fastpath allows the common case to be fully partitioned, without requiring that the entire algorithm be fully partitioned. This allows scarce design and coding effort to be focused where it will do the most good.

Parallel Fastpath combines different patterns (one for the fastpath, one elsewhere); it is therefore a template pattern. Reader/Writer Locking, Hierarchical Locking, and Resource Allocator are special cases of Parallel Fastpath that occur often enough to warrant being separate patterns.

6.6 Reader/Writer Locking

Problem How can programs that rarely modify shared data improve their speedup?

Context You are working on an existing program in which much of the code is contained in critical sections but the read-to-write ratio is large.

The synchronization overhead must not dominate, the contention must be high, and the read-to-write ratio must be high. Low synchronization overhead is particularly important: most implementations of Reader/Writer Locking incur high synchronization overhead.

Use specialized forms of Reader/Writer Locking when synchronization overhead dominates [Andrews91, Tay87].

Forces **Read-to-Write Ratio (+++):** Reader/Writer Locking takes full advantage of favorable read-to-write ratios.

Speedup (++): Since readers proceed in parallel, very high speedups are possible.

Contention (++): Since readers do not contend, contention is low.

Overhead (+): The number of synchronization primitives required is about the same as for Code Locking, but the reader-side primitives can be cheaper in many cases.

Complexity (–): The reader/writer concept adds a modest amount of complexity.

Economics (– –): More CPUs are required to achieve higher speedups.

Solution Use Reader/Writer Locking to greatly improve speedups of programs that rarely modify shared data.

```
/* Global lock for looktab_t manipulations. */

srwlock_t looktab_mutex;

. . .

/* Look up a looktab element and examine it.*/

S_RDLOCK(&looktab_mutex);
p = looktab_search(mykey);

/* insert code here to examine the element. */

S_UNLOCK(&looktab_mutex);
```

FIGURE 9 Read-side locking

The lookup-table example uses read-side primitives to search the table and write-size primitives to modify it. Figure 9 shows locking for search, and Figure 10 shows locking for update. Since this example demonstrates Reader/Writer Locking applied to a code-locked program, the locks must surround the calls to `looktab_search()` as well as the code that examines or modifies the selected element.

Reader/Writer Locking can easily be adapted to data-locked programs as well.

Resulting Context The result is a program that allows CPUs that are not modifying data to proceed in parallel, thereby increasing speedup.

FIGURE 10 Write-side locking

```
/* Global lock for looktab_t manipulations. */

srwlock_t looktab_mutex;

. . .

/* Look up a looktab element and examine it. */

S_WRLOCK(&looktab_mutex);
p = looktab_search(mykey);

/* insert code here to update the element. */

S_UNLOCK(&looktab_mutex);
```

Design Rationale   If synchronization overhead is negligible (that is, if the program uses coarse-grained parallelism) and only few of the critical sections modify data, then allowing multiple readers to proceed in parallel can greatly increase speedup.

Think of Reader/Writer Locking as a modification of Code Locking and Data Locking, with the reader/writer locks assigned to code paths and data structures, respectively. It is also an instance of Parallel Fastpath.

Reader/Writer Locking is a simple instance of asymmetric locking. Snaman [Snaman+87] describes a more ornate, six-mode asymmetric locking design used in several clustered systems. You may use asymmetric locking primitives to implement a very simple form of the Observer Pattern [Gamma+95]—when a writer releases the lock, the primitives will notify all readers of the change in state.

6.7 Hierarchical Locking

Problem   How can you obtain better speedups when updates are complex and expensive but infrequent operations such as insertion and deletion require coarse-grained locking?

Context   You are working on an existing sequential or parallel program suffering from high contention due to coarse-grained locking combined with frequent, high-overhead updates. Hierarchical Locking works best with programs that have hierarchical data structures.

You must need a large speedup badly enough to invest the development, maintenance, and machine resources that the more aggressive parallelization requires.

Forces   **Contention (++):** Updates proceed in parallel. However, coarsely locked operations are still serialized and can result in contention.

Speedup (+): Hierarchical Locking allows coarsely locked operations to proceed in parallel with frequent, high-overhead operations. Contention still limits speedups.

Read-to-Write Ratio (0): Readers accessing a given finely locked element proceed in parallel. However, readers traversing coarsely locked structures are still serialized.

Overhead (–): Hierarchically locked programs execute more synchronization primitives than do code-locked or data-locked programs, resulting in higher synchronization overhead.

Economics (–): Greater speedups require bigger machines.

Complexity (---): Hierarchically locked programs can be extremely complex and subtle, since they are prone to deadlock problems.

Solution   Partition the data structures into coarse- and fine-grained portions. For example, use a single lock for the internal nodes and links of a search tree, but maintain a separate lock for each of the leaves. If the updates to the leaves are expensive compared to searches and synchronization primitives, Hierarchical Locking can result in better speedups than can Code Locking or Data Locking.

For example, allocate a lock for each hash line in the hash line header data structure,[7] as shown in Figure 11. These separate locks allow searches for noncolliding, independent elements in a single table to proceed in parallel.

In this example, Hierarchical Locking is an instance of Parallel Fastpath; it uses Data Locking for the fastpath and Code Locking elsewhere.

You can combine Hierarchical Locking with Data Locking (for example, by changing the search structure from a single linked list to a hashed table with per-hash-line locks) to further reduce contention. This results in an instance of Parallel Fastpath that uses Data Locking for both the fastpath and the search structure. Since there can be many elements per hash line, the fastpath is using a more aggressive form of Data Locking than is the search structure.

Resulting Context   The result is a more heavily parallel program that is less similar to its sequential counterpart but exhibits much lower contention and thus higher speedups.

Design Rationale   If updates have high overhead, then allowing each element to have its own lock will reduce contention.

Since Hierarchical Locking can make use of different types of locking for the different levels of the hierarchy, it is a template that combines other patterns. It also is an instance of Parallel Fastpath.

6.8 Allocator Caches

Problem   How can you achieve high speedups in global memory allocators?

---

[7] In object-oriented programs, this level of data locking results in many independent critical sections per instance.

```
slock_t looktab_mutex;
looktab_t *looktab_head;
typedef struct looktab {
      struct looktab_t *lt_next;
      int      lt_key;
      int      lt_data;
      slock_t lt_mutex;
} looktab_t;

looktab_t *
looktab_search(int key)
{
      looktab_t *p;

      S_LOCK(&looktab_mutex);
      p = looktab_head;
      while (p != NULL) {
          if (p->lt_key > key) {
                S_UNLOCK(&looktab_mutex);
                return (NULL);
          }
          if (p->lt_key == key) {
                S_LOCK(&p->lt_mutex);
                S_UNLOCK(&looktab_mutex);
                return (p);
          }
          p = p->lt_next;
      }
      return (NULL);
}

/* . . . */

    /* Look up a looktab element. */

    p = looktab_search(mykey);

    /* examine or update the element. */

    S_LOCK(&p->lt_mutex);
```

FIGURE 11 Hierarchical locking

Context   You are working on an existing sequential or parallel program that spends much of its time allocating or deallocating data structures.[8] You must need a high speedup badly enough to invest the resources needed to develop, maintain, and run an allocator with a per-CPU cache.

Forces   **Speedup (++):** Speedups are limited only by the allowable size of the caches.

Contention (++): The common-case access that hits the per-CPU cache causes no contention.

Overhead (++): The common-case access that hits the per-CPU cache causes no synchronization overhead.

Complexity (–): The per-CPU caches make the allocator more complex.

Economics (– –): High speedups translate into more expensive machines with more CPUs.

Read-to-Write Ratio (N/A): Allocators normally do not have a notion of reading or writing. If allocation and free operations are considered to be reads, then reads proceed in parallel.[9]

Solution   Create a per-CPU (or per-process) cache of data-structure instances. A given CPU owns the instances in its cache (Data Ownership), and therefore it need not incur overhead and contention penalties to allocate and free them. Fall back to a global allocator with a less aggressive locking pattern (Code Locking) when the per-CPU cache either overflows or underflows. The global allocator supports arbitrary-duration producer-consumer relationships among the CPUs. Such relationships make it impossible to fully partition the memory among the CPUs.

Resulting Context   The result is a more heavily parallel program with an allocator that is quite different from its sequential counterpart but exhibits much lower contention and overhead and thus higher speedups.

You do not need to modify the code that calls the memory allocator. This pattern confines the complexity to the allocator itself.

Design Rationale   Many programs allocate a structure, use it for a short time, and then free it. These programs' requests can often be satisfied from per-CPU/process caches

---

[8] Programs that allocate resources other than data structures (e.g., I/O devices) use data structures to represent these resources. The Allocator Caches pattern therefore covers general resource allocation. For ease of exposition (but without loss of generality), this section focuses on memory allocation.

[9] Perhaps changing the size of the caches or some other attribute of the allocator would be considered a write.

of structures, eliminating the overhead of locking in the common case. If the cache hit rate is too low, you may increase it by increasing the size of the cache. If the cache is large enough, the reduced allocation overhead on cache hits more than makes up for the slight increase incurred on cache misses.

McKenney and Slingwine [McKenney+93] describe the design and performance of a memory allocator that uses caches. This allocator applies the Parallel Fastpath pattern twice, using Code Locking to allocate pages of memory, Data Locking to coalesce blocks of a given size into pages, and Data Ownership for the per-CPU caches. Access to the per-CPU caches is free of synchronization overhead and contention. In fact, the overhead of the allocations and deallocations that hit the cache are several times cheaper than the synchronization primitives. Cache-hit rates often exceed 95 percent, so the performance of the allocator is very close to that of its cache.

Other choices of patterns for the caches, coalescing, and page-allocation make sense in other situations. Therefore, the Allocator Caches pattern is a template that combines other patterns to create an allocator. It also is an instance of Parallel Fastpath.

6.9 Critical-Section Fusing

Problem How can you get high speedups from programs with frequent, small critical sections on machines with high synchronization overheads?

Context You are working on an existing program that has many small critical sections (so synchronization overhead dominates) but is not easily partitionable. You must need additional speedup badly enough to justify the cost of creating, maintaining, and running a highly parallel program.

Synchronization overhead must dominate, and contention must be low enough to allow increasing the size of critical sections.

Forces **Overhead (+):** Fusing critical sections decreases overhead by reducing the number of synchronization primitives.

Speedup (0): Fusing critical sections improves speedup only when speedup is limited primarily by overhead.

Read-to-Write Ratio (0): Fusing critical sections usually has no effect on the ability to run readers in parallel.

Economics (0): Fusing critical sections requires more CPUs if speedup increases.

Contention (–): Fusing critical sections increases contention.

Complexity (––): Fusing otherwise unrelated critical sections can add confusion and thus complexity to the program.

Solution Fuse small critical sections into larger ones to get high speedups from programs with frequent, small critical sections on machines with high synchronization overheads.

For example, imagine a program containing back-to-back searches of a code-locked lookup table. A straightforward implementation would acquire the `looktab_mutex` lock, do the first search, do the first update, release the `looktab_mutex` lock, acquire the `looktab_mutex` lock once more, do the second search, do the second update, and finally release the `looktab_mutex` lock. If synchronization overhead dominates this sequence of code, eliminate the first release and second acquisition, as shown in Figure 12, to increase speedup.

In this case, the critical sections being fused use the same lock. Fuse critical sections that use different locks by combining the two locks into one, and make all critical sections that use either of the two original locks use the single new lock instead.

FIGURE 12 Critical-section fusing

```
/* Global lock for looktab_t manipulations.*/

slock_t looktab_mutex;

. . .

/* Look up a looktab element and examine it. */

S_LOCK(&looktab_mutex);
p = looktab_search(mykey);

/*
 * insert code here to examine or update the
 * element.
 */
p = looktab_search(myotherkey);

/*
 * insert code here to examine or update the element.
 */

S_UNLOCK(&looktab_mutex);
```

Resulting Context The result is a program that has fewer (but larger) critical sections and is thus less subject to synchronization overheads.

Design Rationale If the overhead of the code between two critical sections is less than the overhead of the synchronization primitives, fusing the two critical sections will decrease overhead and increase speedups.

Critical-Section Fusing is a meta pattern that transforms Data Locking into Code Locking and Code Locking into Sequential Program. In addition, it transforms more-aggressive variants of Code Locking and Data Locking into less-aggressive variants.

Critical-Section Fusing is the inverse of Critical-Section Partitioning.

6.10 Critical-Section Partitioning

Problem How can you get high speedups from programs with infrequent, large critical sections on machines with low synchronization overheads?

Context You are working on an existing program with a few large critical sections (so contention dominates). The critical sections might contain code that is not relevant to the data structures they protect, but it is not easily partitionable. Contention must dominate, and synchronization overhead must be low enough to allow decreasing the size of critical sections.

This situation is rather rare in highly parallel code, since for most computer architectures the cost of synchronization overhead has decreased more slowly than instruction or memory-access overhead. The increasing relative cost of synchronization makes it less likely that contention effects will dominate. You can find this situation in cases where Critical-Section Fusing has been applied too liberally and in code that is not highly parallel.

If the program is large or unfamiliar but is not being maintained in sequential form by another organization, you should consider applying other patterns, such as Data Locking. The effort of applying the more difficult and effective patterns can be small compared to the effort required to analyze and understand the program.

Forces **Contention (+):** Partitioning critical sections decreases contention.

Complexity (+): Partitioning "thrown-together" critical sections can clarify the intent of the code.

Speedup (0): Partitioning critical sections improves speedup only when speedup is limited primarily by overhead.

Read-to-Write Ratio (0): Splitting critical sections usually has no effect on the ability to run readers in parallel.

Economics (0): Splitting critical sections requires more CPUs if speedup increases.

Overhead (–): Splitting critical sections can increase overhead by increasing the number of synchronization primitives. There are some special cases where overhead is unchanged (such as when a code-locked program's critical sections are partitioned by data structure, resulting in a data-locked program).

Solution   Split large critical sections into smaller ones to get high speedups in programs that have infrequent, large critical sections and run on machines with low synchronization overheads.

For example, imagine a program that is parallelized using "huge locks" that cover entire subsystems. These subsystems are likely to contain a fair amount of code that does not need to be in a critical section. Splitting the critical sections to allow this code to run in parallel might increase speedup.

If you think of a sequential program as a code-locked program with a single critical section that contains the whole program, then you can see how critical-section splitting results in a code-locked program.

Resulting Context   The result is a program that has more (but smaller) critical sections and is thus less subject to contention.

Design Rationale   If the overhead of the non-critical-section code inside a single critical section is greater than the overhead of the synchronization primitives, splitting the critical section can decrease overhead and increase speedups.

Critical-Section Partitioning is a meta pattern that transforms Sequential Program into Code Locking and Code Locking into Data Locking. It also transforms less-aggressive variants of Code Locking and Data Locking into more-aggressive variants.

Critical-Section Partitioning is the inverse of Critical-Section Fusing.

ACKNOWLEDGMENTS

I owe thanks to Ward Cunningham and Steve Peterson for encouraging me to set these ideas down and for many valuable conversations; to my PLoP '95 shepherd, Erich Gamma, for much coaching on how to set forth the patterns; to the members of PLoP '95 Working Group 4 for their insightful comments and discussions; to Ralph Johnson for his tireless championing of the use of active voice in patterns; and to Dale Goebel for his consistent support.

REFERENCES

[Andrews91] G. R. Andrews. "Paradigms for Process Interaction in Distributed Programs." *ACM Computing Surveys*, *23*(1)(1991): 49–90.

[Gamma+95] E. Gamma, R. Helm, R. Johnson, and J. Vlissides. *Design Patterns: Elements of Reusable Object-Oriented Software*. Reading, MA: Addison-Wesley, 1995.

[Lavender+95] R. G. Lavender and D. C. Schmidt. "Active Object: An Object Behavioral Pattern for Concurrent Programming." Chapter 30, this volume.

[McKenney95] P. E. McKenney. "Differential Profiling." In Patrick Dowd and Erol Gelenbe (eds.), *MASCOTS '95: Proceedings of the Third International Workshop on Modeling, Analysis, and Simulation of Computer and Telecommunications Systems*. Los Alamitos, CA: IEEE Computer Society Press, 1995, pp. 237–241.

[McKenney+93] P. E. McKenney and J. Slingwine. "Efficient Kernel Memory Allocation on Shared-Memory Multiprocessors." In *USENIX Conference Proceedings*. Berkeley, CA, February 1993, pp. 295–305.

[Snaman+87] W. E. Snaman and D. W. Thiel. "The VAX/VMS Distributed Lock Manager." *Digital Technical Journal* (September 1987): 29–44.

[Tay87] Y. C. Tay. *Locking Performance in Centralized Databases*. New York: Academic Press, 1987.

[Zajcew+93] R. Zajcew, P. Roy, D. Black, C. Peak, P. Guedes, B. Kemp, J. LoVerso, M. Leibensperger, M. Barnett, F. Rabii, and D. Netterwala. "An OSF/1 UNIX for Massively Parallel Multicomputers." In *USENIX Conference Proceedings*. Berkeley, CA, February 1993, pp. 449–466.

Paul E. McKenney can be reached at Sequent Computer Systems, Inc., 1975 N.W. Albion Court, Beaverton, OR 97006; mckenney@sequent.com.

REACTIVE SYSTEMS

PART 8

A *reactive system* is a system whose behavior is driven by changes in the real world, outside the computer and its programs. Many of these systems exhibit concurrency because time progresses on independent "clocks" inside and outside the processor, so we see many reactive system patterns interacting with those in Part 7. Many of the authors in Part 8 also wrote distributed processing patterns for Part 2 of the first volume of this series [Coplien+95]. Many of these systems are also real-time systems that must meet prescribed response deadlines. These systems present some of the most difficult problems of practical computer programming today, in the sense that they lead to some of the most pernicious bugs. And you can't find these patterns readily at hand in a college textbook either, though they underlie some of the largest and most widely used computer systems in the world.

Chapter 32, by Amund Aarsten, Giuseppe Menga, and Luca Mosconi, builds on the G++ pattern language [Aarsten+95]. The goal of their pattern language is to isolate external interfaces to a program built on the G++ framework, so the same software can be used for simulation and production. Some of the patterns cut the system in interesting dimensions: instead of thinking of firewalls just for external communication mechanisms, the authors propose organizing external resources by type, each one of which encapsulates the differences between simulated and production semantics. The pattern language is reminiscent in many respects of Barry Rubel's chapter from Volume 1 [Rubel95], which tried to mirror the structure of the hardware world in the software.

The pattern language by Michael Adams, Jim Coplien, Bob Gamoke, Bob Hanmer, Fred Keeve, and Keith Nicodemus captures highly specialized patterns from fault-tolerant telecommunication systems (Chapter 33). These patterns are specific to a small but growing domain: high-availability, fault-tolerant systems such as telecommunications systems. Many of the patterns—such as Leaky Bucket Counter—have trivial implementations, yet you can see how they are effective and why they offer insight on making systems reliable. These patterns are unusual in several respects: their technical content is all prior art in the citable literature, and none of them is object-oriented. Many of the patterns focus on issues of human comfort and convenience, both for the person maintaining the switching equipment and for the telephone subscriber—a hallmark of good patterns in the Alexandrian tradition.

Chapter 34, by Bill Wake, Doug Wake, and Ed Fox, makes the point that interactive programs—particularly programs that use interactive graphics—are real-time programs. They present four patterns, based on event queuing, to enhance the responsiveness of such programs. The patterns range from low-level optimizations that "batch" processing for sequences of related input characters, to grand architectural patterns for asynchronous output processing (as in most Emacs editors). The patterns point to the GOF patterns [Gamma+95] as analogies and as building blocks. These are delightful patterns because they are a little bit unfamiliar and startling, yet the authors take care to substantiate their application from practice and from the literature. Though most other chapters in this section are attuned to human comfort, the connection is graphically clear and direct in this chapter.

Gerard Meszaros, in Chapter 35, brings us another collection of telecommunication patterns, but these focus directly on real-time problems. It's fascinating to compare and contrast these patterns with those presented by Kent Beck and Ken Auer in Part 1. Whereas Kent and Ken's patterns focus on shaping the program so it does what it does quickly enough, Gerard's patterns include mechanisms for the program to change what it does to achieve performance objectives. Work-shedding is a strategy that can keep a real-time system meeting objectives for at least some fraction of its customers; without work-shedding, an otherwise perfectly optimized system serves all of its clients poorly, or is unable to serve them at all because spreading the real time around causes all the applications to break real-time deadlines. The pattern language includes strategies ("Fresh Work Before

Stale") that help the designer decide how to shed work—a counterintuitive solution, but one that is widely used in high-availability computing. These patterns don't invalidate Kent and Ken's patterns, but they expand them into a different context. Gerard's pattern language also recalls the patterns of Part 7, taking advantage of a distributed architecture to balance load across processors.

Not only are the two telecommunication pattern languages related, but they also overlap and weave together at interesting points. Gerard's Leaky Bucket of Credits builds on Leaky Bucket Counter in the preceding chapter. They also weave with many of the patterns of Volume 1 and the distributed processing patterns that Doug Schmidt and other authors have published in the periodical literature. We will likely see continued growth in the pattern literature for these areas for years to come.

REFERENCES

[Aarsten+95] A. Aarsten, G. Elia, and G. Menga. "G++: A Pattern Language for Computer-Integrated Manufacturing." In J. Coplien and D. Schmidt (eds.), *Pattern Languages of Program Design*. Reading, MA: Addison-Wesley, 1995.

[Coplien+95] J. Coplien, and D. Schmidt, eds. *Pattern Languages of Program Design*. Reading, MA: Addison-Wesley, 1995.

[Gamma+95] E. Gamma, R. Helm, R. Johnson, and J. Vlissides. *Design Patterns: Elements of Reusable Object-Oriented Software*. Reading, MA: Addison-Wesley, 1995.

[Rubel95] B. Rubel. "Patterns for Generating a Layered Architecture." In J. Coplien and D. Schmidt (eds.), *Pattern Languages of Program Design*. Reading, MA: Addison-Wesley, 1995.

32

Object-Oriented Design Patterns in Reactive Systems

Amund Aarsten, Giuseppe Menga, and Luca Mosconi

INTRODUCTION

In some application domains, such as computer-integrated manufacturing (CIM) and embedded controllers, the control software must often interface to a *reactive* and *event-driven* system [Garland+93]. A reactive system receives stimuli from the outside world and responds to it by updating its state and giving feedback. An event-driven system is a special kind of reactive system, in which the interaction between the external world and the system (consisting of stimuli and feedback) takes place through events. Reactive and event-driven systems are usually of a concurrent nature. In addition to the events, the control software must usually access the system's state for monitoring and control.

Developing object-oriented (OO) software for event-driven systems presents some difficulties, since the event-driven and object paradigms are fundamentally different. We want to take advantage of the OO environment's support for complexity management, the availability of reusable components, and our pattern language's guidance through the design process. On the other hand, we don't want to lose the event-driven system's component independence, decentralization, and dynamic reconfiguration support.

The Importance of Simulation

In the application domains mentioned above, there is a particular need for simulation. For instance, one cannot test and debug a factory-control application using the actual controllers and machines at the factory. It is especially important to verify the correctness of concurrency and synchronization before the control software is interfaced to the real world.

For the simulation to be of any value, the evolution to a real system must be as seamless as possible. If too many changes are made, we can no longer trust the results obtained by testing the simulation. The changes that are made must also be of a local nature; nonsimulated components should remain unaffected by the transition.

These factors must be taken into account when we try to bridge the object-oriented and event-driven paradigm.

This chapter presents a small pattern language for software control of reactive and event-driven systems, with emphasis on the evolution from a simulation to a real system. The structure of the pattern language is shown in Figure 1. The first pattern gives general directions. The remaining patterns apply to concrete problems encountered in the transition to the real system.

The patterns can be seen as an addition to the G++ pattern language for concurrent and distributed systems [Aarsten+95], and we rely on a few things from that language:

- The possibility of the G++ objects' broadcasting and listening to events through a publish/subscribe mechanism in addition to normal method calls (see Pattern 2—Visibility and Communication Between Control Modules—in Aarsten et al. [Aarsten+95]).

- The patterns for structuring concurrency at different levels of granularity (see Patterns 3 through 6—Categorize Objects for Concurrency, Actions Triggered by Events, Services "Waiting For," and Client/Server/Service—in Aarsten et al. [Aarsten+95]).

FIGURE 1 Simulation and Reality pattern language

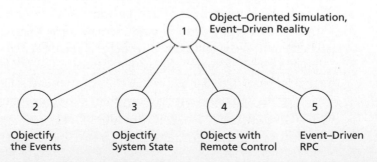

The patterns presented here grew from recent work in which we implemented distributed control systems over two fieldbus communication systems: FIP [Leterrier92], a network protocol specialized for factory instrumentation, and BASEstar Open [Digital93], which we will use for examples.

BASEstar Open

BASEstar Open is an automation-integration framework developed at Digital Equipment Corporation. It is used to manage and distribute information from the shop floor to the other areas of an enterprise and provides transparent and uniform access to data, events, and devices throughout a network.

BASEstar Open runs on a variety of different platforms, ranging from Microsoft Windows (3.1, 3.11, and NT 3.5) to OpenVMS and OSF/1. It uses TCP/IP services as network support.

BASEstar Open provides services (through a C language API) for the management of different kinds of objects. Objects are identified by a global (networkwide) name that can be used to access them regardless of their location. The BASEstar Open fundamental object classes are

- *Data Point*, a distributed variable of a definite type. BASEstar Open enables users to read and write a data point regardless of whether its value is stored in computer memory or in a plant floor device such as a control word of a programmable logic controller (PLC). A data point can be either a basic, built-in type (BOOLEAN, INTEGER_16, etc.) or a user-defined type (array and structure).

- *Event*, a significant happening that may occur at any time. Users can subscribe to notifications of one or more events. Users can also declare the occurrence of an event; BASEstar Open automatically delivers notifications of such events to any user subscribed. A user who declares an event needs no information on existing subscriptions or the users who receive notifications.

- *Enbox*, an *event notification box*, or receipt point for event notifications. Users subscribe to an event, specifying the enbox that will receive the event notifications; they then connect to the enbox in order to receive the notifications. Enboxes provide a First-In, First-Out (FIFO) queue for pending notifications.

Although the examples given here are from BASEstar Open, the patterns should be applicable in most situations where OO programs and event-driven systems must be integrated and where a smooth evolution from simulation to final system is important. In fact, most event-driven systems can be characterized (from a software-integration point of view) by variables and events; BASEstar Open differs only in that it requires events to be received through enboxes.

PATTERN 1: OBJECT-ORIENTED SIMULATION, EVENT-DRIVEN REALITY

Context   You are developing software to control a reactive, event-driven system. You have access to a pattern language and a framework of classes that support concurrency for logical design and simulation. You want to separate logical and physical design but also exploit an evolutionary development process.

Problem   Which architecture should you select for the logical design, and how do you move from prototype to reality?

Forces   Using OO programming, we can quickly build a high-quality simulation by following the pattern language and reusing library classes.

   The simulation will be based on concurrency and synchronization mechanisms such as threads, active and blocking objects, and so on. These mechanisms are not compatible with the asynchronous, event-driven nature of the external world that the final system must interface to, however. Therefore, we may have to make significant changes to the code when making the transition to a final implementation. But this would eliminate the value of the simulation and defeat the purpose of an evolutionary approach.

Solution   Design the simulation using the OO approach. Ensure that the changes made during evolution to a real system are of a local nature by maintaining two representations of the objects that will later interface to the external system, as advised by Aarsten et al. [Aarsten+95] for their Pattern 9, Prototype and Reality. To perform the transition from prototype to reality, replace the simulated objects of the prototype with the objects that will interface to the external system. A suitable creational pattern such as Abstract Factory (from [Gamma+95]) should be used to isolate the rest of the prototype from the replacements.

   In the simulation, a PLC or robot is a program object like the others, accessed by method calls and logical events. In the final program, it is still accessed by method calls and logical events, but its implementation holds references to the needed variables and events of the external system. These are accessed through a framework of basic classes that implement a "glue" layer between the program objects and the external system, as shown in Figure 2. (The details of this figure will be explained by the following patterns.)

The glue layer ensures that the program's view of the system state is consistent with reality, that events in the external system result in logical events, and that the necessary logical events are relayed to physical events in the external system. This translation of events allows us to keep the advantages of event-driven systems without sacrificing the advantages of OO programming.

Usually, introducing an extra layer into an architecture adds overhead, both in space and time, especially when the layer is used to bridge two incompatible programming models. In our experience, however, this was not a problem. Communication with the external system was significantly slower than the data structure lookups and call indirections in the glue layer. Also, in these application domains most software is developed on a custom basis. The cost of more powerful hardware is usually small relative to the time and labor saved in software development.

Implementation   We defined an abstract class, called `BstrObject`, whose main responsibility is to maintain the identity of a BASEstar Open object. Its constructor accepts

FIGURE 2 Object-oriented prototype and event-driven glue (example from BASEstar Open)

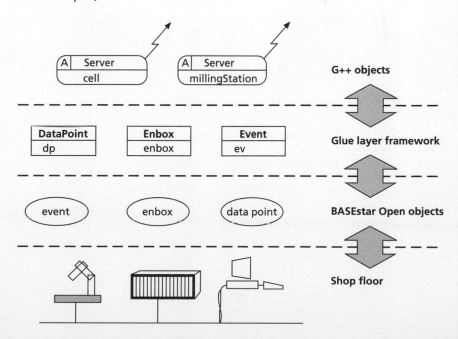

the global (networkwide) name of the object and calls the BASEstar Open API to obtain a handle for it. All the other classes that wrap BASEstar Open objects inherit from `BstrObject`.

Related Patterns The "glue" layer can be seen as a continuation of the Adapter pattern from [Gamma+95]: instead of an adapter object, there is a framework of objects that together perform the adaptation.

The other patterns describe how to implement the glue layer.

PATTERN 2: OBJECTIFY THE EVENTS

Context Objects in the prototype communicate by exchanging events, in addition to the usual method calls.

Problem The logical events in the prototype are just a communication mechanism; they are not first-class objects, as in the external system. We must find a way to associate the external event objects with the logical events in the prototype.

Solution Create a class `Event` to wrap real-system events, as shown in Figure 3. The class will have two attributes:

- `name`, the logical event it corresponds to (identified by an object of class `Symbol` in G++)

- `owner`, the object that will broadcast the logical event when event notifications arrive from the real system

And it will have two methods:

- `declare()`, which raises the corresponding event in the external system

FIGURE 3 Objectifying events

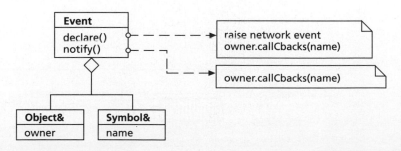

- `notify()`, which makes `owner` broadcast the logical event `name` when the corresponding external event is received.

Implementation   The class `Event` is the "bridge" between the BASEstar Open and G++ events. It maintains the association between the two kinds of events. In addition, a BASEstar Open enbox object is needed for receiving the event notifications; it is wrapped by the class `Enbox`. Each `Enbox` object maintains a collection of subscribed `Event`s; when a BASEstar Open event is received, the corresponding `Event` object is retrieved from this collection and notified.

Since BASEstar Open does not offer an interrupt or callback service for event notifications, the `Enbox` objects must check for pending events periodically.

Related Patterns   Pattern 4, Objects with Remote Control, shows how the objectified events are used to control the external system.

PATTERN 3: OBJECTIFY SYSTEM STATE

Context   In the real system, the objects that represented the physical process in the prototype will depend on the state of the external system. The state of the external system is characterized by variables of different types, whose values change according to the dynamic behavior of the physical process.

All types of variables are accessed through a common mechanism.

Problem   In the simulation, variables that characterize the external system state are implemented as usual programming language variables. When going from prototype to real system, to avoid changing the algorithms that access these variables, we cannot change the way of accessing them. Therefore, we must find a transparent way to access the external system state.

Also, the format of a data type can be different in the application program and the external system.

Forces   To achieve transparent data access, we should define a logical type for each data type in the external system. However, we don't want to duplicate the code for accessing the system state in all the different classes.

To avoid duplicating this code, we could make a single class that knows all the different data types and their internal and external formats. This solution defeats fundamental OO principles, however, and it relies on a runtime–type identification system.

Solution   Create a class for each type of data that will be accessed in the external system, and give it methods to get and set the external variable it wraps. Each class should know how to convert its own data type between the internal and external formats.

The need to duplicate the code to access the external system can be avoided by making all the data-type classes inherit from a `DataPoint` base class, as shown in Figure 4. This class offers, as protected methods, type-generic implementation of the access mechanism.[1]

Implementation   The `DataPoint` class wraps the basic functionalities of data point reading and writing using the BASEstar Open API.

Classes that wrap a specific type of data point (say, `T`) inherit from class `DataPoint` and use its methods to access the data point. They also define `operator=` and `operator T` to mimic the corresponding C++ variable (or G++ object), thus enabling transparent substitution of variables and objects with data points from the prototype to the real system. For instance, the class `Integer16DP`, which wraps an `INTEGER_16` BASEstar Open data point, defines `Integer16DP& operator=( int )` and `operator int` to mimic a C++ `int` variable.

Related Patterns   This pattern is a concrete application of the G++ pattern Prototype and Reality, described by Aarsten et al. [Aarsten+95]. Together with Pattern 2, it forms the base for Patterns 4 and 5.

FIGURE 4 Wrapping the external system state

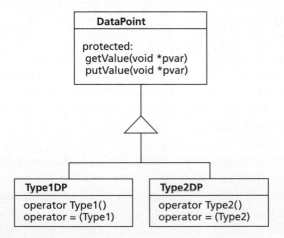

---

[1] More elegant solutions can be found if the compiler supports templates.

PATTERN 4: OBJECTS WITH REMOTE CONTROL

Context   In the prototype, there are active objects representing physical entities. In the real system, these physical entities are remote and communicate by exchanging events and state information. You are applying Patterns 2 and 3 to objectify events and system state.

Problem   The software control objects must be interfaced to the external entities they control.

Forces   Active objects in G++ are created by subclassing the class `Server`. As mentioned in the section on Pattern 2, they communicate with logical events.

   The real-world interface objects must interface to the external system using the objectified events and system state discussed in the sections on Patterns 2 and 3. They must therefore act as "event gateways." Logical events must be tied to their objectified counterparts, so that the events are reflected in the external system.

   At the same time, the reality interface object must be compatible with the prototype objects they replace, to avoid impacting the rest of the application.

   We could reimplement the basic G++ event-handling mechanism to associate an `Event` object with each logical event, thereby ensuring that it is reflected to the external system. However, there are many events in the logical prototype that should not be reflected to the external system. Duplicating all events would greatly increase the load on the communication network.

Solution   In G++, logical events are broadcast by the method `callCbacks (Symbol&)`, which is inherited from the root of the class hierarchy, `Object`. Create a new class (e.g., `BstrServer`) that inherits from `Server`, and add a `callCbacks()` method that takes an `Event&` as its parameter instead of `Symbol&` (see Figure 5). The reality interface object is then derived from the `BstrServer` class. The needed `Events` are declared in the scope of the class, using the same identifiers as those used by the global `Symbol` events. This way, the global events are hidden from the class; thus the `Events` and the new `callCbacks()` are used instead. The class structure before and after the switch from prototype to reality is illustrated in Figure 6.

Related Patterns   This pattern can be seen as an application of the G++ pattern Prototype and Reality [Aarsten+95], with a few extra twists.

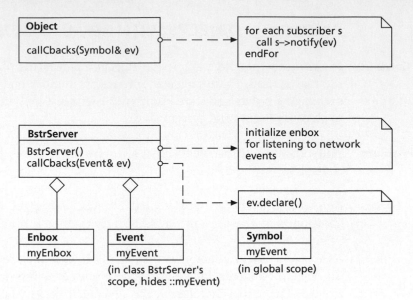

FIGURE 5 Redefining event broadcast

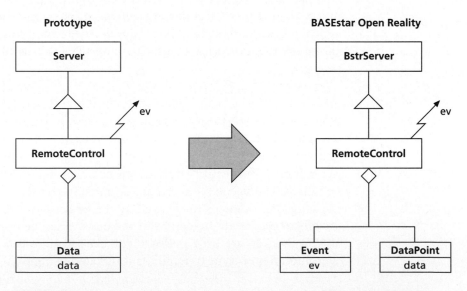

FIGURE 6 Class structure for remote—prototype and reality (example from BASEstar Open)

PATTERN 5: EVENT-DRIVEN RPC

Context   You need to make distributed method calls through the external system.

Problem   The external system provides no support for method calls or standard network protocols.

Forces   The G++ framework defines the classes `Stub` and `RemoteContext`,[2] which support method invocation between remote objects. Their implementation, however, is based on a socket network interface. Obviously, implementing a socket layer on top of an event-driven interface is both cumbersome and inefficient.

Solution   For each object that will receive remote method calls, define a compatible stub class. In the stub class, define two `Event`s for each method, one to represent the call and the other for method return. Also, define a variable in the external system for each method parameter and return value. Implement the method call by setting the system variables according to the parameters, generating the call event, waiting for the return event, and reading the return value from the system.

   Analogously, define a remote context for each object that will receive method calls over the network (the remote context must have visibility of the object in question). The remote context waits for method call events, reads the parameters from the system state, calls the object method that corresponds to the event, writes the return value to the system state, and generates the method return event.

   This process can be performed automatically by a specialized RPC generator.

Related Patterns   This pattern is a different implementation, on a different platform, of the concept from Pattern 10, Distribution of Control Modules, in Aarsten et al. [Aarsten+95].

SUMMARY

In this chapter we have presented a small pattern language that shows how standard architectural elements of concurrent and distributed applications

---

[2]   G++ remote contexts correspond to the *skeletons* in the CORBA [OMG92] reference architecture.

can be reused successfully when developing control software for reactive, event-driven systems.

This way, the logical design and prototypes can be built without worrying about the particulars of the target platform, allowing separation of logical and physical design. At the same time, the patterns presented here ensure a smooth evolution from prototype to real system.

In developing software for reactive and event-driven systems, there are two possible approaches for structuring the control architecture:

- The control of a remote entity, as described by Pattern 4
- The distribution of control objects in a CORBA-like manner, as described by Pattern 5

This pattern language supports both approaches.

ACKNOWLEDGMENTS

This work has been supported by the European Commission, DGIII/A funds, under contract ESSI no. 10070, the AEFTA application experiment.

REFERENCES

[Aarsten+95] A. Aarsten, G. Elia, and G. Menga. "G++: A Pattern Language for Computer-Integrated Manufacturing." In J. O. Coplien and D. C. Schmidt (eds.), *Pattern Languages of Program Design*. Reading, MA: Addison-Wesley, 1995.

[Digital93] Digital Equipment Corp. *BASEstar Open Reference Guide.* (Order number AA-PQVRB-TE.) November 1993.

[Gamma+95] E. Gamma, R. Helm, R. Johnson, and J. Vlissides. *Design Patterns: Elements of Reusable Object-Oriented Software*. Reading, MA: Addison-Wesley, 1995.

[Garland+93] D. Garland and M. Shaw. "An Introduction to Software Architecture." In V. Ambriola and G. Tortora (eds.), *Advances in Software Engineering and Knowledge*. World Scientific Publishing Company, 1993.

[Leterrier92] P. Leterrier. *The FIP Protocol.* Nancy, France: Centre de Competénce FIP, 1992.

[OMG92] Object Management Group. *The Common Object Request Broker: Architecture and Specification.* Framingham, MA, 1992.

Amund Aarsten, Luca Mosconi, and Giuseppe Menga can be reached at `amund@polito.it`, `menga2@polgm1.polito.it`, and `menga@polito.it` respectively.

Fault-Tolerant Telecommunication System Patterns

33

Michael Adams, James Coplien, Robert Gamoke, Robert Hanmer, Fred Keeve, and Keith Nicodemus

INTRODUCTION

The patterns presented here form a small, partial pattern language within the larger collection of patterns in use at AT&T. We chose them because of their interconnectedness and the diversity of their authorship, and because they are probably well known to the telecommunications programming community. Many of these patterns work in other domains, but for this chapter we expect telecommunications designers to be our primary audience.

Two of the unique characteristics of telecommunications software are its reliability and human factors. Many switching systems, including the ones referred to in these patterns, are designed to be in virtually continuous operation—they may be out of service no more than two hours in forty years. In many cases this requirement limits design choices.

The systems must also be designed so that maintenance personnel efforts are optimized. This can lead to largely automated systems or systems in which remote computers monitor and control the switching equipment.

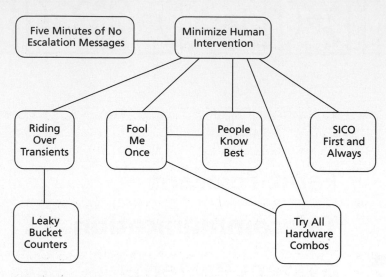

FIGURE 1 Pattern map

GLOSSARY

1A: A central processor for telecommunications systems.

1B: A second-generation central processor based on the 1A architecture.

4ESS Switch, 5ESS Switch: Members of the AT&T Electronic Switching System product line.

Application: The portion of systems software that relates to its call processing function.

Call Store: The system's memory store, used for static or dynamic data.

CC: Central Control (the central processor complex), either a 1A or a 1B processor.

FIT: Failures in a Trillion, a measurement of the failure rate of hardware components (one FIT equals one component failure in 10^9 hours).

PC: Processor Configuration, the initialization and recovery mechanisms (independent of the application) that deal with the common underlying hardware/software platform. *PC* is also used as a verb, to indicate a certain level of system reboot.

Phase: A level of system recovery escalation.

Program Store: The memory stores used for program text.

SICO: System Integrity Control.

Stored Program Control: A term used to differentiate between central control–based switching and the older relay- and crossbar-based systems.

Transient: A condition that is transitory in nature. It appears and disappears. Lightning might produce transient errors.

PATTERN: MINIMIZE HUMAN INTERVENTION

Problem   History has shown that people cause the majority of problems in continuously running systems (wrong actions, wrong systems, wrong button).

Context   Highly reliable, continuously running digital systems for which downtime, human-induced or otherwise, must be minimized.

Forces   Humans are truly intelligent; machines aren't. Humans are better at detecting patterns of system behavior, especially among seemingly random occurrences separated by time. (See the pattern People Know Best.)

Machines are good at orchestrating a well thought out, global strategy; humans aren't.

Humans are fallible; computers are often less fallible.

Humans feel a need to intervene if they can't see that the system is making serious attempts at restoration: A quiet system is a dead system. Human reaction and decision times are very slow (by orders of magnitude) compared to computer processors.

Human operators get bored with ongoing surveillance and may ignore or miss critical events.

Normal processing (and failure) events happen so quickly that it is infeasible to include the human operator.

Solution   Let the machine try to do everything itself, deferring to the human only as an act of desperation and a last resort.

Resulting Context   The result is a system less susceptible to human error. This will make the system's customers happier. In many organizations, the system operator's compensation is based on system availability, so this strategy actually improves the operator's lot.

Application of this pattern leads to a system in which patterns such as Riding Over Transients, SICO First and Always, and Try All Hardware Combos apply as well, providing a system with the ability to proceed automatically.

Rationale   A disproportionate number of failures in high-availability systems are due to operator errors, not primary system errors. By minimizing human intervention, overall system availability can be improved. Human intervention can be reduced by building in strategies that counter human tendencies to act rashly; see patterns like Fool Me Once, Leaky Bucket Counters, and Five Minutes of No Escalation Messages.

Notice the tension between this pattern and People Know Best.

Authors   Robert Hanmer and Mike Adams

PATTERN: PEOPLE KNOW BEST

Problem   How do you balance automation with human authority and responsibility?

Context   A highly reliable, continuously operating system that tries to recover from all error conditions on its own.

Forces   People have a good subjective sense of the passage of time, how it relates to the probability of a serious failure, and how outages will be perceived by the customer.

The system is set up to recover from failure cases. (See the pattern Minimize Human Intervention.)

People feel a need to intervene.

Most system errors can be traced to human error.

Solution   Assume that people know best, particularly the maintenance folks. Design the system to allow knowledgeable users to override automatic controls.

Example: As you escalate through the 64 states of processor configuration (see Try All Hardware Combos), a human who understands what's going on can intervene and stop it, if necessary.

Resulting Context   People feel empowered; however, they are also held accountable for their actions.

This is an absolute rule: people feel a need to intervene. There is no perfect solution to this problem, and the pattern cannot resolve all the forces well. Fool Me Once provides a partial solution in that it doesn't give humans a chance to intervene.

Rationale   Consider the input command to unconditionally restore a unit: what does "unconditional" mean? Let's say the system thinks the unit is powered down; what should happen when the operator asks for the unit to be restored unconditionally? Answer: Try to restore it anyhow, no excuses allowed; the fault detection hardware can always detect the powered-down condition and generate an interrupt for the unit out of service. Why might the operator want to do this? Because the problem may be not with the power but with the sensor that wrongly reports that the power is off.

Notice the tension between this pattern and Minimize Human Intervention.

Author   Robert Gamoke

PATTERN: FIVE MINUTES OF NO ESCALATION MESSAGES

Problem   Rolling in console messages: The human-machine interface is saturated with error reports rolling off the screen, or the system is consuming extreme computational resources just to display error messages.

Context   Any continuously operating, fault-tolerant system with escalation and where transient conditions may be present.

Forces   There is no sense in wasting time or reducing the level of service trying to solve a problem that will go away by itself.

Many problems work themselves out, given time.

You don't want the switch to use all of its resources displaying messages.

You don't want to panic users by making them think the switch is out of control (see Minimize Human Intervention).

The only user action related to the escalation messages may be inappropriate to the goal of preserving system sanity.

There are other computer systems monitoring the actions taken. These systems can deal with a great volume of messages.

Solution   When taking the first action in a series that could lead to an excess number of messages, display a message. Periodically display an update message. If the abnormal condition ends, display a message that everything is back to normal. Do not display a message for every change in state (see Riding Over Transients).

Continue to communicate trouble status and actions taken to the downstream monitoring computer system throughout this period.

For example, when the 4ESS switch enters the first level of system overload, post a user message. Post no more messages for five minutes, even if there is additional escalation. At the end of five minutes, display a status message indicating the current status. When the condition clears, display an appropriate message.

Resulting Context   The system operator won't panic from seeing too many messages. Machine-to-machine messages and measurement provide a record for later evaluation and make the system's actions visible to people who can deal with them. In the 4ESS switch overload example, measurement counters continue to track overload dynamics; some downstream support systems track these counters.

Other messages, not related to the escalating situation that is producing too many messages, will be displayed as though the system were normal. Thus the normal functioning of the system is not adversely affected by the volume of escalation messages.

Note the conflict with People Know Best.

Rationale   Don't freak out the user. The only solution to 4ESS switch overload for an on-site user is to resort to the command "Cancel Overload Controls," which tells the system to ignore its overload indicators and behave as though there were no overload.

This is a special case of Aggressive Versus Tentative.

Authors   Robert Hanmer and Mike Adams

PATTERN: RIDING OVER TRANSIENTS

Alias   Make Sure Problem Really Exists

Problem   How do you know whether or not a problem will work itself out?

Context   You are working with a fault-tolerant application in which some errors, overload conditions, and so on may be transient. The system can escalate through recovery strategies, taking more drastic action at each step. A typical example is a fault-tolerant telecommunications system using static traffic engineering, for which you want to check for overload or transient faults.

Forces   You want to catch faults and problems.

There is no sense in wasting time or reducing the level of service while trying to solve a problem that will go away by itself.

Many problems work themselves out, given time.

Solution Don't react immediately to detected conditions. Make sure a condition really exists by checking it several times, or use Leaky Bucket Counters to detect a critical number of occurrences in a specific time interval. For example, by averaging over time or just waiting awhile, you can give transient faults a chance to pass.

Resulting Context Errors can be resolved with truly minimal effort, because the effort is expended only if the problem really exists. This pattern allows the system to roll through problems without its users noticing them and without bothering the machine operator to intervene (like Minimize Human Intervention).

Rationale This pattern detects "temporally dense" events. Think of such events as spikes on a time line. If a small number of spikes (specified by a threshold) occur together (where "together" is specified by the interval), then the error is a transient. This pattern is used by Leaky Bucket Counters, Five Minutes of No Escalation Messages, and many others.

Author James O. Coplien

PATTERN: LEAKY BUCKET COUNTERS

Problem How do you deal with transient faults?

Context You are working with fault-tolerant system software that must deal with failure events. Failures are tied to episode counts and frequencies.

For example, in 1A/1B processor systems used in AT&T telecommunications products, as memory words (dynamic RAM) get weak, the memory module generates a parity error trap. Examples include both 1A processor dynamic RAM and 1B processor static RAM.

Forces You want a hardware module to exhibit hard failures before taking drastic action. Some failures come from the environment and thus should not be blamed on the device.

Solution A failure group has a counter that is initialized to a predetermined value when the group is initialized. The counter is decremented for each fault or event (usually faults) and incremented on a periodic basis; however, the count is never incremented beyond its initial value. There are different initial values and different leak rates for different subsystems (for example, the leak interval is a half hour for the 1A memory (store) subsystem). The strategy for 1A dynamic RAM specifies that for the first failure in a store (within the timing window), you must take the store out of service, diagnose it, and then automatically restore it to service. On the second, third, and fourth failures (within the window), you just leave it in service. On the fifth failure (again, within the window), you must take the unit out of service, diagnose it, and leave it out.

If the episode transcends the interval, it's not transient: the leak rate is faster than the refill rate, and the pattern indicates an error condition. If the burst is more intense than expected (i.e., it exceeds the error threshold), then it represents unusual behavior not associated with a transient burst, and the pattern indicates an error condition.

Resulting Context   A system in which errors are isolated and handled (by taking devices out of service), but transient errors (e.g., errors caused by excessive humidity) don't cause unnecessary loss of service.

Rationale   The history is instructive: in old call stores (1A memories that contained dynamic data), why did we collect data? For old call stores, the field replaceable unit (FRU) was a circuit pack, while the failure group was a store composed of 12 or 13 packs. We needed to determine which pack was bad. Memory may have been spread across seven circuit packs; the transient bit was only one bit, not enough to isolate the failure. By recording data from four events, we were better able to pinpoint (with 90 percent accuracy) which pack was bad, so the machine operator didn't have to change seven packs.

Why go five failures before taking a unit out of service? By collecting data on the second, third, and fourth failures, you can make absolutely sure you know the characteristics of the error; thus you reduce your uncertainty about the FRU. By the fifth time, you know it's sick and you need to take it out of service.

Periodically increasing the count on the store creates a sliding time window. The resource is considered sane when the counter (re)attains its initialized value. Humidity, heat, and other environmental problems cause transient errors, which should be treated differently (i.e., pulling the card does no good).

See, for example, Fool Me Once, which uses simple leaky bucket counters. This is a special case of the pattern Riding Over Transients. The strategy is alluded to by Downing et al. [Downing+64].

Author   Robert Gamoke

PATTERN: SICO FIRST AND ALWAYS

Problem You are trying to make a system highly available and resilient in the face of hardware and software faults and transient errors.

Context You are working with a system in which the ability to do meaningful work is of the utmost importance, but rare periods of partial application functionality can be tolerated (for example, the 1A/1B processor-based 4ESS switch from AT&T).

Forces Bootstrapping is initialization.

A high-availability system might require (re)initialization at any time to ensure system sanity.

The System Integrity Control program (SICO) coordinates system integrity.

The System Integrity Program must be in control during bootstrapping.

The focus of operational control changes from bootstrapping to executive control during normal call processing.

Application functioning is very important.

The System Integrity Program takes processor time, but that is acceptable in this context.

The system is composed of proprietary elements, for which design criteria may be imposed on all the software in the system.

Hardware designed to be fault-tolerant reduces hardware errors.

Solution Give the System Integrity Program the ability and power to reinitialize the system whenever system sanity is threatened by error conditions. The same System Integrity Program should oversee both the initialization process and the normal application functions so that initialization can be restarted if it runs into errors.

Resulting Context In short, System Integrity Control plays a major role during bootstrapping, after which it hands control over to the executive scheduler, which in turn lets System Integrity Control regain control for short periods of time on a scheduled basis.

See also Audit Derivable Constants After Recovery.

Rationale During a recovery event (phase or bootstrap), SICO calls processor initialization software first, peripheral initialization software second, then application initialization software; finally it transfers to executive control. Unlike a classic computer program in which initialization takes place first and "normal execution" second, the SICO architecture does not make software initialization the highest-level function. System integrity is at an even higher level than system initialization.

The architecture is based on a base level cycle in the executive control. After bootstrapping, the first item in the base cycle is SICO (though this is different code than that run during bootstrapping). So, after the SICO part of bootstrapping is done, the base level part of SICO is entered into each base level cycle to monitor the system on a periodic basis.

The System Integrity Control Program must be alert to watch for failures during both bootstrapping and normal base-level operation. There is a system integrity monitor in the base level that watches timers. Overload control and audit control check in with SICO to report software and hardware failures and (potentially) request initialization, while watching for errors within their own realms.

During bootstrapping and initialization, system integrity employs a number of similar mechanisms to monitor the system (for example, Analog Timers, Boot Timers, Try All Hardware Combos, and others).

Much of the rationale for this pattern comes from AUTOVON, Safeguard, missile guidance systems, and other high-reliability real-time projects from early AT&T stored program control experience. See [Meyers+77].

Author   Robert Hanmer

PATTERN: TRY ALL HARDWARE COMBOS

Problem   The central controller (CC) has several configurations. There are many possible paths through CC subsystems, depending on the configuration. How do you select a workable configuration when there is a faulty subsystem?

Context   You are working with highly fault-tolerant computing complexes, such as the 1B processor.

The processing complex has a number of duplicated subsystems. Each one consists of a CC, a set of call stores, a call store bus, a set of program stores, a program store bus, and an interface bus. Major subsystems are duplicated with standby units to increase system reliability rather than to provide distributed processing capabilities. There are 64 possible configurations of these subsystems, given fully duplicated sparing. Each configuration is said to represent a configuration state.

The system is brought up in stages. First, you need to have the memory units working. Second, you need to talk to the disk, so you can pump stuff into memory (which allows you to run programs to pump the rest of the stores, so code can recover other units). Third, after the base system is configured and refreshed from disk, you can bring up the application.

Forces You want to catch and remedy single, isolated errors.

You also want to catch errors that aren't easily detected in isolation but result from interaction between modules.

You sometimes must catch multiple, concurrent errors.

The CC can't sequence subsystems through configurations, since it may be faulty itself.

The machine should recover by itself without human intervention (see Minimize Human Intervention).

Solution Maintain a 64-state counter in hardware. We call this the configuration counter. There is a table that maps from that counter onto a configuration state: in the 1A, it's in the hardware; in the 1B, it's in the boot ROM. Every time the system fails to get through a PC to a predetermined level of stability, it restarts the system with a successive value of the configuration counter.

In the 5ESS switch there is a similar 16-state counter. It first tries all side zero units (a complete failure group), then all side one units (the other failure group), hoping to find a single failure. The subsequent counting states look for more insidious problems, such as those that come from interactions between members of these coarse failure groups.

Resulting Context The system can deal with any number of concurrent faults, provided there is at most one fault per subsystem.

The state will increment when a reboot (PC) fails.

Sometimes the fault won't be detected right after the reboot sequence (i.e., not until more than 30 seconds after the resumption of normal activities). This problem is addressed in Fool Me Once.

Sometimes, going through all 64 states isn't enough; see Don't Trust Anyone and Analog Timer.

Rationale This design is based on the FIT rates of the original hardware—and on the extreme caution of first-generation developers of stored program control switching systems.

Note that the pattern Blind Search apparently violates this pattern, because it uses a store to hold the identity of the out-of-service module; this is addressed in the pattern Multiple Copies of Base Store.

PC State	CC0	CC1	PS0	PS1	Bus0	Bus1	Other Stores
X000	U	U	U	U	U	U	U
X001	C	C	U	U	U	U	U
X010	U	U	U	U	C	C	U
X011	U	U	A	S	A	S	T
X100	U	U	A	S	S	A	T
X101	U	U	S	A	S	A	T
X110	U	U	S	A	A	S	T
X111	U	U	S	A	A	S	T

X: Don't care; A: Active; S: Standby; U: Unchanged; C: Complemented; T: Marked as having trouble.

TABLE 1 Configurations Established by Emergency Action Switching (Status of Units after a Switch Performed by the Indicated State) [Downing+64, pp. 2006]

Authors   Robert Gamoke; 5ESS switch information, Fred Keeve
    See [Downing+64, pp. 2005–2009].

PATTERN: FOOL ME ONCE

Problem   Sometimes the fault causing a processor configuration (PC) is intermittent (usually triggered by software, such as diagnostics). After a PC is complete, users expect the configuration state display to disappear from the system's human control interface and the system to be sane. If the configuration display state continues to be displayed for more than 30 seconds, users may become concerned that the system still has a problem. But if the system in fact trips on another fault, it may reboot itself (take a phase) and reinitiate the initialization sequence using the same configuration as before (or, worse, start the configuration sequence at the beginning), which raises the probability that the system will loop in reboots ("roll in recovery") and never attempt different configurations.

Context   You are working with a highly available system using redundancy, and you are employing the pattern Try All Hardware Combos.

You're going through Try All Hardware Combos. The system finds an ostensibly sane state and progresses 30 seconds into initialization, beyond boot and into the application. The application "knows" that the hardware is sane if it can go for 30 seconds (using Leaky Bucket Counters). When the system reaches this state, it resets the configuration counter. However, a latent error can cause a system fault after the configuration counter has been reset. The system no longer "knows" that it is in PC escalation, and it retries the same configuration that has already failed.

Forces   It's hard to set a universally correct interval for a Leaky Bucket Counter; sometimes, 30 seconds is too short. The application (and customer) would be upset if the Leaky Bucket Counter were set too long (for example, a customer doesn't want to wait a half hour for a highly reliable system to clear its fault status). Some errors take a long time to appear, even though they are fundamental hardware errors (e.g., an error in program store that isn't accessed until very late in the initialization cycle or until a hardware fault is triggered by a diagnostic run out of the scheduler). People's expectations are among the most important forces at work here. In spite of the potential for some classes of faults to be latent, the application and user feel assured that the system must be sane if it's been exercised for 30 seconds.

Solution   The first time the application tells PC that "all is well," believe it and reset the configuration counter. The second and subsequent times, within a longer time window, ignore the request.

The first request to reset the configuration counter indicates that the application's 30-second Leaky Bucket Counter says that everything is fine. Set up a half-hour Leaky Bucket Counter to avoid being fooled. If the application tries to reset the 64-state configuration counter twice in a half hour, ignore it. This indicates recurring failures that would result in reboots.

Resulting Context   Any subsequent failures will cause the configuration counter to advance, guaranteeing that the next PC will use a fresh configuration. For a single subsystem error that is taking the system down, this strategy will eventually reach a workable configuration. Once the system is up, schedule diagnostics to isolate the faulty unit (see People Know Best). The system will be able to handle repetitive failures outside the shorter window, thereby reinforcing Minimize Human Intervention.

Rationale   See the forces. It's better to escalate to exceptionally extravagant strategies like this, no matter how late, if it eventually brings the system back on line. The pattern has been found to be empirically sound.

Author   Robert Gamoke

ACKNOWLEDGMENTS

Many thanks to Gerard Meszaros of BNR, who served as the PLoP '95 shepherd for these patterns, and to all those who reviewed these patterns in the writers' workshops at PLoP.

REFERENCES

[Downing+64] R. W. Downing, J. S. Nowak, and L. S. Tuomenoska. *Bell System Technical Journal, 43* (September 1964), Part 1, "No. 1 Electronic Switching System": 1961–2019.

[Meyers+77] M. N. Meyers, W. A. Routt, and K. W. Yoder. *Bell System Technical Journal,* 56, 2 (September 1977): 1139–1167.

The authors can be reached at (James Coplien) cope@research.att.com, (Robert Hanmer) r.s.hanmer@att.com, (Robert Gamoke) r.j.gamoke@att.com.

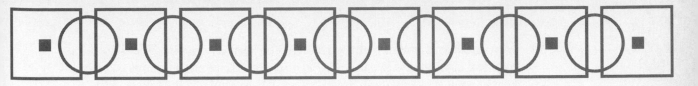

Improving Responsiveness in Interactive Applications Using Queues

34

William C. Wake, B. Douglas Wake, and Edward A. Fox

ABSTRACT

This chapter presents a set of patterns for use in designing the low-level interaction structure of interactive applications.

INTRODUCTION

Programs can be categorized as batch, real-time, or interactive. In a batch application, output is not synchronized with input. The input data is determined before the program is run. In a real-time application, the program reacts to the passage of time, and the utility of a computation depends on when it is delivered as well as its accuracy (see, e.g., Sha and Goodenough's discussion of real-time scheduling theory [Sha+90]). In an interactive application, the program presents output in response to input, and the user's reaction to that output can affect future input to the program [Ambriola+88].

An interactive program must react to the user as quickly as possible. In graphical applications in particular, a timely reaction to user actions is critical to achieving an adequate interactive feel. For example, if the cursor position doesn't consistently reflect the mouse motion, the system will feel sluggish.

The interaction style of an application should be reflected in its structure. Modern programs with a graphical user interface often manage small interactions (e.g., reacting to individual keystrokes), and the program design must accommodate that burden.

The following patterns focus on a design that can help one improve the performance and responsiveness of interactive programs:

1. Event Queue
2. Merge Compatible Events
3. Handle Artificial Events
4. Decouple Execution and Output

PATTERN 1: EVENT QUEUE

Context   You are working on an interactive application (especially one with a graphical user interface). The application receives input as events (such as mouse movement or keystrokes).

Problem   The program must accommodate a modeless user interface where the user, rather than the program, determines what to interact with next. The program must systematically deal with a variety of possible events.

Solution   To accommodate the low-level interaction typical in graphical programs, we can adopt a classical architecture used by simulation programs and build the program around an event queue. (For example, see Pooch and Wall's discussion of discrete event simulation [Pooch+93].) For each event in the queue, information about the type of event (e.g., "keystroke") is augmented with a time stamp and data specific to that type of event (e.g., "shift-A"). Events in the queue are ordered by time.

The event queue object can maintain a count of the number of pending events, retrieve the current event, and remove the current event from the queue. Some implementations may have event filtering, either to prevent certain event types from being fetched from the queue or to prevent them from ever being inserted in the first place. For example, a nongraphical application might choose to ignore mouse motion.

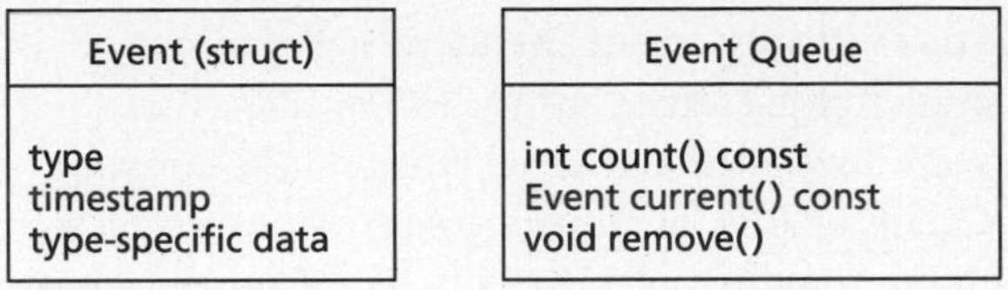

Event (struct)	Event Queue
type timestamp type-specific data	int count() const Event current() const void remove()

FIGURE 1 The event and event queue objects

Event queues are well managed by this typical simulation program structure:

```
done = false
while (!done) do
    e = eq->Current()
    eq->Remove()
    switch (e.type) of
    case type-1: ...
    case type-2: ...
        :
    end (switch)
end (while)
```

Consequences

Flexibility. Applications that respond to events encourage a less rigid interaction model. This program structure lets the user operate in an opportunistic way. The program deals with events one at a time, making a little progress on whichever object is the focus of the user's attention.

Fewer modes. Event-driven applications often strive to minimize the number of modes. For example, a user can resize a window without explicitly leaving the text insertion mode.

Smaller interaction cycles. Traditional applications tend to go through phases (e.g., the input phase). After they complete a phase, they can throw away the context used in that phase. Event-based applications tend to combine phases into a much smaller interaction cycle; thus they must maintain a number of potentially active contexts.

Examples

Simulations. Simulations have long used an event queue structure for overall organization [Pooch+93].

Programming for a graphical user interface. Programs on the Apple Macintosh use an event queue–based design for their basic structure [Apple85]. Microsoft Windows programs use a similar structure [Petzold90]. However, many user interface frameworks, such as PowerPlant [Metrowerks95] hide the event queue by using the Chain of Responsibility pattern [Gamma+95, p. 223].

Related Patterns There is usually only one event queue per application; it might be an instance of the Singleton pattern [Gamma+95, p. 127].

Events are low-level entities. You should consider using the Command and/or Chain of Responsibility patterns described by Gamma and his colleagues [Gamma+95, pp. 223, 233]. The Command pattern can encapsulate an event into an object; the Chain of Responsibility pattern can dispatch the event to the object that should handle it.

Merge Compatible Events (Pattern 2) and Handle Artificial Events (Pattern 3) can be used with an event queue to improve a program's responsiveness. Decouple Execution and Output (Pattern 4) can be used to apply the event queue structure to output as well as input.

PATTERN 2: MERGE COMPATIBLE EVENTS

Context You are working on an interactive program based on an event queue. Performance is important.

Problem Events are arriving faster than the program can deal with them.

Key Question Is it common to have sequences of similar or related events?

Solution Instead of fetching one event at a time, use the event queue's `count()` method to see if there are other events pending. If so, peek into the queue to judge whether the next event is compatible with the current one (in terms of forming a compound event). If the events are compatible, they can be combined into a single compound event. This process can be repeated to merge a sequence of compatible pending events into one.

The timelines in Figure 2 show a typical sequence of events. Events with the same shape are considered compatible. The lower part of the diagram shows the effect of merging events.

Events e1 and e2 were combined when we looked for an event at t_1. Event e3 hadn't yet arrived in the event queue, so it could not be merged with e12. At t_2, event e4 was not compatible with e3, so only e3 was fetched. By t_3, event e5 had arrived and been combined with e4. Event e6 was the only event available at t_4.

This pattern borrows an idea from batch systems and applies it to interactive systems: instead of an on-line sequence, where each command must be executed fully and in order, we get a set of commands that can be optimized together. This improves the performance and responsiveness of the system.

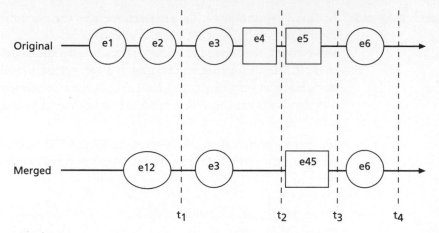

FIGURE 2

Cautions Which events are compatible depends on the program. The important thing is that the effect of operating on the two events together should be the same as the effect of operating on them in sequence. For example, on the Macintosh, the effect of a double click on an object is usually to extend the effect of a single click. We want a distributive law to hold: if *f* is what the program computes, we want

$$\forall e1, e2: f(e1; e2) = f(e1); f(e2)$$

We must make sure to capture the full effect of the combined events. For example, in most editors, "insert-a-character; delete-a-character" is equivalent to "mark the file dirty," not "do nothing."

This pattern should not be applied when the cost of combining the events is more than the cost of simply performing the actions associated with them. If knowing the sequence of events allows little opportunity for optimization, there can be little benefit in combining them. Ideally, the cost would work like this:

$$\forall e1, e2: Cost[f(e1; e2)] \leq Cost[f(e1); f(e2)]$$
$$\wedge \exists e1, e2: Cost[f(e1; e2)] < Cost[f(e1); f(e2)]$$

That is, "it never hurts, and sometimes it helps." If the first inequality doesn't hold, then it will sometimes take longer to handle the combined event. If the second inequality doesn't hold, it never pays to combine events.

There are two escape hatches to this guideline:

1. The definition of "compatible events" can be used to exclude troublesome event combinations.

2. You might make an explicit cost trade-off (e.g., "I don't mind if searching is a little slower, so long as it makes text entry much faster").

Consequences   **Reduced repeatability.** This pattern reduces the repeatability of a program. Previously, only the *sequence* of events controlled what was done. Using this pattern, the *timing* of events interacts with the sequence of events. This complicates debugging and testing. If a test script just fills the event queue as quickly as possible, compound events may be adequately exercised, but simple events may not. You need to test both simple and compound events.

Increased complexity. Memory management is more complicated, as a compound event has more than one event's worth of information associated with it.

Examples   **Word processor.** Consider typing text into a word processor. As each character is typed, the program must calculate line lengths, check word wraps, and so on. Many of these activities are the same regardless of whether one or several characters are inserted. So, rather than receiving "insert c1" and then "insert c2," we can effectively merge the two events into "insert c1 and c2," to avoid some of the overhead.

Microsoft Windows. Microsoft Windows has a repeat count field in its event record to indicate that a string of several identical keystrokes was combined into one event. (However, Charles Petzold [Petzold90, p. 92] points out that many programs ignore the count.)

PATTERN 3: HANDLE ARTIFICIAL EVENTS

Context   You are working on an interactive program based on an event queue. Responsiveness is important.

Problem   The program has too much work to do in response to some events.

Key Question   Can work be done during idle times that might speed up future interactions?

Solution   Let the event queue contain artificial events. In particular, the event queue should return a "system is idle" event when nothing is pending in the queue. (Do not include idle events when counting the number of pending events, however.) The program should handle idle events by using the extra time for background processing; this may speed up interaction in the future.

Actions in response to an idle event should have a bounded execution time—they shouldn't take so much time to execute that responsiveness suffers.

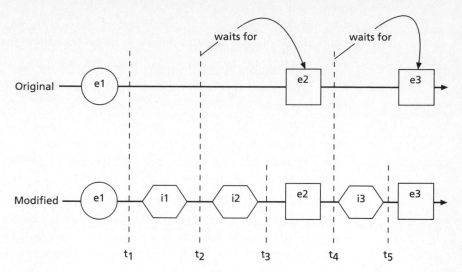

FIGURE 3

The original sequence of events has new events inserted that correspond to times when the system would otherwise be idle. These allow the program to get CPU time rather than blocking until the next true event.

This pattern borrows an idea from real-time systems: let the passage of time affect the program.

Consequences **Improved responsiveness.** Overall responsiveness may improve. The program has done some work it would have had to do anyway, but it has done it *before* the user begins waiting for results.

Slower processing. The computer system may become slower, as idle events steal time that might have gone to other processes. It is necessary to control the rate at which idle events are generated in order to limit the load of the program on the system as a whole.

Increased complexity. The program is more complex; it must often be restructured to allow effective incremental work. Consider a data structure that must be reorganized. It is probably easiest to write this so that the rest of the program comes to a halt; then there is no need to worry about the effect of the data structure reorganization on system use. To reorganize things incrementally, we have to keep track of what pieces are done so far and whether ongoing changes in the data structure affect the partial reorganization that's already been achieved.

For example, suppose we want to search a list. We might maintain the list in two parts: a sorted part and an unsorted part. The sorted part can be searched via a binary search in $O(\log n)$ time, while the unsorted part must be searched via an O(n) search. When we get an idle event, we can use that opportunity to put one more item in its proper sorted position.

Synchronization. Synchronization is important: we must ensure that idle-time processing won't interfere with the main task, either by making sure it is done before the main task resumes, or by standard synchronization mechanisms.

Other events. Events other than idle events are useful, too. For example, we might have events for timers that are expiring, for information coming from the network, or for requests from the operating system.

Reduced repeatability. Both the system load and the event sequence affect the work the program does. (When the system is heavily loaded, fewer idle events will be generated, so the program has less chance to prepare for future interaction.) The speed with which the user interacts with the program thus affects how events are processed.

Cautions   The program should not rely on receiving an idle event—it may never get one.
This technique isn't appropriate for a program that uses threads (lightweight processes). Even if one thread blocks waiting for an event, a lower-priority thread can be scheduled to do background processing.

Examples   LISP systems may perform garbage collection while the system is waiting for user input [Teitelman+81].
An editor can use idle time to write a file that logs the current state (for use in crash and error recovery).
The Macintosh [Apple85] supports idle events, to let the program do work while no user input is pending.

PATTERN 4: DECOUPLE EXECUTION AND OUTPUT

Context   You are working on an interactive program. Performance is an issue.

Problem   Display is expensive or time-critical.

Solution   Rather than strictly alternating command execution and result display, separate the two by introducing an output event. You might let idle events be the system's cue to begin work on clearing the queued output events, or you might schedule output by some other mechanism. (Output events may be kept on the regular event queue, or a separate queue can be introduced.)

Consequences   **Improved responsiveness.** If display is expensive, this lets you improve overall responsiveness, by not requiring the program to wait for output to complete before processing the next input. If display is time-critical, this lets you schedule regular display updates.

Possible instability. This pattern can introduce timing-related instabilities. Since the output is not (always) an accurate reflection of the current system state, the user may overcompensate for the lack of timely feedback. It may be necessary to simplify output to provide the user with current information. For example, dragging a window on a MacOS system causes an outline of the window to be dragged rather than its full contents. This lets display keep up with mouse motion, and it makes the interaction feel smoother (especially on slower machines).

Examples   The Macintosh [Apple85] uses a "dirty region" event (on a single-queue event) to tell an application to update its windows. Craig Finseth [Finseth91] describes Emacs as a pair of processes: one creates the text, and the other tries to keep up with displaying it.

Computer hardware can use this technique: to boost performance, the WM CPU has separate input and output queues for access to memory [Wulf88].

Virtual reality systems can use this decoupling to allow regular updates of the display at a rate independent of the speed at which the virtual world is updated (e.g., see the UVa User Interface Group's discussion of *Alice* [UVa95]).

Related Patterns   Merge Compatible Events (Pattern 2) and Handle Artificial Events (Pattern 3) patterns can be applied to output events.

This is a variation on the Observer pattern [Gamma+95, p. 293]. In the classical Model-View-Controller architecture, views update synchronously after changes are made in the model. This pattern splits view updating from model changes.

CONCLUSION

The event manipulation described in these patterns has the effect of evening out the demands on the CPU. When events are coming quickly, combine them using Merge Compatible Events (Pattern 2); fewer actions are then required. When nothing is happening, use Handle Artificial Events (Pattern 3) to generate idle events, causing new actions to occur.

Many user interface frameworks hide the event queue. They build a layer above the queue and make it seem like messages are being sent directly to interaction objects (using Chain of Responsibility [Gamma+95]). The patterns described here aren't meant to preclude hiding events but rather to suggest ways to change event dispatching to improve system responsiveness.

Applications that do not use a framework may be able to apply these patterns directly. Applications that use a framework may find it worthwhile to change the framework to take these patterns into account.

These patterns are not applicable only to systems with graphical interfaces: even strictly keyboard-based interfaces can make use of them.

Decouple Execution and Output (Pattern 4) represents an old idea that's returning. The Emacs editor has long decoupled the display from command execution [Finseth91]. The idea is achieving prominence again because of the requirements of virtual reality systems.

ACKNOWLEDGMENTS

This chapter benefited from discussions with and criticisms from Steve Wake, John Vlissides, Gerard Meszaros, and other PLoP '95 workshop participants. The first and third authors were partially supported by NSF grant IRI-9116991.

REFERENCES

[Ambriola+88] V. Ambriola and D. Notkin. "Reasoning About Interactive Systems." *IEEE Transactions on Software Engineering, 14*(2)(1988): 272–276.

[Apple85] Apple Computer, Inc. *Inside Macintosh, Volume I.* Reading, MA: Addison-Wesley, 1985.

[Finseth91] C. A. Finseth. *The Craft of Text Editing: Emacs for the Modern World.* New York: Springer-Verlag, 1991.

[Gamma+95] E. Gamma, R. Helm, R. Johnson, and J. Vlissides. *Design Patterns: Elements of Reusable Object-Oriented Software*, Reading, MA: Addison-Wesley, 1995.

[Metrowerks95] Metrowerks, Inc. *Inside CodeWarrior 6.* New York, 1995.

[Petzold90] C. Petzold. *Programming Windows: The Microsoft Guide to Writing Applications for Windows 3.* Redmond, WA: Microsoft Press, 1990.

[Pooch+93] U. W. Pooch and J. A. Wall. *Discrete Event Simulation: A Practical Approach.* Boca Raton, FL: CRC Press, 1993.

[Sha+90] L. Sha and J. B. Goodenough. "Real-Time Scheduling Theory and Ada." *IEEE Computer*, *23*(4)(1990): 53–62.

[Teitelman+81] W. Teitelman and L. Masinter. "The Interlisp Programming Environment." *IEEE Computer*, *14*(4)(1981): 25–34.

[UVa95] UVa User Interface Group. "Alice: Rapid Prototyping for Virtual Reality." *IEEE Computer Graphics and Applications*, *15*(3)(1995): 8–11.

[Wulf88] W. A. Wulf. "The WM Computer Architecture." *ACM Computer Architecture News*, *16*(1)(1988): 70–84.

William C. Wake, B. Douglas Wake, and Edward A. Fox can be reached at `bill@infostation.vtls.com`.

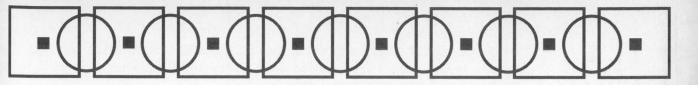

A Pattern Language for Improving the Capacity of Reactive Systems

35

Gerard Meszaros

ABSTRACT

This chapter describes a set of patterns related to improving the capacity and reliability of real-time reactive systems such as telephone switching exchanges. While these patterns are commonly found in telecommunications systems, they can be applied to any reactive system with peak-capacity issues.

INTRODUCTION

A common problem related to increasing the supply of well-documented patterns is the time required to capture them. The people with the most patterns in their heads also have the least time to document them. "*Pareto's Law*," also known as the 80/20 rule, states that 80 percent of the value is attributable to 20 percent of the effort; with this in mind, this pattern language uses the "Coplien form." Jim Coplien has shown us that it is possible to capture very important knowledge with significantly less effort by using a more compact pattern format.

This language refers to a number of patterns that are known to exist but have not yet (to my knowledge) been documented. I invite others to "flesh out" these patterns based on their own experience, and perhaps submit the expanded forms for discussion at future PLoP conferences.

PROBLEM DOMAIN HISTORY

Reactive systems are those whose primary function is to respond to requests from users outside the system. These users may be people or machines. Reactive systems must typically be able to handle a wide range of loads (the number of requests received in a given unit of time) with a high expected rate of request completion.

Examples of reactive systems include

- Time-sharing computer systems
- Telephone switching exchanges (or "switches") and Service Control Points (SCPs)
- Servers (as in client-server architectures)
- On-line transaction processing (such as banking ATM networks, etc.)

These systems all share a need for high capacity at a reasonable cost and high reliability in the face of high or extreme loads, which can lead to system overload.

THE PATTERN LANGUAGE

Capacity Bottleneck (Pattern 1) deals with identifying the limiting factor in a system's capacity. This leads to Processing Capacity (Pattern 2), which describes how to deal with system capacity. Expanding on Pattern 2, three basic strategies for improving system throughput in processing-bound systems are presented: Optimize High-Runner Cases (Pattern 3), which reduces the cost of frequently occurring requests; Shed Load (Pattern 4), which reduces the amount of wasted system effort; and Share the Load (Pattern 8), which increases the amount of processing available.

Shed Load is supported by Finish Work in Progress (Pattern 5), Fresh Work Before Stale (Pattern 6), and Match Progress Work with New (Pattern 7). When Share the Load is used in combination with Shed Load, it is further supported by several patterns relating to efficient implementation of load shedding in a distributed processing environment: Work Shed at Periphery (Pattern 9) and Leaky Bucket of Credits (Pattern 10).

For patterns that are referenced but not presented here, a "fat reference"[1] is included in the footnotes. Figure 1 shows the structure of the pattern language graphically. Several patterns referenced but not presented here are also shown, within dashed borders.

FIGURE 1 The structure of the pattern language presented graphically. Patterns not described in detail here are shown within dashed boxes.

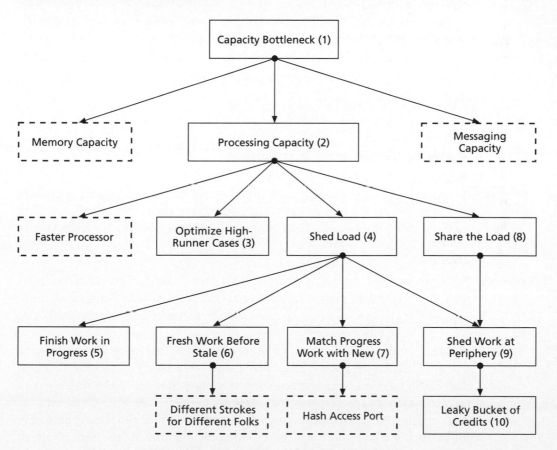

---

[1] A "fat reference" is a short summary of the item referred to, beyond its name and location. It is one of a number of patterns discovered during PLoP '95 that describe factors that make patterns and pattern languages easy to read and digest.

All the patterns contained herein come from the DMS-100 family of telephone switching products manufactured by NorTel (formerly known as Northern Telecom). These products share a common operating system and core processing hardware. They also share a need for very high reliability and availability, even in the face of natural disasters, "mass calling" marketing campaigns, radio station contests, and the like. These natural and man-made events can cause extreme fluctuations in the arrival rates of "service requests" from the phone-calling public; the system must be able to react gracefully in the face of such periods of extreme demand.

Related Pattern Languages   This pattern language deals with handling the need for high system capacity and survivability in the face of system overload conditions. For patterns that describe how to increase the reliability of underlying hardware platforms, refer to Adams et al. [Adams+95]. For patterns related to optimizing Smalltalk programs, refer to Auer and Beck [Auer+95].

CAPACITY PATTERNS

Pattern 1: Capacity Bottleneck

Problem   Customers always want the system to handle the largest possible numbers of users, terminals, requests per hour, and so on, preferably without having to buy more hardware. What is the most effective way to improve the capacity of the system?

Context   You are working with a reactive system that is limited in its capacity by available processing power, number of access ports, connections, other finite physical resources, message reception limits, memory limitations, and so on.

Forces   Adding memory, processors, or other resources increases the customer's hardware costs and may reduce available processing time due to extra refreshing, auditing, interprocessor messaging, and the like. Optimizing data structures to reduce memory requirements may increase the processing cost of accessing the data. Optimizing algorithms to reduce processing cost may both increase the data structures' memory requirements and result in duplicated logic. Most optimizations increase development effort and system complexity. Increased complexity could result in reduced flexibility and reliability as well as increased maintenance cost.

Solution   Understand what determines your system capacity and the circumstances that affect it. Determine both the nature of capacity limits (memory, processing, messaging, etc.) and their location (i.e., in which processing context—core, peripherals, clients, servers, the network, etc.). Only optimize those elements that truly limit the system's capacity. Engineer the system in such a way that these limits can be avoided automatically, or ensure that the system can withstand circumstances in which the demands on its resources are exceeded.

Apply Processing Capacity (Pattern 2) if the limiting factor is the processing cost of the necessary number of transactions. Use Memory Capacity[2] if the limiting factor is the amount of memory required to handle the load. Use Messaging Capacity[3] if the limiting factor is the messaging system's inability to deliver messages between processors in a timely manner.

Related Pattern   Processing Capacity (Pattern 2) is the entry point for a set of patterns used to increase available processing capacity and reduce the cost per transaction.

Pattern 2: Processing Capacity

Problem   The throughput of a system is limited by the capacity of its processor(s). How can you increase this capacity without installing a faster processor?[4]

Context   You are working with a reactive system in which the capacity is limited by the available processing power, and work arrives from external sources in a stochastic fashion. There are predictable peaks and valleys in the arrival rates. As the number of requests received exceeds the system's processing capacity, the number of requests successfully handled actually decreases because of the effort wasted attempting to handle all the requests.

The system's available processing capacity can be summarized as follows:

Total number of cycles per second – reserved headroom.[5]

---

[2] Not included here. This is the first pattern in a yet-unwritten pattern language describing techniques for reducing the amount of memory required by a system. Sample patterns include Overlay Spare Bits and Allocate Only What You Use (a.k.a. Waste Not, Want Not).

[3] Not included here. This is the first pattern in a yet-unwritten pattern language describing techniques for reducing the amount of messages passed between processors. Sample patterns include Message Bundling and Message Compression.

[4] The use of a faster processor may seem like an obvious alternative. However, many systems are already using the fastest processors available to them, and they must therefore seek alternative means of addressing this problem.

[5] "Headroom" includes any reserve processing capacity required to ensure that system responses are within specifications.

The average cost per request (in seconds) of any particular mix of requests can be computed as follows:

Sum over request type:
Cost per request * Number of such requests per second.[6]

The capacity (the "rated capacity"), in requests per second, for any particular mix of requests can be expressed as follows:

Available processing / Average cost per request.

Forces   The available share of the processing capacity within the existing processor(s) can be increased by reducing reserved processing, but this will reduce the safety margin when too many requests arrive at once. One can make do with a reduced margin if the system is designed to shed excess load reliably, but this increases the complexity of the system and the development cost. And system latency (response time) increases as the size of the buffer is reduced.

The total processing capacity can be increased by adding more processors to the system. This does not provide linear growth in available processing power, however, due to the increased cost of communication between the processors. And, unless the system design already supports distributed processing, extensive redesign may be required, at considerable additional development cost and increased system complexity.

The cost of frequently occurring requests can be reduced by optimizing them, but this requires additional design and may add complexity. Optimizations typically come at a loss of flexibility, which will make future extension of the system more difficult. And there is a cost associated with measuring and analyzing the cost of each type of request.

Solution   Determine the cost-to-benefit ratio of increasing capacity by reducing the average cost per request vs. increasing the available processing horsepower vs. reducing the size of the safety buffer needed in case of surges in requests. Based on the amount of increase required, one or more of these approaches may prove to be insufficient; in the most extreme cases, they may all need to be applied.

If a small number of request types constitute a large part of the processing cost, use Optimize High-Runners (Pattern 3) to reduce the cost of these request types. If a large amount of processing capacity has to be kept in reserve to handle peak loads, use Shed Load (Pattern 4) to reduce the necessary size

---

[6] Another way of calculating this is as follows: Sum over request type: Cost per request * % of this request type (of total requests).

of this buffer. (In extreme cases this can double the available processing power, from 40 percent to over 80 percent.) You can then further tune the system capacity at the expense of latency, using Max Headroom.[7] If the necessary increase in processing capacity exceeds what can be recovered through these techniques (or if you have other reasons to distribute your system), you will have no choice but to use Share the Load (Pattern 8) to increase the amount of processing that can be made available to your system.

Related Patterns   Shed Load (Pattern 4) reduces the number of requests accepted during overload, thus reducing the necessary processing headroom.

Optimize High-Runner Cases (Pattern 3) reduces the cost of frequently occurring requests, thus increasing capacity.

Share the Load (Pattern 8) can reduce the cost of requests by delegating work to other processors, and it may reduce the number of requests any one processor must handle (this can also be viewed as increasing the number of cycles available per second).

Max Headroom describes how to increase the available processing by tailoring the responsiveness of the system to maximize the rated capacity.

Pattern 3: Optimize High-Runner Cases

Problem   The average processing cost of service requests is too high to allow the required capacity target to be met. How can we reduce the average cost of individual requests?

Context   You are working with a reactive system in which the required capacity has not yet been achieved. Available processing power may have already been maximized, and all possible extraneous work may have already been shed.

For example, consider a telephone switch using the fastest available processors, with overload handling mechanisms already in place; the capacity must be increased by 4 percent.

Forces   We need to ensure that the system performs adequately and meets its performance (capacity) targets, but we don't want (or can't afford) to optimize every transaction type. The development cost of optimizations is high (often more expensive than providing the basic functionality). Optimizations

---

[7]   Not included here. Headroom is required to ensure that system responses are within acceptable levels and that work load peaks in do not push the system "over the edge." The more fully loaded a system becomes, the longer the average delays become—hence the need to engineer the headroom.

typically increase the complexity of the implementation or reduce the flexibility of the system when it comes time to handle new requirements. Optimizing the wrong parts of a system will contribute little to capacity but greatly increases project cost and system complexity.

Solution The solution lies in "Pareto's Law" (also known as the 80/20 rule); in most systems, 80 percent (or more) of the processing power is consumed by 20 percent of the use cases (transaction types).

Measure or project the high-runner transactions and optimize only those parts of the system that contribute significantly to their cost. This can be done by characterizing exactly what code each high-runner transaction executes (using "profiling" tools) and ensuring that all this code executes efficiently. Optimize only as much of the code as necessary to meet the capacity targets; optimizing more than is necessary just creates extra maintenance cost and increases the likelihood of having to "undo" the optimizations when greater flexibility is required in the future.

For example, suppose that for a telephone switch in a residential area, 80 percent of all calls are basic "line-to-line" calls with no features involved. You need to recover 4 percent of the switch's call-handling capacity. You can either reduce the cost of these "line-to-line" calls by 5 percent or reduce the cost of all the other types of calls by 25 percent! It takes much less development effort to create a special, "fast" version of parts of the "line-to-line" call software than to save a similar amount of processing on a diverse set of call types.

Related Patterns The following is a list of patterns that may be used to support this pattern; they are all pretty standard techniques, so they are not discussed here. Refer also to [Auer+95] for similar patterns relating to Smalltalk development.

Instructions Cached. Makes instructions execute faster by keeping them in a processor cache. This is typically done entirely under hardware control, during program execution.

Faster RAM for Higher-Runners. Makes frequently used sequences of instructions (procedures or methods) execute faster by keeping them in faster memory (such as SRAM). The decision as to what code to put into faster memory is typically made by the system developer at system design or configuration time.

Method Calls Inlined. Reduces procedure/method call overhead by "inlining" (copying) the code that would otherwise have been called into the source or object code of the calling procedure. This may result in many copies of the object code for a single fragment of source code, but better that than many *clones* of the source code.

Polymorphism Precluded (a.k.a. Fixed Methods). Reduces method call overhead by making methods fixed; this allows the compiler to generate jumps to an address rather than having to look up that address at runtime.

Hardware Traps Exceptions. Moves checking for exceptions like bad pointer contents, divides by zero, and so on, into the hardware, to eliminate the need to check in software at runtime. (Less "defensive coding" also makes the program logic easier to read and understand.)

Pattern 4: Shed Load

Problem   Large numbers of requests arriving from outside systems can easily cause your system to bog down or "thrash." The amount of real work actually getting done can decrease as the thrashing increases. This results in users experiencing degraded (or complete loss of) service, which is neither appreciated by the users nor compliant with many communication protocol standards. In extreme cases, the entire system could crash. How can a system best react to such "overload" conditions to ensure that it continues to function?

Context   You are working on a processing-bound, reactive system faced with more requests than it can handle. Overloads of the system must not allow it to become unavailable.

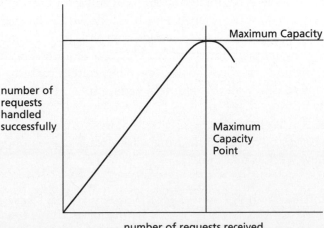

Forces   Efforts to keep the system functioning can use up all its available capacity. Adding more software to handle possible overload situations adds complexity to the system. The cost of trying to shed work could exceed the processing it saves. The cost of determining the overload status of the system may itself reduce the system's capacity. How does the external system behave when work is rejected? (Does the work quietly go away, or does it repeat the requests and hence increase the load on the system?)

Solution   To ensure that the amount of work accepted by the system does not exceed its capacity, shed some requests so that others can be served properly. This is a variation on the system of triage used in hospital emergency rooms[8]: Let the dying die, let those who will heal by themselves heal, and treat only those who really need assistance. In this case, service requests that cannot be properly handled should be shed as early as possible, before a lot of processing is expended on them. By doing this, one can actually decrease the amount of processing power that needs to be reserved for unexpected peaks, thus increasing the available processing and, with it, system capacity. At first glance this seems like "something for nothing," but in fact it carries a very real cost in terms of the increase in system complexity required to handle the peaks with reduced impact.

When the protocols to the outside world have explicit time-outs within which a response must be provided, any received request that is predicted to be delayed longer than the specified time-out can safely be discarded without any change in the visible behavior of the system, and with potentially large savings in processing cost.

Interfaces to humans are a bit more difficult to predict, because human behavior may be affected by the local culture. For example, in some countries people will wait patiently for a dial tone, while in others, if a dial tone is not presented within 2 to 4 seconds, they will hang up and try again or "rattle" the switchhook impatiently. This can require significantly different handling under overload conditions. The Strategy pattern [Gamma+95] is a good way to deal with this required variation.

Related Patterns   Finish Work in Progress (Pattern 5) maximizes the return on investment of processing cycles by ensuring work already in progress gets completed before new work is taken on.

---

[8] Triage is a technique used in medical emergencies to decide how the services of an overwhelmed group of doctors should be deployed when the number of patients exceeds the number of doctors. It determines which patients should be treated first.

Match Progress Work with New (Pattern 7) prevents the deadlock that could be caused by throwing away the wrong work.

Fresh Work Before Stale (Pattern 6) maximizes the number of customers who get acceptable service.

Work Shed at Periphery (Pattern 9) maximizes system throughput by reducing or eliminating the cost of shedding work in a bottleneck processor.

Pattern 5: Finish Work in Progress

Alias   Finish What You Start

Problem   What requests should be accepted, and which should be rejected to improve system throughput?

Context   You are working with a reactive or transaction-oriented system in which user requests are in some way dependent upon one another. A request may build on an earlier request, provide additional information in response to (or in anticipation of) another request, or cancel or undo a previous request.

Forces   Understanding the interdependencies among requests is crucial to shedding work in a productive fashion. Rejecting the wrong work could negate considerable prior investments, or even worse, result in deadlock by "hanging" some transactions along with all the resources they are using. Failing to identify any work that can be rejected prevents improvement of system capacity through the application of Shed Load (Pattern 4).

Solution   Requests that are continuations of work in progress must be recognized as such and given priority over entirely new requests. Clearly categorize all requests into New and Progress categories, and ensure that all Progress requests are processed before serving any New requests. The only exception to this rule is when the time between original requests and follow-up requests is fixed and predictable (e.g., t seconds). In this situation, completely shutting off all new requests will result in a "load dip" t seconds after the system starts shedding new work. This creates an oscillation between an overloaded and underloaded condition; the result is reduced average capacity. This can be countered by "bleeding" a small amount of new work in during the overloaded period to reduce the depth of the dip.

Related Pattern   This pattern supports the application of Shed Load (Pattern 4).

Pattern 6: Fresh Work Before Stale

Alias   Good Service for Some, No Service for Others

Problem   How can you maximize the number of customers who get good service?

Context   You are working on a reactive system that cannot possibly satisfy all the requests it receives. The grade of service (GOS), or performance standard, may be based upon the percentage of requests serviced beneath some threshold (e.g., GOS = percentage of callers receiving a dial tone within 2 seconds).

Forces   When a system is overloaded, users may give up waiting. The system will then have to do extra work to clean up. If the delays are long enough, users may have already given up before the system starts processing their initial request. This can result in a great deal of wasted system resources. But how can you tell whether users are likely to give up, negating all your efforts to serve them?

Keeping track of the age of every request adds memory and complexity to the system. Sorting them could add processing cost to the task of choosing the next request to process. Some requests cannot be ignored and must be given priority handling (e.g., 911 calls and calls from hospitals and police stations).

Solution   If some users get served immediately while others wait a long time, at least some users receive good service; if everyone waits an equally long time, however, everyone gets poor service. So it is better to give good service to as many people as possible and give the remainder poor or no service. This may not seem "fair,"[9] but it is an example of putting the common good before individuals' good.

To maximize the number of users who get good service, put all new requests in a last-in first-out queue: serve the most recently received requests first. These requests are the least likely to be abandoned. Only after the "fresh" requests have been exhausted will you get around to serving the "stale" ones. If users have been patient and are still there, they will be served. If they've given up, there should already be an "undo" (a cancellation of the request) somewhere in the queue with which we can cancel their request entirely.

---

[9]   Since the selection process is random, based on when a request happens to arrive, it actually is equally fair to everybody.

For example, suppose you are swamped with e-mail and haven't been able to read it for a week. When you finally have an hour to read your mail, you must ask yourself, "How can I spend my time most effectively?" Start with the most recently received mail and work backward. What about the ones you never get to? Many requests will have been responded to by someone else. Some will be invitations to meetings long since over. Many of the messages weren't real important; those that were probably re-sent when you failed to respond promptly.

Related Patterns   Match Progress Work with New (Pattern 7) describes how to eliminate some work entirely when the user "cancels" a request.

Different Strokes for Different Folks[10] describes how to guarantee good service for access ports or requests designated as requiring priority handling.

Pattern 7: Match Progress Work with New

Problem   A lot of processing may go completely to waste if users' actions cancel previous ones. How can the system avoid wasting its limited processing capacity handling requests that will be "undone"?

Context   You are working with a processing-bound, reactive system that is under a heavy load and is trying to shed work. Some users are giving up because their requests are not served immediately; this forces the system to "undo" work it just did, at an expense it cannot really afford.

For example, consider the work performed by a telephone network when a user lifts his handset off its hook to initiate a call and then, after waiting several seconds for a dial tone, hangs up the phone before a tone is delivered.

Forces   In many systems, the external actor—be it a live user or another machine—will eventually "time out" on a request and either re-send it or cancel it. It is especially important to detect such duplication or cancellation during periods of peak load, to prevent further degradation of service. Detecting related requests adds complexity to the system. The cost of detecting duplicated or canceled requests must be significantly lower than the processing

---

[10] Not included here. For each access port, designate the queue to which new work requests are to be added when the requests arrive. High-priority access ports can use a different queue, which is served before the "normal" priority "new work" queue. Of course, if too many ports use the high-priority queue, its value is diluted.

cost; otherwise the system will have been made more complex without achieving much capacity improvement.

Solution When "progress" requests are received, pair them up with the appropriate "new work" requests. If the second is a "cancel," the "new work" item can be removed from the queue without having been processed at all! If the "progress" work is something other than a cancel, it should be kept matched with the "new" work in case the "new" work must later be shed. This prevents the system from having to try to figure out what the "progress" work means in the absence of the "new" work.

For example, "threaded" e-mail and news-reading programs collect all the items related to a topic and present them as a bundle to the user. The user can then decide whether to pay attention to a bundle of messages, saving the cost of making this decision on a message-by-message basis.

Related Pattern Work Shed at Periphery (Pattern 9) describes how to avoid the cost of matching the "new" and "progress" work in the bottleneck processor.

Hash Access Port[11] is an efficient way to match "progress" requests with previous requests.

Pattern 8: Share the Load

Alias Move Function Out of Processor

Problem The cost of processing all the requests may exceed the available capacity of a single processor at a specified system capacity. How can the available processing power be increased?

Context You are working on a processing-bound, reactive system that falls short of meeting its target capacity. All other means of increasing the available processing capacity have been exhausted.

Forces Adding additional processors increases the amount of processing power available, but it also makes the system more complex because of the increased messages required to synchronize the work being done. It also increases the amount of memory required. Many of the processors will have

---

[11] Not included here. Assuming that requests from the same (logical) access port are related in some way, one can hash the access port id and detect related requests via "hashing collisions."

the same programs, and they may have common data as well; these will have to be synchronized, requiring further interprocessor messaging. Unless the amount of processing being delegated is significant, the increased interprocessor communications could cost more than they save.

Solution   Given the circumstances, you have no choice but to shift some of the processing to another processor. Select the functions to be moved based on those that are clearly partitioned from what is being left behind, to reduce the amount of synchronization (number of messages needing to be exchanged) required.

Related Pattern   A process for determining suitable partitioning is described in the pattern Context Mapping.[12]

Pattern 9: Work Shed at Periphery

Problem   How does one shed work, at a minimum additional cost, that is beyond the system's capacity?

Context   You are working on a multiprocessor, reactive system that is shedding work to minimize the impact on its capacity of an overload condition (for example, a telephone switch during a rock concert ticket giveaway call-in contest).

Forces   As a request is processed by the system, increased effort is invested in it, contributing to the system's overloaded condition. But the information needed to determine whether the system is overloaded may only be available in the "central processor" (the "bottleneck" processor). Thus by the time the system determines that a request should be shed, it may be substantially complete.

Solution   Detect new work and shed it at minimum cost by moving the detection of new work as close to the periphery of the system as possible. Provide this part of the system with information regarding the available processing capacity of the most limiting part of the system.

---

[12] From Allen Hopley's unpublished pattern language called "Levels of Abstraction." In each processing context, start with the entire model, plus objects representing each of the other contexts. Then, optimize out those parts of the model that are completely unnecessary in this context, based on which function has been assigned to it.

Related Pattern   Leaky Bucket of Credits (Pattern 10) describes how to communicate the status of the system's "bottleneck processor" to its periphery.

Pattern 10: Leaky Bucket of Credits

Problem   How can one processor know whether another processor is capable of handling more work?

Context   You are working with a reactive system in which one processor needs to be aware of the overload state of another processor.

Forces   For a peripheral to be able to reject new work when the system becomes overloaded, it must be able to recognize this condition. But having the bottleneck processor take up valuable processing cycles to inform a potentially large number of other processors of its state would further reduce its capacity. And what happens if it gets so bogged down that it can't send out a "Stop sending me work!" message?

Solution   The bottleneck processor tells the other processors (the peripherals) when it is capable of accepting *more* work. It does so by sending them "credits." Each peripheral holds a "leaky bucket" of these credits. The buckets gradually "leak" until they are empty. When the system is not at capacity, the buckets are continuously refilled with new credits sent from the bottleneck processor until they are full; however, when the system is at capacity, the bottleneck processor will not send out credits, and the peripherals will therefore soon start to hold back new work. When a peripheral sends work to several different and independent processors, it can and must track the credits from each processor separately.

Related Patterns   This pattern is a specialized usage of Leaky Bucket.[13] The amount of work forwarded to the bottleneck processor can be fine-tuned by sending a variable number of credits, based on the remaining headroom.

   This is also an example of applying Context Mapping; each processor keeps a model of "its world," which includes a description of the state of the other processors in the system (i.e., overloaded or not). The credits provide a means

[13] Not included here. The concept of a bucket that leaks until empty and is then refilled (or a bucket that is leaked into until it overflows or is manually emptied) is used throughout high-availability systems to detect all kinds of transient problems. Refer to the pattern by the same name described by Adams et al. [Adams+95].

of keeping the distributed views of any one processor synchronized, in something near real time but at a reasonable cost (especially when the processor is overloaded). This, in turn is an example of Half-Object Plus Protocol, as described in an earlier paper [Meszaros95]; in this case, the "object" that needs to appear in more than one context is the bottleneck processor itself!

ACKNOWLEDGMENTS

I would like to thank all the people who developed the many solutions described in these patterns, and especially Gord Adamyk and Pierre Johnson, who first described them to me.

Special thanks go to Erich Gamma, who was the PLoP '95 shepherd for this pattern language.

REFERENCES

[Adams+95] M. Adams et al. "Fault-Tolerant Telecommunication System Patterns." Chapter 33, this volume.

[Auer+95] K. Auer and K. Beck. "Patterns for Efficient Smalltalk Programming." Chapter 2, this volume.

[Gamma+95] E. Gamma, R. Helm, R. Johnson, and J. Vlissides. *Design Patterns: Elements of Reusable Object-Oriented Software.* Reading, MA: Addison-Wesley, 1995.

[Meszaros95] G. Meszaros. "Half-Object Plus Protocol." In J. O. Coplien and D. C. Schmidt (eds.), *Pattern Languages of Program Design.* Reading, MA: Addison-Wesley, 1995, pp. 129–132.

Gerard Meszaros can be reached at gerard@osgcorp.com.

Index

?